IUI

ALLE ZEIT WACH
1842

Lars Oxelheim

International Financial Integration

With 44 Figures

Springer-Verlag
Berlin Heidelberg New York
London Paris Tokyo
Hong Kong

Professor Dr. Lars Oxelheim
The Industrial Institute for Economic and Social Research
Industrihuset, Storgatan 19, P.O. Box 5501
S-114 85 Stockholm, Sweden

ISBN 3-540-52629-3 Springer-Verlag Berlin Heidelberg New York Tokyo
ISBN 0-387-52629-3 Springer-Verlag New York Heidelberg Berlin Tokyo

Printing in Germany

Printing: Schmidt & Sohn GmbH, Mannheim 61
Bookbinding: J. Schäffer GmbH u. Co. KG Grünstadt
2142/7130-543210

Foreword

There is widespread agreement in the current social and economic debate that the nations of the world are becoming increasingly integrated. Many structural signs in society also suggest that this is so. Integration has become a catchword in the preparations for the internal market of the EC, and a keynote in the debate about association for the European countries which do not belong to the Community. But when we turn to the question of how this integration should be measured, there is very little consensus. Instead there are numerous problems, not only about how to measure integration but even about how to define it.

In this book I shall discuss the import and implications of a particular type of integration, namely financial integration, and then look at the most important problems connected with measuring it. In the empirical investigation reported below I felt the need for an integrated micro-macro approach. Further, I decided to illustrate the measurement problems by studying a small and relatively open economy where exchange controls have been imposed by the government in an attempt to reduce the flow of interest-sensitive capital out of the country, and thus to acquire autonomy for the national monetary policy. An interview study has been carried out with a view to illustrating among other things how expectations are formed among the major actors on the financial market, and this provided additional input for an analysis of the level of financial integration.

For much intellectual support I would like to thank Professor Clas G. Wihlborg, University of Southern California and Professor Thomas D. Willett, Claremont Graduate School. Valuable comments have also been made by many seminar members at the Gothenburg School of Economics, the Industrial Institute for Economic and Social Research (IUI), and the central bank of Sweden (Sveriges Riksbank).

I would also like to thank Professor Gunnar Eliasson, director of IUI, who made facilities available to me for writing this book at the Institute. Moreover, I wish to thank the Banking Research Institute in Stockholm for its role in providing financial support for the translation by Nancy Adler, to whom I also express my thanks.

Any remaining errors and omissions are of course entirely my responsibility.

Stockholm, January 1990
Lars Oxelheim

A note to my readers

This book is the third in a trilogy which describes how disturbances or shocks on the world market are transmitted to the small open economy and then to the individual corporate profit and loss account.

In the present book I discuss the first stage in this transmission, i.e. how the disturbance is transmitted to the small open economy. Oxelheim and Wihlborg (1987) presented a frame for analysing the second stage in the transmission, i.e. how corporate managers should cope with such disturbances or more generally with fluctuations in the conditions on the world market. Finally, in Oxelheim (1985) I discussed the last step in the transmission, i.e. how the effect of the disturbance on the world market should be assessed and reported to external corporate stakeholders.

In this book I am addressing three categories of readers, each with its own store of previous knowledge and its own particular interests. One group consists of *researchers* in economics and business administration, who should find something to interest them in all parts of the book. I have also had this group particularly in mind in writing Chapter 3.

The second category consists of *students* of economics and business administration, particularly those with a special interest in financial markets and international financial and investment analysis. The conceptual side is generally of greatest interest to students, while empirical results are probably less important. I therefore recommend this group of readers to study Chapters 1–2, 4 and 8.1–8.5, including appendices. Students who are particularly interested in analysis should also look at Chapter 3, which describes the analytical problems that have arisen in previous studies, and/or Chapters 5–8, which describe the analytical method adopted here.

The third reader category consists of *business executives, bankers and politicians* interested in empirically grouped conclusions about levels of integration and interest rate autonomy, or in opportunities for profiting from international arbitrage. I recommend this group of readers to look at Chapters 1, 2.3, 2.8–2.9, 4.4–4.5, 5.4, 6.4, 7.5, 8 and 9.

Because I hope to reach such a broad readership, those who decide to read the book in its entirety may find that I have repeated myself in defining the meaning of certain expressions of crucial importance. For this I crave their indulgence.

CONTENTS

List of Figures

List of Tables

CHAPTER 1

The Global Interdependence of National Financial Markets

1.1 Many signs of increasing market integration

In recent decades there have been many signs of increasing integration between the various markets of the world. The liquidity explosion at the beginning of the 1970s and the subsequent worldwide rise in inflation, the reflection of monetary restrictions in the United States in corresponding restrictions in Europe, and the steep rise in the real US dollar rate at the beginning of the 1980s are just a few of many events resulting from the increasingly free movement of international capital. In view of these developments we may well wonder whether any country can isolate itself from the general integration created by the international flows of private capital, even by imposing exchange controls. Rather, it is a question of whether we can measure the level of influence and integration in quantitative terms, instead of simply invoking the kind of "evidence" mentioned above. The present book is intended to answer this question.

To illustrate the problems involved in determining empirically the level of integration and the way in which this level changes over time, I have taken the example of Sweden and Swedish market links with the rest of the world. Sweden, which is claimed by many to possess the most multinational industry in the world, offers a useful sampler of the various links and relationships that ought to be considered in any attempt to measure integration. Thus in relative terms Sweden is a small economy which is wide open to international trade; a high proportion of its industry is located abroad, and it has a big net foreign debt. All these are indications of powerful international links, but to set against this we have the fact that for the last fifty years, up to 1989, Swedish governments have been using exchange controls in their efforts to achieve national autonomy in monetary policy making.

1.2 Previous integration studies demonstrate difficulties in measurement and interpretation

A good deal of research activity has been devoted in recent decades to defining and measuring economic integration. At first the main focus of interest was national integration, or the links between the various markets within a country; now, however, attention has turned instead to the links between markets in different countries. The *theoretical* side of this research activity has been mainly concerned with the concept of economic integration, but there has also been a related interest in the impact of economic integration on the autonomy of national economic policies.

The earliest of these research studies looked at the links between goods markets, and economic *integration* was defined in terms of the *size of trade flows*. More recently researchers have been emphasizing the role of real and financial markets, and economic integration has been defined in terms of *goods and services market integration*, *capital market integration*, and *foreign exchange market integration*.

Whereas the earliest models of economic integration were formulated in terms of actual transactions and flows, the models created over the last ten years or so have been almost exclusively formulated in terms of the expectations and reactions of the market actors. According to these models economic integration can be achieved even though no transactions have been registered. Efficiency in the diffusion of information is now of central interest in defining the concept of economic integration.

A desire to explain the importance of economic integration in a wider context has also inspired an interest in theories about the relationship between this form of integration on the one hand, and political and social integration on the other. Here, however, research still leaves many questions unanswered.

In recent years there has been a good deal of criticism of much *empirical* work on international economic integration. This criticism has been directed mainly at the methods for measuring economic dependence and the way in which the relevant measures and the appropriate data have been chosen. One general objection can be levelled at almost all the internationally reported empirical studies, namely that theories formulated in terms of expected (ex ante) quantities are evaluated in terms of actual outcomes (ex post data). Tests of this kind provide no basis for any conclusions about economic integration, since what they are testing is a composite hypothesis. A possible indication of economic integration is embedded in the results, but it cannot be identified. Testing of the interdependence of capital markets on a basis of similarities in *realized* returns, is an example of testing such a composite hypothesis: one hypothesis about the pricing of financial assets and another one about the appearance of the yield-generating process are both being tested simultaneously, which means that it is only possible to draw conclusions about one of them by making assumptions about the other. And because of the interdependence of the hypotheses, it is not possible to test the plausibility of the assumptions.

Criticism of the empirical approach has also been levelled at the measurement and interpretation of *causality.* The main thrust of this criticism has concerned the problem of distinguishing *actual* signs of economic dependence between countries from *spurious* dependence generated by some common underlying disturbance or factor, such as fluctuations in the business cycle. Thus, if we specify integration from some measure of covariation, we face the difficulty of eliminating from this measure any covariation which could be due to such a common underlying factor. Many researchers recognize that interpretation is a serious analytical problem in the case of large countries such as the United States, West Germany and Japan, whose relationship with their environments can be regarded as one of *mutual dependence.* But most researchers regard the interpretive problem as less serious and more manageable when it comes to countries such as the Scandinavian countries, for example, which are *unilaterally dependent* on, and "influenced" by, their environments.

Nor has anyone succeeded satisfactorily up to now in measuring the economic integration between countries in such a way as to allow for all the market relationships. Analysis has been limited to the dependence between submarkets in different countries. There are thus a great many possible market combinations allowing for many partial analyses; when it comes to the international integration of the country as a whole all this fragmented material can produce contradictory results. Thus in a country with more or less well-functioning exchange controls, for example, financial integration of the money market may differ a great deal from the integration of the markets for long-term investments or loans, or the stock market. This means that an analysis of one market or one market segment justifies conclusions about the national market as a whole only if all the different segments of the domestic financial market are perfectly integrated (perfect domestic integration).

Another problem connected with partial studies is that any conclusions about the links between individual markets in different countries which do not also consider other markets in the same countries, may exaggerate the import of the particular type of integration studied. An apparently strong link between the targeted markets may be due to a *policy reaction.* For example, West Germany sets great store by exchange rate stability, and the country therefore takes pains to adapt to interest movements in the United States. In a study devoted solely to interest rates, strong covariation between the two countries' rates could give an exaggerated impression of their level of integration as a whole.

The few studies which have avoided the pitfalls of partial analysis have almost all been devoted to comparisons between the major OECD countries. Success has been achieved in these studies by circumventing the difficulties that characterize the analysis of small open economies.

1.3 The aim is to measure the level of financial integration

In this book particular attention will be paid to a special form of economic integration – *financial integration.* The idea – after a suitable measuring device has been constructed – is to measure the level of the international integration of a national financial market, to assess the scope for an autonomous national interest rate policy, and to see how this scope has developed over time. And, as was mentioned above, I have chosen to exemplify the measurement process by the case of Sweden.

1.4 Different forms of financial integration

We can distinguish between total, direct and indirect financial integration. Financial integration can also vary in strength from perfect integration to perfect disintegration or segmentation.

Total financial integration thus embraces direct and indirect integration. Perfect (total) integration means that expected real interest rates are the same on the markets concerned. Where total financial integration is not perfect, the reason may be imperfect direct and/or indirect financial integration.

Direct financial integration, which is also called capital market integration, is expressed in deviations from the "law of one price" for financial securities. Under perfect direct financial integration this law obtains, and an investor can expect the same return on investments on different markets (and borrowers the same loan costs), after the requisite adjustment has been made for risk.

If the differential in expected risk-adjusted returns is greater than zero but less than or the same as the transaction cost, we can say that the markets are disintegrated but are nonetheless *efficient.* The concept of efficiency then refers to the market actors, and means for example that these actors have not failed to exploit the possibility of achieving risk-free profits from covered interest arbitrage between markets in different countries. Deviations from this form of efficiency are known as *general market inefficiency.*

Another form of inefficiency or disequilibrium is caused by the controlling devices of economic policy. If a central bank imposes a relatively high cost on a transaction with deterrent purpose, the transaction cost represents an obvious inefficiency in this sense.

The strength of the inefficiency created by such control devices will be manifest in the gap between domestic and foreign interest rates. For example, the extent to which it has been possible to use controls to maintain an interest rate diverging from that of other countries by more than can be explained by risk premiums, exchange-rate expectations and "normal" transaction costs, indicates the *autonomy of a national interest rate policy*. This autonomy does not necessarily mean that the country has achieved independence in terms of monetary policy; rather, it has succeeded in differentiating prices. The distinction is a matter of aggregated versus selective monetary policy.

Indirect financial integration refers to a situation in which the return on an investment in one country is indirectly linked to the return on investments in other countries. The influence is exerted indirectly by way of other markets: by way of the goods market and the foreign exchange market, the capital markets are indirectly disintegrated. Perfect *total* financial integration presupposes perfect indirect integration, i.e. perfectly integrated goods and foreign exchange markets, and such a highly coordinated economic policy that the gap between political risk premiums is zero. If the perfect total integration is global, then the world will consist of *one* financial market composed of perfectly linked national capital markets under strict purchasing power parity. Some researchers claim that the mere fact that a central bank can influence the size of the different risk premiums implies an autonomous national interest rate policy.

As we have seen, indirect segmentation can occur by way of foreign exchange markets, and by "foreign exchange" I refer here simply to an accounting unit. The integration of foreign exchange markets is called "monetary", and should be distinguished from financial integration. A common currency reflects strong *monetary* integration, but does not necessarily indicate *financial* integration. California and New York State, for example, can be regarded as enjoying perfect monetary integration without perfect (domestic) financial integration. We could say that the degree of monetary integration indirectly affects total financial integration.

The presence of exchange risk can be seen as an expression of monetary disintegration. Under imperfect direct integration between capital markets with risk aversion, a price is attached to this risk in the form of a risk premium.

The above-mentioned measures will as compared with the measures traditionally used – degree of capital mobility and degree of substitutability – make it easier to study the extent to which disintegration on various markets contributes to the gap between expected real interest rates and to what we have called disintegrated financial markets in a total perspective. Perfect direct integration is synonymous with perfect capital mobility. Perfect substitutability, however, which is a much stronger condition than perfect capital mobility assuming no risk premiums, differs from perfect indirect financial integration, which in addition to an assumption about no risk premiums also involves an assumption about purchasing power parity (PPP). The two thus have only one element in common (absence of risk premiums).

The concept of financial integration presented here takes into account the markets on which disintegration is generated, but not the exact source of the disintegration. To allow for this we would have to go further and consider different types of barriers to capital mobility such as exchange controls and different taxation or regulatory systems. In this way we would, for example, have found an explanation of a potential disintegration in terms of disintegrated markets for financial services. Measuring financial integration in terms of capital flows directly or indirectly by looking at financial prices, without going into details about financial services for instance, seems still motivated, since capital movements must be seen as the catalyst and indicator of the future integration of all markets.

1.5 Interest rate differential or capital flow as dependent variable?

Studies of interest rates and capital flows are central to the analysis of financial integration. There are three main ways of performing the analysis. One alternative is to measure the *interest rate sensitivity of the capital flows*, which can be done by distinguishing between covered and uncovered interest differentials. A second alternative is to measure the *reflow of capital* and the offset coefficients. A third alternative is to analyse the relationship between interest rates in different countries. It is then a question of studying the *law of one price for financial instruments*, and measuring the difference in level and covariation for different interest rate combinations.

In my analysis below which exemplifies the links between Swedish and foreign capital markets, I will adopt this last alternative and take the gap between Swedish and foreign interest rates as the dependent variable. I was greatly influenced in this choice by the statistical uncertainty that makes it difficult to determine the size of the capital flows over Sweden's borders. Moreover, by taking the interest gap rather than the capital flow as the dependent variable, it is possible to avoid the dubious assumption that the interest rate is used consistently as a policy variable.

1.6 What types of interest rate are relevant to an analysis of financial integration?

Three types of interest rate can be studied: a) *real*, b) *nominal*, and c) *nominal with foreign rates covered on the forward market for foreign exchange.* Starting from these types of interest rates we can distinguish the five common expressions of financial integration which are indicated by numbers in Figure 1.1. The figure describes the links between "prices" on different markets in the form of international equilibrium relationships.

The (total) financial integration of a country's financial market is perfect, if the expected *real* interest rate at home is equal to the expected *real* foreign rate. If this is not so, and the financial integration is thus less than perfect, it is not possible to determine whether the imperfection is of a financial kind, or whether it depends on the imperfect integration of other markets. The level of (total) financial integration is expressed by *real interest rate parity* (alternative 1) and possible deviations from such parity.

If the (total) financial integration is not perfect, we have to focus on the level of direct financial integration. This type of integration can be studied in terms of the law of one price based on interest rates, according to one of the following alternatives.

We can study the difference between *nominal* interest rates (alternative 2). However, this alternative has obvious drawbacks in the case of flexible exchange rates, unless we allow for the proposition of economic theory that interest differentials reflect the market's expectation of a movement in exchange rates during the period to which the interest rate refers.

One way of eliminating the problem of exchange rate expectations and the possibility of premiums for exchange rate risk, is to study the differential between national interest rates and *foreign interest rates covered on the forward market.* If there is no change in the size of possible premiums for political risk, an increase in direct financial integration will show itself here in smaller deviations from international *interest rate parity* (alternative 3) and a smaller flow of arbitrage over the national borders. If the size of the transaction cost is taken into account as well, this last alternative also reflects the efficiency of the market.

A fourth alternative is to add the exchange expectations of the market actors to alternative (2), and to study deviations from *the International Fisher Effect* (alternative 4). If the market actors are averse to risk in some way, the analysis should be extended to consider their demand for risk premiums. The research literature contains relatively few examples of integration studies in which an extended approach of this kind, including premiums for exchange risk as well as political risk, has been adopted.

There is much to suggest, however, that such an approach provides the best conditions, theoretically and operationally, for determining the level of direct financial integration.

A fifth alternative is to study the extent to which the *forward rate is an unbiased estimate of the future spot exchange rate* (alternative 5).

One problem common to all the alternatives is to find foreign equivalents of the domestic interest rate to be analysed. First we have to find instruments which are as similar as possible as regards conditions and risks, but the problem remains of finding explicit expressions of the premiums for the different risks which still distinguish the instruments from one another. It is only when we have considered all the risks that we can say anything about the level of financial integration and the pattern whereby foreign interest movements are reproduced in the domestic rate ("interest transmission").

The most common kind of interest rate used in international studies of direct financial integration and interest transmission, is the rate on treasury bills. Most researchers consider that this rate exhibits the greatest international similarity as regards instrument-specific risks such as default and liquidity risk.

1.7 What interest rates are the "leaders", as the influence of the US rate declines?

In various studies undertaken during the 1960s and 1970s it was generally assumed that interest rates on the US market were unaffected by foreign influence. It was also assumed that they led international trends, which was surely a reasonable assumption in view of the central role of the dollar in the Bretton Woods agreement. However, the influence exerted by the US rate over European interest rates was not complete. Sterilization actions and exchange controls gave Europe a certain freedom. The influence of the US rate has successively diminished, and the results of recent studies suggest that since the middle of the 1970s, i.e. after the collapse of the agreement on fixed exchange rates, there has been a mutual causal relationship between the US rates and their counterparts on the national markets in Europe. This mutual influence is mediated in part by way of the Eurodollar rate.

Results of interest studies carried out in recent years have revealed strong links between the financial markets of the major OECD countries. However, they are not so strong as to leave no chance of using domestic monetary policy to influence interest rates on the national markets. But, as was indicated in Section 1.2, most of the empirical studies ignored exchange rate expectations, or avoided the difficulty of modelling them by comparing the Eurorate with the corresponding national interest

Figure 1.1 Equilibrium relationships[1] between changes in exchange rates, rates of inflation and interest differentials

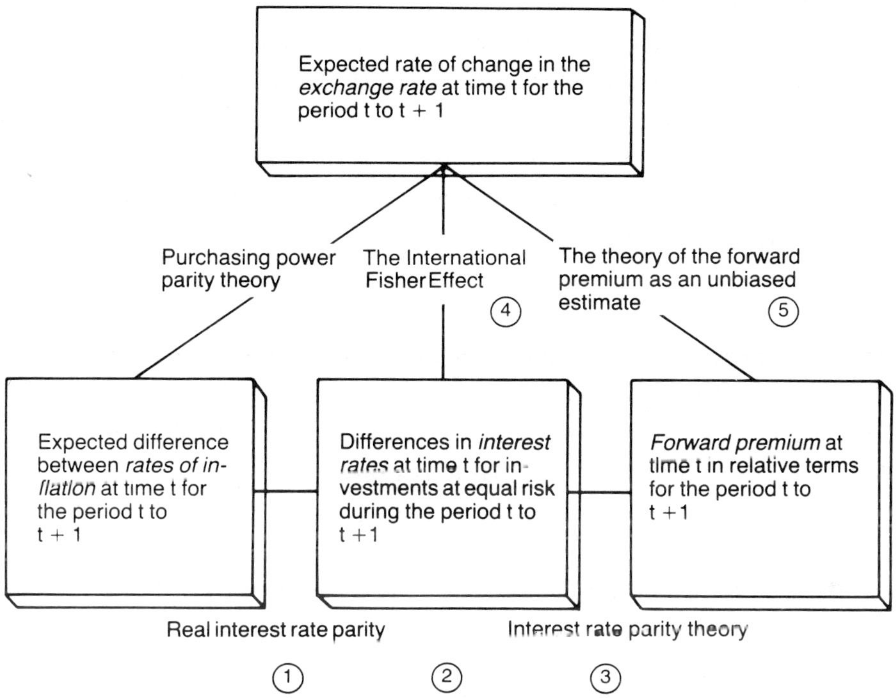

[1] In approximative, but commonly used forms! For a more detailed description and empirical evaluation of these equilibrium relationships, see e.g. Oxelheim (1985). The relationships mentioned in the figure will be presented in greater detail in Chapter 2.

rates. Moreover, most analyses have been limited to a single segment of the financial market. The grounds for any conclusions about the scope for autonomous monetary policies have thus always been weak.

In recent years it has been found that all interest rates are subject to the influence of a common factor which can be called the "global interest level". This can be described as a weighted average of the rates in the largest OECD countries. It has also been shown that the impact of the US interest rates on this global interest level has been gradually declining.

If we want to make an empirical study of the effect of changes in the global interest level on interest rates in a small open economy, the weighting procedure raises an interesting theoretical issue. Should we use trade weights – bilateral or multilateral – or capital market weights? The second of these alternatives would give greater weight to the US rate. Trade weights appear more appropriate, since it can be assumed that capital market weights covariate with the interest rate.

In view of all these measurement problems, we may well ask ourselves: why is it so interesting to measure the level of financial integration and changes in this level? Despite the strong links between the macroeconomy – the economy of a country as a whole – and the microeconomy in which companies and banks are the main actors, I shall nonetheless consider the importance of financial integration in the next two sections under these two separate headings.

1.8 Why is the level of financial integration interesting in a macro-perspective?

What is interesting at the macro-level is the connection between the level of financial integration and a country's ability to influence its own prosperity through an autonomous monetary policy. One way of achieving this autonomy, under fixed exchange rates, is to prevent a state of perfect capital mobility. Figure 1.2 illustrates the links between three elements of policy which can only be combined two and two, and the three possible monetary regimes which these combinations represent.

Figure 1.2 The monetary policy triangle

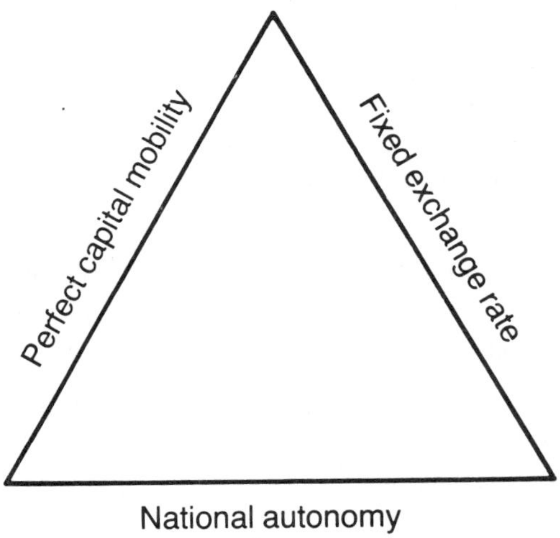

A country's main reasons for protecting itself and conducting an autonomous national policy are the threat of speculative international crises and the high cost to society of financial instability.

The traditional assumption is that greater financial integration promotes greater efficiency in the international allocation of resources, but at the expense of the efficiency of the national stabilization policy. If we step outside this general framework, several other questions arise regarding the efficiency of the stabilization policy. How far can the government keep the domestic real return on a security below the return on the equivalent paper in another currency? How far can it influence the cost of capital within the country and the level of real domestic investment? What can it do to influence the relative cost of capital, and thus also the allocation of capital to various classes of domestic investment? The answer is that under increasing integration their opportunities in these respects remain unchanged, or are reduced. A more exact answer would call for a specification of the kind of integration we are talking about, and a clarification of the prevailing conditions as regards exchange rate systems, capital mobility, the efficiency of information etc.

How can governments exercise autonomy in monetary policy and determine the gap between the expected domestic and foreign real interest rate, with a view to influencing investment and unemployment? By definition perfect total financial integration does not allow governments any such opportunity, whereas if integration is less than perfect, they do have a chance of influencing the size of expected deviations from purchasing power parity and the size of the risk premiums. Thus a gap is created between expected real interest rates, by leaving the market with an impression of greater uncertainty as regards the exchange rate, for instance, and the threat of imminent political interventions. But it is very doubtful whether it is actually possible to help to achieve investment or employment goals by exercising this sort of control.

If even the government is doubtful about the idea of managing developments by increasing the uncertainty on the market, all that remains is to exercise control by influencing the market's exchange expectations and/or by imposing regulations. However, the market will probably not allow itself to be systematically manipulated in its exchange rate expectations, but will recognize the manœuvre for what it is – an attempt at control. In so far as the market does not see through the mechanism, governments do have a chance here of exercising control without incurring too high a "cost". But if the market does see through the control mechanism, there may be high costs to society as a whole. The greater uncertainty on the market can have undesirable results for the country as a whole, perhaps in the shape of postponed investments.

There remains the alternative of using regulations to insert a wedge between domestic and foreign *nominal* interest levels. But even if a government succeeds in achieving this, the question remains of what they have done in real terms. Attempts at disintegration, for example by imposing exchange controls, have a price that is seldom mentioned: by shutting out the effects of international shocks and disturbances, they increase the vulnerability of the home economy to domestic non-policy-related disturbances.

Only a few industrial countries – and Sweden was among them until July 1989 – have functioning exchange controls today. A globally growing network of flows between countries – in manpower, capital, goods, services and information – reinforces our contention that the individual country now has less chance of maintaining an independent stabilization policy by imposing exchange controls and other regulations, even though there are no studies quantifying this possibility or generally indicating – under various market assumptions – the impact of active exchange controls on the level of disintegration of a country's financial market.

1.9 What is the significance of the level of financial integration in a micro or corporate perspective?

As we have seen, under perfect (total) financial integration the expected real interest rates on comparable investments in different countries and different currencies will be the same. Thus, if a (small) country's financial market is becoming more highly integrated, corporate capital costs in the country concerned, and consequently return requirements in real terms, will increasingly adjust to the movements in the global interest level. Greater total financial integration also reduces the corporate incentive to establish operations in a *large* number of different countries.

On a perfect direct integrated capital market the investor cannot increase his expected risk-adjusted nominal return by reinvesting his capital in markets in other countries. A higher expected return converted into the domestic currency is accompanied by a higher risk in his portfolio. The ex ante differentials in nominal interest rates can be expected to compensate for expected exchange rate movements, risk premiums, and transaction and information costs. Thus the profit from the diversification of his investment consists simply of a reduction in a global perspective in the possible non-systematic risk, i.e. the risk for which the investor obtains no compensation. But if the investor is aware of the segmentation of the capital markets, he will have an incentive to seek *excess* return, i.e. a return over and above compensation for the above-mentioned risks and costs, by choosing the "right" national market or combination of markets.

Opportunities for risk-free profits as a result of covered interest arbitrage are an indication that financial markets are not characterized by perfect direct integration. The profits are captured at the corporate level by the cross-border transfer of forward covered capital. Corporate profit opportunities lie in the presence of market inefficiency and/or politically generated inefficiency.

If there is a higher level of direct financial integration, there will also be better opportunities for the market actors to allocate risks and to diversify, and a greater likelihood of increasing welfare because they can achieve the desired trade-off between risk and expected return. Thus the (possible) loss in welfare due to reduced autonomy in the national stabilization policy, has its counterpole in a more efficient allocation of capital in terms of risk and return.

1.10 Is the interest rate in a small open economy determined on foreign markets?

In most models concerned with small open economies it is assumed that the interest rate is determined exogenously. In other words it is often assumed that the "small-country" assumption provides a close approximation. But Aliber (1978b) objects to this, claiming that no country is so small that this assumption can be taken as an acceptable approximation. However, there is much evidence to suggest that the approximation has probably become increasingly appropriate over the last ten years or so.

My point of departure in this book is that the rates in my examples – the Swedish rates – are determined to a large extent by forces outside the country. According to my *hypothesis* capital market integration has increased and the gap between domestic and foreign interest rates, after eliminating risk premiums, transaction costs and exchange rate expectations, has been gradually declining during the period of the study, namely 1974–84; so, too, has the transmission time between foreign interest rate movements and the Swedish rates.

The situation on which I base my hypothesis is that Sweden's financial system has undergone farreaching changes during recent decades. The nature of interest and exchange controls has changed, and during the 1980s a functioning money market has emerged. New money market and capital market instruments have evolved, which have contributed towards a new interest rate structure. At the same time Sweden's structural dependence has clearly increased as a result of internationalization, as will be seen from the argument in the following sections.[1]

1.11 Growing uncertainty raises demands for higher risk premiums

Few events since the end of the war have had such an impact on the evolution of the international financial system as the collapse of the Bretton Woods agreement. Ever since the period just before the final collapse in March 1973 the actors on the market have been working in a competitive environment characterized by growing uncertainty as regards exchange rates, interest rates, rates of inflation and the rules of the market game. And in many cases interest rates and inflation rates have exhibited high levels, historically speaking, in recent years. Actors on Swedish markets have been very exposed to this financial turbulence, which has brought unexpected fluctuations in profit and an aversion to risk.

In its anxiety to ward off financial fluctuations and the accompanying harmful effects on the national economy, the Swedish central bank (Sveriges Riksbank) has, redirected the effects of the underlying "disturbance" in the exchange-rate context, from small successive fluctuations to relatively frequent and sizable devaluations. In any study of the integration of Swedish financial markets it is important to consider the effects of this policy as expressed in investors' demands for compensatory premiums for exchange and political risks.

1.12 The internationalization of trade

Increasing international trade can be seen as a step towards the growing integration of the goods markets and, ultimately, towards higher levels of (total) financial integration. Sweden has been becoming increasingly open to international trade. Exports, measured as a share of GDP have increased by 5–6 percentage points per decade since 1952, and by the middle of the 1980s amounted to 35 per cent. This can be compared with the United States, for example, where the export share remained largely unchanged at about 7 per cent between 1974 and 1984.

A growing number of Swedish companies now invoice their exports in the currency of the recipient country.[2] For many companies with foreign subsidiaries, invoicing in the currency of the recipient country has been part of a strategy of centralizing the exposure of the entire corporate group to the headquarters. This may have increased the currency exposure of the Swedish exporting industries. In the absence of any marked monetary integration, it can be assumed that this increasing exposure has contributed to a greater awareness of risk differentials between different currencies. This awareness must also have helped to generate a more efficiently functioning market when it comes to the pricing of exchange risk, i.e. determining of the size of the risk premium for different currencies.

1.13 The internationalization of financing

The deficit in the current account in the wake of the oil crisis dramatically altered Sweden's net position vis-à-vis the rest of the world from 6.8 per cent of GDP at the end of 1973, to –24 per cent at the end of 1984. Sweden's high rate of foreign borrowing motivates the discussion of a political risk premium for Sweden.

In 1974 there was a change of policy in Sweden at the central bank level with regard to corporate *foreign borrowing.* The system of exchange controls was reorganized and interest rate policy adjusted, with a view to persuading companies to help to finance the growing deficit in the current account by way of foreign borrowing. This succeeded at first, and both corporate and municipal foreign borrowing increased substantially. But after 1977 the picture changed, and the government became the main borrower and net borrower on the international credit market. This was due to the large budget deficit which appeared at this time, and probably also to the companies' experience of exchange risks in the mid-1970s. In 1977 the government's outstanding stock of medium-term and long-term foreign loans amounted to 22 per cent of the total amount borrowed. At the end of 1983 the corresponding figure was 55 per cent.[3] In 1984 the scenario changed once more, and corporate and municipal foreign borrowing rose again.

At the end of 1984 the SEK equivalent of the corporate foreign debt was 109 billion.[4] The net position was about SEK –16 billion. However, in recent years the funding procedure has altered somewhat. An increasing proportion of the banks' foreign operations involves loans taken up abroad and reloaned to Swedish companies. The exchange risk then attaches to the borrower, i.e. the company. This fact dramatically impairs the corporate net position vis-à-vis the rest of the world, compared with that reported above.[5] The issuance of permits by the central bank for direct investment abroad has also changed, in that since 1983 share issues abroad were accepted as a form of financing. 11 per cent of the permits for direct investment abroad in 1983 and 1984 were based on this form of financing.

The proportion of loans in foreign currencies in Swedish non-financial companies increased by almost 10 percentage points from 12 per cent at year-end 1974 up to year-end 1984, while the proportions of loans on the liability side of the balance sheet remained almost unchanged at around 70 per cent. The increasing share of foreign loans in the corporate portfolios may have altered the relationship between risk and return. The more foreign loans there are in a corporate portfolio, the more the company will demand in the way of risk premiums before taking up further loans. Because of the increasing amount borrowed in foreign currencies, it also became gradually easier for companies during the period of the investigation to circumvent exchange controls by making adjustments in their portfolio of foreign loans.

In the wake of this increasing internationalization Swedish companies can also set their growing *foreign assets* off against the higher risks on their foreign loans in the balance sheet. At current prices direct corporate investments abroad increased from SEK 3.8 billion in 1980 to SEK 10.6 billion in 1984.[6] At the end of 1984 their assets amounted to about SEK 93.3 billion.[7]

1.14 The internationalization of production

Another sign of increasing internationalization is the growing number of foreign employees in Swedish companies. In the 40 largest multinational groups[8] the number of foreign employees in 1965 was 170,600, as against 323,000 in these companies in Sweden. In 1984 the number employed in Sweden was more or less unchanged, while the number employed abroad had risen to the same level.

1.15 Design of the analysis

The analysis in this book differs in some ways from its predecessors in the field. To begin with, I have tried to structure the concept of financial integration. Secondly, I have extended a traditional approach to apply to the measurement of capital market integration, and I define a new quantitative measure for this purpose. Thirdly, I formulate a model in terms of expected return and – unlike most previous model-builders – I test my model against at least approximate ex ante data. Fourthly, as a basis for these tests I have collected primary data regarding the process whereby market actors form their expectations.

In the empirical analysis I include interest rates from five sectors of Sweden's financial markets. The theoretical foundations for stock market linkages are different from those referring to interest rate linkages. This fact, together with further forms of measurement and standardization problems, led me to exclude stock market integration from my empirical analysis. This means that I am measuring the international integration of credit markets rather than of capital markets.[9] As in earlier studies of financial integration, the sectorial approach produces a partial or fragmented analysis, in that market influence is not considered in any overall system or general equilibrium model.

The decline in political influence and control on the Swedish market in the form of administratively determined interest rates has probably also affected another factor:

the time lag before influence from abroad takes effect. In order to be able to say something about changes in the level of integration over time, I have also analysed three subperiods.

The data on which the empirical analysis is based refers to the period 1974–84 and includes interest rates on the money and bond markets. The starting date was chosen in light of the collapse of the Bretton Woods agreement. The interest rates studied are the discount rate, the prime rate and the rates on treasury bills, government bonds and industrial bonds. The absence of any formal Eurorate for the the Swedish krona for the period as a whole excluded any short–cuts, such as comparing domestic rates with Eurorates in the same currency, in order to avoid problems in estimating the expected change in exchange rates.

1.16 Plan of the book

Chapter 2 contains a brief survey of the conceptual apparatus and methodological problems in connection with the analysis of financial integration. Here I also introduce my model for analysing the international integration of the Swedish financial market.

Chapter 3 outlines the advantages and disadvantages of different ways of measuring financial integration. In this chapter I survey earlier studies of international financial integration.

In *Chapter 4* various special institutional characteristics of Swedish markets are discussed. The importance of the Swedish exchange controls as an instrument of segmentation is analysed on a basis of the primary data collected. Historical patterns in exchange movements, and the formation of market expectations as regards these movements, are other special aspects which are discussed. I also look at some specifically Swedish measurement problems, for example how to measure the size of non-government capital transactions over the national borders.

Chapter 5 presents an analysis of historical patterns in Swedish interest rates and the correlation between them. With the help of ARIMA models the interdependence of successive interest rate quotations is analysed.

Swedish and foreign interest rates are juxtaposed in *Chapter 6*. I look here for indications of increasing integration in the shape of the adjustment of Swedish interest rates to major shifts in foreign rates. I also illustrate the gap between Swedish rates and the corresponding global rates and US rates.

In *Chapter 7* the analysis is extended to include the correlation between international rates (global rate or US rate) and successive Swedish interest rate quotations.

This analysis of the cross-correlation refers to real interest rates as well as nominal rates without any adjustment for risk or exchange rate effects, either observed or expected. In *Chapter 8* these effects are inserted within the framework of an empirical analysis of my model of the international integration of Sweden's financial market.

In *Chapter 9* the results are summarized. *Supplements* provide lists of designations and key data about the interest rates used in the analysis.

Notes

1 Sections 1.11–1.14 illustrate developments in Sweden during the period of the study, 1974–1984, and are intended to provide the basic material on which readers can build their own interpretations of the results of the study.

2 At the beginning of the studied period over 60 per cent of exports were invoiced in Swedish kronor. By the end of the period this share had dropped to about 40 per cent. The equivalent figure in imports has remained low, at about 25 per cent, with little change throughout the period. (*Source*: Sveriges Riksbank 1988)

3 Sveriges Riksbank, *Kredit- och valutaöversikt* 1984:4, p. 29.

4 The difficulties in estimating this can be seen in *Kredit- och valutaöversikt* 1984:2, p. 20. The figures are taken from the same source 1986:2, p. 13.

5 Sveriges Riksbank, *Kredit- och valutaöversikt* 1986:2, p. 13.

6 According to Sveriges riksbank, *Kredit- och valutaöversikt* 1986:1 and 1987:1, direct Swedish investments per year for the period 1981–84 amounted to SEK 4.6, 6.5, 8.7 and 10.6 million. If we convert this to 1980 prices the investments amounted to SEK 4.3, 5.6, 5.8, 6.1 billion.

7 Sveriges Riksbank, *Kredit- och valutaöversikt* 1986:2, p. 13.

8 See Eliasson et al. (1985).

9 There is a good deal of confusion about these concepts in the literature and in everyday usage, so that some clarification of my own terminology is called for. I regard the *capital market* as a comprehensive designation for the credit and stock markets, where the *credit market* is a comprehensive designation for the money and bond markets.

CHAPTER 2

What Is Financial Integration, and Can It Be Measured?

2.1 Introduction

In this chapter I shall discuss various aspects of financial integration. I shall present my choice of definition and my model, and illustrate the measurement problems we can expect to meet. The theoretical presentation in the first sections is intended to underpin the following discussion of these questions. The aim of the chapter is to provide a theoretical background to the empirical analysis in Chapters 5–8.

Section 2.2 is concerned with price, i.e. the interest rate or the return on various financial instruments. Here I shall address the question of the domestic and foreign determinants of the interest rate. In this section I shall also discuss the link between interest rates in different sectors of the credit market and between interest rates on investments of different maturities.

In Section 2.3 I look at the way capital flows and information link goods markets with the financial markets, i.e. the capital market and the foreign exchange market. In this section, too, financial integration is defined in its various forms. This section reveals the problems which attach to the analysis of total financial integration and underpins my decision to limit the study to direct financial integration. The importance of segmented foreign exchange markets is discussed.

The interest of the international investor in a particular financial instrument depends on risk and expected return. An important aspect of the expected return is the expected movements in exchange rates during the period of the international investment. In Section 2.4 the determinants of the exchange rate are discussed, and the expectations of the market as regards exchange rate movements. Section 2.5 studies various types of risk and the related premiums. The relation between risk and return is studied in Section 2.6.

Section 2.7 is concerned with the possibility of measuring the level of financial integration and interest rate autonomy. The section includes a brief survey of research with reference to the operational definition of financial integration and the related analytical procedures. Here we also look at the problem of basing any conclusions about the level of interest rate policy autonomy on observations of financial integration. In Section 2.8 the definition of financial integration on which the analysis in this book is based, is specified in greater detail. I also describe the model used in the analysis.

The importance of exchange controls as a barrier to financial integration is discussed briefly in Section 2.9. Problems of measurement and standardization are the subject of Section 2.10. A major problem concerns the pricing of risks of various kinds, in comparing markets in different countries. A better understanding of the thought processes of the market actors, should ease this problem. An interview study, aimed at increasing our understanding of corporate preferences and expectations, is presented in Section 2.11. The implications of the chapter as a whole for the design of my empirical analysis are summarized in Section 2.12.

2.2 Are interest rates determined at home or abroad?

The purpose of this section is to examine the determinants underlying the nominal domestic interest rate. We will look at some important "accepted" linkages, and relate the theory of domestically determined interest rates to the corresponding theory of internationally determined rates. Let us start by examining the expectations of the market actors.

2.2.1 Hypotheses about the formation of expectations

What we are interested in here is a hypothesis about the level of integration and the efficiency of financial markets. Market efficiency can be formulated in terms of the extent to which market prices reflect in full all the available information.[1 2]

The hypothesis regarding efficient markets has two parts: one, that the actors are rational and will avoid known errors in forecasting, given the existing information, and secondly that every deviation from expected return is immediately eliminated by arbitrage so that the opportunity for "excess profit" vanishes.[3 4]

Although the hypothesis regarding rational expectations is included in the hypothesis of efficient markets, there is a separate literature for each of the two areas. Perhaps we should therefore clarify the meaning of the hypothesis of rational expectations. In doing so, let us start with the predecessor – the hypothesis of adaptive expectations.

Severe criticism of the hypothesis of adaptive expectations

If we want to model individual behaviour in a world of uncertainty, we have to tackle the modelling of expectations. In studies made during the 1960s and early 1970s this problem was solved by an assumption regarding *adaptive expectations.*[5] It is thus assumed that the individual uses information about earlier forecasting errors to help him revise his expectations. The ideas underlying this concept are derived from control technology, and can be described in the following simple equation:

$$_{t-1}X^*_t = {}_{t-2}X^*_{t-1} + \phi\,(X_{t-1} - {}_{t-2}X^*_{t-1}) \tag{2.1}$$

where $0<\phi<1$.

Thus, we generate today's forecast ($_{t-1}X^*_t$) of a variable X by adding to yesterday's forecast ($_{t-2}X^*_{t-1}$) a fraction (ϕ) of the forecasting error which it has been possible to observe in light of the actual outcome (X_{t-1}).

Criticism of this hypothesis consisted of two main arguments. First, the critics felt it was unrealistic to assume that individuals shaped their expectations exclusively on a basis of historical information. They felt it was a serious drawback to assume that the actors ignore information about future events in forming expectations. The slowness of the market actors to react to their own earlier forecasting errors was also mentioned.

Secondly, the critics objected to the absence of any theory for determining how much of the previous forecasting errors the actors "should" use in forming their new expectations.

Recent studies start from a hypothesis of rational expectations

The objections to the hypothesis of adaptive expectations led to the formulation of *a hypothesis of rational expectations.*[6] The point of departure for this hypothesis is the assumption that individuals do not allow themselves to be consistently deceived. It is assumed that "guesses" about the future must on an average be correct, if people are to be satisfied with their own way of forming their expectations. Thus the existence of systematic errors in expectations is inconsistent with this hypothesis; random errors, on the other hand, may occur.

The use of this hypothesis in an uncertain world is fraught with difficulty. For instance, what information can we assume people possess, when the information about future variables is incomplete? The alternatives are many. For example we could assume that the actors know the structure of an underlying model, or that they know the model's outcome. If a model is stochastic, we can assume that the actors know its statistical characteristics. Given such an assumption, the "true" expectation according to the hypothesis of rational expectations will be the same as the mathematical expectation based on the information which is available when the expectation is formed. The actors behave as though they know the model, and form their expectations accordingly.

It could be objected here that not everybody can understand economic models. But, according to the hypothesis of rational expectations, this does not matter in a world in which information is disseminated quickly and widely, and in which "good" forecasts free of systematic error are continually being published. Given this assumption about the diffusion of information, it is enough for us to model the endogenous behaviour of the "smart" actors whose behaviour on an average proves to be correct.

Objections to the hypothesis of rational expectations

Given this broad interpretation of the hypothesis of rational expectations, it is easy to understand why so many model-builders find it attractive as a substitute for the hypothesis of adaptive expectations. Above all we no longer have to accept that the market actors are beset by systematic errors. But critics of the hypothesis claim that it includes too much. According to Begg (1982) the possible objections are of four kinds: 1) objections concerning calculation problems, 2) objections based on the impossibility of obtaining the information needed for identifying the correct model, 3) objections that question the profit of acquiring the information and consequently the actors' incentive to collect, and 4) objections which emphasize differences in the information of the various groups involved.

To put it slightly differently, we could say that critics object to the *aggregation* of individual people's expectations, i.e. to the assumption of the *homogeneity* of expectations, and that all expectations are equated with those of the smart actor. This idea is based on the implicit assumption that our smart actor acts without systematic error not only in his choice of model but also in his interpretation of information about the values of the variables which provide the basis for his expectations. Thus the smart actor exhibits no systematic *errors in his perception of the model* or *in his perception of the content of the information.* The critics object that according to the hypothesis this circumstance is regarded as applying to other participants on the market as well.

Despite a certain amount of justified criticism, the hypothesis of rational expectations is the only acceptable assumption at present if we want to compare markets in an uncertain world.

Empirical tests of composite hypotheses are always conditional

Two ways of testing market efficiency occur in the *empirical* literature. Both are conditional. One checks whether the expectations are rational rather than adaptive and is dependent on the correct specification of the underlying model. The second seeks to test the assumption of the underlying model and is dependent on the correctness of the hypothesis of rational expectations.

In order to test the hypothesis of rational expectations we need data about the expectations at given points in time. To make things simpler we could as an approximation collect data about the mechanisms used to generate forecasts and about the information base that is continuously used. Even if we trust the truth content of the relevant data, a certain amount of uncertainty attaches to judging the rationality of ex ante expectations by comparing them with actual (ex post) outcomes.

The existence of autocorrelated errors[7] is generally regarded as inconsistent with rational expectations. Against this the "Peso principle" can be invoked.[8] This can be expressed as follows: there is a non zero probability that an event in the form of a powerful discontinuity will occur within a certain period. This event is then included in the expectations, period after period, until it finally occurs. If we make an analysis over a number of periods during which the relevant event does not occur, our evaluation using ex post data will exhibit a systematic error. Thus systematic errors do not provide definite evidence of irrationality in expectations.

With this brief exposition in mind let us now examine the classical premises for interpreting the information content of prices on the financial market.

2.2.2 *A theory of domestically determined interest rates*

The most common point of departure for analysing the interest rate in its domestically market-determined version, is Fisher's Closed Relationship or the Fisher (Domestic) Effect (see Fisher, 1930 or Appendix 2.1). The content of this relationship, as presented by Fisher in the Theory of Interest at the turn of the century, is that the real interest rate, taken over a fairly long period of time, is approximately *constant.*[9] It is assumed that changes in the nominal rate will reflect changes in the expected rate of inflation in a one-to-one relationship. The relationship, in this classical form, was formulated for an economy which included no tax on the yield.

Suppose that everyone knows there is not going to be any inflation. If so, all interest rates are real rates. According to the Fisher Effect the (real) equilibrium rate is then the price at which supply and demand on the financial market are the same size

Figure 2.1 Supply and demand for capital - the real equilibrium interest rate

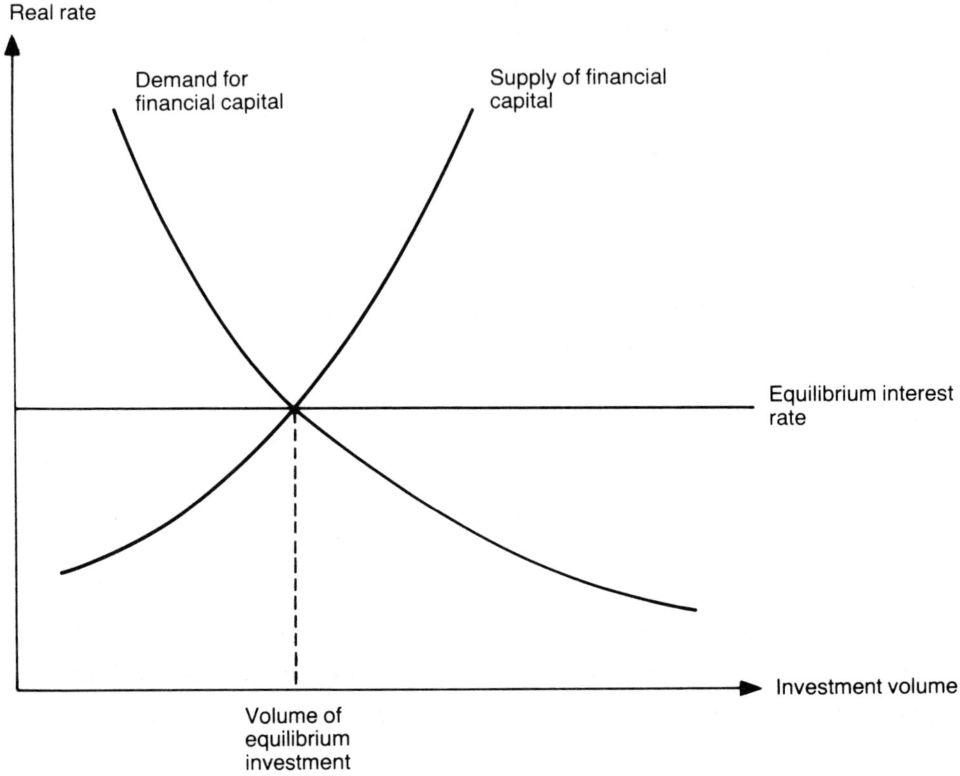

(see Figure 2.1). The supply depends on the propensity to save, i.e. on the willingness of households to postpone consumption. Demand depends on the opportunities for productive investment in a society. It can be assumed that this investment refers to projects whose return will successively decline and that it will continue until the point at which – assuming risk can be ignored – the return is equal to the interest rate. Thus the total demand for capital is a function of the interest rate, and is equal to the sum of the capital requirements of all companies.

Market equilibrium occurs at the interest rate which balances a society's investment requirements with the willingness to save of the individuals in that society. Taxes and the selective interventions of monetary policy can upset the balance.

What will then happen when inflation is to be expected? According to Fisher, the investor will claim a nominal rate which protects his desired real rate. A change of one percentage point in the expected rate of inflation leads to a change of one percentage point in the nominal rate.

The Fisher Effect is paradoxical in being generally accepted as a cornerstone of the classical theory of interest-rate formation without the benefit of any support from empirical studies. Fisher noted the absence of empirical underpinning himself, and tried to explain the empirical deviations by reference to the money illusion.

In recent years, however, some research reports have provided a certain amount of empirical support for the Fisher Effect. Summers (1983) shows that the degree of support varies with the choice of study period, and Virén (1987) that the degree of support depends on the length of the study period. Makin (1983) and Tanzi (1984) claim that the empirical deviations can be explained to a great extent by the choice of method.[10] Others emphasize that support for the Fisher Effect increases when the impact of taxation is taken into account.

Role of tax in the analysis

If we examine the strength of the empirical support for the Fisher Effect as it emerges from the different studies, we find that it varies over time as Summers suggests. Studies of the US market show that in the post-war period up to the beginning of the 1970s, investors demanded higher nominal interest rates simply to protect the desired level of real interest rates against the effect of changes in expected inflation. Empirical studies of later periods suggest that investment behaviour has changed since then. This change could be partly explained by the rate of inflation after the first oil crisis which probably made investors aware of the effect of tax on the real rate of interest.[11] In order to explain the empirical deviations from the classical definition, more attention was thus paid to the effects of taxes in the mid-1970s.[12]

Carmichael and Stebbing (1983) found that a substantial increase in the actual variability of real interest rates can be explained by the fact that, in a financial market perspective, inflation mainly affects the real interest rate. The slight effect on the nominal interest rate is the same in either the long or the short term. In their studies of fluctuations in the rate on US treasury bills, Carmichael and Stebbing show that tax changes are more important than inflation as an explanation of changes in nominal interest rates. They conclude that

> ... not only is inflation not reflected in the after-tax nominal interest rate one-to-one, it is not reflected at all. By extension, it would appear that movements in pre-tax interest rates have had more to do with movements in taxes than with movements in inflation.

The negative correlation between inflation and the real interest rate (the Mundell-Tobin effect)[13], which is emphasized in many theoretical works and which is confirmed, for example, by Fama and Gibbons (1984) and Makin and Tanzi (1983), diminishes when tax is taken into account. Thus if tax is also considered, the empirical underpinning of the Fisher Effect is slightly reinforced.

Tax on interest income – both selective and asymmetrical – probably has a powerful effect on the level of the domestically determined equilibrium rate. In international comparisons of interest rates, of the kind we shall be undertaking in the rest of this book, tax plays a less important role, since the interest income can be expected to be taxed in the home country regardless of where it is earned. But withholding taxes, such as the tax on the return from bond-holdings in the country where the disbursement is made, may alter the situation.

Obvious analytical difficulties

There have been obvious difficulties in the analytical processes associated with the Fisher Effect. As on the exchange rate side, econometric models have generally tended to exhibit weak explanatory value and provided poor forecasts of the development outside the period of estimation.

The inclusion of tax on interest income in the analysis has not explained the empirical deviations satisfactorily. In recent years a great many research reports[14] have been published in an attempt to find other explanations as to why the expected real rate of interest or real interest requirement fluctuate in the real world, and why the relationship between the nominal rate and expected inflation is only a rough approximation. A summary of the results of these reports suggests that the Fisher Effect should be extended or modified to allow for the fact that changes in the level or variability of the nominal interest rate can stem from other causes than

1) a change in the level or volatility of the expected real rate
2) a change in the level or volatility of expected inflation
3) a change in the impact that unit changes in either or both of these variables has on interest rates.

Importance of understanding how actors form their expectations

The greatest empirical problems have arisen from the formulation of the Fisher Effect in ex ante quantities – expected inflation and expected real interest rate. Since these quantities cannot be observed, we have to find acceptable approximations for either or both of them. As we have already seen, actual outcomes provide a poor approximation. Fisher (1930) used an approximation himself. His empirical praxis involved an implicit extrapolation which only acquired its theoretical formulation later as the hypothesis of adaptive expectations.

Saracoglu (1984) and others who claim that the fluctuations in the real interest rate are not random over time, stress the importance of trying to understand the market's expectations with regard to this interest rate within a richer specification. For example, the actors' risk aversion is a crucial factor, and their demands for compensatory premiums for inflation risk and political risk provide a possible explanation of the weak support for the Fisher Effect in the empirical studies.

Deviations from the Fisher Effect have their explanation abroad

Thus the empirical evidence of the Fisher Effect is not convincing, whether or not tax effects are taken into account. It is widely agreed that the relationship must be extended to include several more variables. This can be done either by adding new expressions to the relationship, or by accepting that the real interest rate is not constant but is a function of the investor's view of the investment environment and of the expectations he bases on this view. Thus if he believes that the chances of a higher return under similar risks are better abroad, we can assume that he will adjust his return requirements upwards. An important item in the investor's evaluation will then concern his expectations regarding exchange rate movements. But if the exchange rate is to be allowed for in some way in the domestic interest rate, we come to the question of the link with foreign markets.

2.2.3 A simple theory of the linkage between domestic and foreign interest rates

In classical theory the foreign interest rate is linked to the domestic rate by way of the International Fisher Effect[15] (see Appendix 2.3), which implies that on an efficient and non-controlled capital market the choice of currency for an investment or a loan will ultimately be immaterial. As soon as the relationship is not expected to obtain, the risk-neutral investor – according to economic theory – will find arguments in favour of a particular currency.

Example of speculative transactions under deviations from the International Fisher Effect

The way in which a free market operates can best be described in an example which reveals the link between the risk-neutral actors' expectations and their incentives to speculate.

Let us assume that the nominal interest rate on borrowing on a yearly basis is 10 per cent for the Eurodollar and 8 per cent for the Euromark. An expected change in the USD/DEM exchange rate corresponding to the difference in interest rates, means that costs can be expected to be the same when the loan is taken up. If the market is in imbalance and the appreciation in the Euromark is expected to be less than the difference in interest rates, this will lead to an increase in the demand for the Euromark as loan currency. On the other hand depositors will move their funds to investment in the dollar. As a result of these movements the interest rate on the Euromark is forced up. At the same time sales of DEM in order to acquire dollars on the part of both borrowers and investors, will force down the USD/DEM exchange rate. The argument in favour of Euromarks as loan currency do not disappear until the interest rate on the Euromark has been forced up and the USD/DEM exchange rate forced down to a point at which the Euromark interest rate plus the expected appreciation of the DEM are approximately the same as the interest rate on the Eurodollar. A major objection to this description is that we did not consider the presence of a transaction cost. Because of these costs the state of equilibrium should be represented not by a single point but by an interval within which the argument for speculation does not apply.

The expected effects may be direct or indirect

It has previously been stressed that if we want to get a better idea of interest rate structures, we need to know more about the way market actors form their expectations. An empirical analysis of financial integration calls for a further step, taking both national and international factors into account in our modelling of these expectations. The hypothesis of rational expectations makes heavy demands on the ability of the rationally behaving actor, who should see the links between all the different variables for all future time. This motivates our taking a simple example to illustrate both direct and indirect expectation effects. Let us look at the effect of the budget deficit on the interest rate. In the simplest terms this can be said to consist of two parts. One is the immediate effect of the deficit on the money supply, which may of course have been anticipated. This can be assumed to generate a certain hypothetical level for the domestic interest rate. The second is the indirect effect of the budget deficit, arising from the different inflation expectations generated by the change in the money supply. These effects are then allowed for in the market's exchange rate expectations, giving rise to financial transactions of the kind which led to the market rate observed in the previous example. The trade-off between fiscal policy and monetary policy measures in the action taken will also determine the trade-off between direct and indirect effects.

The International Fisher Effect presupposes risk neutrality

If the market actors are not risk-neutral, there will be a demand for a premium to compensate for risk. If we assume that the market has some form of risk aversion, we will have to extend the International Fisher Effect to include a term for such a premium. This applies to exchange risk when it can be assumed that other risks are matched, as in the case of Eurorates for instance. In any study based on comparisons of national market rates, the relationship would also have to include an expression for political risk.

2.2.4 Links between different sectors of the financial market

We can assume that the rational investor with some form of risk aversion will compare different markets and will allow for risk in his evaluation of the potential return on an investment. We will look at the subject of risk and return in Sections 2.5 and 2.6, but first we can examine the linkages which can be expected between functioning markets not subject to selective monetary policy action.

The linkages refer to different maturities and types of market, and in their simplest form can be described as follows:

$$\begin{array}{ccc} r^{s}_{d} & \longleftrightarrow & r^{s}_{for} \\ \updownarrow & & \updownarrow \\ r^{l}_{d} & \longleftrightarrow & r^{l}_{for} \end{array}$$

i.e. the short-term (s) and long-term (l) interest rates in a country (d) are linked to one another and to corresponding foreign interest rates (for).

Links between sectors in different countries

Figure 2.2 shows the links between national and international markets, and the multiplicity of market combinations to be analysed. Every market has its own specific

Figure 2.2 National and international financial markets

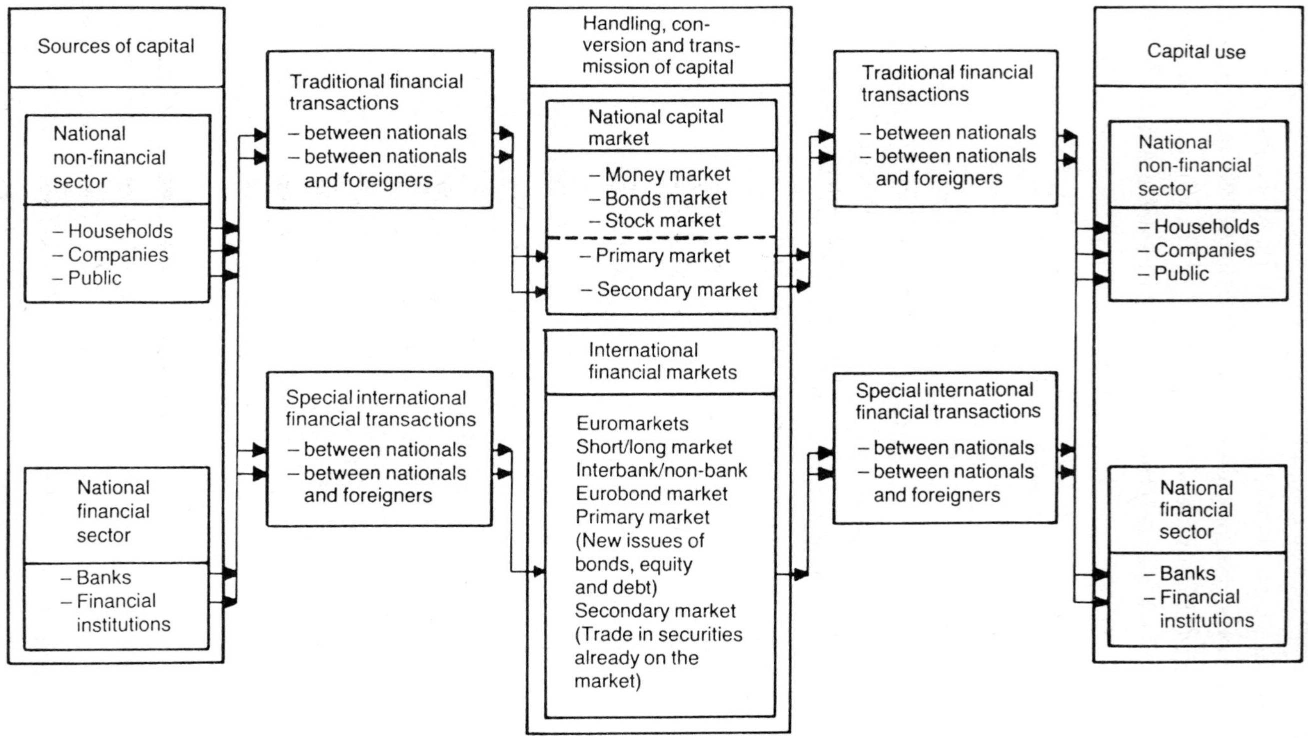

conditions, risks and term structures. And we can also divide markets into those that are controlled and those that are not. The Euromarkets are generally regarded as example of markets without national controls or influence.

Links between Euromarkets and national markets

In order also to illustrate the matching problems connected with the comparison of international interest rates, Figure 2.3 shows the relation between national markets and Euromarkets.

Box A shows the differences to be considered in comparing domestic interest rates and the rate for the corresponding currency on the Euromarket. Box B shows the factors to be considered in comparing interest rates in different currencies on the Euromarket. If the analysis is concerned with comparing national interest rates in different currencies, the elements in both box A and box B must be incorporated into the analysis.

Figure 2.3 Euromarket versus national market

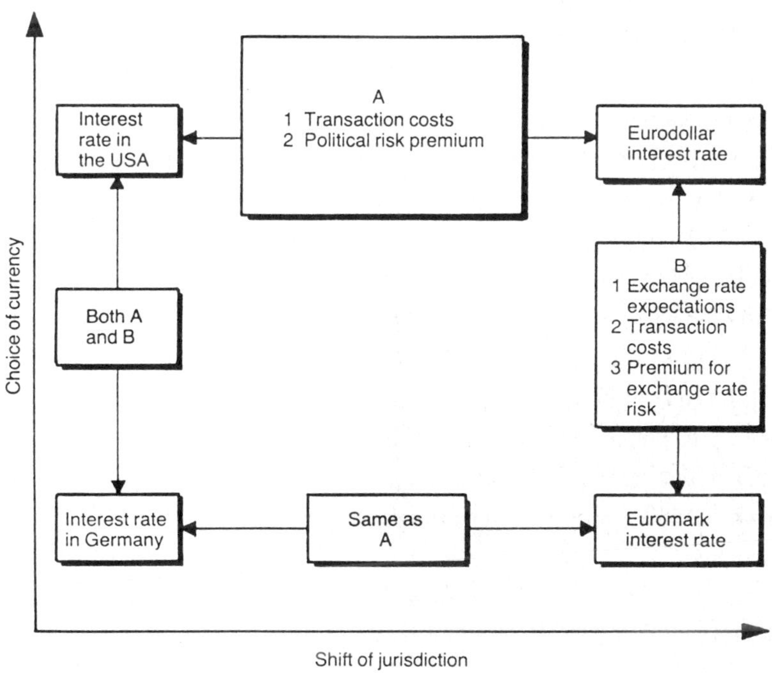

In earlier studies of financial integration and transmission the problem of exchange rate expectations has often been circumvented by comparing the Eurorate with the national rate in the same currency. The absence over a fairly long period of a formal Swedish Eurorate means that an analysis of Swedish integration has to be based on a comparison of national interest rates, taking the elements in both boxes A and B into account.

Links between short- and long-term interest rates

We have seen evidence of the great variety of sectors that go to make up a country's financial market. But is there any clear link between them? The link between the long- and short-term interest rates expresses the difference in information content between them, and it is formalized in the yield curve.[16] There are five theories on the subject of this link, based on assumptions about various kinds of risk premium. One of these theories, the *expectation theory*, says that the difference between long- and short-term market-led interest rates expresses what the investors expect to happen to short-term rates in the future.[17] It predicts that the overall interest rate for two subperiods will exceed the rate in the first subperiod only if the rate for the second subperiod can be expected to rise. A common objection to this theory is based on the strong indication of rising yield curves, and on the interpretation that the market thus expects the short-term interest rate to rise with improbable frequency. Another objection to the theory is that it does not allow for risk.

According to a second theory, the *theory of inflation risk compensation*,[18] the only uncertainty connected with the interest rate is uncertainty about inflation. In the normal case[19] there is a risk in real terms.The lender must thus be offered compensation for accepting a further inflation risk. Due to this compensation, the long-term interest rate should exceed the short-term rate.

A third theory, the *liquidity-preference theory*,[20] is based on the presence of liquidity risk, and the fact that long-term bonds should provide additional return to compensate for it. According to this theory the yield curve should slope upwards more often than downwards. Implicitly it is being assumed that the investor has a relatively short planning horizon. They want to lend short as opposed to companies who want to borrow long. A positive liquidity premium rewards investors who are willing to make make long-term investments.

The fourth theory, the *preferred habitat theory*, is closely related to the previous theory and is the most widely accepted. According to this theory the interest rate on a long-term bond is equal to the average of the short-term interest rates expected to occur during the maturity of the long-term bond, plus a risk premium which corresponds to the supply and demand conditions for that bond. This theory was developed by Modigliani and Sutch (1966, 1967) with an agnostic attitude towards the risk premium. Every investor is assumed to have a preferred maturity, but can be expected to change if he receives compensation. It is only necessary that bonds due to expire in the not-too-distant future should be fairly close substitutes for each other and should carry the same risk premium. The risk premium could also be called an inconvenience premium, in that it is intended to compensate the investor for stepping outside the part of the bond market where he feels at home (his preferred habitat). This theory also explains why the yield curve generally slopes upwards, due to an assumption that the risk premium is positive, since the investor tends to prefer short-term investments.

The fifth theory, the *segmented markets theory*, was originally proposed by Culbertson (1957). The idea underlying the yield curve represents the exact opposite of the idea underlying the expectation theory. According to the segmented markets theory, the markets for different maturity bonds are completely segmented. Different maturity bonds cannot thus substitute for one another, whereas according to the expectation theory they are supposed to be fully substitutable. The interest rate on different maturity bonds is determined by the demand and supply situation for each maturity, without any effect from the expected return on other maturity bonds. This theory can be called in question on empirical grounds: there generally proves to be a certain connection between the returns on different maturity bonds.

The various signals which the five theories send out make it hard to find a clear and indisputable link between the sectors.[21]

The link between the simple annual interest rate and the compound interest rate

Equation (2.2) expresses the simple relationship[22] between the compound interest rate and the simple annual rate.

$$\left[1 + \frac{r_1}{100} \cdot \frac{d_1}{360}\right]\left[1 + \frac{r_2}{100} \cdot \frac{d_2}{360}\right] = \left[1 + \frac{r_3}{100} \cdot \frac{d_3}{360}\right] \qquad (2.2)$$

where r_i = rate of interest per year for period i

d_i = maturity in number of days for investment period i.

If we disregard risk premiums, this equation gives us an opportunity to obtain r_2, and thus to compare our own view of the interest rate in period 2 with that of the market.[23]

From equation (2.2) we can see that the yield curve slopes upwards[24] in the cases where the market has expectations about constant interest rates in the future. This slope provides the investor with something of a point of departure. A steep slope indicates an expectation of rising interest rates. A flatter curve or a curve with a negative slope indicates that the market expects falling rates.

2.3 Capital flows and the links between markets

The level of total financial integration expresses the coordination between financial and real markets. Thus, in order to be able to measure total financial integration, it is necessary to consider simultaneously a multiplicity of markets and the related links in the shape of the flows of goods, money and information.

2.3.1 Capital and information flows under total financial integration

The point of departure for such an analysis could be a model of an open economy in simplified form of the kind shown in Figure 2.4. This figure should make it easier for us to understand the meaning of total financial integration, regardless of whether it is global or bilateral.

The figure describes the link between different markets in the form of important information flows. Further, it shows how direct and indirect integration are linked, and what differentiates the two forms of integration as regards information flows. The imperfect direct integration that is expressed in inefficiency on the market, is represented in the figure by the area designated by the broken line. In an analysis of direct integration we have to assess the extent to which the information flows[25] relating to foreign interest rates, exchange rates and risks exert an influence on domestic financial quantities, such that the "law of one price" is fulfilled and the flows of speculative capital cease. The information that flows into the enclosed area is expressed as a price. The size of this price depends on the expectation structure and risk aversion of the market actors.[26]

What does the difference between interest rates tell us?

We can define the difference between domestic and foreign interest rates as follows:

$$r_d - r_{for} \equiv \hat{s}^* + \text{risk premiums} + \text{inefficiency} \qquad (2.3)$$

where

r_d = domestic nominal interest rate
r_{for} = foreign nominal interest rate
$\hat{s}^*$ = expected relative change in exchange rate.

I shall wait to discuss the nature of the risk premiums and inefficiencies until later, and will simply express the expected relative exchange rate change here in terms of international purchasing power parity, as

$$\hat{s}^* \equiv \hat{P}_d^* - \hat{P}_{for}^* + \hat{u}^* , \tag{2.4}$$

where $\hat{P}^*$ is expected inflation and $\hat{u}^*$ is the expected change in the deviation from purchasing power parity.

Figure 2.4 Information flows and financial links
Country model

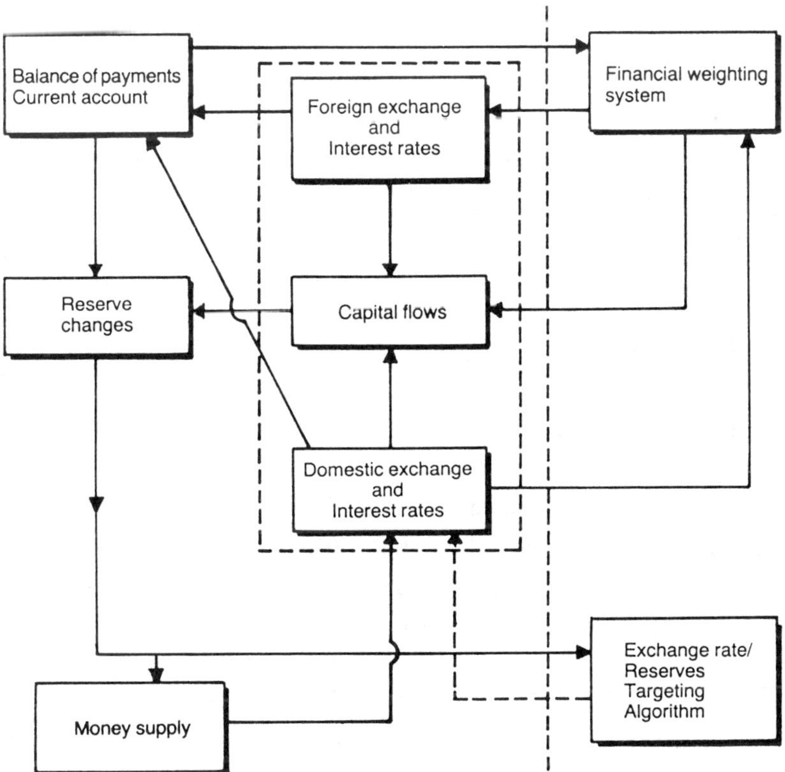

Note: The figure is a modified version of the OECD Interlink model.
Source: OECD (1984)

By combining (2.3) and (2.4) we obtain the following definition of total financial integration:

$$r_d^{R*} - r_{for}^{R*} \equiv \hat{u}^* + \underbrace{\text{risk premiums}}_{\substack{\text{indirect}\\ \text{segmentation}}} + \underbrace{\text{inefficiency}}_{\substack{\text{direct}\\ \text{segmentation}}} \tag{2.5}$$

The left-hand side of (2.5) gives the difference between expected real interest rates. The right-hand side expresses the level of segmentation, direct and indirect. If all the components on the right-hand side are zero, then the total integration is perfect. If the values of $\hat{u}^*$ and the risk premiums deviate from zero, then we have imperfect *indirect* financial integration, while the presence of inefficiencies (values deviating from zero) indicates imperfect *direct* financial integration.[27] Among inefficiencies I include transaction and information costs, general market inefficiency, and inefficiency due to the implementation of economic policy.

The link between financial integration and other forms of integration

Indirect integration is created by links with systems outside the enclosed field in Figure 2.4. Among these are the links with the goods market (in the current account) and with the foreign exchange market where the currency regime is the critical factor. Figure 2.5 provides a simple overview of the way in which total financial integration is linked to different markets.

If financial integration is total and expected real rates of interest are equal, then international purchasing power parity and the International Fisher Effect must obtain. An increase in indirect integration, for example in the shape of a reduction in risk premiums, will mean a higher level of total financial integration due to the greater integration of the markets outside the financial market. An increase in direct financial integration will also mean a higher level of total financial integration. However, it is important to note that we cannot determine from a single observation of greater similarity between expected real interest rates, whether this is due to an increase in direct or indirect integration.

Interest rate, money supply and capital flows

Figure 2.4 revealed the importance of the information flow as a linking factor in the model. The connection between this flow and the increase in the money supply, which

Figure 2.5 Outline of total financial integration under different market assumptions

Form of integration	Market in country A		Market in country B	Effect on level of total financial integration
Political and cultural integration	Politics and culture in country A	<--->	Politics and culture in country B	Political risk premium
Integration of goods markets	Goods market in country A	<--->	Goods market in country B	Deviation from purchasing power parity
Monetary integration	Foreign exchange market in country A	<--->	Foreign exchange market in country B	Premium for exchange risk
Indirect financial integration				Indirect financial integration
Direct financial integration	Capital market in country A	<--->	Capital market in country B	Market inefficiencies
Total financial integration	Expected real interest rates the same in country A and country B			All above components, zero

greatly affects expectations regarding interest rates, can be seen in Figure 2.6. This figure illustrates factors influencing the money supply in Sweden in 1983/84.

The total capital flow can be divided into two parts: one corresponding to the deficit in the current account and one to private capital transactions. There is generally great uncertainty in determining both these flows.

If a country exhibits a smaller foreign exchange outflow than would appear to be motivated by the current account, the reason could be that the domestic interest level is higher than the foreign level, when expectations about future exchange rate movements as well as exchange and political uncertainty, are all taken into consideration. If the outflow of foreign exchange is greater than would appear to be motivated by the current account, it could be because the market actors consider the interest level in the country concerned to be lower than the comparable rate elsewhere. Foreign exchange flows can also be explained by leads and lags of various kinds.

The interest-sensitive capital flow is particularly interesting. This "speculative" capital flow is difficult to isolate, but could perhaps be defined better by the private capital flow than by the total flow. It is in the interest-sensitive capital flows that the lack of direct financial integration and the existence of interest rate autonomy can be revealed.

Figure 2.6 Factors affecting the Swedish money supply in the budget year 1983/84
Billion kronor

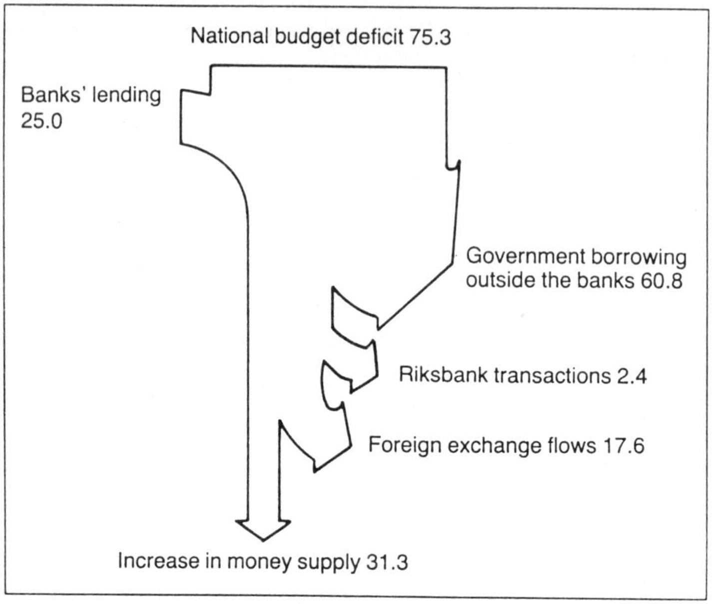

Note: The foreign exchange flow of SEK 17.6 billion operated as a vent which drained the credit market of the excess liquidity due to the large budget deficit of SEK 75.3 billion. Government borrowing outside the banks includes the government's realized foreign exchange losses.

Source: Sveriges Riksbank.

Because of this difficulty in determining the size of the interest-sensitive flow, empirical studies have concentrated instead on the strength of the case for financial transactions, i.e. the law of one price for financial instruments.[28] As soon as the difference in expected risk-adjusted return between two identical instruments is greater than the transaction cost, there is a case for such transactions.

Measurement problems lie ahead

Our discussion of Figure 2.4 gave us some idea of the problems of measurement and standardization which will have to be addressed (see Section 2.10). How, for instance, can we allow for different types of risk linked to a specific instrument or security, so as to obtain full comparability between interest rates? The size of the problem will depend on the complexity of the linkage between financial markets and the multitude of submarkets. The linkage illustrated in the figure is important, since financial consistency is largely achieved by using the effective exchange rate (real or nominal) and multilaterally weighted foreign interest rates as variables explaining the flow of net capital over national borders. The choice of weighting system will be a critical issue here. Exchange rates and interest rate movements in one country will be jointly fed through the model to other countries, endogenously, by means of the weighted foreign financial variables.

2.3.2 The case for arbitrage and speculation

Mobility between securities of different terms and in different currencies, is affected by the widely diverging characteristics of the market actors, providing them with different arguments for arbitrage and speculation. The actors can differ

- in their risk characteristics and risk aversion
- in their expectations
- in the way they react to their expectations
- in their maturity preferences
- in their view of international purchasing power parity.

When it comes to assessing similarities between markets we must somehow make assumptions about the diverging characteristics. This problem is often "solved" by assuming the actors are all the same.

We have previously noted that the theory of market efficiency embraces a hypothesis about the nature of arbitrage. If we want to try to determine at an aggregate level why an apparently motivated arbitrage does not occur, or why there is a chance of risk-free profits from covered interest arbitrage – in other words, why there are evident inefficiencies in the market – we first have to establish the explanatory value of the following non-mutually exclusive factors:

- the diffusion of information – time and costs
- the complexity of the transaction
- the thinness of the market
- tax laws
- any institutional barriers or interventions on the market.

These are the most important factors which can explain the segmentation of markets. They all allow scope for an autonomous interest rate policy. But it is mainly with the help of the last two factors that a central bank can itself generate such autonomy.

2.3.3 Segmentation generated by the exchange rate system

How can institutional arrangements contribute to segmentation? It is generally assumed that the choice of exchange rate arrangements, and in a broader sense the choice of exchange rate regime, determines the level of total financial integration and, ultimately, the scope for a nationally autonomous monetary policy. The desire for a new currency system to replace the Bretton Woods system often emerged as a call for more scope for national economic political action.[29] In a system of fixed (pegged) exchange rates and perfect capital mobility, it is assumed that the investor will relate the domestic interest rate to the global rate, thus robbing the central bank of its interest rate policy autonomy.

A simple model of the scope for national action under fixed exchange rates

In the simplest model of a small open economy with fixed exchange rates and the free movement of capital, government monetary policy is limited to determining how much of the increase in the money supply is to come from domestic sources. The interest rate is determined by the international interest level. If the government in the small country adopts a tight economic policy and the interest rate rises, capital will flow into the country. The central bank should then exchange this foreign currency into the domestic currency, because otherwise the price of the country's own currency will be forced up. New supplies of money force the domestic interest rate down until it returns to parity with the international rate.

If on the other hand the government conducts an expansionary economic policy and introduces substantial liquidity into the system, the domestic interest rate will be forced down and capital will flow out. The central bank should then exchange domestic currency for foreign. The supply of money is thus reduced and the interest level rises to the international level.

In this model the interest rate is determined exogenously, and growth in the money supply is determined by demand. The only thing the government can do, apart from deciding how the increase in money supply should be distributed, is to manage the size of the central bank's reserves of foreign currencies. Under a tight economic policy reserves will increase, and under an expansive policy they will diminish.

If there is an adjustment in the monetary policy, perhaps with a view to improving employment, this will lead – at least in the small country – to capital flows rather than to the desired effect on the policy's real variables. A complementary measure would then be to try to stop the flows with the help of exchange controls.

The choice of exchange rate regime affects indirect financial integration

The choice of exchange rate regime also affects the level of indirect financial integration, by way of the level of monetary integration. Perfect monetary integration means that the exchange rate strictly follows purchasing power parity. If perfect monetary integration obtains, then the premium for exchange risk is zero and the expected exchange rate movement derives from the purchasing power parity relationship. According to formula (2.5) the (total) financial disintegration in this situation is caused by possible political risk premiums and inefficiencies.

An exchange rate regime implying a permanently *fixed* exchange rate between two countries would mean that the two countries must also have coordinated policies and equal inflation.

But if the exchange rate is not to be regarded as permanently fixed, which is a realistic assumption, the risk premium for currencies in a system with an adjustable peg may very well be greater than in a system of completely freely floating exchange rates.

The uncertainty which investors usually express with regard to future exchange rate movements in the form of possible changes in parity, and uncertainty about inflation risk etc. due to switches in national policy, speak against an assumption of perfect total financial integration. Different exchange rate regimes generate different demands for risk premiums,[30] which in turn gives rise to different levels of imperfect (total) financial integration.

In a model context it is usually assumed that future exchange rate movements in a system of fixed rates are known. Alternatively it is assumed that in a system of flexible rates future exchange rate movements are unpredictable.Thus it is being implicitly assumed in this second case that the domestic and foreign interest rates are not systematically linked by the movement of exchange rates. This assumption thus rejects the International Fisher Effect, a fact which has given rise to some criticism.

2.3.4 Focus on direct financial integration

We have now seen the multiplicity of links that could be studied. We have noted that when total financial integration is less than perfect, we cannot immediately determine whether this is due to imperfection in the indirect or the direct integration.

Since it is realistic to expect total financial integration to be less than perfect, I shall concentrate henceforth mainly on measuring the level of direct financial integration. Our starting-point will be formula (2.3). Before embarking on the problems of definition and measurement associated with direct financial integration in Sections 2.7 and 2.8, I shall devote the following sections to problems connected with the different parts of formula (2.3). In Section 2.4 we will therefore look at problems connected with the market's exchange rate expectations, while Section 2.5 will be concerned with transaction costs and risk premiums, and Section 2.6 with the links between risk and return.

2.4 Exchange rate determinants and market expectations

We have already touched on the importance of the "true" model in forming the actors' expectations. To show how ideas about this model have varied over time and with the given assumptions, I shall summarize below the most important features in the evolution of the theory of the determination of exchange rates. I shall then examine the forecasting value of the most important economic equilibrium relationships. And I shall conclude by discussing how the market actors can form their expectations about future exchange rates.

In recent decades many models have been proposed, and the following is necessarily a rough survey only. The number of published models is almost as many as the number of possible combinations of the major explanatory variables (classified as exogenous or endogenous), level of capital mobility, speed of adjustment on the markets, degree of openness in the economy, price flexibility, level of employment, number of goods on the market, number and type of securities, etc. Added to which there are models emphasizing specific characteristics of flexible or fixed exchange rates, allowing for flow and/or stock items, and so on.

2.4.1 Is there any clear-cut model for determining exchange rates?

At the present time there is no clear-cut model for determining the exchange rate, and we are therefore justified in discussing the basic characteristics of several different models. These models differ with regard to the explanatory variables included, the time horizon, and the adjustment process. Different roles are ascribed to the exchange rate in these models. In some it is supposed to create equilibrium in demand and supply on the goods and services markets; the current account is then of central interest. This role is generally ascribed to the exchange rate in a purchasing power parity context. In other models it is a question of creating equilibrium in the supply and demand for financial securities; the capital account is then of central interest. This role is ascribed to the exchange rate in the so-called asset models.

The theory of purchasing power parity

Assuming strict purchasing power parity, the exchange rate maintains a clear link between the international prices.[31] If S designates the price of foreign exchange expressed in a country's own currency, and P_1 and P_2 the price levels at home and abroad for goods in international trade, the absolute version[32] of the purchasing power parity theory can be written

$$S^{12} = \frac{P_1}{P_2} \tag{2.6}$$

and its relative version

$$\hat{S}^{12} \approx \hat{P}_1 - \hat{P}_2 \tag{2.7}$$

The theory has been criticized[33] because the mechanisms whereby the exchange rate is linked to prices have not been specified. Similarly there is no specification of conditions which have to be fulfilled if the theory is to hold.

Monetary models

We can now proceed to study the causes of the price changes. It is generally assumed that prices are determined by the nominal domestic money supply and the real demand for money, which last can be regarded as dependent on the real income and the nominal interest rate. With the help of our assumptions about the character of the prices, we can introduce the money supply and interest rates into the model. We then obtain a monetary model of the exchange rate.[34] From this model we can see that the role of the exchange rate has been altered to involve the creation of equilibrium in the international demand for financial securities rather than in the international goods flows.[35] In this way the monetary model can be classified as an "asset" model.

As we can see in Appendix 2.3 the monetary model gives no clear-cut link between the nominal interest differential and the exchange rate. Depending on the assumptions made about the underlying character of the prices, different results are obtained. In his not entirely uncontroversial[36] model, Frankel (1979a, p. 613) combines the assumption of sticky[37] prices in the short run with an assumption about trends in inflation. According to his model we add a term expressing the differences between expected long-term inflation in different countries to the right-hand side of the monetary equation. In Frankel's model the exchange rate is negatively related to nominal interest differentials, and positively related to expected long-term inflation differentials. Frankel thus claims to have solved the problem of providing a realistic description of the link between the nominal interest differential and the exchange rate, given moderate variation in inflation differentials.

According to Tobin (1969) the drawback of the monetary models – so called because they emphasize the role of the exchange rate in creating equilibrium between the supply and demand for money – is that financial innovations are constantly calling for new measures for the money supply.

Dynamic exchange rate models and rational expectations

Apart from Frankel (1979a) the models mentioned above are based on an assumption of strict purchasing power parity. When this assumption is abandoned, various new models emerge. Among these is the pioneering work of Mundell and Fleming during the 1960s. The introduction of capital mobility[38] into the theory of open economies is often ascribed to Mundell (1963a). Mundell claims that if complete capital mobility obtained, an interest differential deviating from zero would create a potentially infinite capital inflow/outflow, which would have important repercussions on the exchange rate.[39] In Black (1973) rational expectations are integrated into the theory of open economies. Kouri (1976c) introduces these expectations into the models generated by the work of Mundell and Fleming.

Exchange rate models geared to the current account

Parallel with the development of the dynamic exchange rate theory resulting from the introduction of expectations into the model, interest was renewed in the role of the current account. Along with studies of the way in which expectations – and in particular rational expectations – are formed, new ideas have emerged about dynamic exchange rates and about overshooting due to the varying rates of adjustment on the goods and financial markets.[40] Analyses have been made of shocks and disturbances of various kinds – monetary, real, and internationally generated shocks.[41] Among these studies, mention should be made of Dornbusch (1976a). Dornbusch extends Mundell and Fleming's approach, introducing like Kouri (1976c) an assumption of rational expectations.[42] However, in this model imbalances in the current account have no medium-term impact on the economy. The current account is simply treated as a demand component.

The current account has a more active role in Dornbusch and Fischer (1980). These authors assume that supply and demand on financial markets determine the exchange rate at any given point in time, but that the current account determines the movement of the exchange rate over time by way of its effects on the net exchange value of foreign assets and, ultimately, on the financial markets as well.

The model in Dornbusch and Fischer (1980)[43] possesses certain monetary characteristics, but the authors have elaborated the real income measure and introduced a mechanism that links together the current account, the exchange rate and real income. Thus they include interest revenues from domestic net assets ($F = -F^*$) as part of real income. Changes in this asset position ($\Delta F = -\Delta F^*$) occur when the current account is not in balance. The current account is determined by desired domestic net savings, but it also depends on deviations from purchasing power parity calculated from the price index for the domestic production of goods and services. Trade in goods and services is in balance, when purchasing power parity obtains. Thus a desired level of net saving can be achieved only if the exchange rate deviates from PPP. Another component in the current account consists of interest revenues. In order to achieve a transfer of resources corresponding to interest revenues or interest payments, the exchange rate must deviate from purchasing power parity.

Thus $\hat{s} - (\hat{P}_d - \hat{P}_{for})$, the real exchange rate or the deviation from purchasing power parity, here approaches the concept of "terms of trade". The model also includes an interest rate parity equation which is consistent with perfect capital mobility.

It is worth noting that in Dornbusch and Fischer's model an exchange rate based on purchasing power is not necessarily a long-term equilibrium exchange rate. If a transfer of resources has to be made via the balance of trade, deviations in the long-term equilibrium can occur. Here it is assumed that the deviation from PPP adjusts itself in such a way that a transfer consistent with the interest payment (rF) and the savings behaviour (ΔF) is made.

Dornbusch and Fischer argue in favour of the common assumption of a link between the current account and exchange rate movements. However, they include the important warning that anticipated shocks or disturbances on the world markets can obscure the conventional relationship. The assumption of rational expectations can thus combine the asset and the current account theories of the exchange rate, since this assumption can result in a fully anticipated equilibrium path, in which the prices of financial assets are partially adjusted to reflect future current account developments.

Portfolio balance theories

During the second half of the 1970s a portfolio balance approach became increasingly common. The basic assumption was that the demand for money depends not only on income, the conventional transaction variable, but also on wealth. Changes in financial wealth resulting from imbalance in the current account, create monetary imbalances which then generate changes in expectations about long-term price levels and ultimately exchange rate movements. Under uncertainty as regards real return, portfolio diversification makes assets imperfectly substitutable, and can give rise to demands for a risk premium.[44]

The link with relative financial wealth results in a risk premium to the extent that there are differences in consumption patterns and variability in the real exchange rate. The risk premium model is interesting in that, by way of the wealth formulation, it provides a link from the current account to changes in the exchange rate.[45] It also provides a possible link between deficit financing and the exchange rate, by a link to the relative supply of financial assets.

In the "asset" family, models have been developed by Branson (1979) and Frenkel and Rodriguez (1982) based on Kouri (1976c). Like Dornbusch and Fischer, Branson and Frenkel and Rodriguez differentiate between a long-term and short-term equilibrium exchange rate.[46] At the long-term equilibrium exchange rate there are no changes in the country's net foreign assets abroad (flow equilibrium at which the current account obtains). The short-term equilibrium exchange rate, which is asset-related, is determined by the momentary position of the country's net foreign assets. The dynamic path of the real exchange rate depends, as in Dornbusch and Fischer, on the accumulation of net foreign assets due to a deficit or surplus in the current account.

In Branson's model, as in Frenkel and Rodriguez's, financial assets in different currencies are not perfect substitutes for one another. The exchange rate and the domestic interest rate in relation to the global rate is therefore influenced by the domestic quantity of money and the bond supply, i.e. the relative supply of different assets determines the size of the risk premium. A shift in the supply of domestic assets causes a real change in exchange rates. A surplus or deficit in the balance of trade will follow, and an accumulation or liquidation of foreign assets over time. The new long-term equilibrium occurs when the exchange rate is such that the balance of trade is the same as interest payments on foreign assets.

If the model is to provide a basis for exchange rate management the asset approach is an improvement compared with the simple monetary model. In the asset approach the real exchange rate is given an explicit role. However, the approach is unlikely to provide an adequate basis for regulation, when the central bank is concerned about the variability of the exchange rate.

A simplified model approach

This brief survey should provide some idea of the explanatory factors underlying the exchange rate and its role as regards equilibrium. In the first generation of models the exchange rate was assigned the role of creating equilibrium in the international goods flows; in the second, it was expected to create equilibrium in the international demand for financial assets. This shift implied that the exchange rate was regarded as dependent on the substitutability of different financial assets rather than on export/import price elasticity. Where the emphasis in the first generation was on purchasing power parity and the "law of one price", in the second it was on the International Fisher Effect. In the third-generation models, which is where we are today, the emphasis is on wealth effects among other things, and thus on the role of the current account.[47] The recognition of the dynamic element and the varying speed of adjustment on the goods and asset markets has generated several new theories about the course of adjustment from short-term to long-term equilibrium. In the short term the emphasis is on financial equilibrium; in the long term it shifts instead towards equilibrium in the flows on the goods market.[48]

2.4.2 What is the forecasting value of these models?

Advanced economic models have proved inferior to simple partial equilibrium models (see Meese and Rogoff 1983) in forecasting exchange rate movements.

We need not examine the background to Meese and Rogoff's study of exchange rate movements in any great detail here.[49] Suffice it to say that the three models derived from equation (A2.13) in Appendix 2.4 gave less satisfactory results than a simple random-walk model, although the forecasts derived from these models were based on actual values of the explanatory variables.[50]

There could be several reasons for this: the more advanced economic models may have suffered from sampling errors or other data-related errors; structural instability due to oil-price shocks, changes in national economic policy or in the character of exchange rate arrangements, misspecifications or an inability to account adequately for real shocks, may also have played a part. And apart from these more or less technical explanations, new information has also generated new expectations, which causes deviations from the original forecasts of the model.

2.4.3 Market actors' exchange rate expectations

The market's expectations are probably essentially different in systems of fixed or semi-fixed exchange rates and systems of flexible rates. In the first case the expected change in exchange rates is small with a very high probability and large with a very small probability. In a system of flexible exchange rates, on the other hand, expected changes are distributed over a wide interval of varying probabilities.

It is reasonable to assume that the market actors – who accept not being able to beat the market – form their expectations on a basis of some form of systematic processing of simple market information. Their methods may be associated with time-series analysis or the analysis of arbitrage models. In the absence of a general equilibrium model, the actors can base their expectations on the equilibrium relationships in Figure 1.1, i.e. on purchasing power parity, on the International Fisher Effect, on the theory of the forward rate as an unbiased estimate of future spot exchange rates, or on a random-walk model.[51] I shall now briefly review various submodels which actors may use in forming their expectations.

Expectations based on simple projections

Time-series analysis – either long- or short-term – is one alternative. If a long-term analysis is made, some systematic tendencies will obviously become evident in the form of growth trends in the prices of certain currencies. But the long-term projection of such trends provides a dubious forecast. In the short term it turns out that the exchange rate movements can often be described with the help of random models.[52] This result in itself represents a forecast, namely that the best forecast of the exchange rate in a week, for example, is today's spot rate.[53]

Another form of time-series analysis consists of the "technicals" in frequent use especially in American companies for generating forecasts in the short run.[54] The wide use of this technique is interesting in itself, since it endows forecasts with a large element of self-fulfilment. This popularity has no equivalent in Swedish multinational companies. Only three of the nineteen Swedish companies studied express any faith in technicals, or say that they use them for generating a short-term decision base.[55] On a basis of these technicals, the actors might generate speculative bubbles.[56]

Models for arbitrage and speculations as a basis for exchange rate expectations

Another group of forecasting models based on market information consists of models for arbitrage and speculative transactions.[57] These include models which generate forecasts in the shape of forward rates, interest differentials, PPP etc. Only when the individual company believes itself to be in a position to make better forecasts than the market-based forecasts, should the attempt be made. However, the evidence suggests that for most market actors this is aiming too high.

Exchange rate expectations based on purchasing power parity

The theory of purchasing power parity is best suited to generating long-term forecasts. Deviations from purchasing power parity must be carefully assessed and given serious attention as good indicators of the direction and strength of a possible impending change in parity. The degree of openness to international trade and different price elasticities are then important factors that should be considered in an evaluation of the somewhat difficult-to-forecast timing aspect.

Fortune (1985) shows clearly in the longer-term context that market actors are guided by expected deviations from international purchasing power parity, and that to a great extent these expectations determine changes in the exchange rate.

The market actor combines information from different sources

For a currency in a system of fixed or semi-fixed exchange rates, the forward premium as a measure of the market's expectation of exchange rate movements will probably have to be complemented by the cumulative devaluation potential which may be latent in the shape of deviations from PPP. For a trade-weighted Swedish krona, for example, the correlation coefficient between a deviation from PPP and the forward premium is as low as –0.12, which can be taken to mean that this deviation is not allowed for in the forward premium.[58] The market's expectation is probably derived from the forward premium plus part of the cumulative deviation from PPP.

How has exchange rate expectation been handled in other studies?

The problem of exchange rate expectations, as we have already seen, has been circumvented in most studies of financial integration. In those cases where the exchange rate has been considered, it has either been assumed to be constant by citing fixed exchange rates, or a random-walk approach has been adopted. Another way of avoiding the difficulty in studies of countries with a Euromarket rate is to circumvent the exchange rate problem and to study direct financial integration by comparing domestic interest rates and the equivalent rates on the Euromarket.[59] When the market's exchange rate expectations have been considered, they have generally been expressed as the forward rate[60] for the actual currency combination. Some authors[61] have chosen to model exchange rate expectations in the form of interest differentials and/or inflation differentials. Few published studies have modelled the expectation of future exchange rate movements with a term for deviations from purchasing power parity, neither as deviations at the time the forecast is made nor as expected future deviations.[62]

The difficulty in using the forward premium as an expression of exchange rate expectations in a study of direct integration, is that this premium is based on interest differentials. Spurious correlations can then arise. The forward premium is based on the difference between Euro interest rates and is therefore only useful in analysing the gap between other interest rates, whose correlation with the gap between Eurorates is acceptably high. If this is not the case we are justified in assuming that the market is forming its expectations – at least in the short run – on the basis of a random model or on estimated differentials in relative inflation. Any hope of total agreement among the actors about one or the other approach, can be abandoned. This will be confirmed in Chapter 4, where I report on the way in which Swedish companies form their exchange rate expectations.

2.5 Transaction costs and different types of risk premium

In our attempts below to assess the degree of interest rate autonomy in empirical terms, we will have to be able to determine the size of the transaction costs and the risk premiums. Let us therefore examine some of their attributes.

2.5.1 How is the transaction cost determined?

We shall discuss here the determination of the transaction cost in foreign exchange transactions and in interest rate arbitrage. In the simplest case of speculation – foreign exchange speculation – it is a question of the cost of two spot transactions on the foreign exchange market. In the case of covered interest arbitrage it is often a question of the cost of four transactions. In the typical case these can consist of borrowing abroad (in DEM), spot purchase (of SEK against DEM), lending (in SEK), and forward selling (of SEK against DEM).

In estimating the transaction costs for the actual foreign exchange transactions, we can use the difference between spot purchase (S^{pur}) and the selling quotation (S^{sell}) – the bid-ask spread. This differential actually measures two transactions, namely the cost to the bank of buying immediately and of selling later. From the speculator's point of view the transaction cost (T_S) should therefore be written:

$$T_S = \frac{1}{2} \cdot [(S_t^{sell} - S_t^{pur})/S_t^{sell}]. \qquad (2.11)$$

In the case of speculation in buying and selling foreign exchange on the spot market, the transaction cost can be estimated at

$$1 - (1-T_S)^2.$$

If it is a case of covered interest arbitrage, the transaction cost in its simplest form can be written

$$1 - (1-T_S)(1-T_F),$$

where T_F is estimated as half the bid-ask spread on the forward market for foreign exchange.[63]

The cost for foreign exchange transactions is greatest on the forward market

McCormick (1975), Levich (1979) and others who have studied the bid-ask spread for spot and forward exchange transactions, have found that this is always greatest on the forward market and that it is not negligible for currencies whose transaction volume is small. I have found a similar tendency in the case of the Swedish krona.

Higher transaction cost estimated from triangular arbitrage

An alternative way of estimating the cost of foreign exchange transactions is to derive the cost from the triangular arbitrage. We thus compare the actual exchange rate with a rate calculated from triangular arbitrage. If we know the SEK/USD rate, we can compare it with the SEK/USD rate which we obtain when we conduct a transaction via a third currency, i.e. (SEK/DEM) · (DEM/USD). The idea is that if the transaction cost between (at least) the leading currencies is the same, we can expect a maximal differential between observed and estimated exchange rates corresponding to the extra transaction. Frenkel and Levich (1975, 1977) estimated the transaction cost on the forward market in this way and noted that their estimated costs exceeded estimates from the bid-ask spread. However, the uncertainty about the role of the foreign exchange banks as market leaders or as brokers for "odd" currencies, means that this procedure can sometimes produce the transaction cost for two instead of one transaction, thus tending to overestimate the true transaction cost.

Deviations from interest rate parity as an estimate of the transaction cost

Some researchers go so far as to claim that there is no reason to believe in systematic deviations from covered interest parity and market efficiency.[64] According to these researchers the arbitrage cost can therefore easily be estimated as the average value of the absolute deviations from interest rate parity, after the values from speculative periods have been eliminated. Thus implicitly they are assuming that a complete matching of risks has been achieved for the compared assets. Other researchers who have used the same methodology but with other data, reject this simple way of determining the transaction cost.[65] However, I consider that this form of estimate can be used as an upper limit for the transaction cost. This provides a way of mitigating the problem that the difference between the bid and ask-quotation – determined pairwise or triangularly – very probably underestimates the total transaction cost, since it does not contain the arbitrageur's organizational costs and costs for information search.

The transaction cost is linked to the nature of the market

The transaction cost is regarded as being independent of the market actor's motives for undertaking the transaction, but dependent on other market attributes. Fieleke (1975) and others claim that the transaction cost and the bid-ask spread on the foreign exchange market can be regarded as inversely related to the transaction volume and directly related to market restrictions and uncertainty about exchange rate movements. Thus there is every reason for caution in applying to the Swedish foreign exchange market any estimates of transaction costs based on markets which differ from the Swedish market in size, restrictions and so on.

The transaction cost is tending to fall

There is at present a general tendency, which has been pointed out among others by the Bank for International Settlements (BIS 1986), for the transaction cost to fall. Other things being equal, this appears to confirm an increase in direct financial integration.

2.5.2 *Different types of risk in international transactions*

Formula (2.3) included a quantity which I designated the risk premium. We can now look at the risks for which the investor might be expected to demand compensatory premiums.[66] We have to distinguish between *systematic* risk,which cannot be diversified and for which an investor demands compensation, and *non-systematic* risk, which can be diversified and for which there is no compensation.

Four risks to be considered

What risks *apart from* those which are specifically related to the financial instrument, should the investor assess in comparing the yield on different markets?[67] Roughly speaking it can be claimed that one and the same imbalance at the macroeconomic level can manifest itself in effects which can be ascribed to different types of risk. The internationally operating company which is exposed to the most risks, generally faces four types. These are:

- *Country risk.* An expression of the instability in the situation and the general conditions on different markets in a country.[68] The country risk also includes political risk.[69]
- *Financial risk.* An expression of variations in interest rates and capital costs in a given currency. This also includes the risk of default.
- *Currency risk.* An expression of variations in exchange rates – exchange rate risk. The currency risk also includes inflation risk.

These three risks can be called macroeconomic risks, and they must be considered in financial transactions. To this must be added a risk specific to the individual company, namely:

– *Commercial risk.* An expression of variations in relative prices and sales volume.

The various risks are interlinked, as can be seen in Figure 2.7, where the broken line marks the boundary between administrative influence and market influence.

Risk substitutability

A company that fears a devaluation of the local currency may choose to avoid exchange risk and to borrow locally at a variable interest rate. If the central bank in the country concerned decides at the same time to protect its currency by increasing the interest rate, this will increase the rate of the company's loan as well and the company will feel the effect of a financial risk instead of the exchange risk which they have taken measures to avoid. Even the strictly domestic company is exposed to exchange risk. This operates indirectly, and expresses itself by way of the other three risk categories. For example, the exchange risk is related to the commercial risk, in so far as the main competitor products on the domestic market are foreign. An overvalued currency in the home country can mean that the company will be crushed by competition from cheap imported products.

An exchange risk can also be transformed into a political risk if the central bank in a country strangles the outflow of capital as a step in protecting a certain parity for the national currency. In the extreme case the government confiscates assets so that no future transfer of capital from a particular project can occur.

Figure 2.7 Corporate risks

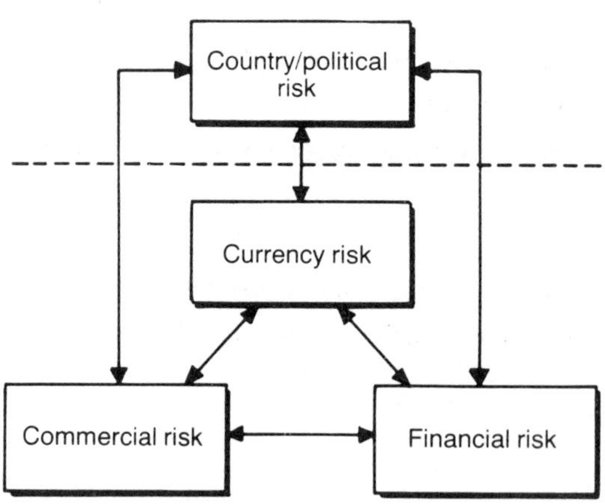

When the individual investor evaluates the investment alternatives on different markets, he then confronts the systematic part of one or more of these risks for which he then sets a price for bearing them – a risk premium.

After matching, only the exchange and political risks remain

As we are concerned here with financial integration, and particularly with direct financial integration, the commercial risk is of no interest to us. Furthermore I have standardized the interest rates in my comparisons, so that I can also ignore premiums for financial risk. This leaves the problem of modelling the market demand for premiums for exchange and political risks.

2.5.3 What determines the size of the risk premium?

If the market actors exhibit risk aversion, it will be necessary to allow for their demands for extra compensation in the form of risk premiums in any analysis of international financial transactions and comparisons of interest rates. The premium represents the market's price for sacrificing safety and accepting risk. It may be *constant* or *variable*. In the second case it can be expected to vary over time, in accordance with certain decision variables.

The point of departure for most studies of the size of the risk premium is a classic article, Pratt (1964), in which the premium is defined and analysed under consideration of the relations between premium, buying and selling rates, insurance premiums and measures of risk aversion.

The definition of the selling price (SP) for a risk (z) is, according to Pratt:

$$U(x+SP) = E[U(x+z)] \text{ or } U(x+\bar{z}-\pi) = E[U(x+z)] \tag{2.12}$$

where x = initial welfare
$\bar{z} = E(z)$ where E is the expectation operator
U = utility function
π = Arrow–Pratt's risk premium.[70]

The selling price represents the minimum selling price which could persuade the decision-maker to sell z with the certainty of obtaining $SP = \bar{z}-\pi$. Arrow–Pratt's risk premium contains an expression for the degree of risk aversion.

In Section 2.6 we will return to the question of different models for the trade off between the size of the expected return and the risk, i.e. variations in this return.

2.5.4 Premium for exchange risk

Towards the end of the 1970s a good deal of interest was shown in the question of a premium for *exchange risk*.[71] The most common way of calculating this premium was to analyse whether the forward rate is an unbiased estimate of the future spot rate. In so far as there was any systematic forecasting error, it was explained by the presence of an exchange risk premium.[72]

It is important to distinguish between constant and variable premiums

In recent years researchers have been trying to determine the character of the risk premium. Is it constant, or does it vary over time? Or does it perhaps have one constant and one variable part? If this is so, then it is important in the present study to distinguish between these two parts empirically and to calculate them both. Otherwise it would be impossible to determine the size of the market's inefficiency.

Attempts have also been made to identify the factors that determine the size of the premium. To a great extent the theoretical discussion about the existence of the risk premium has revolved round *the actual source of the risk.* A view that has dominated in recent years is that the demand for exchange risk premiums is not contingent on the size of the fluctuations in the nominal exchange rate, but rather on relative fluctuations in purchasing power for different currencies, i.e. var($\hat{u}$).[73] Given this clarification of the theoretical base, it becomes possible to test for market efficiency without being compelled to test the combined theory of efficiency *and* a zero risk premium.

It is not only the theory underlying the source of the risk which is complicated. The difficulties also concern the *link* between the source of the risk and the premium. Stockman (1978), Frenkel and Razin (1985) can represent the predominant view here. They claim that the risk premium depends on the appearance of the utility function, i.e. on the intertemporal substitution ratio and on the probability distributions of exogenous variables.[74]

Two main approaches to the empirical determination of the risk premium

In the choice of model the empirical analysis of the risk premium has generally followed one of two routes. One has concerned the analysis of the portfolio balance, in which incomplete substitutability creates a wedge between expected net return on domestic and foreign investments, and gives rise to a risk premium.[75] Empirical analysis along these lines has not produced any obvious results.

The second approach is based on an intertemporal asset pricing model, with discrete points in time.[76] Even here the empirical analysis has been beset by difficulties.

Lucas (1982) and Hodrick and Srivastava (1984) point out that the factors which determine the risk premium in an asset pricing model, make the empirical test complex and difficult to perform. Hansen and Hodrick (1983) and Hodrick and Srivastava (1984) have therefore conducted tests on severely simplified models, which only to a very small degree correspond to the theoretical models. These tests have provided, for example, weak support for a risk premium that varies over time.

International empirical studies provide no clear-cut leads about the character of the risk premium

The results of various empirical studies reflect the difficulties in the theoretical field. Cornell (1977) and Stockman (1978) have tested the occurrence of a constant risk premium. In testing the forward rate as an unbiased estimate of the future rate, neither of them found proof of the existence of such a premium. Tests for constant risk premiums, however, have produced mixed results. Frenkel (1978), for example, found a statistically insignificant constant premium, while Frenkel (1982) reports significance in the case of certain currencies. Like Cornell (1977), Hansen and Hodrick (1983) and Cumby and Obstfeld (1984) found confirmation of serial-correlated forecasting errors, which should be taken to mean that particularly in studies of market efficiency we would be justified in using a risk premium which is allowed to vary over time.

Many researchers have used variable risk premiums in their models. Thus, within the framework of a balanced portfolio model, Frankel (1979b, 1982) and Dornbusch (1982), for example, have formulated the risk premium in terms of outstanding nominal bonds and concavity in the utility function. We could also envisage the risk premium as a function of changes in the variance in deviations from purchasing power parity.[77]

The modelling of the risk premium has no obvious solution

No clear-cut pointers can be discerned in the empirical results presented in recent years with regard to the size and character of the premium for exchange risk. The modelling procedures for a possible premium, such as are necessary to any study of financial integration and market efficiency, remain an open question.

In the presence of obvious analytical problems, however, there is some comfort in recognizing that the premium for exchange risk is probably small in relation to the size of the expected change in exchange rates.[78] The precision in estimating the premium can be assumed to be of minor importance in relation to the uncertainty which dogs the evaluation of the expected exchange rate movement.

2.5.5 Premium for country/political risk

Country risk is not a clear-cut concept. I agree with Leavy (1984) in that I include in the country risk all risks that a foreign investor encounters in a country and risks which are country-specific. It can be described as the risk for changes in the rules of the game on that country's market and expresses the risk for interventions. This broad definition is more or less synonymous to political risk (including sovereignty risk and transfer risk),[79] and is particularly appropriate if one regards the international debt crisis and the way it is handled – as I do – as the source of the overriding systematic risk which is associated with the market in a particular country.[80]

Country risk is often synonymous with the risk of national suspended payments

The literature in this field normally adopts a narrower definition, which comes close to what has traditionally been known as the risk of national suspended payments. A good deal of the literature such as Frank and Cline (1971), Feder and Just (1977), Feder and Ross (1981), Edwards (1984) and, from a theoretical angel, Dufey and Giddy (1984) has been devoted to the question of whether international interest rates reflect the risk of national suspension of payments, i.e. whether the interest rate is a positive function of the size of the debt. As an expression of the country risk Feder and Ross, for example, take the debt-service ratio[81], the ratio between external reserves and imports, the ratio between capital inflow and payments on the debt, and per-capita income.

Oxelheim (1984c) adopts a broader view and identifies leading indicators of country risk. Because industry is slow to adapt and change, the present level and development of the industrial structure foreshadows future risks of intervention and changes in the rules of the game in the country concerned. Measures of the size of industry, its direction, concentration, internationalization and ownership structure, and the diversification of exports, are all examples of such indicators.

Companies demand a compensatory premium for country/political risk

Studies[82] of corporate decision-making about investments or placements abroad, show that decision-makers take political risks very seriously and the international investor has a high aversion to this kind of risk (see Kobrin, 1979, and Oxelheim, 1984a). The risk has a price. Investors demand a premium in the form of a higher expected return. Edwards (1984) regards the interest differential vis-à-vis LIBOR[83] as the premium for country risk. Empirically, however, as is shown in Brewer (1983) for example, the determination of the premium is often more complex than this.

In estimating the political risk premium we are certainly justified in basing our view on a link between rising indebtedness and a higher propensity to political intervention. A country's indebtedness, as we have seen during the 1980s, can result in payment difficulties which seriously reduce that country's economic-political room for manœuvres. Consequently there is a greater likelihood that restrictions and controls will be imposed, implying greater political risk. The premium can be calculated on a basis of the country's gross international debt, its net foreign assets, and some other expression for possible financial difficulties. In a bilateral study of interest differentials, any such difficulties should be expressed in relative form.

This and the previous sections have thus demonstrated the necessity of identifying a satisfactory expression for the source of systematic risk, and of finding ways of converting this expression into a risk premium.

2.6 The link between risk and return

The premium for risk, i.e. the demand for a higher expected returns, can be related to the risk itself in many ways. Before discussing some relevant models let us consider the premium in its simplest form as an *additive* component of the interest rate – a component with one fixed part and one variable. The latter, as we have seen, can be a function of some exogenous variable. For example, the premium for systematic exchange risk can be formulated as a function of the variance in the deviation from purchasing power parity, where this variance is assumed to vary over time.

The difficulties mount up when we cannot assume that the premium is linearly related to the risk but are compelled instead to look for some other mathematical function to describe the relationship correctly. Similar problems arise if we have to consider premiums for several different risks.

2.6.1 The portfolio approach

The portfolio approach was one of the models mentioned above.[84] According to this approach it is assumed that the investor on the market has a portfolio of assets and liabilities in the form of contracts on various conditions: different maturities, in different currencies, and different returns and with future outcomes uncertain. As we have seen, this uncertainty has a variety of sources.

We have already noted that the risk associated with a particular contract has two parts. One concerns the unique risk specific to the contract; the other is the market risk that affects all contracts. The investor can eliminate the unique or unsystematic risk by his own action. But he cannot influence the market or systematic risks. The variance in his portfolio can thus be diminished by increasing the number and spread of contracts, and can be reduced to the average covariance[85] between the different contracts and the market.

The risk and the return on the investment are interdependent. Modern theory on the pricing of investment under risk is based on Markowitz (1952).[86] Markowitz also indicates principles for the choice of efficient portfolios.[87] Underlying the concept of the efficient portfolio is the dual assumption that a) the investor appreciates a high expected return, and b) he does not like risk. The investor is interested in the risk on his *total* portfolio; and the relevant risk is thus the contribution of the specific investment to the overall risk of the portfolio. Appendix 2.4 exemplifies this argument.

In financial theory, diversification to reduce the portfolio risk is described as something desirable for an investor. Moreover, the diversification should be carried out by the investor as the company is not paid for such an activity. But this does not mean that the question of *who* should actually diversify has been solved, i.e. whether it is the ultimate stakeholders (owners/investors) or their representative, the management. Responsibility for the diversification will be a question of choice of target variable, costs, information and administrative barriers.[88]

2.6.2 The capital asset pricing model

Markowitz's principles were developed by Tobin (1958). A further development was introduced in the mid-1960s by Lintner (1965), Mossin (1966), Sharpe (1964), and Treynor (1965). The result was the Capital Asset Pricing Model (CAPM) for the pricing of risk, which is both simple and intuitively attractive.[89]

The basic idea is that the expected risk premium for security , i.e. the expected return over and above the risk-free interest rate, in a competitive market will vary in direct proportion to the security's beta (β_j). See also Appendix 2.5. The expected risk premium for asset j can be written

$$E(r_j) - r_F = \beta_j [E(r_M) - r_F], \tag{2.13}$$

where r_F is the risk-free interest rate and r_M the return on the market portfolio.[90] It is important to note that in CAPM the investor does not receive any risk premium for accepting a unique or unsystematic risk, because – as was stressed before – this risk can be eliminated by way of diversification. The market risk, on the other hand, cannot be reduced by diversification, and every asset or investment is therefore priced in such a way as to compensate the investor for the extra market risk.

Critics of CAPM point out that the model cannot be tested empirically, since the test in itself presupposes that the model holds.[91]

2.6.3 The arbitrage pricing theory

A good deal of research is being devoted at present to refinements of CAPM. And new theories are still appearing, most of them resembling CAPM's structure. Unlike CAPM which follows from an analysis of how investors can construct efficient portfolios, the Arbitrage Pricing Theory (APT)[92] concentrates on how the return on every asset depends on a number of independent factors. APT is less radical in its assumptions, and unlike CAPM requires no measurement of the market portfolio. The expected return can be described as follows:

Expected return on investment =

$$a+b_1(\text{factor } 1)+b_2(\text{factor } 2)+...+b_m(\text{factor } m)+... \tag{2.14}$$

The theory does not specifically identify the factors. It could be a question of an interest rate factor, an oil price factor etc. Like CAPM, APT is based on an analysis of the pricing of shares, but here too the interpretation can be extended.

According to APT the total risk premium of every investment depends partly on the risk premium associated with each factor and partly on the sensitivity of the investment (in its basic form of the share) to every factor, i.e. b_1, b_2 etc. The total risk premium (where r_F = risk-free interest rate) on the investment can be written:

$$r - r_F = b_1(r_{factor_1} - r_F) + b_2(r_{factor_2} - r_F) + \ldots + b_m(r_{factor_m} - r_F) + \ldots \tag{2.15}$$

The difficulty here lies in identifying the factors which affect the size of the return, and then measuring the expected return on each one of them and the sensitivity of the investment to them.[93]

Even if the evaluation[94] of APT is still in its infancy, the model does provide an alternative to CAPM that is worth considering. In the absence of the perfect model it seems that financial theorists anyway agree on two points: the investor demands an extra expected return to compensate for increasing his risk, and the non-diversifiable market risk is the most important. These theories can guide us in formulating tests of financial integration.

2.7 Financial integration and monetary autonomy – some measures and analytical approaches

We have now reached a stage where we stand on firmer ground, when we ask ourselves about the possibility of measuring financial integration. In this section we will examine the measures and analytical approaches that are available to us.

2.7.1 Is it possible to ascertain empirically the political freedom of action?

In the case of a small country with an open economy the level of financial integration tells us how far, in terms of time structure and interest gap, the interest rate on the domestic market is determined by conditions on the corresponding foreign market. It may be a question of the domestic financial market as a whole vis-à-vis the foreign market, or of one market segment vis-à-vis another segment. Under perfect financial integration, the domestic interest rate is determined entirely by exogenous factors. In the other extreme case, under fully segmented national markets, then domestic interest rates are endogenously determined. Between these two extremes we find varying levels of financial integration, depending on the strength of the influence of domestic or foreign factors in determining the domestic interest rate. What, then, is the scope for an autonomous domestic monetary policy in the different cases,[95] and how great is the sensitivity to domestic disturbances.

The freedom of choice in a policy decision must be considered

An empirical study of direct financial integration which is to provide grounds for conclusions about the scope for monetary policy autonomy or in a more narrow sense interest rate autonomy, must also consider the *freedom of choice* under which a political decision has been taken.[96]

Thus, in order to interpret the statistical indications of the convergence of the domestic to foreign rates and thus of the autonomy of the interest rate policy, we have to know something about the goals of economic policy. Table 2.1 shows how this question can be structured. If the observed interest rate is compared with the central bank's targeted rate (TR) and with the global rate (GR) adjusted for risk, transaction cost and exchange rate, we can discern strong or weak indications of interest rate autonomy.

Table 2.1 Indications of interest rate policy autonomy

		Domestic interest rate level in relation to the target (TR)		
		low	**equal**	**high**
Domestic interest rate level in relation to the interest rate in the rest of the world (GR) adjusted for risks, transaction costs and changes in rate of exchange	**low**	weak indication of interest rate autonomy if TR<GR, otherwise no indication	strong indication of interest rate autonomy	weak indication of interest rate autonomy
	equal	strong indication of absence of interest rate autonomy	no indication of interest rate autonomy	strong indication of absence of interest rate autonomy
	high	weak indication of interest rate autonomy	strong indication of interest rate autonomy	weak indication of interest rate autonomy if TR>GR, otherwise no indication

Let us assume, for example, that a government is trying to keep the domestic interest rate at a low and fixed level, perhaps to stimulate real investment and to prevent domestically costly foreign interest fluctuations from reproducing themselves in the domestic interest rate. If in this situation the government succeeds in keeping the rate at its target level (TR) while *at the same time* remaining under the interest level in the rest of the world (GR), it seems to me that we have a *strong* indication of interest rate autonomy. The government has managed to retain sufficient independence *not* to be compelled to maintain the same high interest rate as the rest of the world. Even when the domestic interest rate coincides with the targeted rate but is higher than the global rate, there is a strong indication of interest rate autonomy.

We get a strong indication of a *lack* of interest rate autonomy, however, if the domestic interest level is the same as the level in the rest of the world. The exception would be if the domestic rate is the same as GR while *simultaneously* matching the targeted rate (TR). In such a case we have no indication either way.

There is a *weak* indication of interest rate autonomy if the domestic interest rate is high in relation to the targeted rate (TR) but low in relation to the global rate (GR). The same applies in reverse. In these cases the actual domestic rate deviates from the global rate in the same *direction* as the targeted rate but by a different amount.

If both TR and GR are greater or smaller than the domestic interest rate, we have to look at the size of GR in relation to TR. Where TR and the actual domestic interest rate deviate from GR in the same direction, we can speak of a weak indication of interest rate autonomy; otherwise we have no indication at all.

So is it possible for us to say anything about interest rate autonomy on a basis of observed interest gaps, unless we know exactly what target has been formulated for the domestic rate? The answer is that it might be possible, if for example we can assume that the government is aiming to keep the long-term interest rate down in order to stimulate domestic investment activity. From a Swedish point of view this assumption is reasonable, since this goal was confirmed among other things by the motivation for the Swedish exchange controls. Interest rate autonomy in the form of the *permanent* segmentation will then, when it exists, appears as a negative average "adjusted" interest gap in our analysis.

We do not have equally strong grounds for assuming that the goal as regards the *short-term* interest rates for the whole period has been to keep them low. In the case of short-term rates, interest rate autonomy is thus expressed chiefly in the degree of success in delaying the impact of foreign interest movements on the domestic rate. For these maturities any segmentation is thus most likely to appear in the form of *temporary* segmentation.

2.7.2 *Operational measures of financial integration*

We have thus found that the greatest caution is advisable in saying anything about interest rate policy autonomy solely on a basis of statistically measurable direct financial disintegration. Bearing this in mind, we can now turn to the question of the indicators or variables that should be studied and measured.[97] Let us first discuss the logic behind the definition in (2.3).

Tendencies towards price equilibrium – an expression of integration

The most frequent functional definition[98] of a fully integrated market states that the prices of all production factors – goods, services, labour and capital – are of equal importance and move towards equilibrium. This definition thus also applies to interest rates. Researchers adopting this approach claim that the capital markets are perfectly integrated, when the returns on identical investments in two countries and currencies are *the same at all points in time*. The markets are de facto *one* market. Perfect integration coincides here with Mundell's concept of perfect mobility (Mundell 1963a). Capital movements are triggered by expected interest differentials. Under perfect total integration, expected real interest rates are the same at all times.

The definition of movements towards price equilibrium can never be complete, but it can provide the basis for an operational definition of changes in the level of integration. Thus according to this definition we should be able to claim an increase in international integration if, after exchange rate expectations and risk premiums have been taken into account, the average level of interest rates on a certain instrument *converges* as between two countries, or if the fluctuations in these rates exhibit increased correlation and *move in parallel* with one another. Since it takes time for the convergence to make an impact, it is important to look not only at effects during the present period but also at *lagged* effects.

As I have already mentioned, I limit myself here to the measurement of direct financial integration. My aim in the next part of this section is to illustrate the multiplicity of the financial links which can be measured and analysed as an expression of direct financial integration. Figure 1.1 has already shown how macroeconomic equilibrium relationships provide a basis for such an analysis. I shall elaborate further the definition and my chosen analytical approach in Section 2.8.

2.7.3 *Different ways of analysing direct financial integration*

In a discussion revolving around the concept of financial integration, the analytical alternatives can be described as in Figure 2.8, which illustrates some of the different approaches in terms of key components, such as the choice of dependent variable, the inclusion of transmission effects, the choice of method, the choice of markets to be compared, etc.

Three alternatives in choosing the dependent variable

According to the figure there are three main paths to follow in analysing direct financial integration. The first goes by way of the *interest-sensitivity of the capital flows.* Here the capital flow is the dependent variable and the gaps between nominal interest rates – with or without forward cover – are among the explanatory variables. From the numerous studies which have been conducted we get very little idea about the role of capital flows in linking national markets together. The results from similar studies often contradict one another, due to the many problems connected with measuring the level of capital market integration on a basis of capital flows. Apart from the measurement problems which I mentioned in the introductory chapter, this approach also leads to difficulties when it comes to testing causality, to correctly dealing with the endogeneity of many of the most common explanatory variables, to developing the limited two-country view in a meaningful way, or to distinguishing between endogenous and exogenous policy variables.

The second path goes via the reflow of capital, but the difficulties are the same as those just mentioned.

In following the third main path, the level of integration is derived from *comparisons of the return on equivalent securities* on the markets in different countries, and in some cases on the Euromarket. The dependent variable used here is the gap between domestic and foreign interest rates. By insulating an incentive for arbitrage in terms of opportunities for risk-free profits or incentives for speculation in terms of excess profits, this can be seen as an approximation and alternative to the first of the approaches mentioned above.

Many market combinations to choose from

In comparing the return on equivalent securities, we have many combinations to choose

Figure 2.8 Choice of approach in analysing financial integration

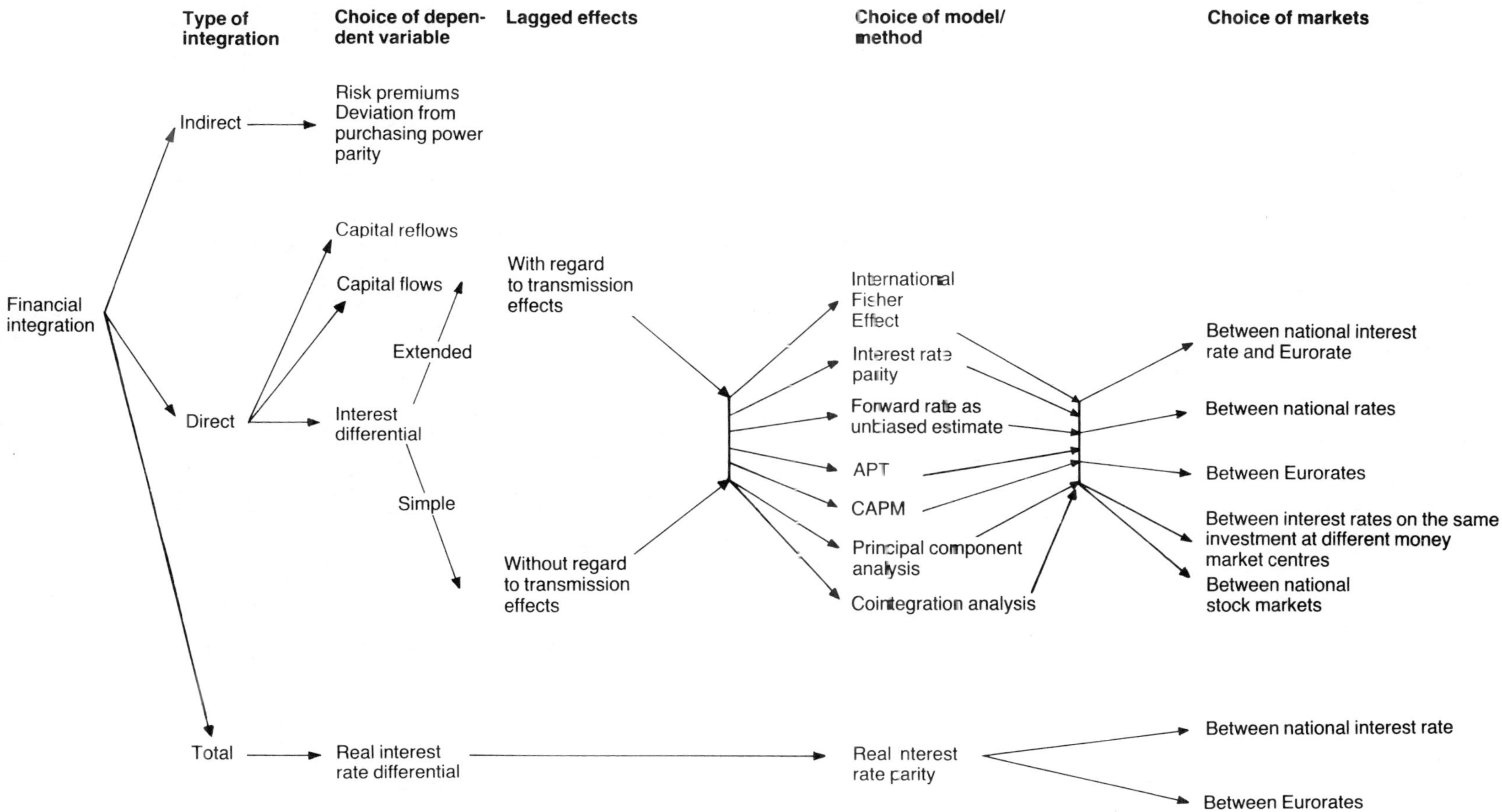

from. The return on a national market can be compared with the return on the corresponding market in another country. Or the return on securities on a national market can be compared with the return on corresponding securities on the Euromarket. Or we could decide to compare the return on securities in the same currency but issued at different market centres. For instance we could compare the return on a dollar investment in New York with the equivalent return in London.[99] The assets to be compared may be shares, bank savings, bonds etc. Or we could compare the cost of loans of various kinds. The common denominator in all these studies is that the "law of one price" shall obtain even on the financial side, if we are to assume that perfect direct financial integration obtains.

We approach the measurement of market efficiency

Comparisons of prices on different markets coincide to a large extent with the analysis of market efficiency. These studies attract particular attention, since all – or almost all – classical theories in financial theory rest on the assumption of efficient markets.[100]

Let us adopt the investor's perspective

If we take the case for speculation as a point of departure in discussing possible demands regarding the gap between two prices so that market efficiency may prevail, we must complement the International Fisher Effect with demands from actors with risk aversion and re-write formula (2.3) as

$$(r_i - r_j) - (\hat{s}^*_{ij} + \text{risk premium}) \leq \text{transaction cost}. \tag{2.16}$$

As long as formula (2.16) holds, there is no argument for speculation in terms of expected excess profits. A special case of this formula is that of covered interest rate arbitrage. By replacing $\hat{s}^*_{ij}$ by the forward rate we can identify a potential pure arbitrage argument (covered interest arbitrage is described in Appendix 2.6). [101] [102] This means that the future exchange rate in the arbitrage is known, and that there is thus no exchange risk. A deviation between the domestic rate and the forward covered foreign rate indicates segmented capital markets. If the deviation is equal to or less than the transaction cost, the market can still be described as efficient. But even if we have eliminated the problem of exchange risk by adopting this approach, there still remains – unless the comparison refers to Eurorates – the question of pricing the political risk.[103]

Efficiency is a prerequisite of interest rate parity.[104] Efficient markets without transaction costs are a prerequisite of perfect direct financial integration. Thus the money and bond markets can prove to be efficient without being perfectly integrated. If, on the other hand, international markets are inefficient in some way, this means that the integration is not perfect.

A diminishing deviation from interest rate parity, given unchanged transaction costs, is not a sufficient condition for assuming an increase in direct financial integration. Before we can say anything about such an increase, we have to know whether the (relative) political risk premium has been constant or, if it has changed, how it has done so.

Can the level of direct financial integration be expressed in a simple measure?

So we now have to ask, can the level of *international* direct financial integration for a single country be expressed empirically in a simple standardized measure? The answer to this question today is, no. There are both theoretical and empirical gaps. But, in my opinion, it is possible to formulate such a measure for individual sectors. A measure of financial integration for the whole financial market of a country then has to be based on some form of subjective evaluation of all these measures together.

The individual measure for each sector should, in my view, provide information about two things.[105] It should express both permanent and temporary segmentation. The measure should also allow for the possibility of comparison over time, thus providing further information about the development and growth of integration and interest rate transmission. In the next section I shall introduce my suggestion for the design of such a measure.

2.8 Applied definition and the choice of model

One of the purposes of the present book is to suggest a way of analysing empirically the international dependence of a national financial market. The analysis will be limited to *direct financial integration* and will be based on comparisons of interest rates.

The *definition* of direct financial integration used here is as follows:

> Market A is perfectly (directly) financially integrated with market B if the interest rate on market A – after exchange rate expectations and risk premiums have been allowed for – is the same as the interest rate on market B at every moment in time, and if the politicians on market A have not themselves decided that this should be so.

I base my empirical analysis on an *assumption* of rational expectations. Provided this assumption is correct, I can concentrate on testing the other constituent of the theory of capital market integration, namely the process of making international financial transactions. The main question here is whether a government by imposing regulations can create permanent and/or temporary segmentation, for instance to prevent the elimination of inefficiencies by way of arbitrage, or speculation.

My *basic model* for the analysis of direct financial integration in this study represents a development of Fisher's approach, as follows:

$$
\begin{aligned}
r_{d,t} - r_{for,t} = \; & \beta_0 + \beta_1 \cdot \text{(expected exchange rate movement)} + \\
& \beta_2 \cdot \text{(exchange risk)} + \beta_3 \cdot \text{(political risk)} + \\
& \beta_4 \cdot \text{(expression of institutional changes)} + \\
& \beta_5 \cdot \text{(expression of lagged effects)} + \\
& \varepsilon \text{ (random term).} \qquad (2.17)
\end{aligned}
$$

The β_0 coefficient is an expression of constant risk premiums, transaction costs, general market inefficiency and a possible average (permanent) segmentation, i.e. a result of interest rate policy autonomy.[106] If the transaction cost, and that part of the risk premium that is included here, remain constant, the comparison of β_0 for different subperiods can reveal whether the general market inefficiency and/or the effects of an interest rate policy autonomy has decreased. It is difficult to distinguish between these two inefficiencies. In order to get some idea of inefficiencies resulting from interest rate policy measures, I will be forced later to make assumptions about the general market inefficiency.

Let us assume, for example, that a country's aim is a low interest rate, lower even than the comparative rate in the rest of the world, in order to promote more rapid economic growth, a higher rate of investment and lower unemployment than other countries. Autonomy in the model will then give a negative intercept, once the transaction cost and constant risk premium have been eliminated.

Other β_i coefficients express the linear addition to the interest gap. The coefficient β_2 is the premium for exchange risk. For each unit of increase in the exchange risk, the interest gap increases by β_2 units etc.

The model I have now chosen exhibits certain similarities with the APT model presented in Section 2.6. In both models it is a case of identifying risks and considering the sensitivity of the return to the respective risk factors. As in APT the measurement is conducted under an assumption of risk-free interest – an assumption that is not always easy to underpin, as will be discussed in Section 2.10.

Coefficients estimated in the model indicate the level of direct financial integration

Under perfect direct integration, the interest gap, adjusted for risk premiums, transaction costs and exchange rate expectations is always zero. In a study of imperfectly integrated markets the analysis of changes in the level of integration must be based on an analysis of the gap and on the adaptation of the domestic interest rate to interest changes in the rest of the world (see Table 2.2). We can measure this propensity to adapt in the form of covariation. Adaptation may not occur straight away, and so we have to look at the strength of the covariation and at the pattern of time lags. For example, if it takes 18 months before a change in a foreign interest rate makes its full impact on the domestic rate, while a later change of equivalent size needs only 9 months before its impact is felt, then we have confirmation of increasing integration, unless the adaptability is an expression of a conscious policy. The shorter the time needed for an external change to reproduce itself on the domestic market, the higher the assumed level of integration between the markets.

The measure of direct financial integration consists of two parts

According to my approach, integration can be expressed by a combination of two parameter values ($\bar{\beta}_0$, t). One of these parameters ($\bar{\beta}_0$) expresses the size of the intercept from which the constant risk premiums have been eliminated. The other parameter (t) expresses the significant lag before a foreign interest rate movement reproduces itself in the domestic rate.[107] Perfect direct financial integration is characterized by the parameter pair ($\bar{\beta}=0$, $t=0$).

We are encountering here a general *analytical problem.* While I am calculating my β-values, I am testing at the same time whether the model is true. Thus non-significant parameter values could mean that it is not. However, by testing the autocorrelation in the residuals, I get some idea as to whether this is the case. But if I find significant autocorrelation, I immediately face a new problem: I have to decide whether this autocorrelation depends on a *misspecified model* or on an improper choice of *proxy variables.*

In such a case, since I find strong theoretical as well as empirical grounds for believing in my model – its functional form and its set of variables – I will have to try some other proxy variables, which are logically motivated and have been included in the preparatory considerations.[108]

The quality of the investigation lends itself to evaluation in aggregate[109] if not in normative form.

Table 2.2 **Indications of increasing direct financial integration**

Factors indicating increased direct financial integration:
- shorter time before foreign interest changes affect the domestic rate
- higher correlation between changes in foreign and domestic rates[a]
- the intercept $\overline{\beta}_0$ declines compared with previous periods.

Factors motivating greater credibility in the above:
- higher multiple coefficient of determination (R^2)
- lower standard error in estimated coefficients[b]
- better Durbin-Watson values[c] (D-W).

To interpret the statistical results in terms of interest rate policy autonomy, we must assume that
- the hypothesis of rational expectations applies
- the results obtained are not a conscious policy choice in a situation where actual freedom of choice has obtained.

[a] Here we have the problem of interpretation mentioned by Kenen (1976). He emphasises that strong correlation between interest rates only tests market integration, after it has been adjusted for correlation which can be ascribed to underlying common factors. If the correlation is zero, this can be interpreted as a sign of segmentation. If this is not the case, the correlation must be "purified".
[b] If the standard errors are small, we can assume that the model contains less uncertainty as a result of multicollinearity i.e. less linear dependence between the explanatory variables and less competition between these variables to express the same information.
[c] These values should be around 2. The existence of autocorrelation will also be measured by a Box-Pierce test for lags of up to 36 months. If autocorrelation obtains, this is among other things an indication that important explanatory variables may have been left out of the model.

How does the model differ from its predecessors?

The chosen model represents an extension of a traditional approach in that the intercept is used to indicate the level of financial integration, that a premium for the political risk is included,[110] and that the modelling of the market exchange rate expectations is based on primary data about market actors.[111]

2.9 Disintegration and monetary autonomy by way of controls

As we have already noted, functioning controls are a sign of financial disintegration and a lower level of interest dependence between domestic and foreign markets. The controls that have a direct effect on the level of integration are interest rate controls and exchange controls.[112]

Exchange controls generate a demand for political risk premiums

The controls affect prices and volumes.[113] Exchange controls, for example, can be formulated either as a tax, perhaps on the return on foreign investments, or as restrictions on the sums which could be transferred for investment abroad. Each such quantitative control has a theoretical equivalent in a tax with the same restrictive effect.[114] Exchange controls on capital flows establish a difference between domestic and foreign interest rates without generating any inflow or outflow of capital. The idea is that it should be possible to vary the monetary policy within reasonable limits without letting exchange rates be affected by capital movements.[115] A functioning system of exchange controls is a signal to the investor that he has to expect market intervention. For this risk we assume he demands compensation. Thus exchange controls give rise to premiums for political risk.

The restricted effects of exchange controls are not empirically confirmed

The theoretical arguments in defence of exchange controls are fairly weak, and there is no convincing proof that such controls generate welfare gains.[116] Rather, after a time such controls even reinforce the disturbances against which they were intended to provide protection.

Hewson and Sakakibara (1975 and 1976) among others have conducted empirical studies which cast doubt on the efficacy of exchange controls to prevent capital outflows and stimulate domestic investment. They have not found any significant effect on capital movements. Johnson (1979), on the other hand, has studied interest differentials and found that certain effects do arise. This apparent contradiction can probably be explained by problems connected with the data for establishing the size of the capital flow. Such problems are common, and will be discussed in Section 2.10.

Many countries have introduced exchange controls, citing the emergency clauses in OECD's capital liberalization agreement regarding balance-of-payment problems. Few countries today, however, implement their controls. It is more a question of preparedness. Those countries which have exchange controls in force – of which until recently Sweden was one – are generally hoping that they will help to prevent high private-economy tax pressure or general economic uncertainty from leading to the flight of capital.

The interesting question is thus whether a country can impose interest controls or maintain autonomous pricing with the help of various types of exchange controls which effectively prevent undesirable capital flows. The opportunities for doing so have been considerably reduced in recent years, as international business enterprise has increased, and – even more importantly – as a result of the emergence of an international credit market.[117] For a small open economy with a large multinational corporate sector, the possibility of controlling short-term flows in a turbulent financial environment seems to be extremely slight. In Chapter 4 we will return to this, and we will look at data about how the earlier Swedish exchange controls were perceived by the market actors.

2.10 Problems of measurement and standardization

Comparisons of international financial markets face many problems of measurement and standardization. The measurement of international capital flows is generally so unreliable that it is impossible to test a model in which the capital flow is a dependent variable. For this and other reasons I have decided to use the interest gap as dependent variable. But there are still difficulties, one of which concerns the comparability of the interest rates on the markets to be compared.

Researchers disagree on what elements should be included in the cost of a financial transaction. Many researchers even include the elusive cost of information search and the effect of controls in the transaction cost.[118] This disagreement about how to measure the transaction cost is unfortunate, since the existence of a transaction cost constitutes a sign of disintegration.[119]

Difficulty in finding comparable interest rates

We have to decide whether the interest rates reflect exactly the same conditions, for example, regarding fundamental risks. We want to compare interest rates which are the same in every respect except for the jurisdiction involved and the currency in which the loan is denominated or the investment is made. The interest rates which can be studied are: day-to-day money rates, rates for treasury bills and treasury discount notes, prime rates, rates on bonds or the official discount rates. In Figure 2.3 we noted the potential sources of error that must be considered in comparing interest rates in different countries, or the Eurorate with national market rates, or the interest rates on investments in different currencies on the Euromarket. Moreover, the administrative regulation of interest rates can produce deviations from international rates in the long run on the national markets, which are difficult to interpret. If the risks are not the same, the differences will have to be priced. In order to simplify the analysis I have therefore tried to go as far as possible in matching factors which are linked to a specific instrument, with a view to having the smallest possible difference for which a price has to be set.[120] With this kind of matching it is possible to avoid the problem of the liquidity premium for example.

In so far as the risk premiums are not constant, we still have the problem of finding unambiguous measures for them. The source underlying the premium, i.e. the risk, then has to be quantified, a problem which I shall be addressing in Chapter 8, where we will be discussing the econometric analysis.

Possible links between risk and return have been considered in earlier sections. The size of the risk premium is conditional on the behaviour of the market actors. Can an aggregate portfolio view, for example, be regarded as steering the actors? If so, what form should I give this aggregate in my empirical study? By collecting primary data about the corporate view I acquire some basis for my assumptions regarding the expectation formation and risk attitude of the most important group of market actors. These data underpin the assumptions about the corporate expectation structure that I shall be compelled to make in Chapter 8.

2.10.1 *Sectorial studies of direct financial integration*

As will be obvious by now, any study of total financial integration based on the total analysis of the flows will be very complex, unless we introduce radical simplifications. And the results of the analysis are correspondingly uncertain. Direct financial integration based on the study of risk-adjusted return is also intrinsically difficult to analyse, but the task is nonetheless manageable. If we want to infer anything about direct financial integration and interest rate autonomy for the country as a whole from the sectorial studies, we will have to proceed in two stages. First we must make our inferences about the total market by studying all its segments, and then we must interpret the results in terms of interest rate autonomy.

We have to draw conclusions about the financial market as a whole from studies of several sectors

As there are so many submarkets or sectors, there are also a great many opportunities for comparing returns in a study of direct integration. If the submarkets in a country were clearly linked, we could reduce the analysis to the study of the return on *one* type of instrument. However, there is no such clear link either in theory or practice.[121] As we have seen, several theories claim to explain the relationship between the short- and long-term rates. On the practical side, selective measures of monetary policy, e.g. subsidized interest rates in certain market segments, motivate an extension of the analysis to include comparisons of the returns on many different types of financial investments.

Financial integration then has to be interpreted in terms of interest rate autonomy

As a second stage in a our series of deductions we come up against the problem of basing conclusions about the political freedom of action in a country on an observation of the level of direct financial integration.[122] For example, if a country manages to maintain a lower interest rate than the rest of the world with the help of controls or *selective* interventions, this does not necessarily mean that it has succeeded in keeping itself apart and remaining autonomous in a monetary policy perspective. It has indubitably succeeded in differentiating prices in certain sectors, but before saying anything about the direct financial integration for the country's entire financial market, we have to make inferences about the total market on studies of the various submarkets. This is a tricky and very subjective process and caution is to be recommended. An analysis of a submarket can send out the wrong signals about the total market, particularly if there has been some redistribution between submarkets.

2.10.2 Bilateral or global comparisons?

The types of model described in the literature for different economies generally start, without further analysis, from the standard assumptions about the financial effects of markets on one another. A polarization occurs, in that the financial quantities are assumed to be exogenously *or* endogenously determined. Thus it is often assumed that the United States is sufficiently big to be able to ignore influence from foreign markets. The interest rate in models of the US economy are endogenized. Sweden, on the other hand, is assumed to be one of the countries whose interest rate is wholly determined by influence from foreign markets.[123] Thus the interest rate is regarded as exogenously determined.

As we have already noted, there are no countries small enough to justify the small-country assumption. And Hartman (1984) suggests that in fact there are probably no countries sufficiently large and dominating to remain unaffected by events in other parts of the world.

Hartman shows that previous international studies, in which the rate on US treasury bills was taken as given, failed to consider an important reverse chain of cause and effect, from events abroad to conditions on the US money market. The interest rate on US treasury bills is used in many contexts as an indicator of the state of the US money market. Hartman sees the mutuality as a relatively recent phenomenon. His study covers 1971–78, and it is not until the period 1975–78 that the mutual effects become significant. This can be partly explained by the diminishing importance of the US dollar as the benchmark for price-setting on the global foreign exchange markets.

Although there may previously have been a case for the *bilateral* analysis of the interest rate in a small open economy and the US rate, we now need a broader measure of the "global interest level" than the US rate can provide. Hartman's results (and those of others) leave the choice of a comparative rate open. The interest rate effect on a small economy such as Sweden's can be envisaged in the following form:

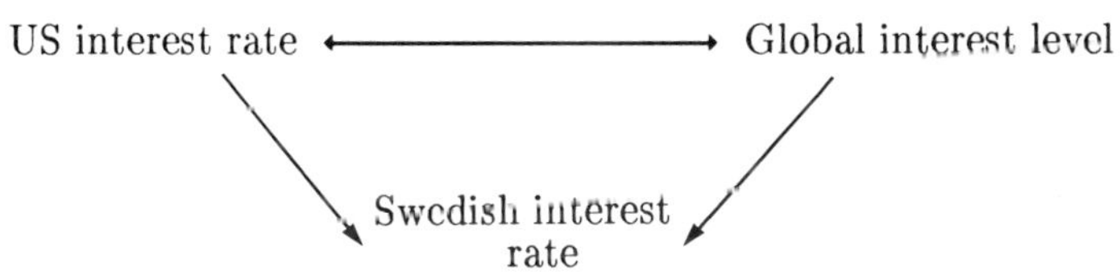

In the case of our present study, it is possible that the US interest rate was the leader at the beginning of the study period, and the "global level" in the form of an aggregate of interest rates was the leader in the later years. For this reason I shall analyse the gap between the Swedish rate and both these interest rates in parallel.

Measurements of the global interest level raises a problem of definition

An advantage of *bilateral* studies is that they provide an opportunity to investigate in detail the factors that distinguish markets from one another. For example, it is easier to model the transaction cost. An even more important advantage of the bilateral study is associated with the difficulty of finding a suitable definition of the "global interest level". An aggregate interest of this kind can be created by combining the interest rates in the world's largest and economically most important countries; but we then encounter a weighting problem.

The weighting of the different interest rates can be based on *trade weights* of some kind or on *capital market weights.*[124] Trade weights are to be preferred, since their correlation with interest rate movements can be assumed to be weaker than that of the capital market weights. The situation is further complicated in that we have to decide between *bilateral* or *global weight systems*. IMF's MERM is an example of a system based on global weights. However, according to various studies in the foreign exchange field, where experience on these questions is greatest, the choice does not seem to have any significant effect on the results or reliability of the analysis.[125]

An analysis of the deviation from the global interest level is motivated

On a perfectly functioning market it can be assumed that the investor is an international actor, i.e. the political risk in one country must be weighed against the political risk in other countries where an equivalent investment could be made. This means a further complication in the analysis, in that political risks in several countries have to be estimated, and the difference must be ascribed an explanatory value.[126] The use of the global interest level has a certain technical merit here, since we can assume that only the non-diversifiable country risk and exchange risk now remain. This effect, whereby my analysis begins to resemble APT analyses, is definitely weaker in comparisons with individual countries than in comparisons with the global interest level. The fact that the capital flows are global in character also speaks for using an aggregate interest rate for purposes of comparison rather than the rate of any individual country.

2.10.3 The transient nature of arbitrage causes measurement problems

In any analysis of the level of financial integration, the time aspect is going to be important. Arbitrage and speculation are a question of hours and minutes. However, it is difficult to study such short-term transactions at least in a structural model. Access to data represents a restriction. We are not very likely to be able to specify such a model in such a way as to allow for the running of monthly data and for really short time horizons. Obviously the timing aspect will be expressed less satisfactorily, the longer the period covered by the individual observations. And this in turn adds uncertainty to the interpretation of observations of the level of financial integration. However, by using market data and testing actual arbitrage situations I have tried at least to some extent to overcome the drawbacks of having to base my analysis on quarterly data.

2.11 Collecting primary data

I have chosen to adopt the investor's perspective. The empirical study of Swedish markets thus calls for an understanding of the behaviour of the market actors.

Admittedly I assume rational expectations, but the validity of this assumption is difficult to test. However, by collecting and analysing primary data I increase my understanding of the actors' expectation structure and the adequacy of the rational expectation assumption.

A survey of the most important actors on Swedish financial markets will be presented in Chapter 4. Here I will simply point out that the largest Swedish multinational companies, taken as a group, constitute the most important single actor.

In order to get some idea of the way these actors, for example, form their expectations with regard to financial variables and of their attitude to the Swedish exchange controls then in force, an investigation[127] was carried out during the autumn of 1983 and the spring of 1984.

The population consisted of companies and groups whose total turnover was in excess of SEK 1 billion in 1981, and which fulfilled the three following conditions for international dependence:

1. the company/group should be among the country's 50 largest exporters
2. the company/group should be among the country's 50 largest sellers abroad
3. the company/group should be among the country's 50 largest foreign employers.

A total of 26 companies/groups fulfilled these requirements. For practical reasons a fourth criterion was added, namely that the company should be listed on the stock exchange. This eliminated two state-owned companies as well as the Johnson Group and Tetra Pac. A population of 22 companies thus remained, and these are listed in Appendix 2.7. Three more companies (Kema-Nobel, Billerud-Uddeholm and ASEA) were subsequently also eliminated, without affecting the representativeness of my data. The final sample thus consisted of 19 companies, which are underlined in Appendix 2.7.[128]

The study covered all aspects of the corporate decisions under macroeconomic uncertainty. It was based on interviews. Data was collected during visits to the companies concerned. During discussions in seminar form lasting from one to three days, views were aired and then registered in accordance with a written questionnaire with standardized questions. Every question allowed for an open answer outside the alternatives given.[129] Virtually all the relevant decision-makers in the various companies took part in the seminars, which were thus attended by anything from one to six people. Regular members were the senior vice president, the financial director, the treasurer, the head of financial planning and the accounting manager. Others who were called in to discuss particular issues included the president, the manager responsible for export credit assessments, the manager responsible for strategic planning and so on. The results of this investigation provide implicitly as well as explicitly the basis for much of the argument in the rest of this book.

2.12 Concluding comment on the methodological problems

In this chapter I have presented a model for analysing market segmentation. In the choice between the capital flow and the interest gap as dependent variable, I have argued in favour of the latter on several grounds. The idea underlying my model is to eliminate from the interest gap all price components, in order to focus on the presence of inefficiencies. Thus I have eliminated the price for different forms of risk, i.e. premiums for exchange risk and political risk, and the exchange rate movements which the market actors expect to occur during the maturity.

I have also discussed various attributes of risk premiums. Are they relatively small or relatively large? Are they constant or variable? We have found no clear-cut answer to these questions in international research. I have therefore decided to work with both, and to try to model the variable risk premiums.

In this chapter I have also discussed various sources of risk and possible proxy variables for the premiums for these risks. For the country risk I found a reasonable proxy variable in the country's international indebtedness, and for the exchange risk in the variations in deviations from purchasing power parity. The proxy variables will be discussed further in Chapter 8. I have also indirectly found a basis for my choice of proxies in an empirical study of decisions under macroeconomic uncertainty in large Swedish multinational groups. One of the main objectives of that study was to mitigate the drawbacks in the previous studies which I have criticized for testing models containing ex ante quantities on ex post data. By collecting data on how the actors form their expectations, I hope to have increased the possibility of achieving reliable tests. Before embarking on a discussion of various attributes characterizing Swedish markets and market actors, I shall present some of the results and findings of some previously published empirical investigations. This will be the subject of Chapter 3.

APPENDIX 2.1

Fisher (Domestic) Effect

According to the Fisher Effect

$$r_t = r_t^{R*} + \hat{P}_t^* \tag{A2.1}$$

where

r_t = nominal interest rate
r_t^{R*} = expected real interest rate
$\hat{P}_t^*$ = expected inflation.

Thus Fisher assumes the nominal or money rate to be equal to the sum of an expected real interest rate and an expected inflation rate. Fisher's theory emphasizes that the real rate of interest depends on real phenomena. Since the influence of these phenomena probably changes slowly, the real rate is assumed to be constant in the short- and medium-terms.

APPENDIX 2.2

Variability in interest rates after tax

Let us assume that the investor allows for tax when he formulates his goal in terms of real interest rate. The expected real rate after tax can be written[130]

$$\dot{r}_t^{R*} = r_t\,(1-c) - \hat{P}_t^*. \tag{A2.2}$$

If we rewrite (A2.2) to make it comparable with (A2.1), we obtain

$$r_t = \frac{1}{1-c}\,[\dot{r}_t^{R*} + \hat{P}_t^*]. \tag{A2.3}$$

If tax rate c is considered by the investor, the variability in the interest rate will be

$$\sigma_r^2 = [1/(1-c)]^2 \, \sigma^2_{\dot{r}^{R*}} + [1/(1-c)]^2 \, \sigma^2_{\hat{P}*} + 2[1/(1-c)]^2 \, \rho_{\dot{r}^{R*}, \hat{P}*} \cdot \sigma_{\dot{r}^{R*}} \cdot \sigma_{\hat{P}*} \tag{A2.4}$$

where, thus,

$\sigma^2_{\hat{P}*}$	=	the variance in expected inflation
$\sigma^2_{\dot{r}^{R*}}$	=	the variance in expected real interest after tax
$\rho_{\dot{r}^{R*}, \hat{P}*}$	=	the correlation coefficient between expected real interest rate after tax and expected inflation

If the tax is not taken into account, the variance will instead be

$$\sigma_r^2 = \sigma^2_{r^{R*}} + \sigma^2_{\hat{P}*} + 2\rho_{r^{R*}, \hat{P}*} \cdot \sigma_{r^{R*}} \cdot \sigma_{\hat{P}*}. \tag{A2.5}$$

A comparison between the variances in (A2.4) and (A2.5) reveals certain clear effects. If the correlation between $\dot{r}^{R*}$ and $\hat{P}*$ can be ignored, it can be stated that the variability in the real interest rate after tax leads unmistakably to higher variability in r, since for every tax rate higher than zero

$$[1/(1-c)] > 1.$$

Let us assume, for example, that the average tax rate on interest earnings is 50 per cent. An increase of 1 per cent in the variance in expected real interest after tax then generates four times as great an increase in the variance in the nominal rate before tax. The higher the tax rate, the greater the impact of variability in r, other things being equal. It is then assumed that there is no fiscal illusion, but that the investor recognizes the tax effects in full. Thus the general uncertainty prevailing today with regard to the tax situation particularly in the financial area, can have a strong effect on the variability of the market interest rate, r. Taking tax into account also means that the effects of an increase in the variance in the expected inflation will be reinforced.

APPENDIX 2.3

The International Fisher Effect

The International Fisher Effect deals with the international equilibrium for interest rates after adjustment for expected exchange rate movements, and it represents the financial market's equivalent of the purchasing power parity theory. The relationship, which is also known as Fisher's open relationship, can be written

$$\frac{S^*_{t+n} - S_t}{S_t} = \frac{r_d - r_{for}}{1 + r_{for}} \tag{A2.6}$$

where

S_t = the spot rate at time t

S^*_{t+n} = market expectation at time t regarding the future spot rate at time t + n

r_d = domestic n-months nominal interest rate

r_{for} = foreign n-months nominal interest rate

On an efficient non-controlled international capital market, the International Fisher Effect (Fisher 1930) implies that

$$r_1 - r_2 \approx \hat{s}^*_{12} \tag{A2.7}$$

where

$\hat{s}^*_{12}$ = expected relative rate of change in the exchange rate (currency in country 1/currency in country 2).

According to the theory of purchasing power parity, the change in exchange rates can then be estimated on a basis of the expected inflation:

$$\hat{s}^*_{12} \approx \hat{P}^*_1 - \hat{P}_2. \tag{A2.8}$$

Assuming risk neutrality, purchasing power parity, homogeneous expectations and immediate response to changed incentives, the real interest rates can be expected to be equal, i.e.

$$r_1 - \hat{P}_1^* \approx r_2 - \hat{P}_2^*. \tag{A2.9}$$

The loan cost for a Swedish company, for example, borrowing in DEM can be written

$$r_{Sw} = r_{WGer} + \hat{s}_{Sw,WGer} \tag{A2.10}$$

where

r_{WGer} = nominal interest rate on the loan in DEM

$\hat{s}_{Sw,WGer}$ = relative rate of change in the exchange rate.

The real interest rate in its simplest form can be written

$$r^R_{Sw} = r_{WGer} + \hat{s}_{Sw,WGer} - \hat{P}_{Sw} \tag{A2.11}$$

where $\hat{P}_{Sw}$ = inflation in Sweden.

However, provided that the purchasing power parity theory holds, we get

$$r^R_{Sw} = r_{WGer} - \hat{P}_{WGer} \tag{A2.12}$$

where $\hat{P}_{WGer}$ = inflation in West Germany.

Thus, assuming that the purchasing power parity theory holds, inflation in Sweden is not expected to affect the real interest rate for the loan in DEM, since the loss in real value caused by inflation in Sweden, is counteracted by an appreciation of the German mark.

The International Fisher Effect represents an example of financial equilibrium relationships, implying that a Swedish krona can be expected to give the same return on investment with equal risk, wherever it is invested. The theory should be formulated in Eurorates, to eliminate the disturbances that national exchange controls can generate. Empirical studies have confirmed the validity of the theory for the major Eurocurrencies.[131]

The interest differential, relative inflation and the exchange rate are linked to one another (cf. A2.7 and A2.8). However, there is no agreement in the theory about the appearance of this link. There is the monetary school which claims that the exchange rate fluctuates in order to create equilibrium in the demand for wealth in the form of financial assets. Against this there is the traditional view that the exchange rate fluctuates in order to create equilibrium in the international demand for the goods flows. Thus, for example, an increase in the money supply can lead to increased inflation, and according to the purchasing power parity theory to a depreciation in the currency of a country. The International Fisher Effect, on the other hand, can advocate an appreciation of the currency, if inflation in the country has forced up the domestic level of interest so that it generates an increased inflow of international capital.

Within the monetary school there are two views about the relationship between interest differentials and exchange rate movements. The first of these has a *Keynesian* base, in that it is assumed that prices are sticky at least in the short run, and that the nominal interest level consequently reflects the tightness of the monetary policy adopted.[132] Domestic interest rates rise in relation to foreign rates due to a contraction in the domestic supply of money in relation to the demand, without there being an equivalent drop in prices. Domestic rates which exceed foreign rates result in capital inflow, which is accompanied by an immediate appreciation of the domestic currency. An appreciation means that the price of the foreign currency falls. A *negative* relationship is thus advocated between the exchange rate movements and nominal interest differentials.

The second view stems from the *Chicago school*, in that it is assumed that the prices are completely flexible[133] (PPP always holds), and that changes in the nominal interest rate reflect changed expectations regarding future inflation. Thus when the Swedish interest rate rises in relation to other rates, for example, this is said to be a result of the fact that the Swedish krona is expected to lose in value as a result of inflation and depreciation. The demand for the Swedish krona drops compared with other currencies; the Swedish krona is depreciated with immediate effect. This sequence of events describes a *positive* relationship between exchange rate movements and nominal interest differentials.

These two views are thus based on different assumptions regarding the speed with which prices adjust. According to Frankel (1979a), the description based on the Chicago school is realistic when the variation in the inflation differentials is great, as for example during the German inflation of the 1920s, while the view based on the Keynesian school is valid when the corresponding variation is small. According to Frankel, the problem is to find a description that is realistic, when the variation is moderate and of a size such as prevailed among most industrial countries during the 1970s. Frankel[134] has combined the two schools in a real interest rate model, and has shown that the exchange rate can be regarded as negatively related to the nominal interest differential and positively related to the expected difference in long-term inflation rate.

APPENDIX 2.4

Model for determining the exchange rate

I present below a monetary model which can serve as an overall summary of the entire monetary model family. Different models can be extracted from it. The overall model specification used by Meese and Rogoff (1983), among others, in testing three important model variants is as follows:

$$e_{12} = a_0 + a_1(m_1-m_2) + a_2(y_1-y_2) + a_3(r_1^S-r_2^S) + a_4(\pi_1^*-\pi_2^*) + a_5\overline{HB}_1 + a_6\overline{HB}_2 + u \tag{A2.13}$$

where, in terms of the Swedish krona,

e	=	logarithm of the SEK price of foreign currency
m_1-m_2	=	logarithm of the ratio of the Swedish money supply to the foreign money supply
y_1-y_2	=	logarithm of the ratio of Swedish to foreign real income
$r_1^S-r_2^S$	=	short-term interest rate differential
$\pi_1^*-\pi_2^*$	=	expected long-run inflation differential
$\overline{HB}_1$	=	cumulative Swedish trade balance
$\overline{HB}_2$	=	cumulative foreign trade balance
u	=	disturbance term.

Frenkel and Bilson's model[135] is one of the models that can be extracted from this. It is based on the assumption that $a_1 = 1$, i.e. that the exchange rate exhibits first-degree homogeneity in the relative money supplies. An assumption which is also made for the other two models mentioned below. This model also assumes purchasing power parity and has the restrictions $a_4 = a_5 = a_6 = 0$. One of the other two tested models is often known as the Hooper and Morton model.[136] It allows for a change in the long-term real exchange rate, and should be regarded as an extension of Dornbusch and Frankel's model[137], which is the third model to be tested. Hooper and Morton's model has none of the restrictions on the zero value of the coefficient a_i in the above equation. In Dornbusch and Frankel's model the slow domestic price adjustments are taken into account, with accompanying deviations from purchasing power parity. In this model $a_5 = a_6 = 0$.

There is much evidence that the model in formula (A2.13) captures the most essential variables, i.e. there is no misspecification as regards content. That the model nonetheless fails to give us an acceptable value for the coefficient of determination can be explained in many ways: for instance a result of multicollinearity, insufficiently long periods with homogeneous conditions,[138] poor quality of data,[139] self-fulfilling prophecies and so on.

APPENDIX 2.5

Example of a portfolio approach

Let us assume that the investor has two alternative investments with which to build up his portfolio. One of these has an expected return of SEK 50 and a standard deviation of SEK 15. The other has an expected return of SEK 60 but a standard deviation of SEK 30. Provided that the investor is not risk-neutral, and thus uninterested in the variance in the returns, he should invest in both alternatives. Assume that the investor divides his input 50-50 between the two investment alternatives. The expected return on the portfolio will then be the same as the average of the expected returns. Thus, the expected returns on his portfolio can be written

$$0.5 \cdot 50 + 0.5 \cdot 60 = 55.$$

Generally it can be said that

> the *expected return* on the portfolio is the same as the weighted average of the expected return on the respective investments.

The portfolio variance depends on the variance in the return on the respective investments and the covariance between them. The portfolio variance in the example can be written:

$$X_1^2 \cdot \sigma_1^2 + X_2^2 \cdot \sigma_2^2 + 2X_1 \cdot X_2 \cdot \rho_{12} \cdot \sigma_1 \cdot \sigma_2 =$$

$$0.5^2 \cdot 15^2 + 0.5^2 \cdot 30^2 + 2 \cdot 0.5 \cdot 0.5 \cdot \rho_{12} \cdot 15 \cdot 30 \qquad (2.14)$$

where

X_i = proportion of portfolio invested in alternative i
σ_i^2 = variance in return on investment i
ρ_{ij} = correlation between return on investments i and j.

The correlation is +1 if the return on the two investments match one another perfectly in the same direction and –1 if the same applies but in opposite directions. The covariance is $\rho_{12} \cdot \sigma_1 \sigma_2$. It is thus determined not only by the correlation but also by the variation in the returns on the respective investments. If the correlation coefficient in the example is assumed to be 0.6, the variance in the portfolio will be 416.25, and the standard deviation 20.4. The return on the portfolio as well as its variance lies between the values of the two individual investments. However, it is possible to reduce the portfolio's variance below the individual variances, if the correlation is sufficiently low.

Assume now that the investor chooses to keep asset 1, i.e. the one whose expected return is 50 with a standard deviation of 15. What, then, will be the addition to the portfolio variance if asset 1 at the margin is exchanged for asset 2, i.e. the one whose expected return is 60 and its standard deviation 30? To begin with, when the investor only holds asset 1, the variance is 225. Let us say that the investor exchanges 1 per cent of his input in order to keep asset 2. The portfolio variance then changes to:

$$0.99^2 \cdot \sigma_1^2 + 0.01^2 \cdot \sigma_2^2 + 2 \cdot 0.99 \cdot 0.01 \cdot \rho_{12} \cdot \sigma_1 \cdot \sigma_2$$

and the relative change in the portfolio variance is

$$\frac{0.99^2 \cdot \sigma_1^2 + (0.01)^2 \cdot \sigma_2^2 + 2 \cdot 0.99 \cdot 0.01 \cdot \rho_{12}\sigma_1\sigma_1 - \sigma_1^2}{\sigma_1^2} = 0.004$$

From the case with asset 1 alone in the portfolio, the expected return increases from 50 to $(0.99 \cdot 50 + 0.01 \cdot 60) = 50.1$. As a result of the substitution, the expected return on the portfolio rises by 0.2 per cent, while the portfolio variance increases from 225 to 225.96, i.e. by 0.4 per cent. The standard deviation on the portfolio increases from 15 to 15.03, i.e. by 0.9 per cent.

The increase in the portfolio variance by the addition of asset 2 is proportional to the weights of the investment and to $\rho_{12}\sigma_1\sigma_2/\sigma_1^2$, according to formula (A2.15), where we obtain $2 \cdot 0.99 \cdot 0.01 \cdot \rho_{12}\sigma_1\sigma_1/\sigma_1^2$, since $(0.99)^2 \approx 1$ and $(0.01)^2 \approx 0$. This term is the relative covariance for asset 2 with the original portfolio (asset 1). Generally it applies for marginal changes in the portfolio that

the *marginal risk* for asset j = the relative increase in the total portfolio variance of a marginal increase in the proportion of asset j in the portfolio.

The substitutability between the two assets in the example can be illustrated by Figure A2.1. Two points can easily be identified. They are $E(r_1) = 50; \sigma_1 = 15$ and $E(r_2) = 60; \sigma_2 = 30$, which represents the alternative of concentrating the investment to one of the assets only.

The portfolio to be chosen will depend on the investor's attitude to risk. By moving along the curve in Figure A2.1, a suitable balance can be found.

The method can easily be extended to a portfolio consisting of N different assets. In such a case the

$$\text{expected return on the portfolio} = \sum_{i-1}^{N} X_i r_i \qquad \text{(A2.16)}$$

and

$$\text{the variance in the portfolio} = \sum_{i=1}^{N} X_i^2 \sigma_i^2 + \sum_{i \neq j}^{N} X_i X_j \rho_{ij} \sigma_i \sigma_j \qquad \text{(A2.17)}$$

Figure A2.2 shows the choice situation when the choice is between a larger number of investment opportunities. If the investor is in favour of a high return and dislikes high standard deviations, he should choose a portfolio along the curve. Markowitz (1952) calls these portfolios "efficient portfolios". The practical problems of finding the highest expected return for a given standard deviation with a large number of investment alternatives is generally solved with the help of quadratic programming.

The proportion of the risk which can be ascribed to an individual investment (j) can be measured by $X_j \cdot \text{cov}(r_j, r_P)/\sigma_P^2$, i.e. as the proportion which is invested in the relevant asset with a relative risk such as was expressed before. The total proportion of the risk which can be ascribed to all investments in the portfolio must be 1.0. If the ratio $\text{cov}(r_j, r_P)/\sigma_P^2$ is greater than 1.0, then asset j is unusually sensitive to changes in the average portfolio's return. A marginal increase in the proportion of this asset will therefore increase the portfolio risk. Let us assume that the investor puts together a portfolio that agrees with the market portfolio or the average portfolio held by all investors. The ratio $\text{cov}(r_j, r_M)/\sigma_M^2$ can then be called investment j's beta value.

$$\beta_j = \frac{\text{cov}(r_j, r_M)}{\sigma_M^2} \qquad \text{(A2.18)}$$

where M refers to the market portfolio. Beta is consequently a measure of the investment's marginal relative addition to the risk of the market portfolio. Investments with beta values greater than 1 have an effect on systematic (market) risks which is over the average, and investments with beta values less than 1 have an effect less than the average.

An investor also has the alternative of lending or borrowing at a risk-free interest rate. Possible efficient combinations of risk and return can be obtained from a combination of loan activity at risk-free rates and the efficient portfolio. These combinations, as can be seen from Figure A2.2, lie along the line from r (risk-free) through P to Q.

Figure A2.1 Expected return and standard deviation on portfolios based on two assets

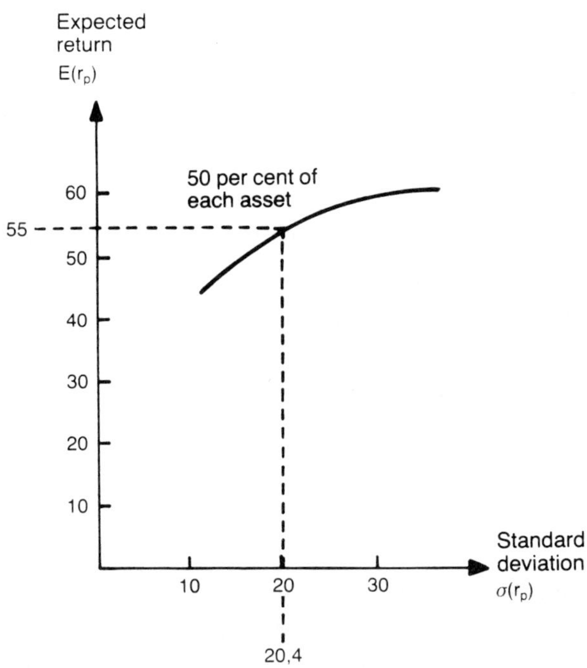

The importance of a risk-free alternative is that the investor must first choose the "best" portfolio (point P) by combining risky securities and then deciding the *size* of his portfolio, by borrowing or lending with a view to achieving the desired combination of risk and return. This addition to Markowitz's principles can be ascribed to Tobin (1958).

Figure A2.2 Efficient portfolios

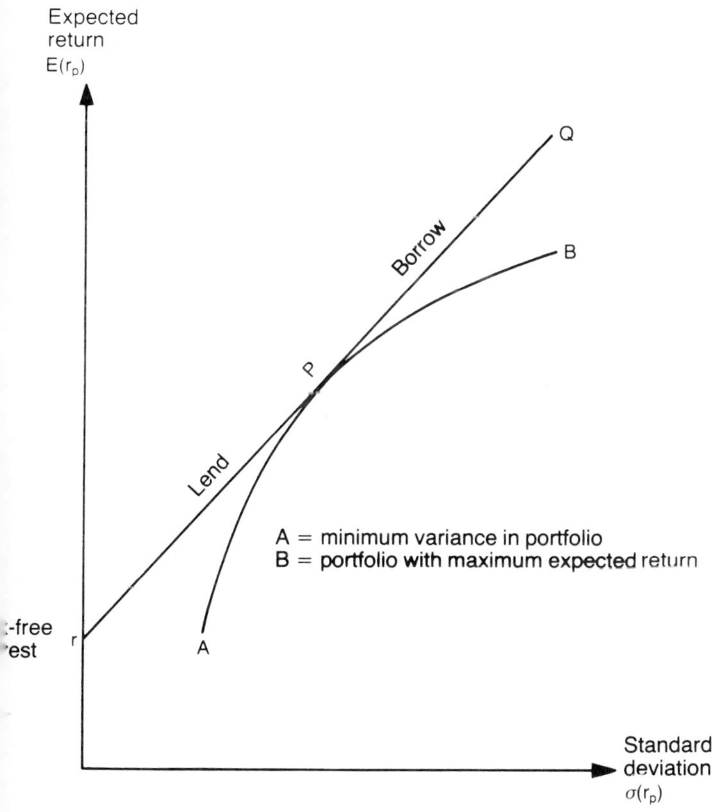

APPENDIX 2.6

The interest rate parity theory

The interest rate parity theory combines forward exchange rates with interest differentials for similar securities or instruments in different currencies. The relationships refer to the Euromarket. Interest arbitrage can be regarded as constituting the link between the spot and forward markets, where the streams of arbitrage funds contribute to equilibrium between the spot and forward markets.

As early as 1923 Keynes demonstrated the importance of interest rate arbitrage in determining the link between the forward exchange premium and the domestic and foreign interest rate respectively. The interest rate parity theory gives the following equilibrium premium on the forward market:

$$f = \frac{F_t - S_t}{S_t} = \frac{r_d - r_{for}}{1 + r_{for}} \tag{A2.19}$$

where

f = forward premium in relative figures

F_t = forward rate

S_t = spot rate

r_d = domestic rate of interest

r_{for} = foreign rate of interest.

The interest rates refer to securities or loans which can be regarded as identical in everything except the choice of currency. The state of equilibrium is stable in the sense that all points which do not satisfy the relationship activate market forces which result in a return to equilibrium.

The following table shows examples of transactions with accompanying costs and the direction of partial adjustment at covered interest arbitrage:

Transaction		Partial adjustment	Transaction cost
Borrowing	r_{for}	↑	T
Purchase of SEK, spot	S_t	↑	T_S
Lending in SEK	r_d	↓	T_L
Selling SEK, forward	F_t	↓	T_F

Interest arbitrage results in the following costs and revenues for the above operations, given a borrowed sum of X foreign currency units:

$$\text{Cost} = X \cdot (1 + r_{for}) \qquad \text{(A2.20)}$$

$$\text{Revenue} = X \cdot (1 + r_d) \cdot \frac{S_t}{F_t} \cdot Z \qquad \text{(A2.21)}$$

where $Z = (1 - T)(1 - T_S)(1 - T_L)(1 - T_F)$ is an expression of the total transaction cost of arbitrage. If the marginal cost is equated with the marginal revenue, we obtain the upper limit to the forward premium $\bar{f} = (F_t - S_t)/S_t$, at which arbitrage is profitable:

$$\bar{f} = \frac{Z \cdot (1+r_d) - (1+r_{for})}{1 + r_{for}} \qquad \text{(A2.22)}$$

If there are no transaction costs, the form of the equilibrium is as before. The lower limit for interest arbitrage ($\underline{f}$) can be calculated in a similar way for the outflow of capital.

Thus according to the interest rate parity theory equilibrium should be represented by an interval rather than by a point, and can then be described as in Figure A2.3.

Point A in Figure A2.3 represents a value whereby, in the absence of transaction costs, interest arbitrage can be profitable according to the above. The four operations in the loan process and the four factors for partial adjustment from the above arrangement, lead to an equilibrium for the forward premium $A_1 < f_A < A_2$. However, if there are transaction costs which give the upper limit for profitable arbitrage at $\bar{f}$, then point A implies a state at which arbitrage is not profitable.

Figure A2.3 Arbitrage argument - deviations from interest rate parity

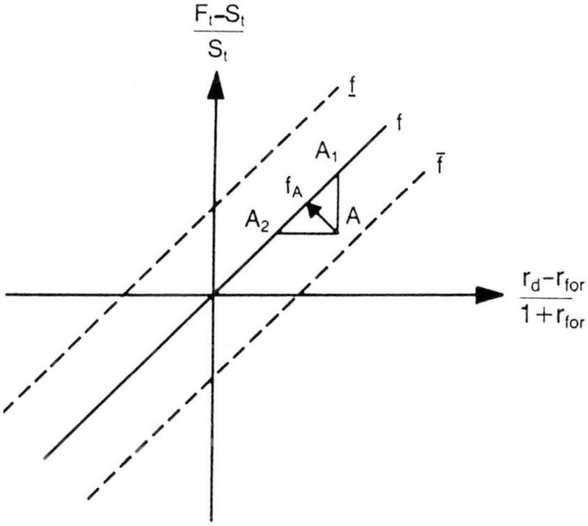

The existence of economically exploitable risk-free profits can be interpreted as a lack of integration. By economically exploitable is meant that transaction costs have been taken into account, and that the investment refers to securities which are comparable in all respects except the choice of currency.

APPENDIX 2.7

Swedish industrial groups with a turnover exceeding SEK 1 billion in 1981

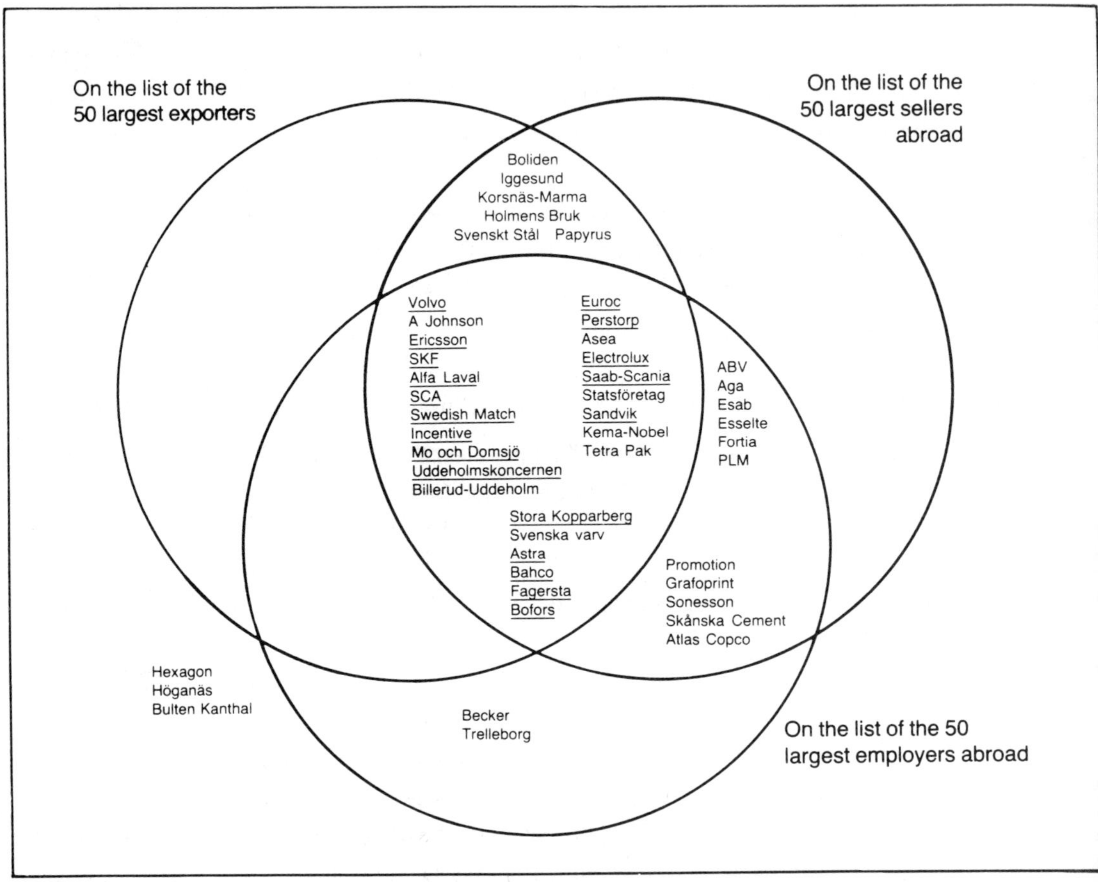

Note: The 19 companies included in the interview study are underlined.

Source: Oxelheim (1984a).

Notes

[1] Fama (1970), building on Roberts (1967), distinguishes three forms of efficiency depending on what kind of information is being considered. If all historic information is taken into account, the efficiency of the markets is *weak*. Their efficiency is *semi-strong* if all public information is reflected in the prices, and it is *strong* if even insider information is taken into account.

[2] A measurement problem also arises from the very definition of market efficiency. We cannot claim that the market prices should reflect all information at any given point in time. Small changes do not motivate immediate price changes, and arbitrage can in itself be expected to take a certain time. But if we work with data collected at certain intervals, the problem is reduced, in that the hypothesis on market efficiency is then based on the fact that the arbitrage process itself has occurred during the period. This means that we can analyse whether all available information is fully reflected in the market prices we have assembled, without having to model the arbitrage process itself.

[3] The discussion of efficient markets can be traced back to Bachelier (1900). However, what we mean today by efficient markets is generally ascribed to Samuelson (1965) and Mandelbrot (1966).

[4] Grossman and Stiglitz (1976, 1980) emphasize that these "excess profits" fulfil an important function, by creating an incentive for the individual to collect and analyse new information.

[5] The concept is attributed to Cagan (1956).

[6] The hypothesis of rational expectations is ascribed to Muth (1961), in his formulization of ideas launched in Modigliani and Grunberg (1954).

[7] Correlation among lagged deviations between expected and actual outcome.

[8] This goes back to a case in which it was expected that the Mexican peso would be devalued against the US dollar with a non-zero probability. This probability was taken into account in the expectations. Thus when the devaluation was overdue, an evaluation with ex post data revealed autocorrelated errors and the existence of systematic errors.

[9] Mundell (1963b) argues that the real interest rate cannot be expected to be constant, but that it falls with rising inflation.

[10] Makin (1983) among others points out the importance of using expected rather than actual inflation. An empirical investigation of the difference between these two quantities can be found in Jonung (1981).

[11] An example of the impact of taxation effects on the investor's return requirements is given in Appendix 2.2.

[12] See, for example, Darby (1975), Feldstein (1976).

[13] From Mundell (1963b) and Tobin (1965).

[14] Carmichael and Stebbing (1983), for example, use an inverted Fisher effect. Roley and Walsh (1984) emphasize the effect of the money supply on inflation expectations, while Hoelscher (1983) looks at the effect of domestic borrowing. Hendershott (1984) sees unexpected changes in expected inflation as an important explanation. Saracoglu (1984) examines the effect of monetary policy on the inflation expectations of the market actors.

[15] Also known as Fisher's Open Relationship.

[16] The yield curve expresses the relationship among interest rates of different maturities, and can be indicated in terms of simple or compound annual rates. Variations in transaction cost can affect the shape of the curve.

[17] This theory was originally presented in Lutz and Lutz (1951).

[18] See, for example, Brealey and Schaefer (1977).

[19] Some instruments can be regarded as providing guaranteed real return.

[20] This theory was originally presented in Keynes (1936) and Hicks (1939). A theoretical development of the theory appears in Roll (1970).

[21] Apart from these five theories it is also possible to formulate the interest rate theory on a basis of a general equilibrium model. See, for example, Lucas (1978, 1982) and Svensson (1983, 1985).

[22] The relationship shows the yield during two consecutive periods of d_1 and d_2 days respectively. The combined length of the two periods is d_3 days, and for this period the simple annual rate of interest r_3.

[23] According to the expectation theory.

[24] Given compound interest rates the yield curve is horizontal, when the market expects constant interest rates.

[25] The information flows on actual or predicted values.

[26] The actors' *risk aversion* is an expression of their attitude towards the trade-off between expected return and risk. The actor who is unconcerned about risk is said to be *risk neutral.* He is thus interested only in expected return. The other extreme approach is to be found among actors who are concerned only about risk and disregard expected return. This attitude is justifiably known as *risk paranoia.* Most actors experience some form of risk aversion, and thus weigh a potential increase in expected return against the accompanying increase in risk.

[27] When it comes to measuring the level of financial integration later in this book, I shall distinguish between *permanent* and *temporary* segmentation. By permanent segmentation I mean that the gap between interest rates is of a systematic kind. Temporary segmentation means that the adaptation to changes in the foreign interest level occurs after a certain time-lag.

[28] The international financial transactions can be of two kinds: *Arbitrage* refers to transactions in different markets at virtually the same time in order to take advantage profitably of different prices and rates without any risks (exchange risk) involved. *Speculation* refer to financial transactions involving risk, i.e. buying and selling with a view to buying and selling later at a profit, when prices have changed.

[29] The Bretton Woods system of fixed exchange rates was based on cooperation in economic policy. McCullogh (1983) found that the collapse of this system clearly increased national sovereignty as regards opportunities for conducting an independent stabilization policy, but McCullogh considers that it contributed only slightly to the achievement of national goals by individual countries. The system of flexible exchange rates could not compensate for the structural dependence that had evolved on the world markets.

[30] The relation between exchange rate regime and exchange risk is discussed by Wihlborg (1978) among others. The premium refers to compensation for variability in real exchange rates.

[31] Purchasing power parity is abbreviated as PPP. The choice of price index determines whether we are to regard PPP as a current-account or a monetary approach. If it is based on a price index for goods and services in international trade, PPP is geared to the current account, while it implies a monetary approach if it is based on a general price index. The theory is fully described in e.g. Officer (1982) and empirical problems connected with the analysis of PPP in e.g. Oxelheim (1985). The law of one price, which is to be seen as a subcase of PPP, states: if two countries produce an identical good, the price of the good should be the same throughout the world no matter which country produces it. Thus the theory of purchasing power parity will be identical with the "law of one price" for a country as a whole, if all countries manufacture the same goods, if all these goods participate in the same proportions in international trade, and

if there are no barriers to free trade.

32 The theory of purchasing power parity can be traced back to the 16th century and the Spanish economists of the Salamanca school. Renewed interest in the theory in our own century is generally ascribed to Cassel. Both Cassel (1922) and Keynes (1923) build on purchasing power parity in a relative version.

33 See, for example, Frenkel (1981). However, it is generally accepted that PPP should be interpreted as an identity in the short term and as an equilibrium condition in the long term.

34 The building blocks of the simplest monetary model consist of a stable money demand function, exogenous money supply, money market equilibrium, the International Fisher Effect, and PPP.

$$p_1 = m_1 - ky_1 + hr_1 \qquad (2.8)$$
$$p_2 = m_2 - ky_2 + hr_2$$

where
p = logarithm of prices
m = logarithm of nominal money supply
k = income elasticity of real money demand
y = logarithm of real income
h = semilogarithmic interest-sensitivity of real balances
r = nominal interest rate.

By combining the above equations with absolute purchasing power parity, we obtain the exchange rate equation for the monetary view:

$$\ln S^{12} = p_1 - p_2 = (m_1 - m_2) + h(r_1 - r_2) - k(y_1 - y_2) \qquad (2.9)$$

35 It is thus a question of an asset-flow mechanism, whereby the goods flows create equilibrium in stocks on the financial markets.

36 Criticism was chiefly concerned with the uncertainty in the estimate that arises as a result of multicollinearity. See, for example, Haynes and Stone (1981).

37 Sticky prices according to the Keynesian model versus flexible prices according to the Chicago School approach.

38 Turnovsky and Bhandari (1982) provide a review of the importance of capital mobility.

39 This view differs from that of the advocates of portfolio adjustment theory, according to which an interest differential is said to give rise to an initial flow as a result of the need to adjust the portfolio. This flow then moves gradually towards zero.

40 See, for example, Frenkel and Rodriguez (1982).

41 See, for example, Frenkel and Aizenman (1982) and Kimbrough (1982).

42 Assuming perfect substitutability between securities, Dornbusch regards the actual rate of depreciation as the sum of anticipated depreciations (which he equates with the nominal interest differential $r_d^* - r_{for}$) and the effect of news about monetary trends, which is expressed in the differential between actual and anticipated depreciation.

43 In order to reproduce this model we have to drop the assumption of PPP, and the following components are added to the monetary model.

$$S - I = \Delta F = f[\hat{s} - (\hat{P}_d - \hat{P}_{for})] + rF = -\Delta F^* = \text{net savings}, \qquad (2.10)$$

where
S = saving
I = investment

Y = Y'+ rF with Y = real income and Y' = exogenous real production
S–I = f(Y)
rF = interest payments.

44 As was indicated above, a portfolio diversification model can be based on the International Fisher Effect, with the addition of a risk premium. The risk premium can in turn be regarded as an expression of variability in the real return, resulting from uncertainty regarding future inflation and changes of the exchange rate.

45 The inclusion of balances of trade in formula (A2.13) in Appendix 2.4 can be regarded to some extent as an expression of risk circumstance.

46 The short-term and long-term characteristics in Branson's, Frenkel and Rodriguez's and Dornbusch and Fischer's models are the same. There real exchange rates and purchasing power parity concepts are also the same, and are based on producer prices in different countries. Just as in the monetary model, it is assumed in all the models that the price index in the function for money demand is the same as the one used in determining the balance of trade.

47 This is where we find the "cash-in-advance" models. See, for example, Lucas (1978, 1982), Stockman (1980) and Svensson (1983, 1985).

48 Artus (1978) demonstrates three ways of determining the long-term equilibrium interest rate, which agree well with my summary here. These three alternatives are determination on a basis of purchasing power parity, the balance of payments, and equilibrium on asset markets.

49 Meese and Rogoff's study was conducted for USD rates in such a way that problems arising from Jensen's inequality (see, for example, Siegel 1972 or McCullogh 1983) would be avoided. The inequality says that the best estimate of the USD/SEK is not necessarily the best for SEK/USD.

50 The analysis refers to the period from November 1976 to June 1981, with forecast horizons up to 12 months. The exchange rates involved were USD versus DEM, JPY and GBP, respectively

51 For a discussion of the usefulness of these in forecasting SEK exchange rates, see Appendix 2.6 and, e.g., Oxelheim (1985).

52 By this is meant that there is no correlation between historical exchange rate movements, which can be used as forecasts or trading rules for future actions. See, for example, Levich (1978) for the US dollar rate and Oxelheim (1981) for the SEK rate.

53 With possible additions of drift parameters.

54 Technicals are simple statistical techniques for processing and converting historical information into buying or selling signals. New information about future values of fundamental variables is not considered.

55 See Oxelheim (1985).

56 Frankel and Froot (1986) summarize their empirical study of the exchange rate expectations of the market actors by stating that the actors think that "I know that in the long run the (dollar's) exchange rate must decline, but in the short run I will ride the current trend a little longer. I only have to be careful to watch for the turning-point and to get out of the market before everyone else does."

57 Oxelheim (1985) reports on an evaluation of different forecasting models based on the Swedish krona. The study concerned the three-month rates, and the *forward premium* gave the best results for most currencies vis-à-vis the Swedish krona in the shape of average value and standard deviation in forecasting error.

58 The above-mentioned correlation indicates that the multicollinearity which can intuitively be feared to disturb a study of integration which includes both purchasing power parity and the forward premium among its explanatory variables, can probably be ignored.

59 i.e. with the same currency.

60 Forward premium/discount rate as alternatives.

61 See, for exampel, Frankel (1979b).

62 Although Hooper and Kohlhagen (1978), for example, suggest the use of PPP as a suitable approach for further research.

63 The transaction cost at covered interest arbitrage is discussed in Appendix 2.6. Few studies show empirically the size of the transaction cost. In Oxelheim (1981) the direct costs of covered interest arbitrage is estimated at around 0.5 per cent, in Frenkel and Levich (1975) to 0.15 per cent for the early 1960s, and in Frenkel and Levich (1977) at about 1.5 per cent for the early 1970s with flexible exchange rates. My own estimate concerns two exchange transactions, while Frenkel and Levich's transaction cost embraces four transactions: two exchange transactions and two securities transactions. The figures in the three studies are not directly comparable, since they concern different currency combinations and periods, but they do provide a rough estimate of the order of magnitude.

64 See, for example, Branson (1968), Frenkel and Levich (1981). Market efficiency is here the same as the absence of opportunities for risk-free profits.

65 See, for example, McCormick (1979).

66 There is some uncertainty, above all between practitioners and academics, about the concept of risk. To the investor risk is an expression of unexpected variations in his target variable. The cash flow is one common variable of this kind. Thus, given this target variable, exchange rate risk is a measure of the fluctuations in the cash flow resulting from unexpected fluctuations in the exchange rate.

67 Liquidity risk, for example, can be regarded as specifically related to the instrument.

68 This definition is somewhat broader than the usual, and leaves the difference from political risk very vague. Thus from now on we will use the term country risk and political risk synonymously, which seems appropriate in this context.

69 According to Robock (1971) political risk exists when:
- there is discontinuity in the decision environment
- the discontinuities are difficult to anticipate
- the discontinuities are the result of political changes.

70 See also Arrow (1965).

71 Solnik (1974b), Grauer, Litzenberger and Stehle (1976), Kouri (1977), Fama and Farber (1979), Frankel (1979b) and others.

72 In a more complete model framework it would be necessary to analyse the characteristics of the error term, ε, in the following equation:

$$F_t = E(S_{t+3}) + \text{risk premium} + \text{transaction cost} + \text{intervention effect} + \varepsilon.$$

73 Solnik (1974c) adopts another view, and claims that the exchange risk expresses differences in consumption patterns.

74 For example, on the concavity of the utility function.

75 Frankel (1979b, 1982), Dornbusch (1982), Dooley and Isard (1982) and others have followed this path.

76 Lucas (1978, 1982), Brock (1982), Hodrick and Srivastava (1984) and others have followed this path.

77 Fama and Farber (1979) and others claim that the premium for systematic risk must be regarded as a function of differences between currencies with regard to the variance in the deviations from purchasing power parity.

78 See, for example, Frankel (1986). Even here, however, we find results in the opposite

direction, as in Fama (1984) for example.

79 It can reflect involuntary *loss of control* over assets in a particular country as a result of expropriation, confiscation etc., as well as *reducing the value of expected return* as a result of interventions which put the market forces out of action.

80 I agree with Lessard's view (Lessard 1983) that a country's international relative indebtedness constitutes the fundamental source of the country risk for the country concerned. Like Dooley and Isard (1986) I see this not only apply to LDC countries but also to industrial countries.

81 Interest payment and amortizations as a percentage of the country's export earnings.

82 See Aharoni (1966), Basi (1963), Kobrin (1979), Kobrin et al. (1980), Oxelheim (1984a).

83 London Interbank Offered Rates.

84 Llewellyn (1980), adopting this approach, expresses the level of financial integration as a combination of:

a) the degree at which the actors on a market try to maximize their portfolio target by diversification,
b) the degree at which they are allowed to do this, and
c) the degree of efficiency in the information transfer.

85 The covariance is here a measure of the way the return covariates with the market risks.

86 Markowitz showed how an investor can reduce the standard deviation in the return on his portfolio by choosing shares which do not completely covariate.

87 Efficient portfolios are those whose return cannot be increased without the portfolio variance also increasing, and whose variance cannot be decreased without the return of the portfolio being reduced.

88 See, e.g., Oxelheim and Wihlborg (1987).

89 Applications in international financing were originally developed by Grubel (1968), Grubel and Fadner (1971) and Levy and Sarnat (1970). The international CAPM (ICAPM) was developed by Solnik (1974a) and Grauer, Litzenberger and Stehle (1976) independently of each other. The model is constructed for the evaluation of shares, but its application can be made broader than this. In Roll and Solnik (1977), for example, there is a direct application of CAPM to determining premiums for exchange risk.

90 Assume for example that the risk-free interest rate is 8 per cent, the average return on the market portfolio 14 per cent, and β_j for a particular investment 1.60. At equilibrium the expected return on investment j will then be equal to $8 + 1.60(14–8) = 17.6$ per cent.

91 See, for example, Roll (1977) and Sharpe (1978) for CAPM and Solnik (1977) and Dumas (1977) for ICAPM.

92 This theory is ascribed to Ross (1976). Solnik (1983) has answered for the development of the International APT (IAPT), i.e. for an adaptation of the model for the analysis of international factors.

93 A critical review of APT appears in Dhrymes, Friend and Gultekin (1984).

94 See Roll and Ross (1980).

95 Since the linguistic usage can vary, it would be as well to explain that by monetary policy is meant policy concerning the management of money and interest rates including allocation measures, rationing of capital etc. The measures adopted within the framework of the policy can be selective (e.g. subsidized domestic interest rates for certain segments) or aggregated and applying to all markets. The alternative to monetary policy measures within the framework of economic policy as a whole, is fiscal policy measures.

96 For example, the domestic interest rate can follow the foreign rate altogether, and yet give a false impression that there has been no monetary freedom of action, if the country in question has *chosen* to follow just that international interest rate trend because, for the moment, foreign exchange policy has been given priority.

97 The measurement problems in connection with financial integration are regarded by many researchers as a key issue for future research. See, for example, Adler and Dumas (1983).

98 Another – but not this time a functional – definition of an integrated market is based on the absence of discriminating institutional arrangements such as tariffs and quotas. Functioning controls of various kinds on the market are often used to support the argument that the market is segmented. Such a definition is not operational in that it does not lend itself to direct measurement. Indirectly, however, the actual efficiency of the controls is a measure of the level of financial integration: the greater it is, the lower the level of integration. The problems of interpretation are easily overcome, as for example when the controls are related to rationing. As has already been pointed out, a transaction cost can be regarded as a tax, and like exchange controls can be interpreted as an indicator of disintegration.

99 See, for example, Herring and Marston (1976).

100 See, for example, Grauer, Litzenberger and Stehle (1976), who make assumptions about a world in which there is no form of deviation from perfect financial conditions.

101 This argument is common for instance in models for price-setting options, in the classical Modigliani–Miller theorem of 1958, in the analysis of the term structure of interest rates, etc.

102 In Oxelheim (1981 and 1985) it is shown that during the second half of the 1970s there were plenty of opportunities for risk-free profits from covered interest arbitrage between financial instruments on the Swedish market and the foreign markets. By profit is meant net profit after account has been taken of transaction costs. By covered interest arbitrage is meant transactions with a view to exploiting the difference between domestic interest rates and some corresponding international rate in a forward covered form.

103 As political risk may exist it is of course a little bit dubious to call the transaction "arbitrage", but nevertheless this is the convention.

104 In comparisons of national interest rates, the premium for relative political risk must be taken into account. In studying interest rate autonomy, there is reason to look beyond interest rate parity. In recent years, for example, governments have tried to conduct stabilization policies with help of the forward premium.

105 Within the framework of these two circumstances, the individual measures can express many characteristics, such as the average risk-adjusted interest gap, deviations from interest rate parity, correlations between domestic interest rates and lagged foreign interest rate quotations, lagged impact on domestic interest rates of a change in foreign rates, and various elasticity rates expressing the influence of the explanatory variables on the domestic rate.

106 In a modelling context caution in the interpretation of the intercept β_0 is generally recommended. Here, however, it is a question of interpolation, i.e. the value 0 is included in the range of all my explanatory variables, and β_0 has an economic meaning.

107 How we should define the effect of the delay on this measure is an open question. Here t refers to the highest number of immediately preceding three-month periods which we have had significant lagged effects on the current interest gap.

108 If this is not so, then we are touching on a question of statistical ethics, and what is generally known as data mining.

109 See Johnston (1972). To produce forecasts Johnston mixes together residual variance and standard error into an expression $\sigma^2 \cdot [1+Z(x^Tx)^{-1}Z^T]$.

110 This premium is included in some models, for example Frankel and MacArthur (1987).

111 As there is no formula for the Eurokrona rate, modelling of the exchange rate expectations and of the premium for exchange risk is necessary, if the approach is to be complete.

112 Indirectly controls of real markets, such as protectionism, also have an impact on financial integration.

113 Exchange controls can also be reflected in the coefficients for risk, which can complicate the interpretation of the effects.

114 This applies in strict form under perfect competition. See Bhagwati (1969) for a discussion of the relation between taxes and quantitative controls.

115 However, the exchange rate can be affected in the longer term in that the price level is affected and changes the development of the current account. As Phylahtis and Wood (1984) have shown, exchange controls can also affect the way in which the exchange rate moves from one equilibrium state to another. However, there is no reason to believe that one way is better than another from the welfare point of view.

116 See, for example, Greenwood and Kimbrough (1987) and Wood (1985).

117 However, the growth of the Euromarket can point in the opposite direction. Some researchers claim that the growth in this market is a sign of the need to circumvent controls on segmented markets. Thus the growth of the Euromarket should be interpreted as a sign of increasing national segmentation.

118 For a discussion of the cost element in covered interest arbitrage, see Appendix 2.6 and, e.g., Oxelheim (1985).

119 One reason for the existence of a transaction cost may also be that the government wants to discourage the transaction.

120 Part of the matching problem also consists of seeing that a simple annual rate is compared with the equivalent simple annual rate abroad.

121 As regards the Swedish market, it is often claimed in banking circles that there are links between the short and long-term interest rates which can be used in an analysis. It is claimed that the interest on the day-to-day market, i.e. the absolutely shortest part, strongly affects trends in interest rates on short-term government securities, which in turn exert an influence on other interest rates on the money market. The central bank has also acknowledge that in recent years it has recognized that its best and possibly only opportunity for influencing the long-term interest rates has been by influencing the short-term rates.

122 At this last-mentioned stage it is also necessary to take into account whether segmentation is the result of capital rationing. If this is so, then the domestic rate of interest will to some extent be irrelevant, and the success of the segmentation can be questioned in so far as it has unintended wealth effects. Capital acquisition by way of foreign borrowing leads to a higher risk premium, which in turn affects the investment volume. We can obtain a measure of this rationing, for instance in the shape of the length of the issuance time. This measure can then be analysed together with the interest gap.

123 Sweden is regarded as a price-taker.

124 These are the major alternatives. We can also envisage weighting systems based on consumption patterns, for example.

125 In a preparatory study for this report, differences in outcome based on trade and capital market weights, with bilateral and multilateral weight systems, were studied. The differences were not found to be systematic and were of apparently negligible size.

126 One way of eliminating this problem is to use Eurorates in creating the global rate. However, the absence of such rates for some countries involved in the comparison

– during some or all years included – forced me to look for other alternatives.

[127] Some of these results are reported in Oxelheim (1984a, b and 1985).

[128] In 1981 the 19 companies included in the analysis represented around 50 per cent of the total domestic value added in Swedish manufacturing industry.

[129] See Oxelheim (1983).

[130] Interest after tax is designated $\dot{r}$ and the tax rate c.

[131] See, among others, Giddy (1976) or Levich (1979).

[132] See, for example, Dornbusch (1976b), Kouri (1976b) and Mussa (1976).

[133] See, for example, Frenkel (1976) and Bilson (1978).

[134] Frankel's approach has been criticized by Driskill and Shefferin (1981) and Haynes and Stone (1981).

[135] Characterized by flexible prices.

[136] Characterized by sticky prices and explicit consideration of the current account. See Hooper and Morton (1982).

[137] Characterized by sticky prices.

[138] To solve this problem would call for too many dummy variables.

[139] Data at the micro-level are often "polished" a little, in order to moderate fluctuations in corporate results. If these data are then later used as input into the model, there will obviously be a lot of interpretation problems. See, for example, Oxelheim (1985).

CHAPTER 3

Results and Findings from Earlier Studies of Financial Integration

3.1 Introduction

In this chapter I shall present a number of important research works which together constitute a useful frame of reference for the analysis and measurement of direct financial integration.[1] The disposition of this chapter is based on the structure of Figure 2.8, in which studies of direct financial integration were roughly divided into two categories.[2] In one of these the dependent variable is the capital flow or reflow, and in the other it is the gap between domestic and foreign interest rates. Interest transmission can be included in both these categories, which means that even lagged foreign interest rates or interest differentials are among the explanatory variables.

In Section 3.2 I shall present some studies of financial integration which focus on the capital flow. Section 3.3 concerns studies in which the arguments for interest arbitrage and speculation have been interpreted as indicators of incomplete financial integration, and which look at deviations from interest rate parity and from the International Fisher Effect. Some of these studies include lagged effects. I have classified the studies according to the markets they consider. In Section 3.4 the general tendencies in this research area are summarized, and I refer to findings and conclusions of importance to my own empirical investigation.

3.2 Studies of the interest-sensitivity of capital flows

3.2.1 Two views

Two views have predominated in studies of the interest-sensitivity of capital flows. One represents a portfolio approach, implying that a change in the gap between the domestic and foreign interest rates initially generates a flow of foreign exchange which subsequently declines. The foreign exchange flow occurs because investors want to adjust their portfolios in light of the change in the interest rate gap. For a further discussion of this point, see Appendix 3.1. According to the other view, a change in the interest rate gap results in an infinite flow, provided there is no alteration in the fundamental conditions.

3.2.2 The hypothesis to be tested

The point of departure is that the greater the capital flows following a certain percentage change in the interest differential, the less the scope for an autonomous domestic monetary policy. The hypothesis to be tested concerns the sensitivity of capital flows. Most studies have related these flows to changes in various monetary variables. The explanatory variables used are interest rates and growth rates in the money supply, as well as income and wealth variables. The analysis involves estimating coefficients which are stable over time for the independent variables. In many cases a comparison of coefficients in different countries is also undertaken. How far regression analysis here justifies any conclusions about the level of financial integration varies from case to case. There are many measurement as well as political factors that affect the interpretation of results, perhaps particularly if the analysis is supposed to indicate the interest level at which political action to prevent an unwanted flow of capital can be regarded as motivated. There is then the added difficulty of allowing for a government's opportunities for neutralizing or sterilizing the domestic monetary consequences of a capital flow.

3.2.3 Major impact of US interest rates before the mid-1970s

During the 1960s and 1970s, almost all models of the interest-sensitivity of capital flows assumed that the US interest rates were unaffected by foreign influences. But reduced trade barriers and the internationalization of the credit market in recent years (Figure 3.1) has given us grounds for assuming that even the US financial markets are exposed to foreign influence. According to the results available to us today,[3] this also seems to have been the case since the middle of the 1970s.

Studies of the interest-sensitivity of the capital flows have been reported in Branson (1968), Branson and Hill (1971), Kwack and Schinkl (1975) and Kenen (1978) among others. The results, referring to different countries, show that the capital flows

Figure 3.1 Nominal financial balances in relation to trade flows, 1963-84

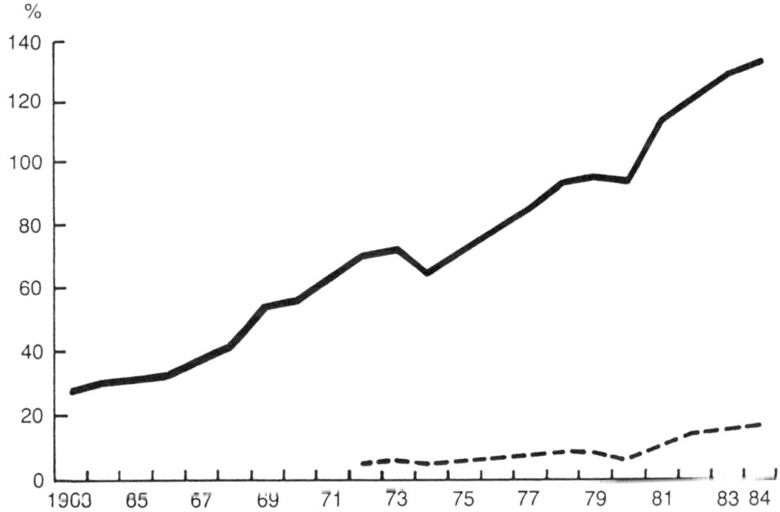

—— Bank system's foreign debts as a percentage of the world trade flow

---- Loan operations on the international capital market as a percentage of the world trade flow

Source: UN, IMF, OECD.

are interest-sensitive. However, this sensitivity is far from reaching the infinite elasticity which would occur, at least initially, under perfect market integration.

3.2.4 A well-known example of the earliest models

An oft-quoted model was presented in Branson and Hill (1971).[4] These authors also reported on empirical tests of their model, based on quarterly data from the 1960s.[5] The results supported the assumption of portfolio adjustments following changes in interest rates. A change in the interest rate differential produces a big new capital-flow effect, which quickly diminishes rather than remaining constant.[6] Their conclusion is that during the period of the study there was some scope for national monetary autonomy, in that every one-off change in the interest differential led to a finite rather than an infinite flow.

3.2.5 Kouri and Porter's model has established a school

Kouri and Porter (1974) studied the effect of monetary policy on the capital account. Their approach is a synthesis of the stock equilibrium approach to capital flows developed by Branson (1968) and the monetary approach to balance-of-payments theory as developed for example in Mundell (1968). They estimated capital flows, taking the following as key explanatory variables: changes in domestic income, the current account balance, changes in domestic monetary instruments, and changes in foreign interest rates. But capital flows arising from movements in expected exchange rates were neglected. Kouri and Porter's analysis referred to Germany 1960-70, Italy 1964-70, the Netherlands 1960-70 and Australia 1961-72, and was based on quarterly data. They concluded that capital flows respond to changes in money-demand/money-supply relationships and to changes in monetary policy. They also stressed that while it may appear that capital movements respond mainly to changes in interest rate differentials between countries, a closer analysis would reveal that a more fundamental source of capital flows consists of fluctuations in the demand and supply for money, and that income fluctuations are an important factor in explaining shifts in money demand.

Moreover they emphasize that the current account balance tends to induce offsetting capital flows, thereby stabilizing the balance of payments. Thus, according to these authors, the behaviour of the balance of payments is dominated by factors that affect capital flows, i.e. changes in income and monetary policy instruments, changes in the world (global) interest rate, and changes in exchange rate expectations. They use the 3-month Eurodollar rate as the world-determined interest rate.

They claim, in light of their results, that despite the strong impact of monetary policy on the capital account in all four countries, there is still room for an independent monetary policy, if only in the short run, provided the central bank is willing to tolerate the large reserve movements which that policy entails.

Using a reduced model of the kind developed by Kouri and Porter, Hodjera (1976) analyses the capital flows for Austria and France. Hodjera's analysis also provides indications of a certain monetary policy autonomy, by demonstrating imperfect capital mobility and relatively low interest elasticity in the countries studied.

Herring and Marston (1977) estimated the capital flows in the German balance of payments as a function of a yield variable (the net of changes in the Eurodollar interest rate, the domestic German interest rate, and the forward exchange rate) and a wealth variable. They introduce a new approach by separating the capital transactions of German residents and non-residents. They concluded that, although capital mobility was high, the Bundesbank had succeeded in limiting the effect on German interest rates by means of sterilization. One of the weaknesses of their approach is that they compare the domestic interest rate with the Eurorate, without taking into account the gap in political risk that then arises. Another weakness, which is common to all the studies I have mentioned in this section, is that the models do not explicitly allow for exchange risk and the impact of the risk premium on the capital flow. A third weakness of the same general character is that the interest data and the capital account data are not in the same dimension. The capital flow data is *global*, while the interest data is *bilateral*.

3.2.6 *Recent models allow for the effect of risk on the capital flow*

Eaton and Turnovsky (1983a) among others point out that when the role of capital mobility is discussed in macroeconomic analyses of open economies, the effect of exchange risk and political risk is often disregarded. Both these risks reduce capital mobility, but in different ways. The exchange risk creates a deviation between the forward exchange rate and the spot rate expected to prevail when the forward contract matures, which in turn creates a deviation between the expected rates of return on covered and uncovered foreign bonds. But the exchange risk does not affect the relation between the covered foreign interest rate and the domestic rate. The political risk, on the other hand, affects this second relationship but not the first. Eaton and Turnovsky state that an increase in capital mobility as a result of the reduced role of either type of these risks, augments the sensitivity of the domestic interest rate to the foreign interest rate and the sensitivity of the domestic price level to the foreign price level. An increase in capital mobility in the form of an increase in the elasticity of speculation augments the steady-state effect of a change in the money supply on the domestic price level. However, an increase in capital mobility that takes the form of decreasing the divergence between the domestic and foreign covered interest rates, has an ambiguous effect on the relationship between money and the price level.

3.2.7 *Swedish studies of the interest-sensitivity of the capital flows*

There have been some studies of the direct integration of Swedish financial markets based on the interest-sensitivity of the capital flows, and the same applies to the financial markets of Sweden's Nordic neighbours, which on the whole have the same type of economy.

Empirical studies of the interest sensitivity of Swedish capital flow

Zetterberg (1980) finds that Swedish capital movements are interest-sensitive, but only as far as *changes* in interest levels are concerned. Zetterberg's study provides some support for the portfolio approach, and thus for the hypothesis that the effects of changes in interest rates on capital movements are a one-off affair. A high level of interest does not guarantee the continuous financing of potential deficits in the current account. An ongoing need for the country to borrow can consequently be satisfied only by constantly raising the relative domestic interest level.

Franzén and Markowski (1985) use a monetary model and quarterly data from 1971:2 up to 1981:4 to show that the leakage[7] (the offset coefficient) is in the order of 0.3–0.4.[8] This means, for example, that a reduction in the domestic liquidity supply by SEK 10 billion results in a currency inflow of SEK 3–4 billion. According to Franzén and Markowski an increase in the interest rate in Sweden in relation to the rest of the world, (here the Eurodollar rate) by one percentage point, results in an inflow of SEK 2.5 billion during the same quarter, calculated at 1981 prices. The effect is a short-term one, and is regarded as the result of portfolio adjustments.

The capital flow examined in a recent study by Englund et al. (1987) shows very much weaker interest-sensitivity. These authors find that an increase in the differentials between Swedish and foreign interest rates by one percentage point can be expected to result in an inflow of foreign exchange amounting to SEK 28.5 million within one month. Their results suggest almost complete Swedish autonomy with regard to monetary policy. Englund et al. express reservations about the result, however, pointing out the difficulties associated with choosing the capital flow as dependent variable when there are obvious measurement problems.

Studies using Swedish data suggest that scope for an autonomous Swedish interest rate policy does exist. Like Franzén and Markowski (1985) and Englund et al. (1987), Åkerholm and Tarkka (1987) fall in with this view.[9] But I feel a certain caution should be maintained since these studies take the capital flow as the dependent variable with all the problems this involves, and they all disregard the political risk and the market's demand for premiums to compensate for the differences in terms of this risk.

3.2.8 *What can we learn from earlier studies of the interest-sensitivity of the capital flow?*

Taken together these studies of changes in capital flows and their relation to interest rate movements or other financial variables suggest that financial markets are neither perfectly integrated nor perfectly segmented.

Perfect substitutability means that the elasticity of the capital flows vis-à-vis changes in the interest differential is very high, and that the domestic monetary policy will have no effect. The studies we have discussed above do not give us any clear idea of the perfection or otherwise of this substitutability. And the studies of the Swedish market are certainly no better in this respect.

Nor is there any agreement in the literature about the appropriate form for an analytical model. Generally speaking, empirical studies in which the capital flow is the dependent variable assume many different forms, due to the great variety of conditions in different combinations that can apply. The main problem, which also goes a long way towards explaining the sometimes contradictory conclusions, is to find a reliable measure of the size of the capital flow.

In the following section we will look at some studies in which direct financial integration has been measured simply by comparing the interest rate on securities in different currencies and/or on different markets.

3.3 Equal expected returns as an indicator of direct financial integration

When direct financial integration proves impossible to analyse on a basis of the interest-sensitivity of the capital flow, several possibilities based on comparisons of expected return suggest themselves. In Figure 2.8 we distinguished various ways of making such comparisons. We will devote the rest of the present chapter to discussing some studies representing each of these approaches.

A *first* group of studies finds a conceptual base in the International Fisher Effect in its simple form.[10] *The point of departure is that under fully integrated markets the expected returns should be the same.*

A *second* group of studies is concerned with covered interest arbitrage,[11] i.e. the analysis of the gap between domestic and foreign interest rates covered on the forward market for foreign exchange. *The view here is that the presence of deviations from interest rate parity indicates imperfect integration.*[12]

The next three categories differ from these two in that they look not only at deviations in the shape of gaps but also at the interest transmission itself. And here the studies are based on the view *that the more quickly a foreign interest movement is transmitted to the domestic market, the greater the integration with the foreign market.*

A *third* group of studies consists of transmission studies based on the return on investments on national markets. Here the subject of the comparison is the way in which fluctuations in the return on a security in one country or group of countries is transmitted to the return on the corresponding security in another country. Here, as in studies of the International Fisher Effect, the main problem is how to estimate the market's exchange rate expectations.

A *fourth* group of studies consists of those which have circumvented the problem of exchange rate expectations by studying the causal link between the interest rate on the Euromarket and corresponding domestic rates.[13] Most researchers using this approach believe they have eliminated all risk. Unfortunately the political risk has been disregarded in most studies in this group.

The *fifth* group which I shall be discussing, looks at differences in the return on investments in shares in different countries.

My survey of the various studies starts with the "law of one price" on financial markets. This can be studied in terms of the empirical validity of two expressions of the law: the International Fisher Effect and the interest rate parity theorem. I shall then continue my survey by discussing differences in the transmission process of different types of interest rates in those market combinations which have proved empirically interesting. Finally I shall discuss studies of stock market integration.

3.3.1 Studies of the International Fisher Effect

The International Fisher Effect dates back to the turn of the century, but what we can call the standard theory of the pricing of *international* financial securities did not really begin to evolve until the late 1960s and early 1970s.[14] Let us start by examining some important stages in the empirical analysis of the International Fisher Effect.

What is meant by the concept of expectation?

Conceptual confusion can often arise in analysing the International Fisher Effect. This concerns the concept of expectation, two types of which will figure in the following discussion. In analysing the validity of the studied equilibrium relationships, I shall employ the concept of *mathematical expectation* and the term "unbiased" will be used.[15]

In the International Fisher Effect, which was described in some detail in Appendix 2.3, another type of expectation is included, namely *market expectation.*

When the term *unbiased* is used in connection with the International Fisher Effect, the implication is generally that there are no systematic differences between market expectation in the shape of this relationship and actual outcomes. For various reasons the market expectation can differ from that indicated by Fisher. When comparisons are made between the interest differential and the actual exchange rate movement, we are thus testing the two hypotheses in the right-hand side of equation 3.2.

$$S_{t+n} - IFE_t(n) = [S_{t+n} - S^*_{t+n}] + [S^*_{t+n} - IFE_t(n)] \qquad (3.2)$$

The deviation between the actual future spot rate (S_{t+n}) and the forecast from the International Fisher Effect [$IFE_t(n)$] can thus be subdivided into a deviation between the actual future rate and market expectation (S^*_{t+n}) and a deviation between market expectation and the forecast [$IFE_t(n)$].

The subdivision according to formula 3.2 shows that conclusions about integration based on ex post analysis can be difficult to interpret. For example, the market expectation may be correct, even though the actual exchange rate does not assume the relevant value. This can come about, within the limits of efficiency, if the transaction costs are so great that the financial transaction is not economically defensible. The source of the interest gap – whether it depends on the market expectation deviating from the International Fisher Effect or on the presence of transaction costs – will determine any conclusions about the inefficiency and disintegration of the markets. The difficulty lies in judging the relative weight of the two causes. Yet another source of systematic deviation is to be found in the investor's risk aversion and his demands for a risk premium to compensate for the exchange and political risks. Thus any conclusions about the inefficiency of the market must also allow for an evaluation of these premiums.[16]

Analysis of the International Fisher Effect is often a question of the size of premiums for exchange risk

Many empirical studies of the International Fisher Effect have been concerned with the extent to which a systematic deviation between the forecasted and actual exchange rate change can be explained by the presence of a risk premium.

Test of real interest rate parity

When we combine an assumption about no deviations from the International Fisher Effect with an assumption about purchasing power parity we get equal expected real rates of interest and perfect total financial integration. There have been several studies of this form of integration based on real interest rate parity, e.g. Mishkin (1984a, 1984b), Cumby and Obstfeld (1984), Mark (1985b), Cumby and Mishkin (1986), Gaab, Granziol and Horner (1986) and Frankel and MacArthur (1988). These studies all report that there is a gap between the real interest rates, and that these rates are far from perfectly correlated between countries. Thus, they indicate a fairly low degree of (total) financial integration.

Frankel and MacArthur use a set of forward rate data for 24 countries to decompose the real interest differential into two parts: the covered interest differential or political premium, and the real forward discount, or currency risk premium. The latter is further decomposed into the exchange risk premium and expected real depreciation.[17] This analysis produces some counterintuitive results: it appears that even in the 1980s and even in industrialized countries capital mobility remained low. Frankel and MacArthur find some explanatory value in the political premium, but in general the currency premium appears to be a more important determinant of the real interest differential. Of the two currency factors the authors find the expected real depreciation to be as large and variable as the exchange risk premium: They also find it to be the more important determinant of the real interest differential. They conclude that the imperfect integration of goods markets rather than of financial markets may be responsible to this extent for the fact that real interest rates are not equalized.

Early empirical studies of the nominal interest rate differential

Porter (1971) based his discussion of financial integration on tests of the predictive power of different yield differentials. He analysed the interest rate differentials between the United States and Canada for securities with maturities of 3 months, 1 year, 2 years and 10 years, to determine whether they reflect "anticipations" regarding the time path of the exchange rate. In the case of the maturities of two years Porter found a strong relationship, but for maturities either shorter or longer than this, he found no obvious relationship. He takes this to mean that the markets may be integrated, but that there is still scope for monetary autonomy. However, Porter's analysis includes no explicit measure of risk premiums.

Aliber (1974), on the other hand, suggests that the systematic difference between the interest differential and the observed exchange rate change must be analysed in terms of two risks, an exchange risk and a political risk. Aliber concentrates on the information content in different rates of interest, and emphasizes the differences which were illustrated in Figure 2.3 above. It is assumed that national interest rates, unlike Eurorates, contain premiums for political risks. Thus, by using the forward rate, Aliber felt able to distinguish the premium for exchange risk from the premium for political risk. He found the premium for both risks to be about the same size, and took the presence of risk premiums to mean that we can expect the interest differential to give a biased estimate of future exchange rate movements. Aliber thus shows that the International Fisher Effect must be extended by the inclusion of terms for the premiums for exchange and political risk.

A capital asset pricing model as a way of incorporating the exchange risk

Roll and Solnik (1977) applied a capital asset pricing model (CAPM) to the international money market. [18] [19] In their analysis of eight countries they use the term "extraordinary exchange return", which they express in the form of the relationship between the forward and spot rates. They assume that for every currency the extraordinary exchange return reflects the addition to the risk in the portfolio caused by that currency. Roll and Solnik conclude that the actual premiums are positively related on average to the portfolio risk, but that the individual premiums differ significantly from those forecast by the model. Their conclusions should be interpreted with caution in view of the choice of securities in the market portfolio, the method of estimating the extraordinary return, the neglect of premiums for political risk, and the presence of autocorrelation with resulting uncertainty in the estimates. Roll and Solnik mention the analytical difficulties themselves, and they claim that their empirical results do at least indicate – as is generally accepted today – that exchange risk and political risk must be considered in any theory of international financial transactions which can be regarded as realistic.

Deviations from the International Fisher Effect in an analysis based on Swedish interest rates

No published study has so far analysed the International Fisher Effect using ex ante data and Swedish interest rates, either as a way of analysing financial integration or for any other purpose. In Oxelheim (1985) I describe an analysis of ex post deviations from the International Fisher Effect based on Swedish interest rates. Big deviations from the relationship were observed during the period 1974–84.[20] The forecasting value of the interest differential for this period was low. The systematic errors were few, however. It was not possible to confirm the occurrence of a constant exchange risk premium.

Hörngren and Vredin (1986), however, find a risk premium in the shape of a systematic deviation between the forward premium and the exchange rate change over the covered period. Whereas from my own tests of corresponding relationships I was unable to find any *significant* indication of a risk premium (Oxelheim 1985). However, the explanation of these contradictory results may be that we were using data for different periods, and that I studied bilateral rates while Hörngren and Vredin use a Swedish basket index. My result, i.e. with deviation from the International Fisher Effect and deviation from interest rate parity theory, but with the forward premium as an unbiased estimate of the future exchange rate change, supports the conclusion that in demanding a premium for risk, the market is mainly concerned about *systematic* political risk and less about *systematic* exchange risk.[21]

Together these *studies* indicate that the market is averse to risk and that it is necessary in any study of the international integration of the Swedish market to extend the International Fisher Effect to allow for premiums for political as well as for exchange risk. The risk attaching to the investor's positions in various currencies should thus be linked up with other risks on the financial and commercial contracts in the investor's portfolio.[22] At the present stage the theory provides no convincing basis for considering all these risks at the same time. But, as has been stressed before, the problem of establishing the size of the risk premium is only one of several difficulties which has hitherto vitiated any attempts to understand direct financial integration by analysing the International Fisher Effect.

3.3.2 Studies of interest rate parity

One group of studies examines direct financial integration on a basis of observed deviations from interest rate parity. But the interest rate parity theorem, which was described in some detail in Appendix 2.6, is not entirely uncontroversial.

Two schools regarding the arbitrage underlying interest rate parity

Two schools of thought can be distinguished as regards the interest rate parity theorem and the nature of the forward premium. One school consists of the supporters of the "Modern Theory" (see, for example, Stoll 1968 and Kesselman 1971). According to this theory (MT) the equilibrium forward rate generally falls between the exogenously determined forward rate according to interest rate parity and the expected future spot rate. It can be regarded as a weighted average of the interest-rate-parity-determined forward rate $S_t[(1+r_d)/(1+r_{for})]$ and the expected future spot rate S^*_{t+n}.

In MT the market actors are divided into groups according to their motives. The main categories are arbitrageurs on the one hand and actors with speculative motives on the other. According to MT the first of these demand a forward contract when the forward rate deviates from interest rate parity, thus linking the forward rate to the interest rates. The speculative actors adopt open forward positions, thus linking the forward rate to the expected future spot rate.

MT assumes that the interest rate is entirely determined exogenously, by the actions of the central banks, and that it is completely independent of any expectations. Under interest rate parity it is assumed that the demand for arbitrage is infinitely elastic. According to this view no change in the market actor's expectations regarding the future exchange rate – due perhaps to government counter-speculation – has any effect on the arbitrageur's demand curve or on the forward rate generated by the interest rate parity. The volume of arbitrage changes automatically to meet the speculative demand. This gives a false impression that a government can successfully control capital flows by intervening on the forward market. Because of the exogeneity of the interest rates, the demand curves for forward contracts among different groups of market actors will be completely independent of one another.

By including expectations, the advocates of MT believe they can explain the deviations from interest rate parity. To put it another way, they claim that arbitrage does not in itself tell the whole truth about the relationship between premiums and differentials; the expectations of the speculators must be included. MT has thus been regarded as helping to explain observed deviations from interest rate parity. However, market data over the last few years indicates that interest rate parity holds for the best-matched case, viz. interbank trade on Euromarkets, and that the gaps between domestic rates and forward covered foreign rates increasingly rarely fall outside the arbitrage interval.[23] This applies even if we include the very turbulent period of the early 1980s.

Among the opposing theories is the Capital Asset Pricing Model (CAPM).[24] According to this model, different categories of market actors should be identified not according to motives but according to price deflators. It is assumed here that the interest rate differential reflects expectations regarding future exchange rates. At the same time the forward rate is determined according to the interest rate parity theorem. Thus interest rates and the forward rate can be regarded as endogenized and as functions of exchange rate expectations. The deviation from interest rate parity arises as a result of the demand for compensation for political risk. The demand for contracts cannot be broken down according to transaction motives, as in MT; rather it must be regarded as multiplicative or interactive. Thus the forward rate cannot be subdivided into two parts, one determined by interest rate parity and one by expectations regarding the future exchange rate.

A good deal of empirical evidence has been cited against MT. Using US and Canadian data and assuming rational expectations, McCallum (1977) takes into account the autocorrelation in the residuals and finds that expected future spot rates make no difference. He thus concludes that MT contributes nothing of explanatory value. Phaup (1981) criticizes MT, showing that if the forward rate is to deviate from interest rate parity, alternative forms of speculation must not freely substitute for one another.

My own observation that in the case of the Swedish krona the correlation between the forward premium and the deviation from purchasing power parity is –0.12, might also be interpreted as evidence against the Modern Theory (see Section 2.4 above). We thus have good reason to complement the forward premium by an explicit term for the market's exchange rate expectation. This can assume the form of a term for the deviation from purchasing power parity – the cumulative appreciation/depreciation potential.

Different explanations of deviations from interest rate parity

Good surveys and further arguments for and against the validity of the interest rate parity theorem can be found in Frenkel and Levich (1975) and Herring and Marston (1978) among others. There are many explanations in the literature for observed deviations from interest rate parity. Branson (1969) and Frenkel and Levich (1975) explain the deviations in terms of the presence of transaction costs. They claim that these costs are often underestimated, since information costs are seldom included. Institutional constraints or controls are suggested as an explanation by Einzig (1961), Canterbery (1965) and Sohmen (1969). Kenen (1965), Prachowny (1970) and Frenkel (1973) explain the deviations by saying that the interest rate can be regarded as functionally related to the transaction volume. Grubel (1966) and Stoll (1972) cite the risk of default and Aliber (1973) and Dooley and Isard (1980) the political risk.

There is thus no consensus on this point. Since my view here is that an indication of direct integration can be obtained only after the price of various risks has been deducted from a possible deviation from interest rate parity, this list can serve as a basis for the construction of a "price list".

New techniques in the analysis

Most studies of interest rate parity have used fixed-period regression analysis. The interest rate differential has been regarded as an exogenous variable. However, there is good reason to take into account a possible two-way interaction between the forward premium and the interest differential as well. McCallum (1977) allows for simultaneity by using the two-step least-square method, and Pippenger (1978) by using frequency-based spectral analysis.[25] Browne (1983) follows Pippenger's line in a test of interest rate parity between Ireland on the one hand and Germany, Great Britain and the United States on the other. For the Ireland-United States relationship Browne finds perfect interest arbitrage with unlimited arbitrage funds and instantaneous response. For the Great Britain-Ireland relationship the response is slow, but funds that are in infinitely elastic supply permit interest rate parity in the long term. For the Germany-Ireland relationship interest rate parity does not seem to hold, since funds are not unlimited. Alternatively the explanation could be that the relevant markets are too "thin".[26]

The time aspect causes difficulties in the analysis of interest rate parity

Levich (1979) emphasizes the time aspect in interpreting deviations from interest rate parity. He notes such deviations in the case of USD and claims that these can probably be explained in terms of timing, i.e. the time-lag between transmission of information and implementation of a transaction. A certain amount of time is needed to exploit the information that signals the possibility of risk-free profit from covered interest rate arbitrage. Sometimes four transactions have to be carried out. The fact that an ex post analysis indicates risk-free opportunities does not necessarily mean that a potential investor was equipped with ex ante rules for exploiting them. An efficient market presupposes rational investors, i.e. investors who convert information into transactions without delay.

It is reasonable to assume that some time passes between the investor obtaining the information and his being able to exploit it; due to this lag his chances of profit may have vanished. Thus, the existence of deviations from interest rate parity in an ex-post analysis is not necessarily a sign of market inefficiency. It would therefore be interesting to know whether the risk-free opportunities are still available one period later, i.e. given that the investor has had a chance to exploit them. To investigate this point, the observations in our analysis should refer to hours and minutes rather than to the weeks and months that are often used in structural models.

It is difficult to analyse the level of direct financial integration with the help of the interest rate parity theorem

Any attempt to infer the level of financial integration – and possible changes in this level – on a basis of observed deviations from interest parity, will be dogged by the problem of estimating the transaction cost and the premium for possible political risk. Opinions are divided about the breadth and structure of the neutral band around the interest rate arbitrage line (cf. Figure A2.3 in Appendix 2.6). Traditionally the band has been regarded as a function of the transaction cost only, but in any study of markets with risk aversion the premium for the systematic political risk will also have to be incorporated.

Analysis of interest rate parity, based on Swedish interest rates

Attempts to analyse deviations from interest rate parity based on the Swedish krona and Swedish instruments and to examine the role of these deviations as possible signs of segmentation, can be found in Oxelheim (1981, 1985), and Englund, McPhee and Viotti (1985) among others. These works give some indication of the increasing integration of Sweden's financial markets from observations of the deviations from interest rate parity, which appear to have declined in frequency and size. However, if we are to interpret these observations in terms of direct financial integration, we still face the problem of measuring explicitly the size of the premium for political risk.

3.3.3 Transmission of interest rate effects between markets

Whereas the analysis in the earlier sections has investigated differences in levels of return, the following analysis is more concerned with the strength of various links and interdependencies. A strong market link is a necessary if not a sufficient condition for integration.

As before the exposition refers back to Figure 2.8 and includes three types of market dependency. The analysis is concerned with interest transmission, i.e. with the way in which the interest rate in one country affects the rate in another country or group of countries, straight away or with a time lag. Is there, for example, a global interest effect, and does the global interest level affect the interest level in individual countries? If so, how great is this influence and what pattern does it follow? We can claim that *the higher the level of integration between markets, the greater is the explanatory value of this global rate for the interest level in the individual country.* Market expectations about future exchange rates and the premiums for exchange and political risk should also be taken into account. These three difficult elements vary in strength in the different market dependencies studied below. We shall also see that they have been tackled by researchers with varying success.

3.3.3.1 Transmission of interest effects from one country to another

Fase (1976) applies the principal-component technique to short-term interest rates, to determine whether the rates moved in a manner consistent with perfect substitutability. His analysis covers three-month treasury bills in 11 industrial countries[27] and is based on data for the period January 1961 – December 1972. Fase concludes that the variation among uncovered interest rates was explained fairly well by three principal components and among covered interest rates by two of these components.

The first of the components which the two cases have in common is the "international" or "global" interest rate. The results indicate, however, that perfect substitutability does not obtain. The other significant component, according to Fase, is identified with political risk. When he bases his analysis on uncovered interest rates, he also finds that a third component becomes necessary, which reflects exchange risk. However, he emphasizes that the quantitative importance of this aspect does not seem to be very great, presumably because it has sometimes been absorbed by the first principal component of uncovered interest rates. It should also be noted that the analysis referred to a period which lacked the kind of turbulence we have seen in the 1980s. Fase also found support for the hypothesis that interests in the United States had a dominating influence on the "global interest level", which in view of the period he was studying accords with the results of many other studies.

The existence of a significant common international factor or global effect which reproduces itself in all economies, is also reported by Logue, Salant and Sweeney (1976). These authors tried to discover whether there was a common international factor affecting interest rates in different countries. Their analysis concerns the interest rate on medium and long-term government bonds in the United States, France, West Germany, the Netherlands, Switzerland, Great Britain and Sweden. The analysis is based on quarterly data for the period 1958:1–1973:2. The greater the covariation between the common factor and the particular interest rate, the greater the integration was assumed to be. Logue, Salant and Sweeney found that 82–85 per cent of the variance in the level of interest rates and 41 per cent of the variance in the first differences in these levels from one period to another, could be explained by a common world-wide factor. Their analysis also revealed several regional country constellations.

One constellation centres around West Germany and another around the United States, Great Britain and France.

Even though their analysis concerned a period of calm on the exchange rate front, it has one weakness: the market expectation of future exchange rate movements was ignored. This may give a downward bias to the estimates of the extent of integration. However, since the analysis referred to medium- and long-term interest rates rather than short-term interest rates, the bias was probably small.

It is popularly believed that Japan has succeeded in isolating itself by imposing restrictions. But Fukao and Okubo (1982) show that the yield on Japanese domestic long-term bonds is determined not only by domestic factors such as the short-term interest rate and the quantity of outstanding long-term bonds, but also by foreign factors such as the foreign long-term interest rate, the inflation differential, and the cumulative imbalance in the current account. The authors conclude that the yield on bonds in Japan is determined in no small measure by the long-term interest rate in the United States and by the market's exchange rate expectations. An analysis of data from the last few years shows these links particularly clearly.

Weaknesses in these studies

Generally speaking the investigations in this group of transmission studies lack a structural basis, for example in the shape of an extension of the International Fisher Effect. In fact most studies of capital market relationships even lack any explicit modelling of expected exchange rates. Admittedly the problems involved in such modelling are daunting. But the absence of any consideration springs from an implicit assumption that the anticipated spot rate does not differ significantly from that of today, or that changes in expected exchange rates are not related in any systematic way to the change in the interest differential.

Can we proceed from an analysis of the global interest rate?

The reduction in inter-market barriers and the observed increase in international financial transactions both suggest that there could be a "global" rate which exerts influence on markets all over the world – something which the studies in this group also indicate.

And the studies also confirm that an analysis of the level of direct financial integration of a small open economy which has no formal Euromarket quotations, should be based on the transmission of changes in the global interest rate to the particular economy concerned and should take the political risk into account.

3.3.3.2 The link between national interest rates and Eurorates, and between Eurorates

Many researchers see the Eurorate as an intermediary for the foreign disturbances whose effects we are considering here. This view can put us on the wrong track, for instance if domestic disturbances first affect the Eurorate and after that the domestic rate. We might then wrongly conclude that the domestic rate had been influenced by conditions on the Euromarket rather than by the domestic disturbances which were really the root cause. Such an interpretation of events might occur if the domestic interest rate is regulated. In this group of transmission studies, the problem of exchange rate expectation and exchange risk has been eliminated by the choice of interest rates. All that remains is the political risk, except when two Eurorates are being compared.

The fundamental question in this section is whether the national interest rates and the Eurorate for a particular currency develop together, i.e. with causality in both directions with or without time-lag, or whether they are simultaneously determined by each other. Earlier analyses of this question have produced contradictory results.

Role of the Eurorate as intermediary between national markets

Studies published in the 1960s and early 1970s such as Hendershott (1967), Kwack (1971), Mills (1973) and Argy and Hodjera (1973), support the proposition that *changes in the Eurodollar rate adapt after a certain time-lag to changes in the interest rate on treasury bills in the United States.* But they also show that the adjustment is not total. Mills finds that European interest rates are "occasionally instrumental" in determining the level of the Eurodollar rate. But Giddy, Dufey and Min (1979) claim that the Eurosterling rate is more sensitive to changes in market conditions than the domestic rate is, i.e. the interest rate in Great Britain adjusts itself more slowly to changed conditions than the Eurosterling rate. Thus, we have two major categories of results, and in studies based on data up to the mid-1970s there was no consensus as regards either of the two transmission processes, not even when the same interest rates were used. Three explanations for these contradictory results suggest themselves, all connected with technical factors: different choice of period to study, different choice of data, and different choice of method. In addition, we can also expect modelling problems.

Analysis of cross-correlation with filtered series

Volker (1980) demonstrates that the effect of external fluctuations varies between countries of different size, and he shows the extent to which small countries respond more quickly to external influence than large ones. This is thus a test based on Mundell (1968), which claims that in a world where capital mobility obtains, the maintenance of fixed exchange rates in a small open economy means that the country's interest rates are dominated by events outside its borders. Volker's analysis is based on data for the period 1961 to the end of 1970. He investigates transmission and the related structure of time-lagged effects. Unlike other studies[28] which have allowed for time-lagged effects, Volker assumes a less restrictive structure and studies the cross-correlation between filtered series.[29] With covered interest rates the US rate turns out here to have more influence than the Eurodollar rate on the rates in Great Britain and Canada. But the Eurodollar rate has greater influence on interest rates in West Germany, France, Switzerland and the Netherlands. Unlike most of the other researchers in the area[30] Volker finds no lagged relationship between the Eurodollar rate and the US rate.

Mutual influence between US rates and other rates

During the 1960s and 1970s it was generally assumed that the interest rates on the US market were unaffected by foreign influence. In recent years results have emerged suggesting that since the mid-1970s influence has flowed in both directions between these interest rates and the Eurodollar rate. Many researchers using causality tests extend this mutuality to include also the link between the US rates and other interest rates on major national markets.[31]

Hartman (1984) finds it strange that the possibility of *mutual causality* between national interest rates through the interest rates on the Euromarket has received such scant attention. Indirect influence from the national rates of the major countries on the national US rate by way of the Eurodollar rate must be regarded as probable, in view of the evidence adduced by Argy and Hodjera (1973), Mills (1973), Kwack (1975) and Min (1976) for the influence of the European rates on the Eurodollar rate.

Need for an equation system to allow for mutuality

Herring and Marston (1977) extended the research in this contest from the effect of the European interest rates on the Eurodollar rate, to a simultaneous equation system for the Eurodollar market and different European financial markets. Their research is based on data up to 1971, and it shows that the Eurodollar rate has a significant effect on conditions on European financial markets. Since rates on the US market have also proved to be a determining factor for the Eurodollar rate, this implies that fluctuations in the US market rate also have an indirect effect on the European rates. As in most other studies during the 1970s on this topic the US rate is taken as given, i.e. unaffected by events in the rest of the world.

As I have already mentioned, many studies since the beginning of the 1980s have been sought to demonstrate the reciprocal relationships between domestic markets and foreign interest rates by referring to the relationship between national interest rates and Eurorates. Among them Kaen and Hachey (1983), Hartman (1984) and Cumby and Mishkin (1984), for example, have described the relationship between the markets in an equation system on the following lines:[32]

$$r_t = \sum_{i=1}^{m} \alpha_i r_{t-i} + \sum_{j=1}^{n} \beta_j r^*_{t-j} + \varepsilon_t \tag{3.3}$$

$$r^*_t = \sum_{i=1}^{m^*} \alpha^*_i r_{t-1} + \sum_{j=1}^{n^*} \beta^*_j r^*_{t-j} + \varepsilon^*_t \tag{3.4}$$

Summation is made over the number of time-lagged periods. r_t refers to the domestic interest rates which according to equation (3.3) are determined by previous values for the domestic rate and the Eurorate. The influence of other factors is summarized here in ε_t. If, as in this case, the researcher has decided to compare national markets with the Euromarket, then ε_t will contain a term for political risk, or some form of sovereignty risk (see Figure 2.3). In so far as this risk is correlated with historical interest rates, there will be an estimation problem as soon as we try to estimate a structural model. However, in the case of equation (3.3), and if we are only interested in isolating sources of disturbance, these problems will not be so great. Similarly the Eurorate (marked with an asterisk) depends on previous values for the domestic rate and the Eurorate. The effects of other factors on the Eurorate are summarized in ε^*_t. In a model based on the equation system, a rejection of the null hypothesis H_0: $\beta = 0$ implies sufficient evidence to indicate the influence of the Eurorate on the domestic rate. Similarly a rejection of H_0: $\alpha^* = 0$ implies that the domestic rate affects the corresponding Eurorate.

Studies by Hartman (1984) and Cumby and Mishkin (1984) show that the US rates are far from unaffected by the sequence of events abroad. The first of these studies is concerned with nominal interest rates and the latter with real rates. These studies refer to conditions during the 1970s and they also serve to confirm the assumption that this influence has been increasing in recent years. The studies were concerned with the US capital market, i.e. with a market which up to the beginning of 1974 was to some extent controlled as a result of restrictions on capital flows. The abolition of these restrictions and the growth of the Euromarket can certainly go a long way towards explaining the significant increase in foreign influence on the US market. And we can assume that this influence will have been growing even stronger during the early 1980s.

Hartman shows that up to 40 per cent of the variation in the Eurodollar rate during the period 1975-78 can be traced to events on the US financial markets. What is interesting in his study compared with other investigations, is its high explanatory value. The variation in interest rates on the US financial markets that comes from foreign markets by way of the Eurorate, is in the order of 20–60 per cent, which must be regarded as surprisingly high in view of the fact that this influence was previously thought to be negligible.[33] One obvious conclusion is that the US financial markets are no longer as isolated as was previously assumed. Thus, the use of the US rate as an approximation for the global interest rate no longer seems motivated.

Kaen and Hachey (1983) have used a Granger or Granger-related technique[34] and data for the period 1974–81 and find strong empirical support for the conclusion that since the collapse of the Bretton Woods Agreement and the start of a general abolishment of exchange regulations, domestic market rates adjust more quickly than the Eurorate in the same currency to changes in monetary or economic conditions.[35]

In view of the frequency with which feedback causality was observed, Kaen and Hachey find it difficult to claim that all monetary or economic changes arise on the domestic market. Instead they suggest that the domestic rate responds more quickly than the Eurorate to changes in external market conditions, rather than vice versa. Their result directly contradicts Giddy, Dufey and Mins (1979), who found that the Eurosterling rate responded to changes more quickly than the domestic rates in Great Britain. Kaen and Hachey's result is consistent with the presence of market imperfections and/or transaction costs. The overall results of combined one-way and feedback causality indicate financial disintegration by way of structural phenomena on the market and/or transaction costs that hamper or reduce the incentive to make immediate price adjustments.

The global rate as an aggregate of national rates determines the trend

We thus appear to have convincing confirmation from the various studies that the US interest rate can no longer be regarded as unaffected by other rates; rather, there is a mutual relationship between the US rate and other national rates as well as between the different Eurorates. Support has been found for both mutual and unilateral relationships. But, as Kaen and Hachey have pointed out, when the relationship is unilateral we will always find the influence going from the US market to the Eurodollar market. These authors come to the same conclusions as regards Eurosterling vis-à-vis the market in Great Britain. There is thus much to suggest that domestic financial markets in the large economies adjust more quickly than the Euromarkets to changing conditions.

In studying the transmission in recent years of interest effects to small open economies, we have found good reason to consider a global effect consisting of the effects of aggregate interest rates in the major OECD countries, as well as effects from the US rate.

3.3.3.3 Comparisons of national stock markets

Financial integration includes integration of stock markets. Under total financial integration the expected real return on individual shares is the same on different markets. However, unlike the credit market there is no simple theory about how the national stock markets in terms of aggregated returns are linked to each other. There are also many ways studying the direct integration of the national stock markets. One way is to look at the opportunities that are open to the investor for diversifying his portfolio by buying foreign securities in addition to domestic ones. If the business cycles or the movements in security prices at home are not perfectly correlated with those abroad, a diversification of the portfolio over national borders can reduce the risk to the portfolio, i.e. the variance in its return. The view here is that *the lower the reduction in the risk as a result of this diversification, the greater the similarity between domestic and foreign investments as regards risk and return, and the higher the level of direct financial integration.*

Another way of studying integration is to investigate the price of risk in different countries. The "law of one price" can then be applied to portfolios. The price of risk is the increased return that is combined with a certain increase in risk. The hypothesis is that *the existence of perfect correlation between these price changes indicates that the markets are perfectly directly financially integrated.*

Four analytical paths can be discerned up to the beginning of the 1980s

Adler and Dumas (1983) surveyed empirical studies made before 1983 and commented on the lack of progress in developing an appropriate analysis; there was still no distinct empirical method for measuring the level of integration in this area. They discuss four possible paths for a meaningful analysis:

- One way is by studying *the correlation between national stock market indices.* Many studies equate low correlation and segmentation under the assumption that integrated national markets can be expected to fluctuate together. However, such conclusions may be wrong, perhaps because selective policy interventions in different countries affect production operations differently. Random shocks may affect specific sectors selectively. Thus the industrial structure may be an important explanation of the low correlation. If the link is to be justified, many variables must be matched. If they are not, then according to Adler and Dumas a low correlation between national stock market indices can generally be regarded as consistent with perfect capital market integration.

- A better way is to analyse *the correlation between national consumption rates.* It can be assumed that consumption risks, unlike production risks, are mutualized in an integrated and Pareto optimal capital market. In such a market, small and random (unanticipated) fluctuations in domestic consumption rates should be perfectly correlated with the aggregate random consumption rate. One not insurmountable difficulty is to define the aggregate consumption risk, when differences in taste result in deviations from international purchasing power parity.[36]

- A third way is to analyse *the price of securities.* Instead of inferring the degree of segmentation direct from the correlation structure, we can derive alternative CAPM models, with and without segmentation. These are then confronted with data to see which fits best.

  An alternative method is to use Arbitrage Pricing Theory (APT) and to test whether random factors which are common to stocks in different countries are assigned the same price on the different national stock exchanges. Stehle (1977), for example, tried to test the hypothesis that the US market is completely isolated against the hypothesis that it is completely integrated with the rest of the world. Under complete segmentation the market portfolio for US investors would be represented by the US index, while under complete integration the world index would take on this role. However, in his empirical analysis Stehle did not succeed in distinguishing significantly between the two competing models.

  Solnik (1977) recommends comparing actual and optimal return portfolios, rather than comparing actual return with their theoretical values. However, he claims that optimally composed portfolios under segmentation or integration would not be sufficiently unalike to allow for any clear conclusions to be drawn.

– The fourth and last approach is based on CAPM concepts and was first proposed by Black (1974). A developed version can be found in Stulz (1981). Instead of assuming complete segmentation or integration, the idea here is to study *a continuous parameter of segmentation in the form of a proportional tax.* Black regards the tax as based on the investor's net holding (long-term minus short-term) on risky foreign assets, while Stulz's tax is positive for both long- and short-term positions. Borrowing at home and abroad is risk-free and without tax in both the models. The obviously small differences in the specification nonetheless produce two quite different CAPMs, but with one common attribute: the global portfolio will not be efficient for any investor in either of these models.

According to Adler and Dumas (1983) the segmentation test would consist essentially of fitting the derived CAPM to the stock price data. After which the values of the implied tax rate are calculated, or its effects are evaluated in a security market line analysis.

Early portfolio studies of stock market integration indicated the existence of segmented markets

Levy and Sarnat (1970) developed optimal international portfolios for five different risk-free reference interest rates, based on mean rates of return and standard deviations for common shares in 28 countries. The analysis covered the period 1951–67. The authors found that the risk/return relationships differed significantly between countries, and that the stock markets in these countries were not fully integrated. However, they have not explicitly allowed for the fact that the return on investment to investors from different countries is affected and changed by a change in the exchange rate.

Agmon (1972) came to a different conclusion. He applied regression analysis to data from Germany, Japan, Great Britain and the United States, to show that a zero hypothesis regarding integrated markets cannot be rejected. He found that stock prices in Great Britain, West Germany and Japan responded immediately to changes in the share index in the United States, and he took this to mean that there is a "global market" for shares.

Panton et al. (1976) come to the same result as Agmon. They employ factor analysis to investigate the structure of equity return in order to identify groups or subgroups of countries in which the returns are of the same character. They also investigate the intertemporal stability of the return, and in their analysis of the period 1963–72 they find a certain stability from one year to the next; but the stability becomes less, the longer the period studied. Because the returns are not fully correlated between countries, return in relation to risk can be increased by means of international portfolio diversification. According to this study, the return also increases with the length of the investment period.

Lessard (1976) tested the opportunity cost of restraining international investment under two market assumptions: one that the market is segmented, and the other that it is integrated. He found that all investors except those in the United States and Canada would experience a considerable loss if they limited themselves to domestic investment and that the evidence is more nearly consistent with the assumption of segmented markets. Diversification pays, since the markets are segmented and the pay-offs are higher for investors domiciled in smaller countries, which appear to have an essentially different relation between risk and return than that obtaining in larger countries. A remarkable feature of Lessard's results is that the small-country assumption does not seem to have any great importance for stock market relations between small countries and large ones.

Rugman (1976) looks at opportunities for investors to diversify internationally and assumes that there is reason for a company to diversify, unless the investor has eliminated the possibility of the company doing so. In a study of American companies Rugman shows that as companies increase their foreign sales they also become able to reduce the variation in their earnings. He takes this to mean that domestic and foreign stock markets are not fully integrated and that the companies internalize their capital transfers over the national borders, since the similar transfers from investors have failed to integrate domestic and foreign markets in full. If the inverse relationship obtains between country size and a domestically generated variance in corporate earnings, then companies in small countries should have a stronger motivation to expand abroad than companies in larger countries.

Recent portfolio studies indicate that segmented stock markets still prevail

In many recent portfolio studies it is claimed that stock markets are still segmented. Eun and Resnick (1987) provide an example of this. The authors carried out a portfolio study of investments in 15 countries and found that national investors in these countries would be able to make potential profits from international diversification, which indicates that the stock markets are segmented. Swedish investors are among those liable to make the smallest potential profits from such diversification. Eun and

Resnick also compare the ex post results of the three most common diversification strategies with the result in the respective domestic portfolios. In the case of four of the fifteen countries in the study, among them Sweden, the authors find that the domestic portfolio is superior to the internationally diversified portfolios.[37]

Problems in analyses based on international CAPM

Solnik (1974a) based his analysis on international CAPM (ICAPM) and calculates the systematic international risk for 234 common stocks in eight European countries[38] and 65 shares on the US markets. He finds a strong international factor in the pricing of risky securities, which can be taken as a sign of a high level of stock market integration. However, national factors are still important.[39] These domestic factors are "diversified away" in the global context, so that a strong correlation appears between realized return and systematic international risk.

The application of CAPM in an international context is associated among other things with the problem of identifying the denomination currency or base currency. In CAPM as in Solnik's model, for example, the investor in different countries is identified by a single price index. Investors who live in different countries, however, probably also have different consumption bundles. Thus each group of investors would like returns to be calculated in its own home currency. As the exchange rate moves, the real return on a given portfolio changes for investors living in different countries. Solnik tries to get round the exchange problem by assuming that investors in different countries can cover their exposure by leading and lagging payments. But the problem still remains, since the returns will be the same only if the cost of cover is identical.

International Arbitrage Pricing Theory and integrated stock markets

Cho, Eun and Senbet (1984) test the international Arbitrage Pricing Theory by carrying out an interbattery factor analysis. They reject the combined hypothesis that the international stock markets are integrated and that the international APT theory holds.

The time structure in the link between stock markets

Hillard (1979) conducts a spectral analysis and finds that the different sectors of the world market react to financial crises independently of one another, despite the existence of a certain correlation between changes in the markets in the different continents.

As a result of major structural changes we would like to believe that this pattern has changed during the 1980s, something which is confirmed by Khoury, Dodin and Takada (1987) among others. They have analysed the lagged effects of one national stock market on another. In the period 1975–83 they found that the US market led developments and that the Japanese, the French and the German markets were one day behind the American. These three markets also show a strong covariation among themselves. The authors also found that the US stock market index can provide a good approximation for the global index which a CAPM analysis requires. However, their analysis is not sufficiently standardized as regards risk to allow any inferences about stock market integration.

Isolating market imperfections for testing purposes

Solnik (1977) claims that market segmentation is caused by investment barriers, and that the most efficient way of testing the degree of imperfection is to isolate one market imperfection and to investigate its effect on the pricing of risky assets.

Errunza and Losq (1985) examine this question with the help of a cross-sectional regression analysis. They set out to analyse a hypothesis of "mild" segmentation, i.e. securities in country A can be purchased by investors in country B, but the reverse does not hold. They examine nine developing countries on the one hand, and the US market on the other for the period 1976–80. They conclude that the securities in country A are priced as if the market were integrated, and that the securities in country B entail a super-risk premium which is proportional to the conditional market risk involved – a premium which in my terminology can be regarded as a premium for political risk. However, since the tests were not conclusive, further empirical investigation was recommended.

Stock market interdependence allowing for macroeconomic variables

Bhandari and Genberg (1989) analyse the dependence of relative stock market developments on real exchange rate changes. They find developments depend on changes in real exchange rates. However, they also find substantial instability in the relationship over time. The authors argue that the instability stems from the existence of permanent real shocks that have different effects on the countries in their sample. According to these authors it appears either that some degree of explicit coordination of economic policies or that certain shared shocks are necessary to explain the positive correlation, they suggest that the effect of different shocks – permanent and transitory – should be studied, and they conclude that a lot could potentially be learnt about economic interdependence by establishing exactly which foreign variables affect domestic stock prices, and how they do it. Goodwin, Farsio and Willett (1989) argue along the same lines and claim that the sign of the exchange rate's effect on stock prices could be different depending on the origin of a shock – nominal or real. Starting from the relation between exchange rates and interest rates, they identify disturbances as either nominal or real and allow the coefficient for the exchange rate to differ between the two cases. By using this procedure they are able to improve the explanatory value of the exchange rate substantially.

Oxelheim and Wihlborg (1987) argue that a stable relation cannot be expected between any one of the macroprice variables mentioned and corporate performance, since typically these variables change simultaneously within a general equilibrium framework. Thus, the discovery of exchange rate sensitivity in a company's cash flows does not necessarily imply that there is any independent exposure to exchange rate changes. A wide range of domestic and foreign variables must be taken into account simultaneously before any such conclusions can be drawn.

Arbitrage Pricing Theory (APT) provides a framework for analysing the way in which exogenous factors contribute to the risk of particular securities. Macroeconomic factors and the pricing of risk associated with uncertainty about such factors have been analysed, by Chen, Roll and Ross (1986) among others. However, these authors include only domestic factors. The value of APT tests declines if foreign factors or any important factors are left out. The tests involve testing the joint hypothesis of APT and the underlying factor model. As Oxelheim and Wihlborg (1987) point out, the stability of the coefficients in a factor model can be doubted even if a complete set of factors is included; it is also necessary that these factors be truly exogenous. The reason is that if a set including both foreign and domestic macroprice variables is used, for example, but these factors are not exogenous, then the coefficients for the macroprice variables would depend on the frequency with which the "true fundamentals" have changed.

Ibrahimi, Oxelheim and Wihlborg (1989) analyse the stability of regression coefficients for stock market rates of return on macrovariables in Japan, Sweden and the US under different macroshock specifications for 1979-87. The sensitivity of stock market prices to unanticipated exchange rate changes was found to be negligible after interest rates and inflation rates had been taken into account. Thus if the differences in exposure to macroeconomic shocks are allowed for, we might be led to conclusions about much higher interdependence between rates of return on different stock markets, due to the influence from the global interest rate, than have been found hitherto.

The international integration of stock markets is not perfect

Overall these diverse studies of the relationship between stock markets in different countries suggest that national markets are not segmented, nor are they fully integrated. Here, as in the other tests of integration, the empirical choice of measures and analytical methods has not yet been satisfactorily developed. Further, political risk in the broader sense of the term has been disregarded in most of these analyses.

3.4 Observations from the literature – a summary

There have been major changes over the last ten years or so when it comes to the pattern of fluctuations in various real and financial variables. Conclusions about the level of financial integration have therefore been gradually revised. In some cases comparisons referring to the same periods and securities have led to different results, due to the choice of explanatory variables and methods of analysis. We thus have to ask ourselves: what is the truth today and how robust are the results? From the published material it appears that the world's financial markets are at present in an intermediate state, neither perfectly segmented nor perfectly integrated. It could also be that the short markets (money markets) are segmented, while the long markets (bond and stock markets) are perfectly integrated. Transaction costs and exchange risk presumably affect short-term investments more than long-term investments.

There is no evidence that the small country assumption is a good approximation for any countries, nor is it possible to find examples of countries large enough to be uninfluenced by external disturbances. International studies based on data from 1975 onwards show no example of any extreme cases today. In studies published during the 1960s and 1970s it was generally assumed that the interest rates on the US market were unaffected by foreign influence – a conclusion which probably had some justification. The integration on the markets now appears to have reached a stage at which mutual causality obtains between US interest rates and the corresponding rates on the various national markets in Europe. This mutual influence can then be transmitted via the Eurorates. Generally speaking integration has gone so far that changes in a "global interest level" appear to have a significant effect in most countries. But even if the financial variables studied behave as though the market were largely integrated, no one denies that there is still some scope for a certain amount of domestic monetary autonomy. Admittedly the studies suggest that "global effects" predominate, but they demonstrate country and regional effects as well.

No study of equivalent returns in different countries provides unequivocal support for the assumption of full substitutability between domestic and foreign assets. No study denies the possibility of some scope for an autonomous domestic monetary policy. All the studies are consistent in finding that financial markets are linked to one another and are subject to similar forces, but not to an extent that completely eliminates the scope for an independent national monetary policy.

One drawback of the studies published over the last few decades is that with few exceptions they all concern single sectors of the financial market, and that the grounds they provide for any inferences about the autonomy of national credit and monetary policies are weak. Many studies have also circumvented the problem of estimating market expectations of future exchange rates. In some studies this impaired the value of the published results. Few studies have adopted the kind of extended Fisher approach that might seem called for in analysing the market in a country which lacks formal Euromarket quotations for its financial quantities. No published investigations have provided any indisputable quantitative measures of financial integration or of the changes in the level of integration over time. And no studies seem to have been devoted to the analysis of the behaviour of market actors.

Certain points which emerge from the results of these studies are worth bearing in mind in connection with the empirical analysis of direct financial integration which will be reported in Chapters 5-8 below. In particular the following points have emerged:

- the analysis should be based on ex ante data
- the influence of the global factor or "global interest level" needs to be examined
- national US dollar rates should be used in preference to Eurodollar rates when the dollar rate is the global factor
- it should be noted that in recent years the US dollar rate has diminished in importance as a global factor in comparison with an aggregate global interest level
- the market's risk aversion should be taken into account
- an extension of the International Fisher Effect should be adopted, so that the price of exchange risk and political risk can also be included in the model
- a model of the market's formation of exchange rate expectations is necessary
- all the compensation which the market can claim for uncertainty in the rules of the market game should be included in the premium for political risk.

APPENDIX 3.1

Adjusting portfolios in an open economy

Disturbances of various kinds arouse in the investor a desire to adjust and modify his portfolio.[40] The adjustment can be made in two ways, and we can speak of a flow-based and a stock-based version. The two versions differ with respect to the immediate response to a disturbance in the variables which are to create equilibrium, and with respect to the subsequent adjustments until a state of acceptable stability is achieved. The differences vary according to the assumptions regarding exchange rate regime and the degree of capital mobility. In a closed economy there is no difference; the main differences in an open economy are shown in Table A3.1. The difference between the two versions in their response to disturbances lies in the initial changes of the market-clearing variables and in the subsequent paths of adjustment to the common steady state.

Table A3.1 Differences between the stock and flow versions as regards the short-run response to disturbances

	Fixed exchange rate	Flexible exchange rate
Perfect capital mobility	Any disturbance affecting the stock demand for money, directly or through changes in national income (output) at factor cost (Y) and the interest rate on government bonds (r), lead to an immediate exchange of bonds and money with foreigners according to the stock version, while it leads only to a gradual exchange of bonds and money with foreigners according to the flow version. In both versions saving leads to the gradual accumulation of both types of asset.	No difference
No capital mobility	According to the flow version any disturbance creating a trade deficit and an outflow of reserve currency produces a higher interest level and a lower output level than in the stock version. The reverse applies to disturbances which generate a trade surplus and an inflow of reserve currency.	No difference
Closed economy	No difference	

One conclusion which can be drawn from Table A3.1 is that the central bank must adjust its open market operations to the nature of asset demands. The differences and similarities in the table are based on the assumption that the central bank has an immediate stock demand for bonds in the stock version, and a long-run stock demand for bonds in the flow version, and that it implements the latter at the same rate as households implement their long-run demand for money. The presence of differences between the short-run responses in the two versions depends upon which assets, if any, are being exchanged internationally and upon the terms of the exchange.

Notes

1 Readers who are interested exclusively in the empirical side of the analysis and measurement process, can move straight on to Chapter 4.

2 I treat studies of capital flows and capital reflows as a single category.

3 See, for example, Hartman (1984) and Cumby and Mishkin (1984).

4 These authors adopted a monetary model based on stock adjustment in order to estimate the capital flows of the major OECD countries. The model was as follows:

$$\Delta K_t^i = \alpha_0 + \alpha_1 \Delta R^i + \alpha_2 \Delta V^i + \alpha_3 \Delta MI^i + \alpha_4 \Delta R^f + \alpha_5 \Delta TB^i + \varepsilon_t \qquad (3.1)$$

where

ΔK_t^i = net capital flow for country i in period t
R^i = a set of current and lagged interest rates in country i
V^i = current and lagged income velocity of money (GNP/money stock) in country i
MI^i = indicator of monetary tightness in country i (e.g. Jaffee and Modigliani 1969; index for credit rationing)
R^f = a vector of foreign interest rates
TB^i = country i's trade balance
ε_t = error term

5 The greatest number of quarters considered in the model in terms of lagged effects is six. Velocity (except for Canada) and monetary tightness such as rationing, did not prove to be significant in any country.

6 The cost of forward cover was also introduced as an alternative explanatory variable, and in the case of England proved to be highly significant as an explanation of capital movements in and out of the country.

7 If the government tightens up its monetary policy, the domestic interest rate rises and foreign exchange flows into the country. In order to avoid an increase in the exchange rate, the central bank changes the currency into Swedish kronor. This means that the money stock increases and the interest rate falls. Thus the monetary tightness is counteracted by the inflow of foreign currency; and this circumstance is known as monetary leakage (Dornbusch 1980). Under perfect direct integration this leakage is 100 per cent, i.e. 1.0.

8 Lybeck (1975) shows an offset coefficient of 0.45.

9 Åkerholm and Tarkka (1987) analyse the period 1974:1–1985:4.

[10] This does not include risk premiums and lagged transmission effects.

[11] See previous footnote.

[12] It has become common to regard the absence of deviations from interest rate parity as a sign of *perfect capital mobility.* Similarly the absence of deviations from the International Fisher Effect is regarded as a sign of *perfect substitutability.*

[13] In a study of the integration of the Swedish financial market it is not possible to circumvent the difficulty in this way, because of the lack of long enough series of historical data for a formal Eurorate for the krona.

[14] See, for example, Grubel (1968), Grubel and Fadner (1971), Levy and Sarnat (1970), Solnik (1973), Adler and Dumas (1975) and Grauer, Litzenberger and Stehle (1976).

[15] Unbiasedness means that the mathematical expectation of an estimator is equal to the parameter. At a repeated number of estimations with a particular estimator, the average of the estimates will be the same as the "true" value, i.e. the parameter. In the analysis of the International Fisher Effect unbiasedness means that the average value of all deviations can be expected to be zero. Given unbiasedness there will thus be no *systematic* deviations.

[16] The presence of a risk premium means that the markets are not perfectly totally financially integrated. Nor are they perfectly indirectly financially integrated. On the other hand they may still be perfectly directly financially integrated.

[17] Meese and Rogoff (1986) use co-integration analysis. They explore the relationship between real interest rate differentials and real exchange rates by testing to see whether the two series can be represented as a co-integrated process (see Granger 1983). The evidence they find suggests that there is no common influence inducing non-stationarity in both real interest rate differentials and real exchange rates.

[18] The ideas underlying CAPM have been described in Chapter 2 and its appendix.

[19] Roll and Solnik hypothesized that interest rates should, over and above the expected exchange rate change, contain a term expressing the covariance between the exchange rate in the analysis and the exchange rates in all other countries, or – as they put it – "plus a term depending on exchange risk covariances".

[20] Lybeck (1975) tests differences between nominal interest rates and shows that during the period 1957–72 Swedish interest rates followed the foreign rates. The relationship was far from complete, however.

[21] The analysis concerns bilateral interest comparisons.

[22] For a link between the macroeconomic risks and the market actors' investment decisions, see, for example, Oxelheim and Wihlborg (1987).

[23] The arbitrage interval has been discussed in Appendix 2.6.

[24] See Sharpe (1964), Lintner (1965), and Mossin (1966), or the brief presentation in Chapter 2 in the present book.

[25] According to Pippenger (1978) many of the above-mentioned studies fail to differentiate between interrelated short-term and long-term characteristics of the forward premium and the interest differential respectively. Pippenger comes to the remarkable conclusion that the supply elasticity for arbitrage capital increases from almost zero in the short run to infinity in the long run. There is thus a simultaneity here between flow and interest differential which makes the placing of these studies in the categories listed above rather arbitrary.

[26] The analysis was performed on data from the beginning of 1981 to the middle of February 1982, a total of 284 observations. Browne motivates his choice of period by the fact that before 1981 data can be disturbed by central bank interventions, which in turn disturb the way the market forces maintain interest rate parity.

[27] The member countries of the Group Ten and Switzerland.

[28] Herring and Marston (1977) assume a first-degree polynom; Hendershott (1967) and Kwack (1971) assume partial adjustment models with geometric decay patterns etc.

[29] Volker looks at the interest rates for the Eurodollar and for investments on financial markets in the United States, West Germany, France, Great Britain, Canada, Switzerland and the Netherlands, and examines how alternative measures of changes in the global rate (here the Eurodollar rate and the US rate) are reflected in domestic interest rates.

[30] The absence of any significant lagged effect on the Eurodollar rate from the US rate agrees with Argy and Hodjera (1973) but conflicts with the structure in Hendershott (1967) and Kwack (1971).

[31] A technique often used in analysing the structure in time-lagged interest changes is Granger's test of causality, which has often proved useful in other financial areas as well (Granger 1968). See, for example, Caves and Feige (1980), Feige and Pearce (1979) or Sargent (1978). Zellner (1979) analyses limitations of this test.

[32] Using the variant of the Granger-Sim causality test that has been discussed, for example, by Sargent (1978).

[33] Hartman finds the significance of his results surprising, in view of the fact that the difference in interest rates on these markets leads to arbitrage movements within the space of hours rather than the days or weeks required for a pattern to become clear. He also shows that the relationship between the expected week-to-week changes in the Eurodollar and the domestic interest rate respectively, is only weakly correlated. However, it is sufficiently strong to cause difficulties, according to Hartman, when it is a case of deciding which part of the variation in domestic rates can be traced to foreign events.

[34] See Granger (1968) and Caves and Feige (1980).

[35] Their data consisted of Eurosterling and Eurodollar rates, and domestic interest rates for these currencies. Their conclusions were based on the existence of numerous examples of one-way effects from the domestic markets to their respective Euromarkets, while there was never any indication of such effects in the other direction.

[36] See e.g. Breeden (1979) and Stultz (1981).

[37] The other three countries were Japan, Singapore and the United States.

[38] The study was based on daily prices and dividend data. A market-value-weighted world index was constructed from 10 national indexes. All national indexes and security returns were studied with regression analysis against the world index return. The contribution of the global factor to the percentage variation was calculated, as well as the systematic international risk on individual shares. The relationship was then calculated between international risk and return.

[39] For Sweden (1966-71) Solnick found that 45 per cent of the variance in price on a share can be explained by national factors and 18 per cent by international factors.

[40] See, for example, Tobin (1958) and Markowitz (1959).

CHAPTER 4

Characteristic Features of the Financial Market in a Small Open Economy – the Case of Sweden

4.1 Introduction

In this chapter I describe conditions and markets in the country to be used in our examples, namely Sweden, in order to provide the reader with the background and insights necessary to a better understanding of the subsequent empirical analysis of the integration of the financial market in a small open economy. I will thus highlight the institutional and structural changes which have taken place during the studied period 1974-84. In some cases I will also mention changes outside this period, if they appear to be closely linked to what has happened within it.

Sweden's financial system has been undergoing a number of radical changes in recent decades. A functioning money market has evolved and new securities have become available. All this has contributed to a change in the interest structure. At the same time there have also been successive changes in the interest and exchange control regulations. Sweden's international dependence as a borrower has been growing ever since the middle of the 1970s, due to substantial imbalances in the country's current account. In this chapter we will thus be looking at ways in which characteristic aspects of the Swedish financial market have been changing. Various features of the market with implications for the level of direct financial integration will be discussed below, while interest rates will be analysed in the next chapter.

Section 4.2 introduces the actors on the Swedish financial markets. Section 4.3 examines the occurrence and significance of various administrative control mechanisms. Section 4.4 is concerned with the efficiency and cost of the Swedish exchange control regulations. Primary data on the largest Swedish multinational groups and their attitude to exchange controls will also be presented in this section.

In Section 4.5 we will look at fluctuations in exchange rates in a Swedish perspective. This section is important to our interpretation of the market's exchange rate expectations and its possible aversion to exchange risk. An interesting question in connection with the formation of expectations on the market is: how important are the exchange rate arrangements? The answer to this and other related issues will be explored in this section with the help of primary data about how companies generate their exchange rate forecasts. This section provides an empirical basis for specifying the market actors' learning function.

Section 4.6 contains measurement problems specific to the analysis of Sweden's financial markets. Most of the problems are concerned with measuring non-government capital flows over the national borders.

4.2 Actors on the Swedish financial market

It is assumed that a functioning financial market in a closed economy apportions the savings in the country in such a way that they will be used to the best economic effect. It is also assumed that the market apportions risk-bearing in the economy, so that every actor can carry the amount of risk he chooses. As financial integration increases, the expression "best economic effect" acquires a global dimension. However, different types of controls can make it difficult for the market forces to find the "best" effect.

In Sweden controls of various kinds were in force during the period under investigation, and in so far as they were effective the country's financial markets were unable to function altogether as described above. The actors on these markets were prevented to a greater or lesser extent from using the particular market to achieve a satisfactory trade-off – such as the free market forces permit – between risk and return. In July 1989, the exchange controls were abolished and most foreign transactions were allowed. However, there are still restrictions on how such transactions should be conducted. With few exceptions it is obligatory, for purposes of statistical registration and tax control, to use a Swedish bank with a currency licence. But let us see what opportunities were available to various categories of actors during the period under investigation.

4.2.1 Many actors hampered by controls

The actors on Sweden's financial markets are the Swedish central bank (the Riksbank), the National Debt Office, the municipalities, the commercial banks (both Swedish and foreign), the cooperative banks, the savings banks, the finance companies, brokerage firms, industrial companies, trading companies (Swedish and foreign) and households.

The *central bank* seeks to influence the markets via the general and selective credit policy instruments at its disposal. Among the general instruments are changes in the discount rate and penalty rate, open market operations and cash requirements. By these means the central bank can influence the economy by controlling both the price (the interest rate) and the amount of credit available. Its selective credit policy includes such instruments as interest rate controls, issuing controls, investment requirements, lending regulations and cash ratios. However, these selective means have been used very much less in recent years. All that remained at the end of the period under investigation were the cash requirements imposed on the banks, the gross investment requirement aimed at the insurance companies and pension funds, the gross investment requirements imposed on the banks with regard to housing bonds, and the regulation of insurance company interest rates on index loans. The dates when the various monetary policy restrictions were abolished are given in Appendix 4.1.

The central bank also operates on the spot market and the forward market for foreign exchange by intervening to protect a parity level for the Swedish krona. Until 1985 the central bank imposed a secret interval or band[1] within which deviations from current parity levels were tolerated. The bank changed the interval in 1985, at the same time proclaiming openly that it would not tolerate deviations from the parity level[2] greater than ± 1.5. In Section 4.3 we will return to the question of the central bank's opportunities for controlling interest rates.

The *National Debt Office* raises loans to finance the national budget and to administer the national debt. The methods for financing the national loan requirement have varied a great deal from year to year (see Table 4.1). Interest rates and the money supply are both affected by the Debt Office's choice of method for government borrowing. There has thus been a lot of discussion recently about the need to coordinate national debt policy and credit policy. The Debt Office influences the liquidity supply on the market by regularly issuing treasury discount notes and other government securities, or by taking up loans abroad.

Previously the central bank and the Debt Office together determined the issuance rates, which were then regarded by the market as an expression of the central bank's interest rate policy. However, after 1982 a change took place and at the end of the period under investigation the market was determining the issuance rates on treasury discount notes and government bonds by way of a tendering procedure. But the central bank still had the opportunity to influence the interest rate through its buying and selling operations on the second-hand market.

Policy as regards the foreign exchange flows[3] has varied a good deal over time. The directives that provide the basis for foreign borrowing have also varied. The period 1949–73 was characterized by tight exchange controls and small capital movements.

Table 4.1 **Financing the government borrowing requirement**
Distribution among lending sectors
Billion kronor

	Stock changes								Position
	1979	1980	1981	1982	1983	1984	1985	1986	1986-12-31
Central bank	14.5	-0.6	11.9	8.6	-14.6	28.6	2.9	27.6	103.3
Banks	3.0	17.5	25.7	-0.2	17.3	-6.0	-18.4	-19.9	51.2
Borrowing outside the banks	17.4	15.5	19.1	52.9	54.6	40.3	57.6	30.6	350.7
Insurance companies	3.6	3.8	4.8	10.2	11.7	10.7	2.6	-2.7	56.9
Pensions funds	5.0	6.5	8.2	8.3	10.4	7.1	5.4	-5.2	69.1
Households	5.9	7.9	4.0	5.8	9.2	14.5	18.7	27.4	114.1
Companies etc.	2.9	-2.7	2.1	28.6	23.3	8.0	30.9	11.1	110.6
Domestic financing	34.9	32.4	56.7	61.3	57.3	62.9	42.1	38.3	505.2
Foreign	9.1	22.0	7.5	17.6	19.7	0.4	11.3	-6.4	125.6
Total borrowing requirement	44.0	54.4	64.2	78.9	77.0	63.3	53.4	31.9	630.8
Realized exchange losses	0.0	0.0	1.8	2.6	6.1	11.1	8.0	3.6	
Budget deficit	44.0	54.4	66.0	81.5	83.1	74.4	61.4	35.5	

Source: Sveriges Riksbank

The capital movements which did occur were mainly commercial credits and the financing of direct investment abroad. The borrowing requirement proper was introduced in 1973/74. The point of the borrowing policy formulated in 1974 was that corporate foreign borrowing should help to cover deficits in the current account. Until 1977 the idea was that the government should not borrow abroad. Between 1977 and 1979 a policy evolved whereby the government should borrow so long as it did not borrow more than the corresponding deficit in the current account. In 1984 a new policy was adopted as regards foreign exchange flows, which should not henceforth be negative. If there is a deficit in the current account, it is to be financed by private foreign borrowing.

The *municipalities* have operated on various markets mainly as borrowers. Many municipalities have borrowed abroad and thus indirectly affected the conditions on the Swedish markets. Some of these municipalities have acquired a reputation for innovative thinking in their foreign borrowing. On Sweden's financial markets the importance of the municipal treasurer's office is often undervalued.

As a group the *commercial banks, the cooperative banks, the savings banks, the financial institutions, the commission agents and brokers* mediate market contacts for other actor categories such as companies and households. Within this group there are two types of transaction, those between banks and those between banks and customers. As a result of inter-bank trade this group of actors can adopt positions of its own, and can thus exert an influence on the market over and above the effect of its bank-customer transactions.

The regulation of borrowing and lending interest rates and the volumes of credit previously limited the scope of the Swedish banks substantially. As we have seen, little of this credit control system remained at the end of the period under investigation. More problematic have been the exchange controls, which have reduced the banks' opportunities for operating on international markets and have thus indirectly affected Swedish market conditions. During the period of investigation the banks were not normally allowed to give credit to foreign borrowers who had no connection with Sweden.

The exchange controls did even more to reduce the possibility of *foreign banks* operating on Swedish markets, by acquiring Swedish government bonds for example. A change took place in 1986 when foreign banks were in fact able to open subsidiaries in Sweden, but their opportunities for doing business with Swedish companies were circumscribed compared with those of the wholly Swedish banks. The following are some of the restrictions which they still had to face:

- only a *Swedish* bank could convert currency into Swedish kronor and engage in possible forward hedging
- only a *Swedish* bank could lend in Swedish kronor
- only a *Swedish* bank could transfer money to a customer as payment for a debt or deposit in interest-bearing accounts in Swedish kronor.

At the end of 1986 the foreign banks accounted for 8.5 per cent of the trade on the Swedish foreign exchange market.

During the 1980s *Swedish companies* enjoyed better opportunities for operating on financial markets. As a result of the introduction of new instruments, companies were able to issue capital direct from the market, without having to go via a bank as before. A tendency has emerged whereby only companies with dubious credit rating employ banks or financial institutions as credit agents.

In other respects, too, companies have been taking over traditional banking functions. Several large corporations such as Volvo, Alfa Laval, ABB and Swedish Match, have established some form of internal bank. Some of these companies also supply external services. The exchange controls have certainly helped to hasten this development, since the rules have forced companies to "lock up" the excess liquidity generated by the increase in growth margins that followed the devaluations in 1981 and 1982[4]. The implications of the exchange controls for the opportunities of Swedish companies to operate with optimal economic effect will be examined in greater detail in Section 4.4.

Traditionally *foreign companies* have had little opportunity to operate directly on financial markets in Sweden. However, a foreign investor had some opportunities for investing in his own country while also buying Swedish kronor on the forward market, thus creating an investment structure bearing the same return and the same risk as an investment in Swedish securities with a corresponding term. This construction presupposes interest rate parity and the absence of political risk.

The opportunities for *households* to operate on financial markets have been limited to choosing between consumption or saving[5] in various forms. During the period under investigation they have had no opportunities for financial arbitrage in any form. Similarly, households had extremely limited opportunities for buying shares on foreign stock exchanges, although by buying trust units they were able to find a desirable combination of risk and return as an alternative to the risk-free interest on their bank savings.

Since the abolition of the Swedish exchange controls foreign investors have acquired almost unlimited access to the Swedish capital market. Swedish actors have acquired access to foreign capital markets, and investors such as households who have traditionally had little opportunity to invest in foreign currencies, bonds or shares, can now do so. However, they have to put their deposits in the foreign currency into an account in a bank in Sweden authorized by currency licence.

4.2.2 The market actors and direct financial integration

It has become increasingly difficult in recent years to evaluate the importance to the market as a whole of any individual actor or group of actors, because of the many new instruments which have appeared and which are difficult to trace in the balance-sheets of companies or banks.[6] This difficulty is particularly noticeable when it comes to evaluating bank commitments and the size of the accompanying future liabilities.

Table 4.2 gives us some idea of the size and distribution of non-government capital transactions, and thus also tells us something of the relative position of the Swedish and foreign actors during a great part of the period under investigation. The foreign contribution to these capital transactions consists of long-term loans and the short-term financing of exports and imports to Swedish borrowers. In more recent years in the table, foreign actors have also been able to make portfolio investments by investing in

Table 4.2 Non-government capital transactions
Billion kronor, net

	1977	1978	1979	1980	1981	1982	1983	1984	1985	1986
Direct investments										
in Sweden	0.4	0.3	0.5	1.1	0.9	1.2	0.4	1.3	2.2	4.9
abroad	-3.3	-1.9	-2.6	-2.5	-4.3	-6.1	-8.1	-8.7	-10.4	-22.5
Long-term loans										
from abroad	11.3	4.5	0.9	3.0	9.8	11.5	2.0	9.0	9.1	23.9
to other countries	-2.3	-1.5	-1.2	-1.2	-4.0	-6.4	-4.0	-1.5	-0.5	-4.2
Short-term financing of exports and imports	-0.4	0.2	1.5	2.5	4.2	5.5	5.5	7.3	16.3	7.3
Trade credits	–	-1.9	0.7	-3.1	-1.9	-2.4	-9.0	-3.1	5.0	3.6
Residual items and other capital transactions	-0.5	3.3	-1.2	-3.2	1.8	0.8	6.8	-7.1	-8.6	-10.6
Total	5.2	3.0	-1.4	-3.4	7.4	5.2	-6.4	-2.8	13.1	2.4

Source: Sveriges Riksbank.

Swedish shares. Apart from loans, Swedish actors have also been able to invest in foreign shares by making use of switch-currencies. The export of Swedish shares has increased substantially since 1982, but so many of the shares have then been repatriated that the net export for the whole period 1982–86 remained at around SEK 15 billion.

The formal links between Swedish and foreign financial markets were limited. In practice, however, the exchange control regulations left plenty of scope for the exchange flows stemming from the actors' consideration of interest rates and risk. This applies to both short-term and long-term flows. It seems to me that the opportunities for legally circumventing the intentions of the exchange controls in short-term transactions were good, particularly for large multinational groups. But the opportunities were less good when it came to long-term capital transactions.

It is important that we should take account of the norms for the government's foreign borrowing in our analysis. For instance, it is easier for us to evaluate the level of autonomy by applying statistical measures if we know something of the government's intentions in this respect. When the central bank wants companies to borrow abroad, it accepts the credit policy consequences of a deficit in the current account in the shape of a domestic rise in interest rates, which stimulates borrowing abroad.

In the periods when companies have been responsible for foreign borrowing, there is reason to assume that the gap between Swedish and foreign interest rates corresponds at least to the actors' exchange rate expectations and their demand for risk compensation. Companies have greatly improved their opportunities for taking action here, with their large and (in 1974-84) growing volume of debts. This situation recalls many of the conditions described in Errunza and Losq (1985). According to these authors' results we could expect a super-risk premium on the Swedish interest rate – a premium which in my terminology can be called a premium for political risk.

The large Swedish corporations account for a growing share of the financial activity, both within Sweden and with other countries. They have to be regarded as the major group of actors on the Swedish financial markets. BIS (1985) has also noted that the large companies have become major actors on the global financial markets, and describes the growing number of financial transactions outside the banking system as a global phenomenon.[7]

The emergence of Swedish second-hand markets has paved the way for an interest rate more closely adjusted to the market, and gives us reason to expect a higher level of direct financial integration. In the next section we will look a little more closely at the mechanisms associated with interest-rate formation in Sweden.

4.3 Rates of interest and administrative control mechanisms

In this section I shall concentrate on the interest rates which are relevant to my analysis. As we have noted, these are the official discount rate, the rates for treasury discount notes and treasury bills, prime interest rates, the rates for government bonds and notes, and the rates for industrial bonds. In the course of my argument I shall also touch on the concepts of interest rates for certificates of deposit and penalty rates. Among other things this section will show how the central bank has tried to steer Swedish interest rates. I shall return in a later section to the question of how far the control can be seen as effective.

4.3.1 Market development and new interest-bearing securities

Developments in the Swedish financial system in the 1980s were accompanied by the introduction of new interest-bearing papers. In March 1980 the certificate of deposit was introduced, thus launching a series of novelties. In July 1982 the treasury discount notes appeared with a functioning second-hand market. With these instruments the

National Debt Office was addressing a new category of investors. Previously treasury bills had been aimed mainly at the banks. Companies occasionally invested in these papers, but the interest rate was often too low to attract them.[8] The introduction of certificates of deposit and treasury discount notes laid the foundations for a functioning money market in Sweden. The development of the outstanding sums in the respective instruments on the money market can be seen in Figure 4.1. By the end of 1985 the money market had grown to a size corresponding to 17 per cent of Sweden's GDP. A similar development began on the bond market in 1983, with the introduction of government notes. The auction procedure on the issuance of government notes was introduced in 1984. The interest on these papers is thus adjusted automatically to the yield requirements obtaining in the current market situation.

As a result of these developments many of the central bank's traditional instruments of monetary policy lost their effect.[9] Monetary policy acquired a new thrust, in which buying and selling in open market operations occupies a central role. Regulations and administrative controls of various kinds seemed to have lost much of their impact. However, at the end of the period of investigation, Sweden was going through a transitional stage, during which some controls remained and the central bank still believed that it could steer interest movements to some extent by administrative means.[10] The change in the level of this interest rate autonomy is the subject of my empirical analysis.

Since the mid-1980s open market operations – buying and selling treasury discount notes and government bonds – have become the most usual instruments adopted by the central bank. Variations in the penalty rate and the discount rate are second to these. Changes in the discount rate were used chiefly in a structural context, for example to mark a change of course in economic policy or in connection with more long-term adjustments to the international interest level. Since December 1985 the penalty rate has been replaced by the an "interest rate scale" for controlling the costs of the banks' borrowing from the central bank.

4.3.2 More open market operations

During 1950 market operations were replaced as an instrument of monetary policy by changes in administratively determined interest rates. The fact that the central bank returned to the use of direct market operations during the 1980s, must be considered in light of the evolving money market in the wake of the great budget deficit in Sweden and in light of the new capital market perspective. With the help of open market

Figure 4.1 Outstanding sums for different instruments on the Swedish money market 1980-85

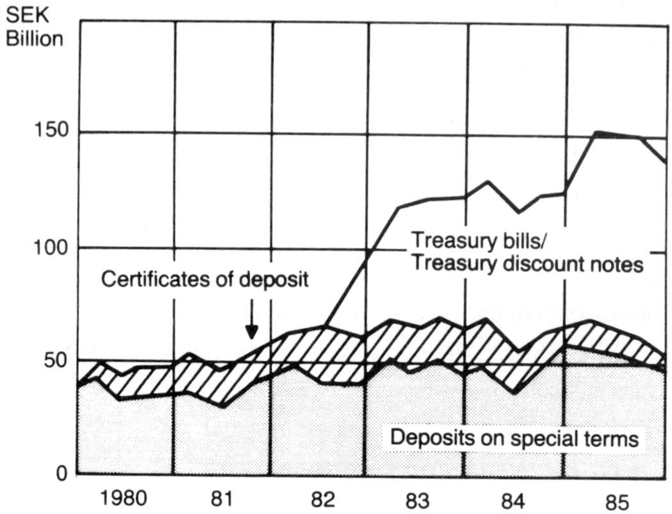

Sources: ETLA, IUI and others (1987).

operations the central bank hoped to influence the banks' cash liquidity and the general interest level. These operations were first employed by the central bank in their attempts to influence the effect of the penalty rate on money market rates. Even this way of controlling cash liquidity was much more flexible and easier to apply than the system of cash requirements. Since December 1985 the use of the interest rate scale for the banks' borrowing in the central bank has meant a further step in the same direction.

Thus, the interest rate at which the banks finance their day-to-day cash deficit[11] is of decisive importance to the interest level on the money and bond markets. Several factors affect the extent of the banks' borrowing in the central bank. The foreign exchange inflow and the government expenditure surplus reduce bank borrowing, while government borrowing on the domestic market works in the opposite direction. The central bank employs two different techniques to reduce or increase bank borrowing from the central bank:

- direct buying or selling of government securities
- repurchase agreements in government securities.

The central bank employs repurchase agreements mainly to parry the considerable fluctuations in cash liquidity that arise in the banking system. This type of transaction generally means that the central bank buys government securities from the banks and commissioning agents with an agreement about resale after a certain time, e.g. seven days. The interest conditions for these transactions can be established either by the central bank setting a particular rate or by an auction procedure.

As a result of the direct buying and selling of government securities combined with repurchase agreements, the central bank hopes to be able to influence more exactly the extent of bank borrowing from the central bank, and thus the interest rate on the money market. In this way it influences both the banks' and other borrowers' short-run financing costs, as well as corporate foreign exchange transactions. When the central bank makes a change in the short-term financing costs, this change – if it is regarded as permanent – tends to have an effect also on the interest rates for long-maturity financial assets.

Market operations are effective only in periods when the banking system is not borrowing at penalty rates from the central bank or investing surplus liquidity with the National Debt Office.

Up to a point the central bank's operations on the open market can be inferred from its weekly balance, although this is only reported as a net position. The central bank's purchases of government securities lowers the interest level, while its sales have the opposite effect. To have any effect the size of these operations should be equivalent to at least a few billion kronor. For comparison it should be noted that in the middle of 1986 the central bank had at its disposal domestic government securities to a sum just over SEK 80 billion.[12]

The general tendency during the 1980s was away from administratively determined interest rates. Since this tendency emerged at the beginning of the 1980s, the market forces have been increasingly allowed greater scope in interest formation and, as we have noted, controls tend increasingly to consist of the central bank countering these forces by engaging in operations on more markets. Over and above the new instruments that have appeared during the 1980s, we should also mention that since 1980 the parties on the market have been free to determine the interest rate on industrial bonds. The interest on new issues of industrial bonds (the comparative rate) is now determined by the banks as a result of interest rate movements on the second-hand market. Furthermore, apart from the so-called real interest loan, controls over the insurance companies' lending rates were abolished in 1982. Interest controls were imposed on bank lending rates between April 1980 and April 1983, after which they were replaced by a recommendation. Although the content of the recommendation recalled the former regulations, it offered a certain flexibility. In May 1985 even the recommendation was abandoned.

4.3.3 From discount rate/penalty rate to the interest rate scale

During the period of our investigation the discount rate/penalty rate[13] gradually lost its importance as an instrument in the control of interest rates. With the introduction of the interest rate scale, the discount rate/penalty rate also came to mean something different. Since my empirical study covers a period in which both the discount rate and the discount rate/penalty rate functioned as active instruments of control, there is justification in discussing them both. We can also look briefly at the interest rate scale.

For a long time the base for a bank's borrowing right in the central bank was the taxed equity of the bank in question. However, banks have different accounting strategies in their annual reports, which meant that a more competition-neutral base was required. Thus since 1 June 1986 a bank's taxed equity plus 50 per cent of its valuation reserves have represented the base for its borrowing right.

Influence exerted through the discount rate/penalty rate

The penalty rate in its former version had a steering effect on short-term investments, i.e. on money market rates. But if the penalty rate were to achieve this effect, the banks' borrowing in the central bank had to reach a level where the penalty rate applied, as it had to do whenever their cash liquidity was squeezed.

Thus the effects of the penalty rate on the market rates was determined by the level of liquidity in the system. In a very liquid market an increase in the penalty rate was expected to have little effect, at any rate to begin with. In a tight liquidity situation an increase in the penalty rate was expected to have a very powerful effect, which was more or less fully reflected in the market rates.

The central bank could affect the liquidity situation by buying or selling government securities on the money market, or by influencing issuances of government papers on the market. Thus, formally, the central bank exerted control by varying the discount rate and/or the penalty rate *in combination with* conducting market operations intended to affect liquidity.

The discount rate was not changed very often. When changes were made, the idea according to the central bank was to underline a more permanent change in the interest trend. Adjustments in the penalty rate in its former shape, on the other hand, were very much more frequent. See Table 4.3.

An increase in the penalty rate could be introduced, for example, following a large and long-lasting outflow of foreign exchange. Or a decrease could be expected if international short-term rates showed a clear downwards tendency without any promise of a reversal.

Table 4.3 Discount rate and penalty interest rate changes 1980–84

	Discount rate		Penalty rate
1980-01-18	10.0	1980-01-18	13.0
1981-01-21	12.0	1981-01-21	17.0
1981-10-15	11.0	1981-03-27	16.0
1982-03-12	10.0	1981-06-12	15.0
1983-01-21	9.0	1981-10-15	14.0
1983-04-08	8.5	1982-06-18	14.0
1983-06-29	9.5	1982-09-10	15.0
		1982-10-01	17.0
		1982-10-15	15.0
		1983-01-21	12.0
		1983-03-11	11.0
		1983-09-23	12.0
		1983-12-02	11.5
		1984-06-29	13.5

Effect of the penalty rate on different actors

The monitoring of interest rates by the central bank affects the banks' revenue side, which used to mean among other things that the discount rate and the penalty rate always had to be reasonably in tune with one another in the somewhat longer term. The penalty rate after all determined the cost of much of the banks' borrowing, at least when it was effective and when the banks' borrowing from the central bank exceeded a certain level. The banks' borrowing costs in the central bank increased, thus affecting the market rates for certificates of deposit and treasury discount notes and even the interest rates for deposits on special terms. The historical link between money market rates, the penalty rate and the discount rate is illustrated in Figure 4.2.
Although changes in the penalty rate affected many separate parts of the Swedish economy, the direct effects were most obvious in the banks. Indirectly these changes thus affected the interest rates for other market actors.

Let us look at the example of an "effective" increase in the penalty rate and its implications for the banks. When certificates of deposit were issued, the interest rate

Figure 4.2 Money market interest rates in Sweden and the central bank's discount rate 1978-85

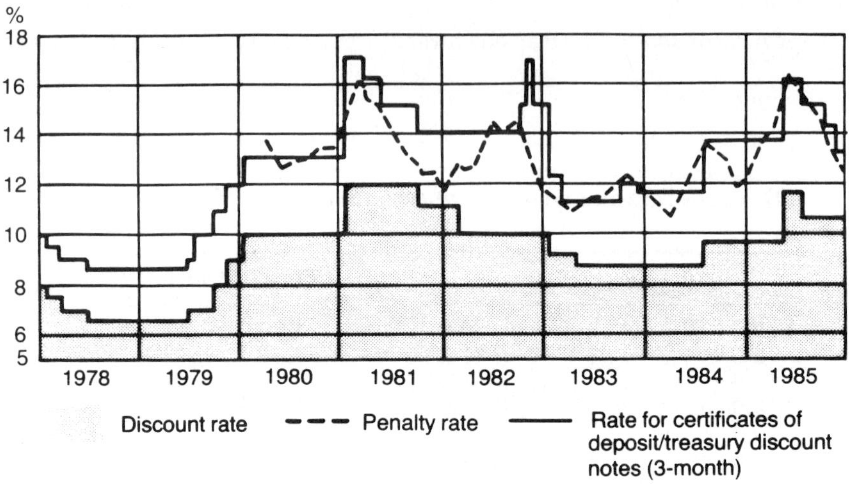

Source: Kredit- och valutamarknaden, Sveriges Riksbank (1985), p.18.

had to be increased to fit the new market situation which had been created as described above. This had a negative effect on the banks' interest margin (provided the discount rate was unchanged). Any other short-term refinancing that was related to the market interest rate was also charged to the banks' results. Banks which had a relatively large proportion of short-term refinancing were hit harder by increases in the penalty rate than banks which based their lending almost exclusively on the household sector (for example savings banks).

The effects of increases in the penalty rates were different for different categories of market actors. The obvious result was that an investor who had a large holding of treasury discount notes, for example, lost relatively more than a company or another institution which had invested its liquid assets in a way that was unaffected by movements in the penalty rate.

Companies that issued their own certificates would find after an adjustment in the penalty rate that their loan costs for new issues had changed. Furthermore such changes affected profitability in so far as they affected inventory costs in the company. Investing in short-term securities could be seen as an alternative to stockpiling. Application of the penalty rate in its old form was thus to a great extent an instrument of selective credit policy.

The interest rate scale

As we have noted the interest rate scale which determines the conditions for the banks' borrowing in the central bank was introduced during 1985. Since then a number of technical adjustments have been made. The principle is that the more the bank system borrows from the central bank, the higher the rate the banks will have to pay. The way the interest rate scale works is exemplified in Figure 4.3 which shows the scale after the adjustment introduced on 1 February 1988. At that date the number of steps in the scale was increased and the height of the steps was halved to one percentage point, while the depth of the steps was halved from about SEK 7.3 billion to about 3.7 billion. If the banks as a whole borrowed up to SEK 3.7 billion, they had to pay 7 per cent interest. If they borrowed between SEK 3.7 and 7.3 billion, they had to pay 8 per cent, etc.

4.3.4 Interest rate formation and direct financial integration

In the previous sections we have seen that central bank regulation of the Swedish

Figure 4.3 Interest rate scale for banks' borrowing from the central bank

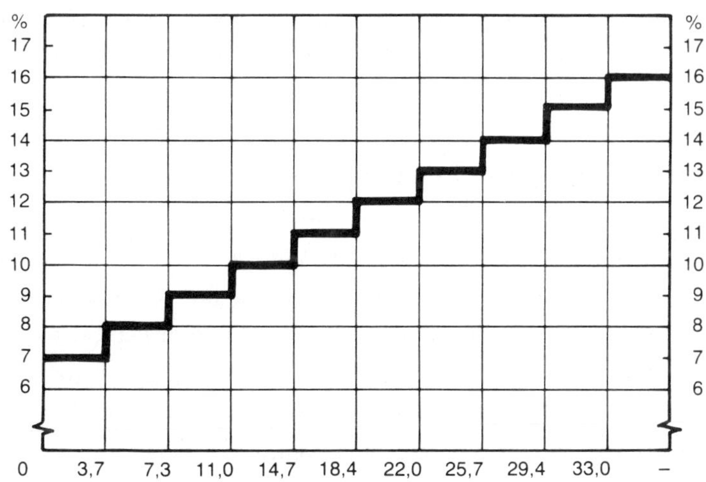

Source: Sveriges Riksbank

interest level changed fundamentally during the period under investigation. The shift away from predominantly administrative controls to operations on the open market can perhaps be interpreted as an acknowledgement of the growing influence of foreign interest movements on Swedish rates. In both types of control a particular interest level can be fixed, but market operations permit the central bank at least temporarily to neutralize disturbances from outside the country. The central bank's opportunities for insulating markets from foreign disturbances constitute the main subject of the analysis in Chapters 5–8. However, we should also note that any changes in Swedish interest rates now occur in small continual steps, unlike the bigger changes introduced at different times which were typical of the administrative interest rate system. Because of the nature of the change in interest formation, indications of a possible increase in direct financial integration in the form of new patterns in the transmission of foreign interest rate movements, may be more difficult to discover.

The new pattern of interest rate formation also had an effect on market expectations. The particular size of a foreign exchange flow no longer provides any clear-cut signal. Before market operations became so common, a foreign exchange outflow, for instance, meant that traders on the market could expect a tighter market and an increase in the interest rate.[14] Since it became known that the central bank exerted influence through its market operations, the picture is no longer so clear. For example, if the central bank is able to sterilize the foreign exchange flow, the interest rate remain constant.[15]

In a research perspective these developments raise the interesting question as to whether the choice of new ways of managing domestic interest rates was initiated by the fact that the market had learnt to circumvent the "old" controls, or whether the change was the expression of a more liberal attitude or an understanding of integration.

4.4 Swedish exchange controls and their effect on segmentation

In previous sections we found that the existence of a functioning system of exchange controls could be seen as a sign of financial disintegration. In order to measure the efficiency of the controls we can try to establish whether the volume of capital movements – given a certain interest differential – is different when exchange controls obtain and when they do not. The comparison is thus hypothetical and the difficulties involved in measuring effectiveness in this way are obvious. Another "softer" way of analysing effectiveness is to look at the way the controls were perceived by those who were subject to them. As a complement to my quantitative integration study I have chosen this second approach, and in this section we will look at the nature of the

Swedish exchange control regulations and how their effects were perceived by the large Swedish corporations during the period studied. We will get some idea of the "extra" costs engendered by the controls and of the restrictions on companies' when it comes to striking an appropriate trade-off between risk and return.

4.4.1 Nature and scope of the exchange controls

The Swedish exchange controls consisted of the central bank's application of the foreign exchange regulations based on the Foreign Exchange Act of 1939.

As a supplementary instrument in an effective monetary policy the exchange controls varied as internal and external imbalances arose. Their paramount purpose, however, was to provide the central bank with an opportunity for managing the export and import of capital, without having to make dramatic decreases or increases in the domestic interest rates. This insulation of the domestic credit market probably called for considerable sacrifices on the part of some companies, while others were favoured as more highly developed international capital markets evolved and internationally "expectation-led" short-term capital flows substantially increased. Many market actors had to bear extra risk, without compensation in the shape of a reasonable risk premium.

The three main purposes of the Swedish exchange controls

The role of the exchange controls in Swedish economic policy varied over the years, but for the 1970s and 1980s its purpose can be summarized under the three following headings:[16]

1. To compel the private sector to help to cover foreign borrowing – without dramatic interest effects on the domestic credit market – and to work for a stabilization of the private amount of debt in foreign currency.

2. To reduce private capital movements which could have given rise to systematic or random disturbances in the external value of the Swedish krona.

3. To provide arguments for investing in Sweden. One such argument concerned employment – albeit not explicitly expressed. It was based on the idea that the investing company should perceive the factor price in Sweden as more advantageous than the factor price plus the exchange uncertainty of a foreign investment.

Portfolio investment v. direct investment

OECD's capital liberalization code, in which a distinction is made between two types of investment – *direct investment* and *portfolio investment* – has been an important factor in shaping Sweden's exchange controls. Sweden's controls were based on OECD's definitions of these concepts. A direct investment, according to this definition, is an investment whose aim is to establish a permanent relationship between the investor and the object, particularly such a relationship as will create opportunities for exercising real influence over the object's operation. Investments which do not fit this description are to be classified as portfolio investments, and are assumed to have had a portfolio purpose. IMF adopts a somewhat broader definition of direct investment, including extended trade credits from a parent to a subsidiary company.

The Swedish exchange controls incorporated in the concept of *direct investment* such things as acquisition of shares, loans from parent to subsidiary companies, a parent company's guarantee of a subsidiary's loan, and self-financing over and above the normal consolidation requirement.

The fundamental principle underlying OECD's capital liberalization code is that a direct investment shall not be hampered on grounds of exchange policy or by other controls. Sweden undertook to adopt this code. Consequently what had to be monitored was the genuineness of the direct investments. However, from time to time Sweden invoked the emergency clauses included in the code. One of these implies that the code can be set aside when a country has balance of payments problems. Sweden's position between 1969 and 1981 was accordingly that for an investment to be permitted, it had to be favourable in a balance of payments context, and not just in light of its direct return. In 1969 a requirement was also introduced regarding foreign financing of direct investment. This requirement was abolished in 1986.

Many features of the exchange controls were also based on other emergency clauses in OECD's capital liberalization code. One of these clauses stated that a direct investment could be stopped if it was of an exclusively financial kind and could be intended to provide entry to a country's foreign exchange market. Another clause provided for the prohibition of direct investments aimed at circumventing the Swedish tax regulations. Yet another clause allowed for refusing direct investments which might have serious effects on the national interest. This clause has been incorporated in § 2a in the Swedish Foreign Exchange Act, where it is related to industrial and employment policy considerations.

On certain points Sweden recorded reservations from the freedom which the code allows its member countries, particularly as regards *portfolio investments.* Thus international sanction was obtained for the basic Swedish rule against this type of capital transaction.

Obviously it was not always easy to distinguish between direct investment and portfolio investment; the boundaries could be blurred both as regards intended influence and the changing nature of the investment over time. A direct investment could not be made abroad without the permission of the central bank because its "genuineness" had to be reviewed. The reasons for a possible refusal had to be given and reference made to the capital liberalization code.

The Höganäs provisions

A similar problem could arise in connection with transactions that do not take place. Perhaps profits have not been repatriated, with the result that a subsidiary enjoys the same kind of financial growth as if it had received capital from the parent company. Transactions of this kind, which really mean that a direct investment changes into a portfolio investment, were regulated by the 1949 *Höganäs provisions.* Among other things it was stipulated that without the permission of the central bank the investing company was not allowed to build up funds from profits in the foreign company beyond the level that the operations, as reported to the central bank, would motivate. Investments in the Nordic countries and developing countries were exempt from this requirement.

In the foreign exchange situation that evolved after 1973 the limit for "normal" consolidation in foreign companies was likely to be so high that in the short term this stipulation had little meaning for the roughly 3,500 of the 7,000 Swedish subsidiaries which were affected by the Höganäs provisions as a whole. In the longer term, however, it had a certain importance in connection with checking on "genuineness".

Barriers to new organizational forms

The regulations also meant that the central bank could require a foreign subsidiary to be owned direct from Sweden. In this way some multinational groups were prevented from achieving the most favourable structure for their operations. A permit was needed to establish a holding company abroad – a form of organization which was often an important component in efficient risk management.

Exchange controls mainly a barrier to portfolio investments

The thrust of the exchange regulations can be summarized rather generally in the following terms:[17]

- Outgoing capital transactions resulting in portfolio investments were generally forbidden; the most important examples were the acquisition of foreign bonds and shares and bank deposits in foreign currencies in other countries.
- Outgoing and incoming direct investments were free but subject to a test of "genuineness"; in the case of outgoing investments there were financing conditions, and the Höganäs provisions applied.
- Trade-related transactions including the financing of loans were exempt from controls, provided the normal trading conditions were adhered to.
- Incoming portfolio investments in kronor were forbidden; in practice exceptions were allowed for the acquisition of Swedish stock- exchange-listed shares.
- Incoming portfolio investments in foreign currencies in the form of Swedish borrowing abroad were subject to liberal regulations; by and large this meant that the minimum term of the loan was two years.

4.4.2 How the multinational groups perceived the exchange controls

The efficiency of the exchange controls can be inferred from corporate attitudes towards them: how restrictive did they appear to the companies? If they completely spoiled a company's chances of acting to the best economic effect, they could cause costs to society as a result of lost investment opportunities on domestic or foreign markets. An exchange control can be regarded as a signal, expressing the government's desire to control the market, thus causing certain market actors to demand a premium for the uncertainty this means, i.e. a political risk premium.

In certain cases multinational groups perceived exchange controls as a barrier

In the study presented in Section 2.11 above I interviewed managers in the largest Swedish multinational groups regarding attitudes towards the exchange controls. Many of the questions raised during the interviews touched directly or indirectly on various institutional restrictions affecting the trade-off between risk and return and the opportunities for the corporations to choose their own trade-off. One general question concerned the perceived limitations on the management of exchange risk. It was worded as follows:

What factors are perceived as restricting exchange risk management in your Group (company)?

Respondents were encouraged to indicate the factors, internal and external, which they perceived as restrictive. They were also asked to evaluate the importance of the factors on a five-point scale, ranging from *very restrictive* to *insignificant.* This last category came into the picture mainly when respondents were asked to say something in conclusion about any alternatives which I had formulated in advance but which they had not mentioned themselves. My list included *Swedish institutional restrictions such as exchange controls.* This limitation was mentioned spontaneously by everyone, and the answers were as follows:

Very restrictive=	1	2	3	4	5	= Insignificant
No. companies	15	3	1	0	0	

Another of the nine sets of questions concerned the importance of various instruments of economic policy to corporate results and position. The question was in general terms and ran as follows:[18]

What experience and what expectations does your Group have of various measures of economic policy in Sweden?

The respondents began spontaneously to rank their experiences. When they had done this, I produced any alternatives on my list which the respondent or group of respondents had not mentioned. This procedure guaranteed that all those interviewed had to air their views on at least 20 alternatives. In one or two cases this "reminder" meant that the original ranking was somewhat revised.

The controls were effective in preventing the long-term export of private capital

The government's inhibiting of private long-term capital export was included by 18 of the 19 companies as a measure that had a negative effect on their company's results and value. This applied both to their experience in the period 1974-83/84 and to their expectation of future effects. In both dimensions – experience and expectations – the rankings were much the same. This can perhaps be taken to mean that the companies had failed to find compensatory measures to counteract the inoptimality in capital management which this measure generated. The inoptimality may thus refer to return on capital and to the effect on corporate exchange risk management. From their own experience the companies ranked government prevention of private long-term capital export as follows:

Ranking:	–1	–2	–3	–4	not mentioned
No. companies	5	4	7	2	1

Exchange controls perceived as restrictive in three important cases

In the section on institutional restrictions I asked the following question about the various elements in the overall exchange regulations:

> **How much do the following exchange control regulations in the form of limitations and rights affect your Group's opportunities for successful exchange risk management?**

The respondents were first asked to mention the most important regulation, and then to evaluate other regulations for their impact on corporate exchange risk management. The importance of the regulations was assessed on a five-point scale, ranging as before from *very restrictive* to *insignificant.* I again closed the interview by asking for an evaluation of any regulations on my own list which had not been mentioned.

The regulation which was spontaneously perceived as the most restrictive was *the requirement regarding foreign financing for direct investment abroad.* This restriction was mentioned as far the most important by 12 of the companies. Four companies mentioned as the most important restriction the fact that *loans in foreign currencies could only be forward covered for the last six months of the maturity.* Three companies mentioned as the most important restriction the fact that *loans could not be preamortized unless a new compensatory loan in foreign currency of the same size was taken up.*

From the discussion that accompanied each question it emerged that the volume of direct investments had been relatively small during the period 1974-83 in those companies that did not mention the requirement regarding foreign financing. This restriction was certainly perceived by these companies as very limiting, but because of the size of the loans already taken up the restrictions on these loans were regarded as an even more serious problem.

In the spontaneous listing of important restrictions many mentioned in very general terms the combined effects of several controls, as can be seen from the following statements:

> We find it very limiting, not to be able to create free flows for matching.
>
> We take a serious view of the limited opportunities for using foreign issues.
>
> The requirement regarding five-year loans for foreign borrowing proves much more expensive than short-term loans renewed over five years.
>
> The rejection of an application for permission to do business with foreign banks has put us in a very difficult position in connection with the tighter conditions on the Finnish credit market.

> The fact that we are not allowed to use SEK wherever we want to, costs us a lot.
>
> We find the regulations connected with the establishment of branches extremely complicated.
>
> The restriction on interest on foreign exchange accounts is troublesome; these accounts should function as special deposits.

Table 4.4 summarizes the overall corporate evaluation of the various restrictions involved in the exchange controls. The requirements that were perceived as the most restrictive are the three which are ranked highest, namely the requirement regarding foreign financing for direct investments, the limitation on the forward cover of financial loans, and the limited opportunities for amortizing foreign loans before maturity. The first and last of these were perceived as very restrictive by 12 companies. All three requirements are intimately related, in that they were all aimed at inhibiting private long-term capital export and at protecting the Swedish credit market. The prevention of a long-term market for the Eurokrona was thought to be important to the success of this aim.

Table 4.4 shows that the restrictions on medium and long–term transactions or transfers worried the companies most – an effect which probably accumulated in the course of the period studied. After all, in the short perspective the Höganäs provisions were to be interpreted so capaciously that they did not actually reduce a company's room for manœuvres very much. Moreover, their effect on short-term contracts was further neutralized by the fact that companies could indulge in non-regulated transactions such as leading and lagging payments, or in de facto regulated transactions such as short commercial credits.

At times when the Swedish krona has been under strong devaluation pressure, the expectation-led capital flows have been so great[19] that the regulation of other flows might seem pointless. The expectation-led capital flow immediately before the devaluations in 1977 was of the same order of magnitude as the total medium and long-term net borrowing for that year. Here we should also remember that only about half of all Swedish subsidiaries abroad were subject to the full Höganäs provisions; the rest were exempt, either because the companies were located in the Nordic countries or in a developing country or because they were established before 1949 when the provisions came into effect.

The corporate "cost" of the exchange controls

The questions listed in Table 4.4 concern perceived restrictions on corporate exchange risk management resulting from the exchange controls. Thus, the respondents had to think in terms of additional cost and opportunity cost. What action do I take? What action would I have taken if there were no exchange controls?[20] A cost-benefit analysis would be needed if we wanted to study the overall effects of the exchange controls. But this in turn would call for studies of elasticity and econometric calculations. However, a first step would simply be to make a list of the cost elements in a company which are generated by the exchange controls. The total extra cost can be subdivided as in Table 4.5.

One inevitable component in the indirect cost of the exchange controls is the time required for the necessary administrative processes.[21] The answers to many of the questions reported in Table 4.4 are widely dispersed. Take, for example *Permission from the central bank to provide guaranties to non-residents*. Those who ranked this requirement "2" on the scale, often emphasized the unavoidable extra cost, as the following comments show:

> This requirement is not all that restrictive, but it takes time.
> This doesn't bother us very much. It's just an administrative process.
> This requirement simply means a lot of paper work.

As regards the more uncertain element in the indirect cost, many respondents spoke of the uncertainty in dealings with the customer due to the delays caused by the provisions; these could sometimes be quite considerable. They referred to the business or investment opportunities they lost while they were busy with what they saw as meaningless paper work.

To quantify the various parts of the cost matrix in Table 4.5 would require a detailed investigation, which lies outside the immediately purpose of the present report. However, without being able to give exact figures, I suggest that the cost of being unable to achieve the best economic trade-off between risk and return by way of international diversification, was the most important factor on the cost side. Thus, the turbulence on the foreign exchange and capital markets probably had some effect on corporate investment behaviour, thus altering the social calculus after the middle of the 1970s.

Table 4.4 Multinationals' view of exchange controls

What is the impact of the following exchange control principles in the form of restrictions and rights, on your Group's opportunities for successful exchange risk management?

a. *Requirement regarding foreign financing of direct foreign investment, for example the acquisition of foreign subsidiaries*

Very restrictive =	1	2	3	4	5	= Insignificant
No. companies	12	4	2	0	1	

b. *Requirement regarding permission for loans in foreign currencies (in most cases)*

Very restrictive =	1	2	3	4	5	= Insignificant
No. companies	0	2	1	5	11	

c. *Requirement regarding permission to have an account in a foreign bank*

Very restrictive =	1	2	3	4	5	= Insignificant
No. companies	1	6	4	3	5	

d. *Requirement regarding repatriation of assets in foreign banks*

Very restrictive =	1	2	3	4	5	= Insignificant
No. companies	2	8	2	2	5	

e. *Requirement regarding permission to provide guaranties to non-residents*

Very restrictive =	1	2	3	4	5	= Insignificant
No. companies	0	6	5	4	4	

f. *Absence of opportunity to amortize loans before maturity, without having to take a new compensatory loan of the same size*

Very restrictive =	1	2	3	4	5	= Insignificant
No. companies	12	5	0	0	2	

g. *Restricted right to make advance payments on imports to Sweden (i.e. without the permission of the central bank)*

Very restrictive =	1	2	3	4	5	= Insignificant
No. companies	3	3	5	1	7	

h. *Requirement regarding permission for netting within a group*

Very restrictive =	1	2	3	4	5	= Insignificant
No. companies	0	2	4	1	12	

i. *Requirement regarding permission from the central bank with conditions regarding financing in foreign currencies for international trading, i.e. trading in large consignments of oil and grain, for example.*

Very restrictive =	1	2	3	4	5	= Insignificant
No. companies	0	0	0	2	17	

j. *The restrictions involved in being unable to cover loans in foreign currencies on the forward market except for the last six months of their maturity*

Very restrictive =	1	2	3	4	5	= Insignificant
No. companies	7	5	4	1	2	

k. *The right to multilateral cover, i.e. forward buying of foreign currencies against another foreign currency through Swedish foreign exchange banks*

Very important =	1	2	3	4	5	= Insignificant
No. companies	3	7	2	2	5	

l. *Another principle underlying exchange controls, namely the interest on foreign exchange accounts*[a]

Very restrictive =	1	2	3	4	5	= Insignificant
No. companies	0	4	2	0	0	

[a] This question was actually an "open" one, and six companies emphasized the low interest rate on foreign exchange accounts.

One of the items in another of the nine sets of questions concerned the uncertainty factors which were most likely to inhibit a planned international investment. These included uncertainty about being able to repatriate profits, uncertainty about exposure to exchange risk, and uncertain access to local capital. As regards the last two of these, it should be noted that even if a company succeeds in borrowing locally to match the asset acquired, there is still the problem of transaction exposure, i.e. of matching greatly varying flows of capital costs with the yield flows from a security or an investment. This can give rise to different types of investment behaviour which must be taken into account in analysing the net effect of the exchange controls.

The cost of the exchange controls – company v. country

What does not appear in Table 4.5 is the important opportunity cost which accrued to the country because the requirements of the exchange controls put companies in a

Table 4.5 **Additional cost to the company due to the requirements of the exchange controls**

	Certainty	Uncertainty
Direct	Cost of buying foreign exchange when another foreign exchange is already available. The transaction cost.	Cost associated with an exchange risk that has arisen, or that could not be covered, due to the exchange controls.
Indirect	The cost of extra work necessary to meet the requirements of the controls.	The cost of maintaining the customer's interest. The cost due to changes in the exchange rate level.

situation where they preferred to refrain from investment. This was certainly not an uncommon state of affairs during the period under investigation, since in an investment situation the regulations sometimes exposed the companies to exchange risk that they were unwilling to take. In answer to the question:

Has your Group abstained from any investments since 1974, because of the risk situation created by violently fluctuating exchange rates?

One company answered that this had often been the case. Seven companies replied that they had abstained from investment at some time during the period. The remaining eleven companies answered in the negative. In three of these cases, no such investment decision had been on the cards. The general impression from these interviews was that their experience of turbulent exchange rates was going to make the companies more likely to abstain from investing in the future, unless an abolition of the exchange controls provided them with the opportunity to find their own desired trade-off between risk and return.

The link between corporate investment behaviour and the "cost calculus" associated with the exchange controls is illustrated in Table 4.6.

After the abolition of the requirement regarding the foreign financing of direct investment abroad, the vertical line disappeared from the picture, as did the economic inoptimalities connected with the application of this provision.[22]

The immediate extra cost of the exchange controls was borne by the private sector. However, not inconsiderable opportunity costs must be considered in the total social calculus. These costs were of such a size as to call for the abolition of the exchange controls.

Table 4.6 Corporate investment behaviour and the cost calculus for the exchange controls

Investment category	Changed investment behaviour as a result of exchange controls			
	Abstain from investing	Transfer investment to Sweden	Invest with local borrowing	Invest with loans in a third currency
1. Production investment				
2. Production investment motivated by requirements of local authorities		*The exchange controls prescribe foreign financing*		
3. Production investment motivated by market requirements	Evaluation in terms of opportunity cost for both company and country		Evaluation in terms of additional cost to the company. Direct capital costs and matching opportunities are taken into acount	
4. Investment in research and development				
5. Investment in marketing companies				
6. Investement in companies with financial operations				
7. Investment in holding companies or equivalent		*The exchange controls forbid this form of foreign investment, with certain exceptions*		
8. Investment in stockpiling	Evaluation in terms of opportunity cost for company and country; also in terms of additional cost regarding the companies' financial part		Evaluation in terms of opportunity cost for company and country; also in terms of additional cost as regards the companies' financial part	
9. Investment in real estate				
10. Investment in securities or equivalent				
11. Other investments of a portfolio character				

4.4.3 Exchange controls and direct financial integration

The attitude of these companies to the exchange controls confirms the view that during the period of the study the regulations as a whole had a disintegrative effect. This disintegration gave rise to inefficiencies in the form of transaction costs, sometimes in the shape of a tax. In certain cases, too, the controls directly prevented the entry of particular market actors on to foreign markets. There is considerable evidence that the disintegration was stronger on the bond and stock market than on the money market. However, the difference between the markets diminished as the Swedish credit market became increasingly securitized.

The companies appear to have had a loan share – usually foreign loans – which exceeded the desirable level in the balance sheet.[23] It can therefore be presumed that companies were demanding an increasingly high risk premium for further loans.

This section has provided examples of a number of cost items which are not normally included in the cost of individual transactions, but which must be considered in a study of financial integration. The restrictions which the exchange controls imposed on corporate opportunities for acting to the best economic effect also led to corporate demands for compensation, i.e. a premium for political risk. The managers in the interview study stated that even if they were seldom denied permission when they applied for it, the mere *existence* of the institutional framework according to which they were forced to apply signalled uncertainty about the outcome of their next application. Thus they used to charge a premium, e.g. for repatriating their capital to Sweden and investing it within sphere of influence of the Swedish government and the central bank.

When it comes to differences between long-term and short-term markets and the demand for a premium for political risk, the results of my interview study agree with the following view as expressed in an official government report (SOU 1985:52, p. 267).

> Interest policy can no longer be aimed primarily at internal stabilization goals. The Swedish short-term interest rate is fundamentally dependent on foreign rates; the aim is to achieve a relationship with the international rates such that destabilizing foreign exchange flows are avoided or limited. In the present situation this means that the Swedish short-term interest level must be higher than the international level. In the case of the long-term rate, the exchange controls allow for greater autonomy, although this has been limited by the long-term financial borrowing which was initiated in 1974 and which linked the Swedish market to the international market. (Our translation)

The continual albeit slow liberalization of the Swedish exchange controls which was taking place during period of the study, should be reflected in indicators of greater direct financial integration. In Chapters 5–8 we shall be looking at the evidence of this supposition in quantitative terms.

4.5 The Swedish krona – historical exchange rate patterns and the formation of expectations on the market

The gap between the fundamental variables which we found to be underlying exchange rate movements (Section 2.4), gradually diminished during the 1980s. Nonetheless, the variability of the exchange rates increased dramatically. One reason for this seems to be the increasing world-wide deregulation of national financial markets. Increased financial activity also meant that trade transactions in goods and services came to represent a declining share of the total turnover of the global foreign exchange markets.[24]

Turnover on global foreign exchange markets has greatly increased

During the 1980s turnover on global foreign exchange markets more than doubled. A study made by the central banks in the United States, Great Britain and Japan shows that during 1986 the turnover in New York, London and Tokyo amounted to about 200 billion per day.[25] The total value of the non-gold reserves in the world's central banks amounted at the end of 1986 to USD 510 billion.[26] If we compare this figure with the figure for daily turnover we are left with the impression that the central banks have little chance of consistently intervening to monitor the foreign exchange market, without at the same time causing other problems such as inflation. If the exchange rate is to be protected, changes in interest rates will have to be used increasingly as the means for achieving this end.

The day-to-day turnover on the Swedish foreign exchange market also showed a substantial increase during the 1980s. The average turnover per bank day amounted to SEK 23 billion[27] during 1986. At the end of 1986 the Swedish foreign exchange reserves, excluding gold, was a little less than SEK 50 billion. On the Swedish foreign exchange market interbank transactions accounted for slightly over 80 per cent. In London and New York the corresponding figures were 88 and 87 per cent.

Imbalances on the Swedish forward market

In Sweden forward trading represented around 26 per cent of total turnover in 1986, as it also did in London. In New York forward trading in foreign exchange accounted for 35 per cent.

On the Swedish forward market the foreign exchange banks sold more foreign exchange than they bought on forward terms, with maturities up to about 6 months. For longer contracts the situation was reversed. This tendency, which has been apparent since the beginning of 1970, is due to the fact that export contracts are often longer than import contracts. Further, the exchange controls, when they still applied, only allowed forward cover for the last 6 months of the maturity of a loan.

Speculative bubbles in pricing

Developments on the global financial markets, with an increasing share of the turnover in the form av speculative trading, give rise to deviations from purchasing power parity. This situation is reinforced by the fact that more trading now takes place between banks, where decisions are based on short-term signals in historical series rather than on expected changes in fundamentals. The occurrence of speculative bubbles depends on the great faith that foreign exchange dealers place in "technicals".

Swedish companies believe in an efficient foreign exchange market

The attitude of the Swedish companies to the efficiency of the foreign exchange market is reflected in the answers to the following question.

What is the predominant view in your Group regarding the efficiency of the foreign exchange market?

	No. companies
The efficiency of the foreign exchange market is *strong*, i.e. the today spot rate reflects all available information including insider information	3
The efficiency of the foreign exchange market is *semi-strong*, i.e. the today spot rate reflects all official information	11
The efficiency of the foreign exchange market is *weak*, i.e. the deviation between the today spot rate and the future spot rate is independent of historical exchange rate movements	2
The foreign exchange market is *inefficient*	3

The standardized alternative answers are based on Fama (1970). The answers show that 16 out of 19 companies believed to some extent in the efficiency of the market. 11 companies believed that the rate reflects all the official information, while another 3 put it more strongly and said that even inside information is fully reflected in the rate.

4.5.1 Central bank management of the krona rate

The price of a currency is determined by supply and demand. According to IMF's constitution, a central bank can and should prevent day-to-day or week-to-week fluctuations. In order to succeed in this, the central bank decides on a parity which it then sets out to protect. It intervenes to moderate the fluctuations around this parity or equilibrium rate. This intervention consists of buying and selling the domestic currency on the spot and forward markets.

Central bank influence is increasing world-wide

Central banks have become increasingly eager to manage exchange rate developments as a growing proportion of foreign exchange transactions have come to be concerned with speculative transactions, while openness to international trade is increasing world-wide. In recent years economies all over the world have been experiencing increasing financial-market-generated deviations from purchasing parity, *while also* becoming increasingly vulnerable to these deviations.

Of the 151 countries which were members of IMF in 1987, the currencies of over a third are linked to another single currency (predominantly USD).[28] Sweden was at that time one of 28 countries whose currency was tied to a basket of other currencies.

Sweden changed its exchange rate arrangements in August 1977

The present exchange rate arrangements for the Swedish krona go back to August 1977. Before that date the Swedish krona belonged to the European currency snake. According to the basket arrangement the effective nominal exchange rate is fixed, although the rate in relation to each of the currencies in the basket can vary. The currencies included in the basket belong to the countries which account for at least 1 per cent of Sweden's total foreign trade. A further requirement for inclusion is that the currency should be quoted daily in Stockholm. Swedish exchange policy in relation to the basket means that by intervening on the foreign exchange market, the central bank maintains the foreign exchange index[29] close to a given value. The exchange rate index is described in Appendix 4.2.

There are many ways of choosing the weighting system for a foreign exchange index. In the long run and in a Swedish perspective, according to Franzén and Rosenberg (1983), the differences between the central bank index[30] and other foreign exchange indexes which can be estimated, are small. In fact they have been so small that any decisions about the timing and size of the devaluations in the currency basket system would probably have been no different if Swedish exchange rate policy had been based on one of the other theoretically possible indexes.

The basket arrangement has simplified corporate risk management

The arrangement of the European currency snake gave companies many opportunities to make profits. We can see how they reacted to the change in the basket arrangement in terms of risk management from their answers to the following statement.

Our Group has had more difficulty in managing risk under the present basket arrangement for the Swedish krona than it had when the krona belonged to the European currency snake.

Fully agree	**=**	**1**	**2**	**3**	**4**	**5**	**= Definitely disagree**
No. companies		0	5	3	8	3	

To judge from these answers companies have found their difficulties to be the same or slightly less as a result of the change. I take this as a possible indication that a fixed exchange premium would remain unchanged by a change in foreign exchange arrangements.

A positive corporate attitude to the basket arrangements can also be inferred from the answers to the following question:

How would your Group like the value of the Swedish krona to be managed in future, so as to simplify risk management?

	No. companies which ranked the alternative "1" (i.e. best alternative)
Clean floating	1
No parity is established, but the central bank tries to keep exchange rate fluctuations within given limits (managed floating)	0

The value of the krona is altered in small steps in relation to predetermined conditions (crawling peg)	1
The value of the krona is tied to a basket system along present lines	10
The value of the krona is tied to some other national currency[a]	3
The value of the krona is linked to some other international currency unit such as SDR, ECU, etc.	2
Association with EMS	2
Some other construction	0

[a] All three companies which ranked this alternative highest, wanted to see the Swedish krona tied to USD.

10 of 19 companies wanted the central bank to go on managing the value of the Swedish krona in a basket system of the present model.

4.5.2 Nominal and real fluctuations in the krona rate

The fluctuation pattern of a currency can be described in many ways: in nominal or real terms, according to long-term or short-term variations, to the number of days per year when a deviation has been greater than a certain value, etc.

Nominal exchange rate movements increased dramatically during the 1970s

Nominal exchange rate movements since the 1970s are described in Figure 4.4. As we shall see later, these are reflected after a time in the interest rate pattern. We see a tendency for the price of most currencies to increase in SEK.[31] The figure also shows a series of violent upsets after 1973. The devaluations of 1977, 1981 and 1982 can be seen with great clarity. What also emerges is the importance of the foreign exchange arrangements and of real disturbances. A good example of the importance of the foreign exchange arrangement is the unchanged SEK/DEM rate which appears in the figure, and which is the result of the Swedish krona being tied to the D-Mark from 1973 until August 1977. This was a trend that by no means reflected the development of fundamentals. The powerful decline in the rate for JPY during the second oil crisis can illustrate the importance of real disturbances.

Figure 4.4 Exchange rate index SEK/foreign currencies 1970-84
Nominal rates, quarterly data, end of period
Index 1969/70 =100

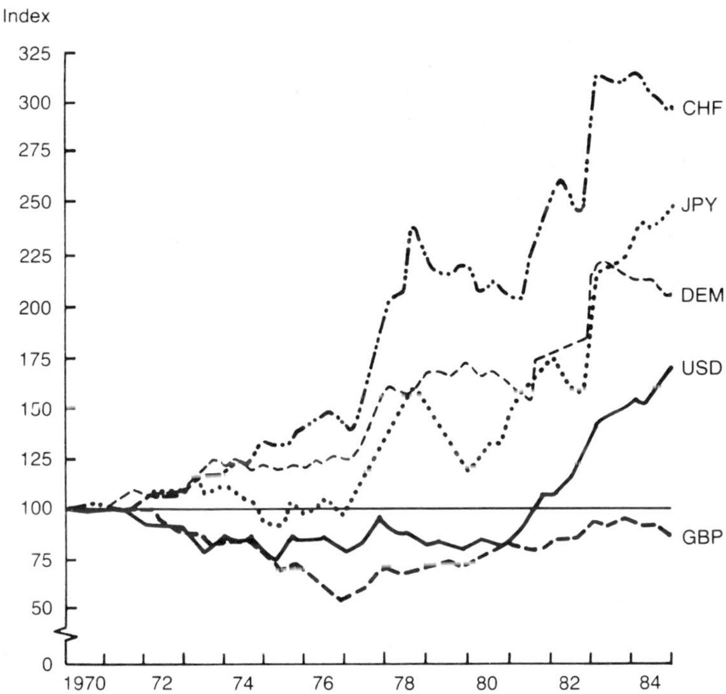

Weekly exchange rate fluctuations have increased

From Table 4.7 we can see the variation pattern on a weekly basis divided into different periods.

The standard deviation increased for all five currencies between 1974–76 and 1978–84. Not unexpectedly the most dramatic increase is in the SEK/DEM rate, even though the standard deviation for this rate is still the lowest of the currencies studied.

Exchange rates exhibit different probability patterns

Figure 4.5 illustrates relative frequencies for weekly exchange rate movements during the period 1974–84. The figure can be regarded as an expression of the probability distribution of weekly spot rate movements. The distance between the lines is 34 per cent for all currencies except FIM. The distributions turn out to be markedly different

Table 4.7 Mean ($\hat{\bar{s}}$) and standard deviation (σ) in weekly percentage change in the spot rate

	1974–84		1974–76		1978–84	
Currency	$\hat{\bar{s}}$	σ	$\hat{\bar{s}}$	σ	$\hat{\bar{s}}$	σ
GBP	0.12	1.41	-0.28	1.15	0.07	1.44
USD	0.11	1.38	-0.10	1.01	0.18	1.47
DEM	0.11	1.20	-0.03	0.45	0.09	1.37
CHF	0.18	1.66	0.12	1.03	0.13	1.87
JPY	0.15	1.59	-0.09	0.96	0.18	1.79
No. observations	546		155		339	

as regards both central value and dispersion as well as skewness and peakedness – an observation that is certainly taken into account in the corporate demand for premiums for exchange risk.[32] As we can see from Table 4.7 and Figure 4.5, the pattern gives us a basis for evaluating exchange risks, if we can assume that the fluctuations are unanticipated. In the weekly perspective this is a reasonable assumption, since according to Oxelheim (1985) weekly SEK exchange rate movements follow a random-walk model.

The pattern of real exchange rate movements depends on the degree of openness in an economy

The deviations from purchasing power parity give us an idea of the degree of over- or undervaluation of a currency. The degree of openness to international trade and the elasticity in a country's foreign trade, determine the durability of the deviation from parity. Transactions on the financial markets can then serve to reinforce the deviation. In recent years deviations have been noted which researchers find difficult to explain, and which have been dubbed speculative bubbles. Figure 4.6 shows the development of a purchasing power parity index for Sweden and some other small and relatively open economies. Figure 4.7 shows this development for some OECD countries with a relatively lower level of openness to international trade. Index 100 is the parity level.[33] Values over 100 indicate the extent of the overvaluation, while values under 100 refer to undervaluation. The choice of equilibrium point and index is important to the calculation of the deviations and can always be debated. Here I have used the wholesale price index.[34]

Figure 4.5 Weekly changes in the (spot) price in Swedish kronor of the most important currencies in the Swedish currency basket 1974-84
Percentage per week

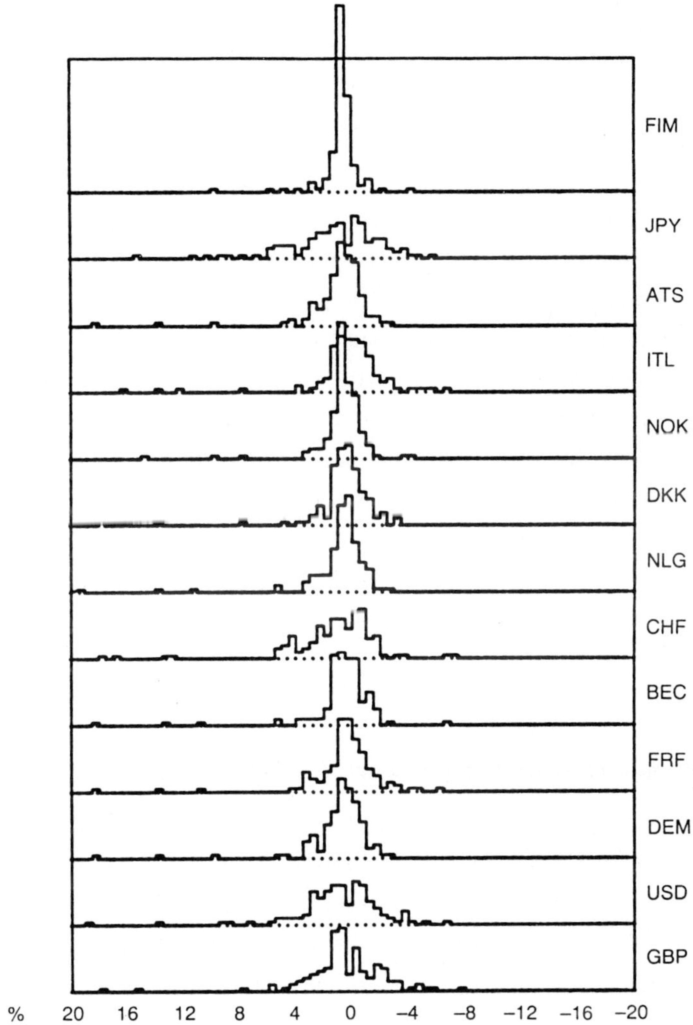

Note: Fat tails imply a more risky currency. On the left side of the figure we can see the effect of the devaluations of the Swedish krona for all currencies

Large and durable deviations from purchasing power parity for certain currencies

Figures 4.6 and 4.7 illustrate two situations. First, we can see that both the size and the durability of the deviations from purchasing power parity are different in the two figures.[35] In the small open economies, the deviations must be kept small and short-term.

Secondly, the figures illustrate the difference in the ability of central banks to keep control over movements in the value of a country's currency. In Figure 4.6 we see the trend for the USD real exchange rate. The picture reflects the general idea of a powerfully undervalued US dollar during the second part of the 1970s, and a correspondingly overvalued US dollar during the early 1980s. The real, effective rate rose by 50 per cent between the middle of 1980 and the beginning of 1985. The deviations since the beginning of the 1970s have been substantial and have lasted a long time.

Figure 4.7 shows the dramatic movements in the real exchange rate for the Swiss franc. The picture reflects the powerful shift in the real effective exchange rate for the Swiss franc in 1977–78, when it rose by over 30 per cent and became greatly overvalued in relation to the most important trade currencies for Switzerland. In a small, open and exchange-sensitive economy like the Swiss, such an overvaluation could not last. By temporarily introducing negative interest on deposits in domestic banks by non-residents, the demand for the Swiss franc for such transactions was reduced, and the deviation from parity eliminated.

The Swedish krona has been overvalued for long periods

The real effective krona rate shows a clear trend during the period 1974–82. In all cases successively increasing overvaluation has led to devaluation. However, between the September devaluation in 1981 and the October devaluation in 1982, the deviation did not have time to become very substantial. The 1982 devaluation changed the pattern, and left the Swedish krona undervalued by a little over 10 per cent.

Disintegrated goods markets resulted in a loss of market shares for Swedish exports

The overvaluation of the Swedish krona during the period January 1974 to August 1977 resulted in a substantially lower export share. During this period Swedish companies lost 15 per cent of their world market shares. The devaluations in 1977, when the August devaluation brought the Swedish krona down to its "equilibrium level", was reflected in weakly rising export shares. The deterioration in relative prices in the second quarter of 1979 following the second oil crisis was reflected in the loss of market shares in 1980. The devaluation in September 1981, which again brought the krona to equilibrium level, put a further check on share losses.

Figure 4.6 Real effective exchange rates - major OECD countries 1976-86
Index: average 1980-82 = 100[1]

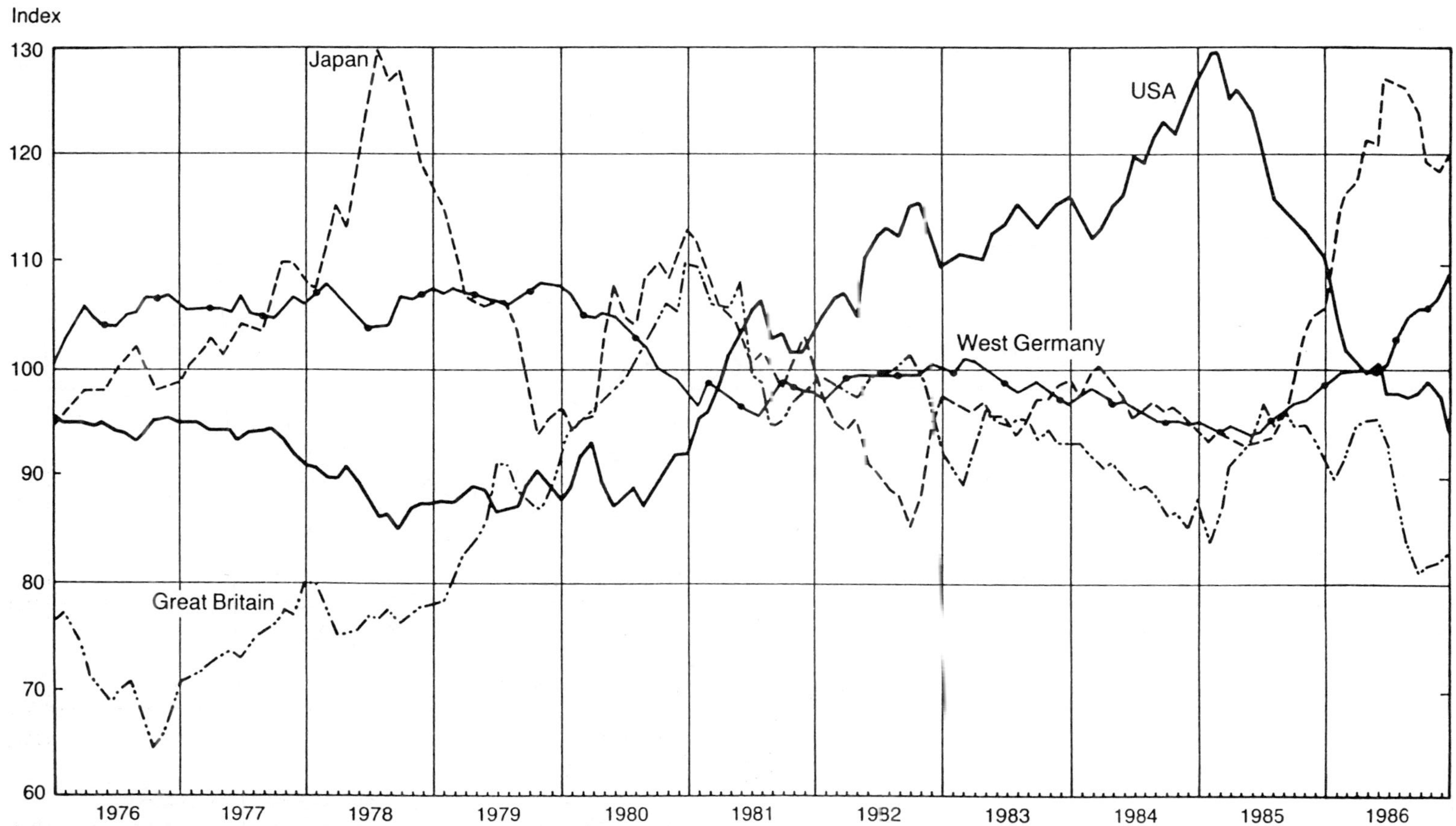

[1] Each index corresponds to the nominal effective exchange rate adjusted for differentials in the wholesale price index.

Figure 4.7 Real effective exchange rates - small and relatively open economies 1976-86
Index: average 1980-82 = 100[1]

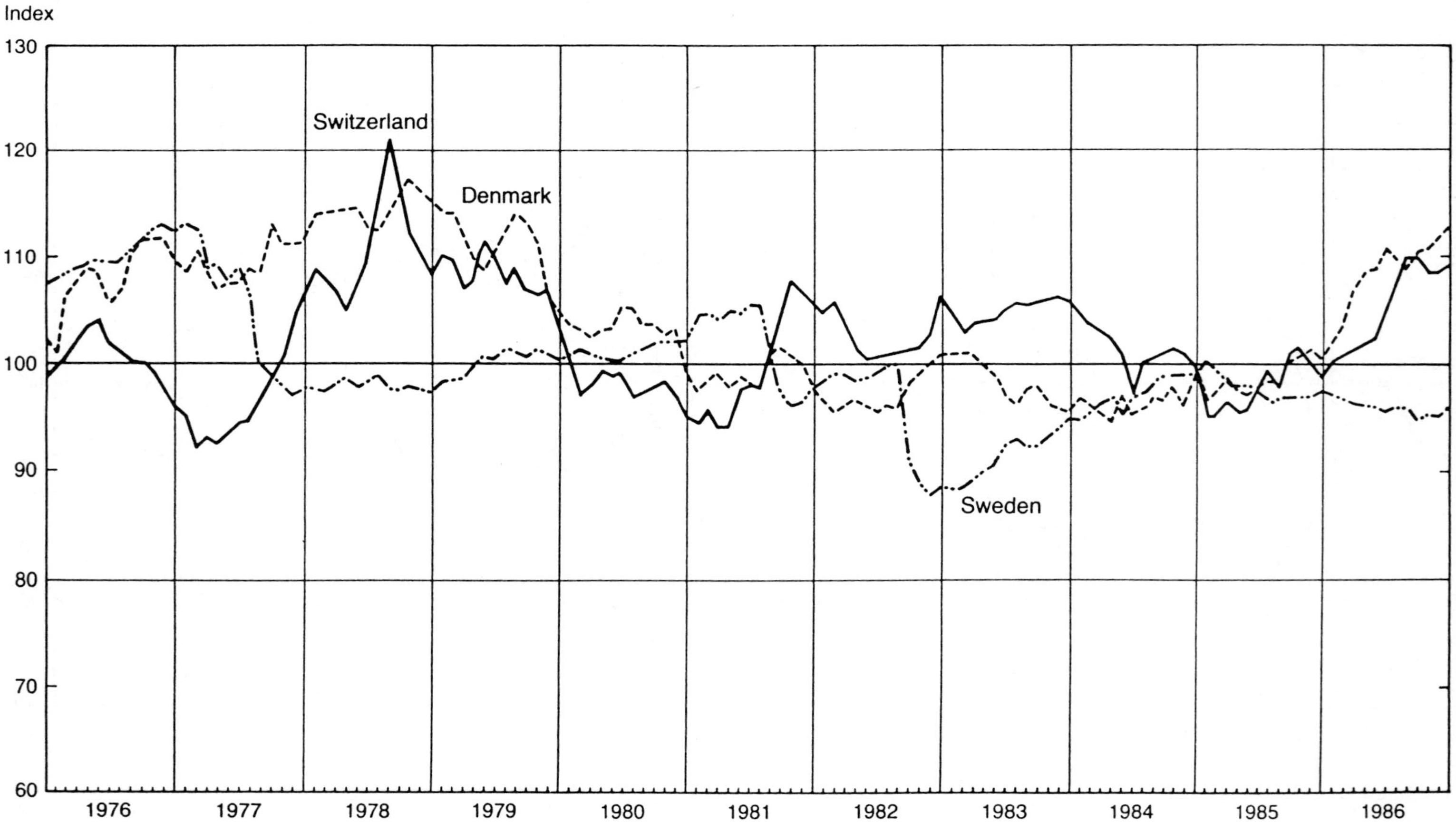

[1] Each index corresponds to the nominal effective exchange rate adjusted for differentials in the wholesale price index.

In an overall perspective the increase in market shares between 1977 and 1979 can be interpreted in various ways. One interpretation is that it did not seem possible to win back the shares so long as the Swedish krona was overvalued. When the krona was at its equilibrium level, volume shares[36] can be stabilized and, at best, increased. But the gain in market shares at the 1982 devaluation was fairly modest. There was certainly a gain in 1983, but no further gain in 1984, while 1985 saw a loss again.[37] The absence of gains in 1984–85 was partly due to the companies choosing higher gross margins in order to consolidate, rather than aiming for market share gains.[38]

The disintegration of the goods markets has not been reduced

The goods markets appear to have been as disintegrated as ever during the period of our investigation, which means that total financial integration cannot be expected to be perfect. If we want to find out anything about direct financial integration, we will have to study the risk and exchange-adjusted interest gap. A line of argument associated with the deviation from PPP should then be an important element in forming market expectations about exchange rate trends.

4.5.3 *How do Swedish multinationals form their exchange rate expectations?*

The interview study previously referred to included one set of questions regarding the way the Swedish market actors formed their expectations of future exchange rate movements. This shows that during the period under investigation no company in the study was using any kind of explicit forecasting model. Instead forecasts were generated on a basis of intuitive assessments unsupported by models.[39] However, at the back of his mind the decision-maker had some sort of macro-economic idea about the variable that was likely to be most important. The forecast of the exchange rate movement was then generated with the help of this variable. The forecaster sifted through the information available – usually from banks – and looked for the forecast which was based most closely on the variable that he set the greatest store by. The Swedish multinationals showed a certain lack of consensus concerning the most important determinants of the exchange rate movements. See Table 4.8.

As part of my investigation the president, or in some cases the senior vice-president, was asked to react to a number of statements, among other things about any change in their forecasting efforts or in the quality of their forecasts during the period under investigation. Only 2 of 18 companies put more effort into making exchange rate forecasts in 1984 than in 1974. One of these companies felt that the extra investment had improved its forecasts. All in all three presidents or senior vice-presidents felt that they had become better at making exchange rate forecasts since 1974.[40]

Table 4.8 Explanatory variables or indicators in generating exchange rate forecasts in Swedish multinational groups

What importance is ascribed to the following explanatory variables or indicators in generating exchange rate forecasts in your Group?

O = the mode, i.e. the most common answer

	Range of answers
a. *Current account* **Very important** = 1 2 ③ 4 5 = **Insignificant**	1–5
b. *Balance of trade* **Very important** = 1 2 ③ 4 5 = **Insignificant**	1–5
c. *Rate of inflation measured by consumer price index* **Very important** = ① 2 3 4 5 = **Insignificant**	1–4
d. *Rate of inflation measured by wholesale price or producer index* **Very important** = 1 ② 3 4 5 = **Insignificant**	1–5
e. *Foreign exchange reserves* **Very important** = 1 2 ③ 4 5 = **Insignificant**	1–5
f. *Government budget balance* **Very important** = 1 2 ③ 4 5 = **Insignificant**	1–5
g. *Money supply growth* **Very important** = 1 ② 3 4 5 = **Insignificant**	1–5
h. *Recent history in exchange rate movements* **Very important** = 1 ② 3 4 5 = **Insignificant**	1–5
i. *Country's energy import* **Very important** = 1 2 3 4 ⑤= **Insignificant**	2–5
j. *Relative unit labour cost* **Very important** = 1 2 3 ④ 5 = **Insignificant**	2–5
k. *Nominal interest level in relation to the rest of the world* **Very important** = 1 ② 3 4 5 = **Insignificant**	1–5
l. *Real interest level in relation to the rest of the world* **Very important** = 1 ② 3 4 5 = **Insignificant**	1–5
m. *Other indicators, i.e. the political situation* [a] **Very important** = ① 2 3 4 5 = **Insignificant**	

[a] This was an "open" question, and seven companies mentioned the political situation as a very important factor.

Table 4.9 Identification and ranking in US multinational groups of the most useful indicators of future exchange rate movements

Selected indicators of future exchange rate movements	Percentage of responding firms [a]				
	Ranking of indicators				
	Degree of usefulness			Important but not ranked	No response
	(1)	(2)	(3)		
Balance of payments					
on a basis of official reserves	8.4	16.8	15.8	11.2	47.7
on a basis of liquidity	7.5	23.4	18.7	4.7	45.8
Balance of trade	11.2	24.3	20.5	9.3	34.6
Rate of inflation (WPI)[b]	17.8	26.1	11.1	9.3	35.5
Rate of inflation (CPI)[c]	15.0	21.4	18.7	11.2	33.6
Gold reserves					
convertible incomes	0.9	2.8	27.1	3.7	65.4
Government budget deficit	0.0	8.4	34.6	5.6	51.4
Money supply growth	5.6	19.6	30.9	8.4	35.5
Recent history of exchange movements	5.6	10.3	32.6	8.4	43.0
Country's energy situation	0.0	0.9	23.4	4.7	71.0
General import trends	0.0	1.9	23.2	3.7	71.0
Other indicators[d]	18.7	7.5	8.4	9.3	56.1

[a] Based on 107 completed questionnaires.

[b] Measured by wholesale price index.

[c] Measured by consumer price index.

[d] Particularly interest rates, but also labour costs, international political developments, parallel rates of exchange (black-market rates), international indebtedness, trade links between countries.

Source: Jilling (1978).

It is significant that the companies set aside relatively little to spend on forecasting exchange rates. They seem to regard purchasing power parity as the "true" model, and are prepared to let experts – bank experts for example – do the calculations on this basis. This procedure of letting the "informed" calculate the model value corresponds to the idea behind the hypothesis of rational expectations discussed in Chapter 2.

Theory-building in the exchange rate field has developed a good deal during the period under investigation, as a result of which companies may have changed the expectation structure. Table 4.9 shows what were considered by US multinationals in the 1970s to be the most important indicators of an imminent change in the exchange rate. It is interesting to see that the interest rate is mentioned only in a footnote, whereas today it is reckoned to be one of the absolutely vital indicators[41] (see Table 4.8). However, according to our interview study, the forecasting procedure seems to have remained fairly intact in the Swedish multinationals concerned.

The multinational groups believe in purchasing power parity

The presidents in the interviewed companies were asked to react to the following statement about the purchasing power parity theorem.

The purchasing power parity theorem provides a satisfactory explanation of long-run exchange rate relationships, by linking relative inflation rates and exchange rates

Fully agree =	1	2	3	4	5	= Disagree entirely
No. companies	4	10	2	2	0	

Purchasing power parity thus seems well entrenched at top managements level. The chief executive in 14 companies out of 18 agreed in full or very nearly so.[42]

The chief executives did not trust the forward premium to give a correct picture, on an average, of the future exchange rate. This can be seen from their reactions to the following statement:

On an average the forward rate provides a correct picture of the exchange rate at the date of maturity

Fully agree =	1	2	3	4	5	= Disagree entirely
No. companies	0	3	2	8	5	

One explanation of this attitude seems to be that people do not trust the forward rate alone to provide an adequate forecast, unless it is supplemented by a "probable" correction of deviations from purchasing power parity.[43]

The answers in the interview study suggest that companies form their expectations about the exchange rate in a year's time or more, on a basis of a general consideration of purchasing power parity. In forming expectations about the exchange rate in the more immediate future, deviations from purchasing power parity that have already occurred are ascribed a probability, to be reversed later. This is then combined with the forecast provided by the forward rate.

Attitudes to the International Fisher Effect are polarized

The presidents or senior vice-presidents were also asked for their views on the International Fisher Effect , by reacting to the following statement:

Interest differentials on loans or investments with the same risk in different currencies balance any exchange rate movements that could be expected

Fully agree =	**1**	**2**	**3**	**4**	**5**	**= Disagree entirely**
No. companies	1	9	0	3	5	

Nobody involved was neutral. Ten agreed in full or with some hesitation that the International Fisher Effect holds, while eight rejected the relationship entirely or had some doubts about it.

4.5.4 *The relationship between the prices of different currencies in Swedish kronor*

A possibly relationship between the prices of different currencies expressed in SEK can be used for judging whether the market actors could adopt a *portfolio approach.* The linear relationship is positive for virtually all currencies during the period 1974–84. It was the major devaluations of 1977, 1981 and 1982 that paved the way for this overall positive correlation. If instead the relationship is measured against the currency basket, where these parity changes have been eliminated, quite a different correlation pattern is obtained. Tables 4.10 and 4.11 show correlation coefficients for periods with different currency arrangements. The difference in correlation pattern for the two arrangements obtaining during the period of the study is slight. Throughout the period there is a strongly negative relationship between the price in Swedish kronor for the EMS currencies and the US dollar. From Table 4.11 we can see that the correlation between the SEK/DEM rate and the SEK/USD rate is –0.82. Since the standard deviations for the relevant subperiod were about the same size for the two exchange rates (see Appendix 4.3), the value can be taken to mean that if the SEK/USD rate rises by one percentage point then the SEK/DEM rate will on an average fall by 0.82 percentage points.

The relationship between the SEK/DEM exchange rate and the SEK/ATS rate is a clear example of the impact of the exchange rate arrangements on the correlation. Table 4.11 shows the correlation between these two rates as 0.96, i.e. an almost perfect linearly positive relationship. The explanation of this strong relationship lies in the fact

Table 4.10 Correlation between the weekly percentage change, compared with the currency basket, in the spot price of different currencies expressed in SEK, 1974–76
Coefficients of correlation for the period 1974–76 based on 155 observations

Currency	GBP	USD	DEM	FRF	BEC	CHF	NLG	DKK	NOK	ITL	ATS	JPY	FIM
GBP	1.00	0.11	-0.56	-0.04	-0.40	-0.42	-0.51	-0.43	-0.56	-0.06	-0.54	0.04	-0.29
USD		1.00	-0.66	-0.29	-0.59	-0.49	-0.62	-0.48	-0.54	-0.06	-0.58	0.33	-0.41
DEM			1.00	-0.06	0.54	0.51	0.52	0.41	0.56	-0.23	0.83	-0.22	-0.42
FRF				1.00	0.03	0.13	0.22	0.00	-0.03	0.11	-0.01	-0.03	0.06
BEC					1.00	0.33	0.60	0.38	0.64	-0.10	0.49	-0.27	0.27
CHF						1.00	0.36	0.29	0.37	-0.02	0.51	-0.18	0.38
NLG							1.00	0.44	0.53	-0.07	0.53	-0.30	0.41
DKK								1.00	0.45	-0.06	0.42	-0.31	0.29
NOK									1.00	-0.09	0.55	-0.32	0.34
ITL										1.00	-0.21	-0.12	-0.02
ATS											1.00	0.26	0.42
JPY												1.00	-0.19
FIM													1.00

Table 4.11 Correlation between the weekly percentage change, compared with the currency basket, in the spot price of different currencies expressed in SEK, 1978–84
Coefficients of correlation for the period 1978–84 based on 339 observations

Currency	GBP	USD	DEM	FRF	BEC	CHF	NLG	DKK	NOK	ITL	ATS	JPY	FIM
GBP	1.00	-0.05	-0.36	-0.24	-0.28	-0.15	-0.30	-0.37	-0.14	-0.34	-0.36	-0.12	-0.05
USD		1.00	-0.82	-0.56	-0.65	-0.58	-0.79	-0.66	-0.06	-0.32	-0.80	0.01	0.20
DEM			1.00	0.49	0.63	0.55	0.90	0.67	0.07	0.38	0.96	-0.09	-0.23
FRF				1.00	0.53	0.27	0.47	0.48	-0.23	0.47	0.50	-0.06	-0.14
BEC					1.00	0.32	0.65	0.63	-0.08	0.28	0.64	-0.13	-0.19
CHF						1.00	0.51	0.28	-0.04	0.21	0.54	0.16	-0.23
NLG							1.00	0.63	-0.09	0.33	0.89	-0.09	-0.23
DKK								1.00	-0.02	0.37	0.67	-0.10	-0.15
NOK									1.00	-0.19	-0.08	-0.06	0.41
ITL										1.00	0.40	-0.04	0.01
ATS											1.00	-0.08	-0.23
JPY												1.00	-0.12
FIM													1.00

that the Austrian schilling is tied to the West German mark in its exchange arrangements. Swedish companies can exploit this strong relationship for matching. For example, a claim in Austrian schillings, can be balanced by a loan in West German marks.

The pattern that emerges from the tables can be used to reduce the risk of various short-term foreign exchange investments. However, during the period under investigation it has been important in a portfolio approach based on negative correlations between different exchange rates, to keep an eye on changes in parity that alter the value of all currencies in the same direction. This threat has materialized in no less than six cases, usually in the form of substantial devaluations.

The portfolio approach in Swedish multinational groups

The correlation pattern offers the market actors an opportunity to improve their risk/return ratio by diversifying efficiently. However, my study of the 19 largest Swedish multinationals shows that none of them were using explicit portfolio models during the period of my study. Rather vaguely specified portfolio ideas, on the other hand, did appear in the decision processes of five of the companies. Thus in the empirical analysis of the period 1974-84 which will be presented in Chapters 5–8, we can assume that the portfolio approach adds little to our understanding of the interest movements during the period. In an analysis of the interest gap, a model incorporating additive risk premiums would seem appropriate.

4.5.5 *The foreign exchange market and direct financial integration*

We have observed that the fluctuations in the exchange rates for the Swedish krona increased during the period under investigation. We have also noted large and frequent deviations from purchasing power parity and have thus found that neither goods market integration nor monetary integration obtained. For the period 1974-84 as a whole the level of goods market disintegration appears to have remained unchanged. Thus, there can be no perfect total international integration of Swedish financial markets.

In anticipating this result, our main focus in this book has been limited to measuring direct financial integration. This will be effectuated by comparing the expected return on different markets. It is interesting in this context to note that the multinationals put their faith in purchasing power parity in a long perspective, and took into account possible deviations from parity when they formed their expectations about future exchange rate movements. Eleven of 19 companies ascribed a value "1" to this variable on a 5-point scale, which means that the variable was regarded as very important. In six cases it was the only variable that was given this high value, which means that it was perceived by these companies as the most important single variable behind exchange rate movements at least for the period under investigation. Thus when we return to the question of the investor's exchange rate expectations in Chapter 8, we will have to include the deviation from purchasing power parity in our model in some form or another.

My study of Swedish multinationals shows that these companies are averse to risk. I have been unable to find any evidence that the great liquidity build-up that most of them have experienced during the 1980s has taught them to see financial market fluctuations as an opportunity rather than a threat. I take this result from our admittedly limited sample to mean that the aversion to risk for the market as a whole was constant during the period under investigation.

The standard deviations in various nominal kronor exchange rates increased, while they for deviations in real effective kronor rates remained constant. To be able to evaluate these variances in terms of risk, we have to compare them with corresponding variances in other countries. We then find that the risk has remained unchanged.

We have noted a correlation pattern which can be used for portfolio investments. But the empirical study shows that explicit portfolio models were not in use in Swedish multinationals during the period covered by the study. In view of this I assume that the premiums for risk can be regarded as additive in the investor's calculations. Since the Swedish kronor was subject to two exchange rate arrangements during our period, 1974–84, I shall use a dummy variable to capture a possible resultant change in the level of financial integration.

4.6 Specific measurement problems

Another problem which complicates the analysis of financial integration is to determine the size of private capital transactions over national borders.[44] It concerns the difficulty of measuring the total foreign exchange flow as well as the interest-sensitive flow. This last varies very much depending on whether it is reported by the Central Bureau of Statistics (SCB) or the central bank. The discrepancies are given in Appendix 4.4.

The difference between the two sources of information regarding the deficit in the current account has often been substantial, which means that the two bodies also judge the private capital flows quite differently, since they both use the transaction change in the foreign exchange reserves as their point of departure.[45]

4.6.1 The Central Bureau of Statistics and the central bank use different methods

The central bank and the Central Bureau of Statistics (SCB) proceed quite differently when they calculate the current account. The *central bank* bases its estimate on customs statistics and currency registrations and tries to produce a summary of current payments and transactions of the kind presented in Appendix 4.4.

SCB tackles the problem from the other end, and derives a capital balance by measuring the net change in Swedish assets and liabilities abroad. As a basis for this measurement SCB uses statistics from the central bank and the National Dept Office, and data from a questionnaire regarding corporate foreign assets and liabilities.

SCB compares its estimate of capital transactions with changes in the foreign exchange reserves, and the current account balance thus becomes that part of the change in the foreign exchange reserves which does not correspond to the registered capital transactions. The reliability of this method is intimately connected with the reliability of the transaction statistics.

Since 1983 SCB bases its reports on a sampling procedure. As a result it is possible to indicate the standard error in the estimate of the current account. For 1984 SCB calculates this error in quarterly figures at SEK 600–800 million. See Appendix 4.5, which also shows the difference between the current account balance in its preliminary and definitive versions.

The main problem in the SCB calculations stems from the effects of violent foreign exchange fluctuations. The value in SEK of foreign assets and debts reported by companies can vary enormously, without there having been any capital transaction. One of SCB's problems is thus to achieve a high level of reliability and consistency in the information provided by the companies.

4.6.2 The central bank uses an adjustment entry

The central bank bases its evaluation of service exports in a particular year on SCB's service questionnaire for the previous year, which is extrapolated by a simple method. This extrapolated entry is known as the adjustment entry. The central bank's report on the accuracy of this entry for the years 1980–83 shows that it deviated from the real state of affairs by something between +18 and –8 per cent. Nominally the adjustment entry is pretty large. Thus in 1984 it amounted to SEK 17 billion, a sum that is split between return on capital and other services.

4.6.3 The central bank's residual item further complicates the question

The central bank's reports contain a residual item, which expresses unexplained foreign exchange flows. In view of the size of the residual item – in 1983 an unexplained inflow of SEK 5.9 billion and in 1984 an outflow of 4.5 billion – this must be regarded as a serious problem. The item represents the difference between the transactions which are reported in the current account and the capital balance on the one hand, and the actual change in foreign exchange reserves on the other. If the reporting were perfect, there would be no residual item, i.e. no difference between the relevant quantities.

Even the "location" of the residual item in the context of the balance of payments is controversial. At present it is reported as including capital transactions only. Probably, however, much of it should be assigned to the current account, but nobody dares assume the task of splitting it between the capital account and the current account.

4.6.4 The choice of data source is an open question

It is not really possible to say that either of these methods is the best. Both have their drawbacks. Thus the central bank has no quick or complete reporting system for service exports, while SCB's reports obviously suffer from having to evaluate foreign assets and liabilities at different times.

For 1984 as a whole the difference in the two estimates of the private capital flow was over SEK 7 billion. Even if we allow for a confidence interval round SCB's estimate, the central bank's estimate would still not fall within it. It is thus a question of a "systematic" rather than a random deviation.

Figure 4.8 shows the non-government capital flows as a percentage of the foreign exchange reserves at the end of the respective quarters. We can see that the differences between SCB's and the central bank's estimates of the capital flow are sometimes very large.

4.6.5 The measurement problem and direct financial integration

Which series is to be regarded as the correct one is thus a question of crucial importance in any analysis of direct financial integration, if the capital flow is the dependent variable in the model. But uncertainty in determining the private capital flows will be of minor importance, if we choose a model that just captures the value of the capital flow as a signal. We can then use the flow as an explanatory variable, and our choice of data source will depend not on the accuracy of the measures but on the value of the flow as a *signal* to the market actors. One argument in favour of using the statistics reported by the central bank is that these provide the basis for the government's economic policy controls. In view of the interest among other market actors in anticipating what the government might do in this context, we can assume that even companies will concentrate on the flow movements reported by the bank. Thus in the analysis in Chapters 5–8 I shall use the flows reported by the central bank.[46]

Figure 4.8 Non-government capital flows according to SCB's and the central bank's estimates 1974-84
Percentage of the foreign exchange reserves at the end of quarters

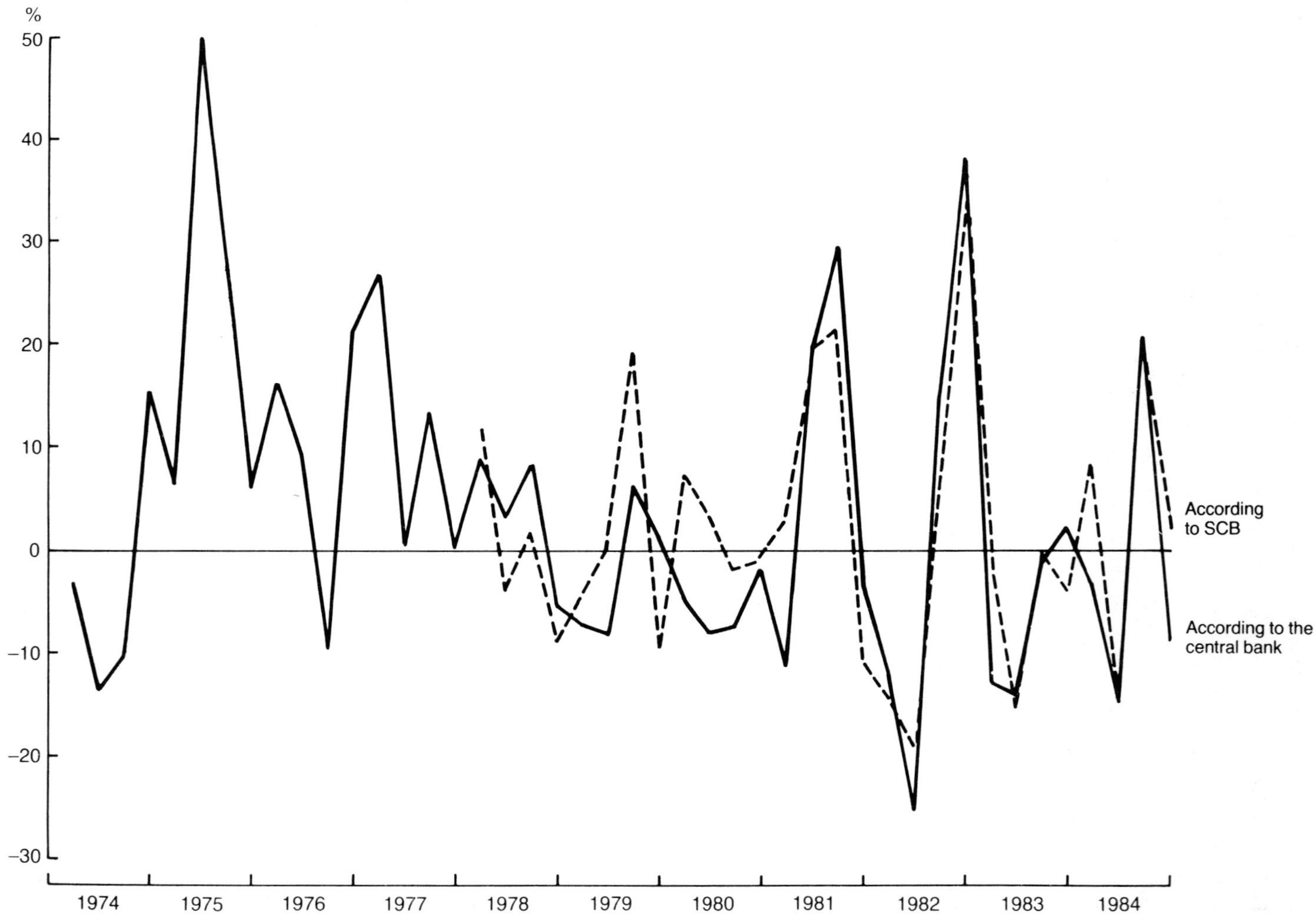

Sources: SCB, Sveriges riksbank (central bank).

APPENDIX 4.1

Date of abolition of monetary policy regulations, 1978–85

Regulation of rate of interest on bank deposits	1978
Regulation of interest rates on industrial bonds	1980
Regulation of insurance companies' lending interest rates	1982
Liquidity ratios for banks	1983
Net investment requirement for insurance companies	1984
Lending ceiling for finance company leasing	1985
Investment requirement for property insurance companies	1985
Lending restrictions on municipal- and company-financing institutions	1985
Regulation of bank lending rates	1985
Lending ceiling for bank lending in Swedish kronor	1985
Lending ceilings for finance company loans	1985
Loan recommendation for nonpreferential lending by housing-financing institutions	1985

Still in force at year-end 1985:

Cash ratio for banks

Regulation of insurance companies' interest rates on index loans

Gross investment requirement for insurance companies and pension funds

Gross investment requirement for banks regarding housing bonds

Note: The institutional changes during 1985 have been incorporated, since it is realistic to assume that some of them had already been anticipated by the end of the period under investigation, and may thus have influenced the figures reported here for the period.

APPENDIX 4.2

Exchange rate index

The goal of the Swedish government's exchange rate policy is to maintain a fixed rate for the krona. The krona is not tied to any single currency, but is held fixed against an average of 15 currencies, the so-called exchange rate index. The weight of every currency in the index reflects its relative importance to Swedish foreign trade. The weights are based on the last five years' foreign trade, and are adjusted on 1 April every year. The basket construction will hold in check the effect on the krona rate of the powerful movements in individual currencies which have characterized the foreign exchange market in recent years.

Weights in the central bank's exchange rate index

	1977	1984	1989
US dollar	16.0	19.1	2.5
German mark	16.7	16.2	16.4
English pound	13.9	13.2	11.1
Norwegian krona	9.9	9.4	8.7
Danish krona	9.5	8.2	7.6
Finnish mark	7.2	7.2	6.7
French franc	5.3	5.5	5.2
Dutch florin	5.1	5.1	4.6
Belgium franc	3.9	3.8	3.7
Italian lira	3.2	3.6	3.8
Japanese yen	2.1	2.7	3.6
Swiss franc	2.6	2.2	2.1
Austrian schilling	1.9	1.5	1.3
Spanish peseta	1.5	1.2	1.5
Canadian dollar	1.2	1.1	1.2
Total	100.0	100.0	100.0

Source: Sveriges Riksbank.

The parity value of the exchange rate index after the devaluation in 1982 is 132. A rise in the index implies a weakening of the krona, and vice versa. The system allows some flexibility, in that fluctuations around the parity value are allowed. The fluctuation band is between the index values 130 and 134, i.e. +/– 1.5 % in relation to the base value. When necessary the central bank intervenes, i.e. buys or sells foreign exchange. The need for such intervention is determined by the foreign exchange flows generated by private and municipal sector net transactions with other countries.

APPENDIX 4.3

Standard deviations in the forward and spot rates

Table A4.1 shows the standard deviations in various exchange rates. It is interesting to see how these standard deviations can vary substantially between currencies, and how the currencies might thus be essentially different in a risk perspective.

The table also shows standard deviations in forward rates. Here it is interesting to note that the difference between standard deviations in the forward and spot rates respectively for a single currency are negligible. Thus the use of forward contracts only reduces risk under very severely specified assumptions. One such assumption is that the forward contract is of the same length as the investment horizon. If this is the case, a forward transaction means that the exchange risk is reduced to zero. It this is not the case, the risk is reduced by a factor which is inversely proportional to the square of the discount factor.[47]

APPENDIX 4.4

Foreign exchange flows 1974–84

Table A4.2 shows total foreign exchange flows as well as non-government capital flows for the period 1974–84.

Where Sweden has a foreign exchange flow smaller than could be regarded as motivated by the current account, the reason may be – after allowing for expectations regarding future exchange rate movements – a higher interest level in Sweden than abroad. If the foreign exchange outflow is greater than would be motivated by the current account, the reason – aften allowing for exchange rate expectations – may be that the market actors find the risk-adjusted interest level lower in Sweden than in the rest of the world. The foreign exchange flows can also be explained by various types of leads and lags.

Table A4.1 **Standard deviation in three-month relative changes in spot rate and forward rate 1974–84**
SEK/foreign currency
Percentage per quarter, Tuesday closing rates

		GBP	USD	DEM	FRF	BEF	CHF	NLG	NOK	DKK	ITL	ATS	JPY	FIM*
1974–84	σ_S	5.31	5.54	4.74	5.02	4.81	6.52	4.81	4.50	3.20	5.26	4.68	6.84	2.64
n=123	σ_F	5.45	5.26	4.77	4.78	4.94	6.35	4.76	4.30	3.03	5.62	4.53	6.71	2.31
1974–76	σ_S	4.87	5.34	1.51	3.66	1.06	3.43	1.23	1.39	0.96	5.48	1.16	4.92	2.04
n=36	σ_F	5.24	4.82	2.03	3.47	1.22	3.46	1.57	1.42	0.79	6.56	1.52	4.59	2.04
1978–84	σ_S	4.57	5.41	5.46	5.42	5.56	7.11	5.66	5.43	3.74	4.77	5.49	7.30	2.41
n=75	σ_F	4.79	5.31	5.42	5.15	5.78	6.93	5.63	5.25	3.58	4.84	5.26	7.31	2.18

* The number of observations for FIM is 106 (1975–84) and 19 (1975–76).

Note: σ_S = standard deviation in spot rate.
σ_F = standard deviation in forward rate.

Table A4.2 **Current account and foreign exchange flows 1974–84 according to SCB's and the Swedish central bank's (CB) reports**
Billion kronor

	74:1		74:2		74:3		74:4		75:1		75:2		75:3		75:4		76:1		76:2		76:3		76:4	
	RB	SCB	RB	SCB	RB	SCB	RB	SCB	RB	SCB	RB	SCB	RB	SCB	RB	SCB	RB	SCB	RB	SCB	RB	SCB	RB	SCB
A Current account	-1.4		-0.4		0.2		-0.9		-0.2		0.3		-1.8		0.1		-1.5		-1.3		-1.4		-3.1	
B Non-government capital flows	-0.3		-1.1		-0.8		1.2		0.5		2.5		3.3		0.8		2.2		1.4		-1.1		2.3	
C Foreign exchange flow A+B=D-E-F	-1.7		-1.5		-0.6		0.3		0.3		2.8		1.5		0.9		0.7		0.1		-2.5		-0.8	
D Foreign exchange reserves – transaction change	-1.7		-1.5		-0.6		0.3		0.3		2.3		1.7		1.3		0.8		-0.0		-2.5		-0.8	
E Central bank's other foreign transactions											-0.5		0.2		0.4		0.1		-0.1		-0.0		-0.0	
F Government's net borrowing abroad																								

	77:1 RB SCB	77:2 RB SCB	77:3 RB SCB	77:4 RB SCB	78:1 RB SCB	78:2 RB SCB	78:3 RB SCB	78:4 RB SCB	79:1 RB SCB	79:2 RB SCB	79:3 RB SCB	79:4 RB SCB
A Current account	-3.6	-1.9	-3.8	-0.6	-0.8 -1.3	0.1 1.5	-1.5 -0.2	0.6 1.2	-1.0 -1.6	-1.6 -3.0	-4.9 -6.9	-3.2 -1.6
B Non-government capital flows	3.0	0.1	1.9	0.2	1.6 2.1	0.7 -0.7	1.7 0.4	-1.0 -1.6	-1.3 -0.7	-1.4 0.0	1.1 3.1	0.2 -1.5
C Foreign exchange flow A+B=D-E-F	-0.6	-1.8	-1.9	-0.4	0.8	0.8	0.2	-0.4	-2.3	-3.0	-3.8	-3.1
D Foreign exchange reserves – transaction change	0.5	2.5	0.6	1.4	1.1	2.4	0.1	-0.5	-1.3	0.1	-0.9	-0.5
E Central bank's other foreign transactions	0.3	0.3	0.6	-0.4	-0.1	-0.1	-0.1	-0.1	0.5	-0.0	0.1	0.1
F Government's net borrowing abroad	0.8	4.0	1.9	2.2	0.4	1.6	-0.0	-0.0	0.5	3.1	2.9	2.5

	80:1		80:2		80:3		80:4		81:1		81:2		81:3		81:4		82:1		82:2		82:3		82:4	
	RB	SCB	RB	SCB	RB	SCB	RB	SCB	RB	SCB	RB	SCB	RB	SCB	RB	SCB	RB	SCB	RB	SCB	RB	SCB	RB	SCB
A Current account	-4.2	-6.0	-5.5	-7.2	-5.9	-6.8	-3.5	-3.6	-2.6	-5.2	-1.3	-1.2	-5.4	-3.9	-4.7	-3.3	-2.8	-2.4	-1.6	-2.8	-7.3	-5.8	-10.0	-9.2
B Non-government capital flows	-0.6	1.1	-1.2	0.5	-1.2	-0.3	-0.3	-0.2	-2.0	0.5	3.3	3.7	6.4	4.8	-0.7	-2.2	-2.4	-2.8	-5.0	-3.8	2.9	1.4	9.6	8.5
C Foreign exchange flow A+B=D-E-F	-4.9		-6.7		-7.1		-3.8		-4.7		2.5		0.9		-5.5		-5.2		-6.6		-4.4		-0.7	
D Foreign exchange reserves – transaction change	-0.3		0.9		-0.1		-0.5		3.7		-1.4		1.3		-2.5		-0.6		-0.9		0.1		1.7	
E Central bank's other foreign transactions	0.3		0.1		0.2		-0.2		2.1		-1.1		-0.7		-0.0		-0.0		-0.0		-0.0		-0.3	
F Government's net borrowing abroad	4.3		7.6		6.7		3.5		6.2		-2.7		1.1		3.0		4.7		5.7		4.4		2.7	

	83:1		83:2		83:3		83:4		84:1		84:2		84:3		84:4	
	RB	SCB	RB	SCB	RB	SCB	RB	SCB	RB	SCB	RB	SCB	RB	SCB	RB	SCB
A Current account	-1.4	-3.8	2.1	2.4	-4.3	-4.7	-3.5	-5.4	3.2	0.0	0.6	-0.1	-2.9	-3.0	-0.0	-3.2
B Non-government capital flows	-3.2	-0.9	-3.7	-4.0	-0.3	0.1	0.8	2.7	-1.0	2.2	-4.6	-3.9	7.6	7.7	-2.9	0.3
C Foreign exchange flow A+B=D-E-F	-4.7		-1.6		-4.6		-2.7		2.2		-4.0		4.7		-2.9	
D Foreign exchange reserves – transaction change	0.2		0.2		-0.4		5.1		2.1		-3.0		4.3		-3.8	
E Central bank's other foreign transactions	-0.4		-0.2		-0.1		-		-0.6		-		-0.1		-	
F Government's net borrowing abroad	5.3		1.9		4.4		7.8		0.5		1.0		-0.3		-0.9	

Source: SCB, Sveriges Riksbank

APPENDIX 4.5

Current account reporting according to SCB

Table A4.3 Specification of current account outcomes according to SCB 1978–84
Quarterly data

	Quarter	Current account balance		Standard deviation [a]
		Preliminary	Definitive	
1978	1	–1.5	–1.3	..
	2	1.5	1.5	..
	3	–0.4	–0.2	..
	4	0.9	1.2	..
1979	1	–1.8	–1.6	..
	2	–2.5	–3.0	..
	3	–6.6	–6.9	..
	4	–2.0	–1.6	..
1980	1	–6.6	–6.0	..
	2	–5.9	–7.2	..
	3	–7.6	–6.8	..
	4	–3.0	–3.6	..
1981	1	–5.8	–5.2	..
	2	0.5	–1.2	..
	3	–3.5	–3.9	..
	4	–3.0	–3.3	..
1982	1	–3.0	–2.4	..
	2	–2.4	–2.8	..
	3	–6.4	–5.8	..
	4	–8.2	–9.2	..
1983	1	–2.7	–3.8	1.22
	2	2.1	2.4	0.72
	3	–5.3	–4.7	0.68
	4	–2.6	–5.4	0.67
1984	1	–0.6	0.0	0.78
	2	–0.9	–0.1	0.63
	3	–3.5	–3.0	0.68
	4	–3.4	–3.2	0.87

[a] From 1983 only, when a sampling technique was introduced.

Source: SCB.

Notes

[1] This interval amounted to ± 2.25 per cent.

[2] At this time the parity value was 132 – as it had been ever since the devaluation in October 1982.

[3] Foreign exchange flows are defined as the change in the foreign exchange reserve minus the government's foreign borrowing. If the domestic liquidity supply is greater than the demand for liquidity, there will be a foreign exchange outflow. If the demand is greater than the supply of liquidity, there will be a foreign exchange inflow. The foreign exchange flow is an indicator of the tightness of the credit market.

[4] "Excess liquidity" in combination with the exchange controls also explains other developments on the market, such as complex corporate cross-ownership arrangements.

[5] And borrowing as a negative form of saving.

[6] So-called off-balance-sheet items.

[7] For example the large companies borrow direct on the market via their commercial paper programmes. Most of the large companies in my empirical study make use of this opportunity.

[8] Quotations are still made for treasury bills. The interest rates on treasury discount notes which will be used in the empirical analysis later in the book, were quoted for the first time in October 1982 and refer to treasury discount notes with 90 days remaining.

[9] Among the traditional instrument of monetary policy we have *first* changes in administratively determined interest rates, *secondly* changes in the banks' cash ratios, *thirdly* the restrictive instrument of selling new government loans, and finally the *fourth* instrument consisting of operations on the open market.

[10] The notion that the autonomy was regarded as temporarily frozen is expressed in the central bank's Kredit- och valutaöversikt (1984:3) where it is claimed that Sweden "despite improvements in the current account and the national budget, cannot conduct an independent interest policy vis-à-vis the rest of the world until ... the structural imbalances have been substantially reduced ...". The central bank often motivated changes in the administratively determined interest rates by reference to changes in the foreign interest level.

[11] On the day-to-day loan market the banks can buy and sell the deficit or surplus in liquidity that arises in the day-to-day operations. However, the banks need not deal with each other on the day-to-day loan market; if a bank has a deficit in liquidity it can borrow from the central bank. If a bank has a surplus of liquidity, this money can be deposited in an account in the National Debt Office.

[12] The total quantity of money at the time was about SEK 440 billion.

[13] The discount rate and the penalty rate are the banks' borrowing rates in the central bank. Borrowing to a limited extent (25 per cent of equity) took place in this system at the discount rate. Borrowing above that level was at a penalty rate.

[14] The central bank's acknowledgement of their "control" over the foreign exchange flow by intervening on the forward markets caused strong reactions on the market during 1987 and led to much debate.

[15] Previously, too, the central bank was able to sterilize foreign exchange flows, for example by changing the cash ratios. However, the procedure was not as simple as market operations.

[16] To begin with the controls were an instrument of rationing to support trade policy, and later a support for a credit policy aimed at controlling domestic economic activity. During the most recent decades their purpose was rather to support monetary and exchange policy.

investigation.

[18] The question was further elaborated as follows:
"In order to cope with an imbalance in its balance of payments, a country can adopt various measures in its economic policy. Rank the measures which have most affected your Group's results and position since 1974. The action which *has had* the greatest positive effect on the Group is ranked +1 etc. The action which has had the greatest negative effect on the Group is ranked –1, followed by –2 and –3. Indicate at least 3 of each kind. In the column for expected effects the actions are ranked according to the importance which they can be *expected to have* on your Group, regardless of whether you have any experience of it or not".

[19] According to Franzén and Uggla (1978) the expectation-led capital flow immediately before the devaluations in 1977 was about SEK 6–7 billion.

[20] The press release 26/1987 from Sweden's central bank provides the embryo of an opportunity cost analysis. The answers to an interview study conducted by the central bank in a sample of Swedish companies, are reported. The result is that almost half the studied companies declared that the volume of their foreign borrowing exceeded what was *desirable* as a result of the central bank's financing requirement.

[21] Söderström (1980) estimates the administrative costs for the exchange controls at roughly SEK 50 million. The government's own official report (SOU 1985:52) has estimated the reorganization of the reporting of incoming payments at SEK 50 million. My own estimate of the administrative costs is around SEK 120 million at 1987 prices, of which the main part falls on companies and banks.

[22] This provision was abolished in June 1986.

[23] This has been verified by my interview study as well as by the study conducted by the central bank.

[24] IMF estimates this share at about 4 per cent for 1986.

[25] In London it amounted to the equivalent of USD 90 million, New York USD 60 million and Tokyo USD 50 million.

[26] BIS (1987).

[27] Sveriges Riksbank, Kredit- och valutaöversikt, 1986:4, p. 14.

[28] IMF (1987).

[29] For a discussion of different calculation methods in choosing weights for the Swedish krona, see Franzén and Rosenberg (1983).

[30] On theoretical grounds the index should allow for substitutibility conditions or demand and supply elasticities in the trade. Bilateral trade weights, which have been used, have clear practical advantages, given the present quality of the statistics, compared with the theoretically motivated MERM weights (see Artus and McGuire 1982).

[31] The currencies have been chosen with a view to reflecting the exchange rate trends in loan currencies important to the Swedish market actors.

[32] I have already pointed out that the premiums are based on the fluctuation pattern in real exchange rates. However, in a weekly perspective, real and nominal exchange rate movements are approximately the same.

[33] For a discussion of the choice of reference period, see e.g. Oxelheim (1985).

[34] As we have already seen, the choice of index is guided by the purpose of the purchasing power parity index. If it is to provide a basis for central bank control, the producer price index is to be preferred, or – when this cannot be produced consistently – the wholesale price index. Generally speaking we can say that if internal relative price relationships are stable, then the results exhibited in the form of deviations from purchasing power parity are robust for the choice of index.

purchasing power parity are robust for the choice of index.

35 Deviations can arise, for example, due to substantial differences in real interest rates or radical changes in real conditions. An example of the latter could be the importance of North Sea oil to England and Norway. As regards the durability of these deviations from purchasing power parity, the structure of the individual country's economy plays an important part. For a country like the USA, with little foreign trade in relation to its total economy but with gigantic capital movements and financial transactions in dollars, it is possible to have a strongly under- or overvalued currency for long periods. The US dollar was regarded (pretty unanimously) as substantially undervalued against most currencies in the industrial world in the second half of the 1970s. This undervaluation, which can be confirmed by reference to studies of purchasing power parity, largly depended on a systematic differential in expected real interest rates between bloc currencies from 1974 and until the second part of 1980. During the whole of this period the US real interest rate was lower than the West German, sometimes as much as 5 percentage points.

36 Depending on the extent to which companies let the exchange rate adjustment be reflected in relative prices, rather than choosing a rise in the gross margin.

37 National Institute of Economic Research: Konjunkturläget 1986.

38 The answers to my interview study suggest that it was a question of a conscious choice on many good grounds.

39 At the time of the study three of sixteen companies were using so-called technicals as a basis for their buying/selling transactions on the foreign exchange market.

40 Their answers were concerned with corporate ability rather than personal ability. As in many cases there had been exits and entries among the corporate staff.

41 An alternative explanation as to why US multinationals disregarded the forecast value inherent in the interest rate differential may be that the changes in these differentials were not large enough during the first half of the 1970s to be regarded as having any explanatory value. Here I am comparing multinationals from different home countries but I see no reason to assume any geographical differences between the two sets of companies compared.

42 One of the 19 companies in my study is fully decentralized. This company did not take part in the series of questions addressed to the presidents or senior vice-presidents, since the views of the chief executive in such companies do not necessarily reflect attitudes in different parts of the group.

43 In its review, Kredit- och valutaöversikt 1986:4, the central bank reflects the view that the forward premium does not correspond to the interest differential for long maturities.

44 For a detailed discussion, see SCB (1987).

45 In measuring the total foreign exchange flow, the government's net borrowing abroad and other central bank transactions are eliminated from the change in the foreign exchange reserves.

46 As a control, estimates will also be based on the flows reported by SCB. When structural tendencies of a deviating character are noted, this will be indicated in footnotes.

47 See Oxelheim and Wihlborg (1987).

CHAPTER 5

Fluctuations in Swedish Interest Rates – Historical Patterns

5.1 Introduction

In this chapter I shall analyse historical patterns in Swedish interest rates. The idea is to show the extent to which yesterday's interest rates can explain today's. This analysis complements the analysis of fluctuation patterns in exchange rates reported in the previous chapter. Together these two analyses provide a good base for a discussion of the level of international integration on the Swedish financial market.

In Section 5.2 the movements in nominal and real Swedish interest rates will be discussed. I shall analyse the validity of the Fisher Effect and the relations between the Swedish rates included in the study.

Section 5.3 consists of an analysis of correlation patterns between successive changes in each of these interest rates. The analysis is based on ARIMA models.[1] In Section 5.4 the interest rate patterns will be interpreted in terms of the direct integration of the Swedish financial market.

5.2 Nominal and real Swedish interest rates 1974–84

As we have already noted, interest rate formation in Sweden has changed fundamentally since the middle of the 1970s. The changeover from administratively determined interest rates to rates increasingly determined by the market, has probably been reflected in new interest rate patterns.

5.2.1 The pattern of nominal interest rates

Historical peaks

In Figure 5.1 we can see that in a historical comparison interest rates in Sweden during

Figure 5.1 Nominal interest rates 1900-1985
Annual average level

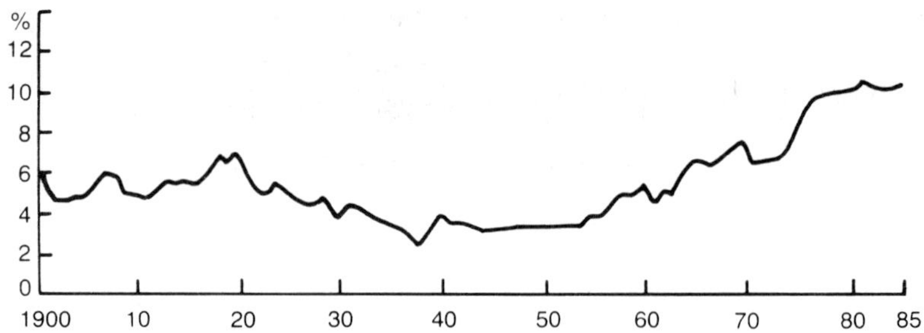

Note: The interest rate is based on four somewhat different series of quotations of discount rate and the rate for government bonds, but it can be regarded as a good approximation of the interest rate trend during the present century.

Source: The figure is based on Ståhl (1980) for the period 1900-1978. The series has been extended by including the interest rate on government bonds/government notes.

the early years of the 1980s were high. The Swedish discount rate was then up to 12 per cent, while the rate for 90-day treasury discount notes reached almost 16 per cent. The long-term interest rate was, at its highest, around 14 per cent. Thus during the period 1981–84 the general interest level was high compared with the beginning of the study period, i.e. between 1974 and 1978. On the other hand the gap between the highest and lowest interest quotations (the range) for all types of interest rates during the respective periods fell somewhat.

Growth trend

For the period 1974–84 as a whole we can identify a trend factor for all types of interest rates. The largest factor is found for the rate on treasury discount notes, where the average monthly growth is about 7 points (hundredths of a percentage). The lowest factor is for the discount rate and is about 3 points.

Variability unchanged

The variability in interest rates can be measured in several ways. I referred above to one such measure in terms of the range. If instead we measure the variability in terms of standard deviation, we can discern some slight indication in Table 5.1 that the variability declined between the 1974–77 period and 1981–84.

For a long time the discount rate led other interest rates

In the 1978–84 period the discount rate was noticeably more variable than between 1974 and 1977. This greater variability is an expression of the growing importance of the discount rate as a control instrument towards the end of the 1970s. The discount rate development is also reflected to some extent in other rates of interest. The relationship varies in strength from one type of interest to another. In Table 5.2 we can see that short-term interest rates showed the strongest covariation with discount rate movements. For instance, the discount rate has had an important effect on the prime rate. Over the period as a whole more than 50 per cent of the variability in the prime rate can be traced to changes in the discount rate. As we have already noted, the role of the discount rate in monetary policy declined during the 1980s, as the penalty rates on the banks' borrowing from the central bank became more common. The close relationship between penalty rates and three-month treasury discount notes is an example of this. See Figure 5.2.

Stronger links between different segments of the Swedish financial market

Table 5.2 shows that during the period under investigation there was also a growing correlation between changes in different types of nominal interest. The weakest link is that between the discount rate and the rate for government bonds. But for the period as a whole the link is significant. Moreover, in view of the investment requirements which the central bank imposed on the commercial banks and the insurance companies, the interest rate on government bonds has lived something of a life of its own. As a whole the correlation pattern suggests a certain, albeit limited, association between movements in the different types of interest. However, for eight of ten possible interest rate comparisons this relationship is stronger in the latest subperiod than in the earliest one. I take this as an indication of increasing integration between the different segments of the Swedish credit market.[2]

Table 5.1 **Mean and standard deviation in Swedish nominal interest rates[a] 1974–84**
Quarterly data, annual rate as a percentage

	No. observations	Mean	Standard deviation
1974–77			
Interest rate on treasury bills/treasury discount notes	16	7.7	2.3
Prime interest rate	16	8.5	1.4
Interest rate on government bonds/government notes	16	8.9	0.8
Interest rate on industrial bonds	16	9.0	0.9
Discount rate	16	6.8	1.0
1978–84			
Interest rate on treasury bills/treasury discount notes	28	10.4	2.9
Prime interest rate	28	11.5	2.0
Interest rate on government bonds/government notes	28	12.0	1.2
Interest rate on industrial bonds	28	11.9	1.4
Discount rate	28	9.1	1.6
1981–84			
Interest rate on treasury bills/treasury discount notes	16	11.7	1.8
Prime interest rate	16	12.7	1.4
Interest rate on government bonds/government notes	16	12.7	0.6
Interest rate on industrial bonds	16	12.9	0.5
Discount rate	16	9.9	1.3

[a] For a more detailed description of the interest rate, see Supplement 1.

Figure 5.2 Penalty rate and interest rate on three-months treasury discount notes 1982-85
Monthly average

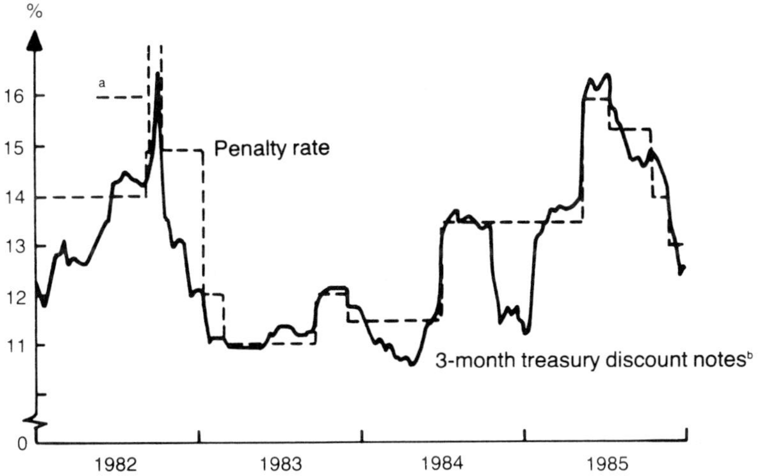

[a] From 18 June up to and including 9 of September 1982 a special fee of 2 per cent was charged for banks who had loans from the central bank at penalty rates for at least six days.
[b] From July 1983, 3-month treasury discount note rate. Earlier 3-month rate on certificates of deposit.

Source: Sveriges riksbank (central bank).

5.2.2 *The pattern of real interest rates*

The real interest level was high in historical terms during the 1980s

Real interest rates in Sweden rose substantially during the first half of the 1980s.[3] For the first time in 50 years they were on a level corresponding to that of the late 1920s and early 1930s. This trend is illustrated in Figure 5.3. After a period of 20 years during which real interest rates were between 0 and 4 per cent, the inflation explosion generated negative real interest rates at the beginning of the 1970s. From the middle of the 1970s there has been a rising trend in real interest rates.

Table 5.2 Covariation between Swedish interest rate movements 1974–84
Pearson's coefficients of correlation, monthly data

	Interest rate on treasury bills/treasury discount notes	Prime interest rate	Interest rate on government bonds/government notes	Interest rate on industrial bonds	Discount rate
1974–84 131 observations					
Interest rate on treasury bills/treasury discount notes	1.0	0.52*	0.33*	0.34*	0.63*
Prime interest rate		1.0	0.21*	0.30*	0.76*
Interest rate on government bonds/government notes			1.0	0.32*	0.17*
Interest rate on industrial bonds				1.0	0.41*
Discount rate					1.0
1978–84 84 observations					
Interest rate on treasury bills/treasury discount notes	1.0	0.50*	0.33*	0.35*	0.62*
Prime interest rate		1.0	0.17	0.27*	0.66*
Interest rate on government bonds/government notes			1.0	0.22*	0.12
Interest rate on industrial bonds				1.0	0.42*
Discount rate					1.0

1981–84 48 observations					
Interest rate on treasury bills/treasury discount notes	1.0	0.53*	0.38*	0.44*	0.67*
Prime interest rate		1.0	0.38*	0.46*	0.71*
Interest rate on government bonds/government notes			1.0	0.23	0.19
Interest rate on industrial bonds				1.0	0.57*
Discount rate					1.0

* Significant positive correlation at 5%-level testing.

Financial investment relatively profitable during the 1980s

Figure 5.4 also shows how the real rate of return on real assets (machinery, building and inventories) actually developed in the manufacturing industry. Up to the middle of the 1970s it had – as expected – been higher than the real interest rate on long-term industrial bonds.[4] The average difference was around 4 per cent. Since 1976 this differential has often been negative and financial investment has proved more profitable than real investment.

Violent fluctuations in the real interest rate

Table 5.3 shows that the *actual* real interest rate has fluctuated a great deal, particularly in the case of short-term rates. The same applies to the *expected* real interest rate.[5] At the same time we can see that over the period as a whole expected real interest rates have fluctuated more than actual rates. However, during the subperiod 1978–84 there is less variation in all cases. Papadia (1984) claims that the ex ante real interest rate can be expected to fluctuate less than the ex post rate, since when inflation is abnormally high or low people expect it to return to the "normal level". A comparison of Tables 5.1 and 5.3 shows that the variation in expected and actual real interest rates is considerably greater than the variation in the corresponding nominal rates.[6]

Thus we find that the assumption in the Fisher Effect regarding a more or less constant "expected" real rate of interest, is not empirically confirmed.[7]

Figure 5.3 Real interest rate trend 1900-1985
Annual average value

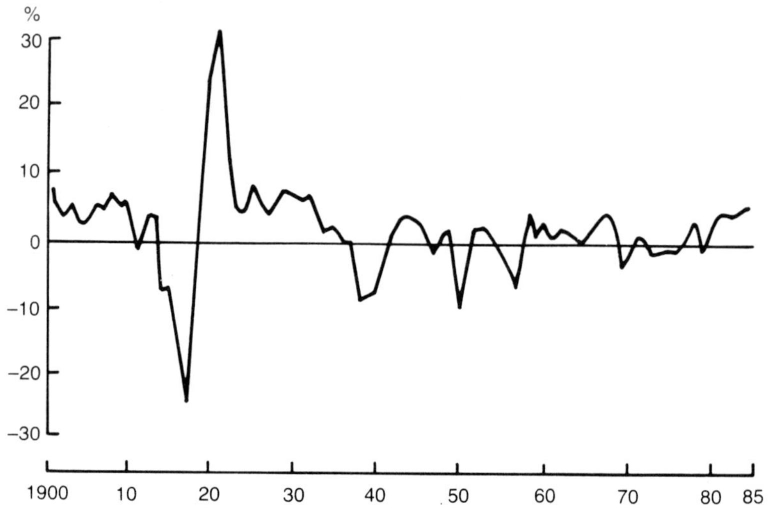

Note: See note to Figure 5.1.

Source: For the period 1900-1978 the figure is based on Ståhl (1980). The updating refers to the real interest rate on government bonds/government notes.

5.2.3 *How do interests rate movements affect Swedish industry?*

Real investment falls as the interest rate rises

In economic theory it is generally assumed that an increase in a country's interest rate will result in a lower level of investment. Increasing interest rate fluctuations are assumed to have the same effect, due to the investors' demands for compensatory risk premiums. Empirically the relationships are difficult to verify, since there are many disturbing factors. Another empirical complication is that the incentive to invest is created by the *expected* return, and as we have seen it is always difficult to replicate in empirical market analyses the way actors form their expectations.

Table 5.3 **Mean and standard deviation in the Swedish real interest rates[a] 1974–84**
Quarterly data, annual rate as a percentage

	Actual real interest rate		Expected real interest rate	
	Mean	Standard deviation	Mean	Standard deviation
1974–77, 16 observations				
Interest rate on treasury bills/treasury discount notes	-2.7	4.1	-1.7	5.2
Prime interest rate	-1.5	4.3	-1.1	4.7
Interest rate on government bonds/ government notes	-1.0	4.6	-0.7	4.8
Interest rate on industrial bonds	-1.0	4.6	-0.7	4.8
Discount rate	-3.2	4.4	-2.9	4.7
1978–81, 28 observations				
Interest rate on treasury bills/treasury discount notes	1.2	5.0	1.1	4.7
Prime interest rate	2.4	4.8	2.2	4.8
Interest rate on government bonds/ government notes	2.8	4.6	2.6	4.5
Interest rate on industrial bonds	2.7	4.8	2.6	4.7
Discount rate	0.0	4.6	-0.2	4.4
1981–84, 16 observations				
Interest rate on treasury bills/treasury discount notes	3.5	3.8	3.0	3.8
Prime interest rate	4.5	3.2	3.9	4.2
Interest rate on government bonds/ government notes	4.7	3.1	4.2	3.8
Interest rate on industrial bonds	4.5	3.2	3.9	3.8
Discount rate	1.7	3.4	1.1	3.9

[a] For a further description of the interest rates, see Supplement 1. The consumer price index is used in calculating the real interest rate.

Figure 5.4 Real rate of return and real market interest rate 1951-85

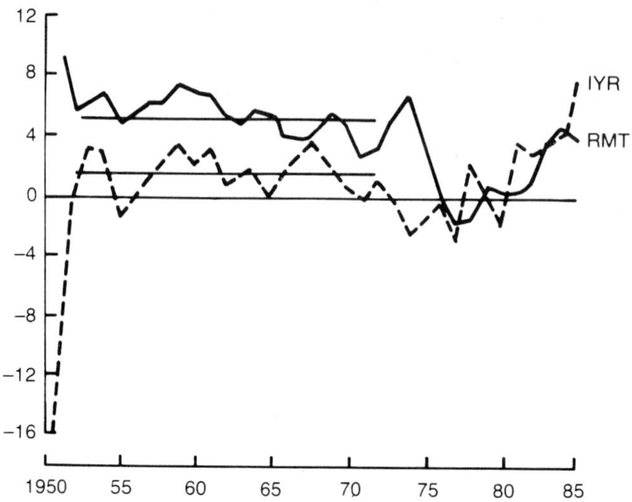

IYR = Real rate of interest of long-term industrial bonds
RMT = Real rate of return on real assets in manufacturing industry

Note: The horizontal lines represent the average for the years 1952-72.

Source: Södersten (1987).

Södersten (1987) shows that changes in the yield relationship between a company's financial and real investments affects its investment ratio. An upturn in the rate of return on real assets by one percentage point in relation to the long-term interest rate on industrial bonds, increases the investment ratio (measured as net investments' share of value added) by 0.5 percentage points the following year.[8] During the period of the analysis the investment ratio amounted on an average to 5.6 per cent, which suggests that changes in profitability were having a powerful effect on industrial capital formation. Thus, since profitability changes are related to the interest rate on industrial bonds in the present study, we can say that capital formation in Swedish industry is determined by events on the world market, to the extent that the Swedish interest rate is partly governed by events on this market.

Stock exchange index falls as the interest rate rises

It is generally recognized that unexpected interest rate movements affect the economic value of a company, and the way it will be evaluated on the stock exchange.[9] In order to illustrate this connection I have conducted a simple regression analysis in which the stock exchange index[10] is the dependent variable and changes in the interest level the explanatory variable.[11] The analysis shows significant links between changes in the stock exchange index in one month and the change in the three-month prime interest rate during the same month.[12] An increase in the interest rate of 1 per cent produces an average fall in the stock exchange index of 1.7 per cent.[13]

If the *entire* Swedish capital market is internationally integrated, changes in the world interest level will determine the development on the Swedish stock exchange, partly by way of changes in the Swedish interest rate and partly by changes in the world's share index. On the other hand if the sectors of the Swedish financial market are disintegrated, the impact of changes in the global interest level on the Swedish stock exchange might operate to a large extent through the global share index only. Since in this case movements in the global interest rate affect both the Swedish interest rate and the Swedish stock exchange index, without any causal relationship between the two, any correlation that might be noted would be spurious.

Ultimately the effect on industry comes from outside

Any further discussion of the link between interest rate fluctuations and the real markets would take me too far from my subject. I have presented these examples simply to illustrate the possible effect on Swedish industry of an increase in financial integration, which would mean that the global interest level would have more impact on the domestic interest level. Growing financial integration means that corporate requirements on rates of return are increasingly dictated by the global interest level.

5.3 Correlation between successive quotations of Swedish interest rates

In this section I shall analyse Swedish interest rate quotations, to see how far there is a covariation between successive quotations of the same type of interest. Thus I shall analyse the correlation between successive quotations of one and the same *Swedish* interest series. The cross-correlation, i.e. the correlation between quotations of foreign interest rates and successive time-lagged quotations of the corresponding Swedish interest rate, will be analysed in Chapter 7.

5.3.1 *Analytical method*

In this analysis I shall use an ARIMA-model of interest determination on Swedish markets. The technical details of the method are described in Box-Jenkins (1978) and have also been discussed in Oxelheim (1980), in connection with an analysis of forward and spot rates on the foreign exchange market. The parameters in ARIMA are p, d, q, where

p = number of past periods for which there is auto-regressive dependence (AR)

d = number of differentiations[14]

q = number of past periods in which there is on moving-average dependence (MA).

The model specification which is compatible with the weakest type of market efficiency (according to the definition in Fama 1970), and which is also the model that provides my working hypothesis in the following analysis, is the random-walk model. This model designates ARIMA (0,1,0) and can be written:[15]

$$r_t - r_{t-1} = \varepsilon_t \tag{5.2}$$

where

r_t = interest rate quotations at time t

ε_t = random error with $E(\varepsilon_t) = 0$, $V(\varepsilon_t) = \sigma_\varepsilon^2$ and $cov(\varepsilon_{t-1}, \varepsilon_t) = 0$.

If there are many possible models, the best model can be chosen according to one of the many competing criteria. Here I have used the Zellner-Palm criterion (1975) and an alternative test, the so-called Akaike-criterion.[16]

Zellner-Palm (1975) recommends tests with a high level of significance, on the lines that the loss will probably be greater if we neglect to include a motivated extra explanatory term than if we include such a term when it is not motivated.

In view of the structural changes that occurred during our period, it seems reasonable to study models for different subperiods.[17] As an indicator of structural or behavioral changes I have used changes over time in the average value and variance in certain financial variables. Changes in level, i.e. changes in average value between periods, can be seen as an expression of structural change, while changes in variance can be regarded as a sign of behavioural and possible speculative change.

5.3.2 In most cases the random-walk model proves to be best

I have applied the ARIMA analysis to three periods. Apart from the period as a whole, I have also analysed two subperiods which are interesting in a structural perspective. The subperiods are January 1978 – December 1984, and January 1981 – December 1984. The first of these periods constitutes a long period for analysis during which Sweden's exchange rate arrangement remained the same (the currency basket). The second of the periods allows an analysis of interest data that has been generated to a great extent on market terms.

An ARIMA analysis covering up to 36-month time-lagged interest rate quotations has been conducted. The analysis, which is based on observations of the market at the end of each month, concerns coefficients of auto-correlation – both total and partial – and a Box-Pierce test.[18]

The results of an analysis of the *first differential* are reported in Table 5.4 in the form of the best model (according to the evaluation methods mentioned above). It appears that the working hypothesis, the random-walk model ARIMA (0,1,0), is accepted almost every time. The "best" forecast of the interest rate a month ahead is the current rate. The results hold here for an analysis of the subperiods 1978–84 and 1981–84, and accord well among others with Volker's observations for domestic short-term interest rates in the major OECD countries (Volker 1980). In the case of longer-term interest rates, and particularly the interest on government bonds, there are indications that an extra term is needed.[19] In the case of the interest rate for government bonds I found a correlation between successive movements, i.e. future movements can be regarded as a fraction of the latest change.[20]

5.4 The interest rate pattern and direct financial integration

The Fisher Effect does not pass the empirical test

According to the Fisher Effect changes in expected inflation should be reflected in the nominal interest rate in a one-to-one relationship. In other words in an empirical analysis we would expect to find a strong correlation between the nominal interest rate and expected inflation.

We can see from Table 5.5 that this correlation is not significant for any of our five interest rate types. Table 5.6 suggests instead that there is a strong negative relationship between the real interest rate and inflation. Given *constant* real interest rate

Table 5.4 The "best" ARIMA model for movements in Swedish interest rates (First differential)
Monthly data

Interest rate	Period	Model
Treasury bills/ treasury discount notes[a]	Jan 1974–Dec 1984	$r_t - r_{t-1} = \varepsilon_t$
	Jan 1978–Dec 1984	$r_t - r_{t-1} = \varepsilon_t$
	Jan 1981–Dec 1984	$r_t - r_{t-1} = \varepsilon_t$
Loans to first-class borrowers (prime rate)	Jan 1974–Dec 1984	$r_t - r_{t-1} = \varepsilon_t$
	Jan 1978–Dec 1984	$r_t - r_{t-1} = \varepsilon_t$
	Jan 1981–Dec 1984	$r_t - r_{t-1} = \varepsilon_t$
Government bonds/ government notes[b]	Jan 1968–Dec 1984	$r_t - r_{t-1} = \underset{(0.07)}{0.24} \cdot (r_{t-1} - r_{t-2}) + \varepsilon_t$
	Jan 1978–Dec 1984	$r_t - r_{t-1} = \varepsilon_t$
	Jan 1981–Dec 1984	$r_t - r_{t-1} = \underset{(0.12)}{-0.32}(r_{t-1} - r_{t-2}) + \varepsilon_t$
Industrial bonds	Jan 1974–Dec 1984	$r_t - r_{t-1} = \varepsilon_t$
	Jan 1978–Dec 1984	$r_t - r_{t-1} = \varepsilon_t$
	Jan 1981–Dec 1984	$r_t - r_{t-1} = \varepsilon_t$
Official discount rate	Jan 1957–Dec 1984	$r_t - r_{t-1} = \varepsilon_t$
	Jan 1978–Dec 1984	$r_t - r_{t-1} = \varepsilon_t$
	Jan 1981–Dec 1984	$r_t - r_{t-1} = \varepsilon_t$

(Standard errors in brackets)

[a] In the tables the interest rate on treasury bills has been described by a series consisting o the interest rate for three-month treasury bills up to September 1982 and the interest rat on 90-day treasury discount notes after that date. If we run a series consisting solely of th interest rate on treasury bills, we get the same model recommendation.

[b] From November 1983 the interest rate on government notes.

according to the Fisher Effect, we should expect a zero correlation between inflation and the real interest rate. I therefore take this observation as evidence indicating that the Fisher Effect does not hold, and that changes in expected inflation affect the expected real interest rate rather than the nominal interest rate.

Carmichael and Stebbing (1983) have dubbed this inverted 1:1 relationship between changes in the real interest rate and altered inflation expectations the "inverted Fisher Effect". The Fisher Effect in its classical version appears to be based on the implicit assumption that financial assets and capital are good substitutes for one another, while financial assets and money are poor substitutes. This assumption can be questioned, and like Carmichael and Stebbing we could even claim that the reverse is true and that we thus have an inverted Fisher Effect. Virén (1987) finds that an extended inverted Fisher Effect provides, due to risk and hedging effects, the best description of changes in the nominal interest rate in the short run, while the classical Fisher Effect gives the best description in the longer term.

Is the interest rate perhaps determined abroad?

It is only to be expected that in periods when it has been administratively determined, the nominal interest rate should exhibit deviations from the Fisher Effect. But it is interesting to note that during the 1980s when interest rates were increasingly market-determined, the deviations were obviously not reduced. A comparison of the subperiods reveals that the strongest grounds for rejecting the Fisher Effect appear in the period 1981–84.

We could of course extend the analysis to allow for taxes and other factors, but instead I shall close this analysis of the Fisher Effect here. My conclusion seems to be that the relationship fails to describe interest rate formation in a satisfactory manner, which means that many new explanatory variables can come into the picture. Some of these lead us to wonder whether the interest rate is not determined outside the country instead.

The correlation pattern does not contradict the idea of influence from abroad

We have noted that the information contained in the historical movements in the domestic interest rate seems to have very little value as an indicator of a future change in interest rates. The best description of interest rate movements is generally obtained with the help of a random-walk model. Long-term interest rates exhibit the same pattern, except that in some periods an autoregressive term of a higher order has been necessary for the interest rate on government bonds.

The results of the ARIMA analysis can encourage us to make a further analysis and to seek for other explanatory variables. My next step will therefore be to see how far the fluctuations in Swedish rates can be explained by movements in foreign interest rates, and how far this can be regarded as a systematic influence.

Table 5.5 **Correlation between nominal interest rate and "expected" and actual inflation in Sweden 1974–84**
Monthly data

Inflation / Interest rate	Consumer price change		Producer price change	
	Actual	Expected	Actual	Expected
Interest rate on treasury bills/treasury discount notes	0.19	0.17	-0.02	0.04
Prime interest rate	0.08	0.09	0.18	0.12
Interest rate on government bonds/government notes	-0.03	0.02	0.20	0.20
Interest rate on industrial bonds	0.01	0.07	0.28	0.24
Discount rate	0.11	0.18	0.20	0.23

Note: The number of observations is 44. No coefficient of correlation is significant at the 5% level.

Table 5.6 **Correlation between actual real interest rate and actual inflation in Sweden 1974–84**
Monthly data

Inflation / Real interest rate	Consumer price change	Producer price change
Interest rate on treasury bills/treasury discount notes	-0.81	-0.85
Prime interest rate	-0.89	-0.89
Interest rate on government bonds/government notes	-0.91	-0.92
Interest rate on industrial bonds	-0.91	-0.93
Discount rate	-0.92	-0.93

Note: The number of observations is 44. All coefficients of correlation are significant at the 5% level.

Notes

1 *Auto*r*egressive* *i*ntegrated *m*oving *a*verage.

2 The possible presence of risk premiums which vary over time may deduct from the value of my interpretation. However, a multivariate approach, with one Swedish interest rate against other Swedish rates, added no explanatory value to my analysis for the periods concerned.

3 The real interest (r^R) is calculated here as

$$1 + r^R = (1+r)/(1+\hat{P}).$$

If, for example, the nominal interest rate is 8 per cent and the inflation is 8 per cent, the real interest rate will be 0 per cent. Given a nominal interest rate of 8 per cent and inflation at 4 per cent, the real interest rate will be 3.84 per cent.

For small values of r, r^R and $\hat{P}$ the simpler formula provides an approximation:

$$r^R = r - \hat{P}.$$

If the interest rates are measured as interest intensities, i.e. we assume continual returns, the relationship will be

$$e^{r^R} = e^{r-\hat{P}} = e^r/e^{\hat{P}},$$

where e is the base for the natural logarithms.

4 Signifying extra scope for return on investment to compensate for the risk connected with real investment.

5 In estimating the expected real interest rate I have used the inflation rate in the immediately preceding period as an expression of the market's inflation expectations. Several authors (e.g. Hooper 1984, Sachs 1985, and Coe and Golub 1986) have used proxies like this naive one successfully – and generally with more success than when sophisticated econometric forecasts are used (e.g. Shaefer and Loopesko 1983).

6 If the covariance between nominal interest rates and expected inflation is zero or negative, the result would be trivial, as can be seen from formula (5.1);

$$\mathrm{var}(r^R) = \mathrm{var}(r-\hat{P}^*) = \mathrm{var}(r) + \mathrm{var}\,(\hat{P}^*) - 2\mathrm{cov}(r, \hat{P}^*) \quad (5.1)$$

According to the Fisher Effect, however, we should expect $\mathrm{cov}(r, \hat{P}^*)>0$.

7 As we found in our survey of interest rate theory, there is great uncertainty in the interpretation of empirical tests of the Fisher Effect. We should be particularly careful when we interpret results based on the long-term real interest rates, since the market's estimate of future inflation can deviate from the procedures – using a latest known inflation rate – which we are using here.

8 The one-year lag in the explanatory variable is supposed to capture the time it takes the company to adjust.

9 The economic value is estimated as the discounted present value of all future cash flows. No distinction is made between the effect of substitution and the effect of a change in corporate cash flow.

10 Veckans Affärer's stock exchange index.

11 I regard this causal relationship as probable; but there are those who claim the opposite, i.e. that changes in the share index lead to interest rate movements.

12 Here I am assuming that all interest rate changes are unexpected.

13 The interest level is described as an index. An interest rate of 6 per cent gives a value 106 on the index. If a new interest rate is 7 per cent, the index change will thus be 0.94 per cent. The stock exchange movement can be calculated in a similar way. The analysis refers to the period 1974–84. There is also significance for the subperiod 1981–84. Here, however, the interest rate's effect on the stock exchange index increases, so that there is a drop of 3.3 per cent when interest rate index rises by 1 per cent.

14 In the process used (ARIMA), it is important that the changes are stationary. If such is not the case, "stationarity" is created with the help of transformation.

15 If there is growth in the interest rate movements, we would need to differentiate further, or to use a drift parameter, i.e. a constant that reflects the average change per period in the mean value of the process. However, earlier in this chapter we noted that we have weak linear growth and can therefore content ourselves with the model description in (5.2).

16 This test is described in Melard and Rouland (1979).

17 The problem of defining periods with homogeneous market conditions has been discussed by Leamer and Stern (1972) among others.

18 As a formal test of the autocorrelations in the residual the Box-Pierce test has been used (see Andersson 1976) on residuals with up to 36 months time-lag. The test function Q is analysed as an expression of whether a statistical serie can be regarded as "white noise". For time-lags up to k periods, the test function Q is:

$$Q(k) = N \sum_{k=1}^{k} \rho_k^2 .$$

Given that ρ_k = estimated autocorrelation with a time lag of k periods, and
N = number of observation in the series.

Q(k) will be approximately χ^2 distributed with k degrees of freedom under H_0: no autocorrelation. Stationary series are assumed.

19 An autoregressive term.

20 In the analysis of periods 1968–84 and 1981–84.

CHAPTER 6

Swedish Interest Rate Fluctuations in an International Perspective

6.1 Introduction

From this chapter onwards we will be looking at the extent to which foreign interest rate movements can explain the fluctuations in Swedish interest rates as identified in the previous chapter. The present chapter includes a description of the interest development on the world market and in Sweden. My purpose is to show how the size of the Swedish interest rate has deviated from the "global interest level", and where possible to seek an explanation in underlying differences in policy. I shall take both the US interest level and a weighted average of the interest rates in the OECD countries as my "global interest level".[1]

I would like to emphasize that the aim of the present chapter is purely descriptive. The chapter is intended to provide the reader with some idea of the *size* of the nominal gap between Swedish and foreign interest rates, and of how this gap develops over time. It should also help to show whether there is a certain pliability about the nominal interest rates, suggesting some degree of international integration in the Swedish financial market. However, such a suggestion should be interpreted with great caution, since we have no opportunity here of allowing for the risk factors that distinguish one country from another.

Section 6.2 describes the nominal interest development, while Section 6.3 looks at the real interest rate development. In Section 6.4 we shall discuss the implications of the various observations in terms of financial integration.

6.2 How Swedish nominal interest rates deviate from foreign interest rates

The five types of interest in my study have different time dimensions. I shall let these determine the order in which I present them, and will start with the pattern of discount rate movements. The chosen order also seems reasonable in view of the long periods when interest rates in Sweden have been largely administratively determined, and to a great extent have reflected movements in the Swedish discount rate.

6.2.1 Developments in the discount rate

The differentials between the discount rates of the OECD countries increased dramatically during the 1970s

Discount rate movements in some of the major OECD countries are illustrated in Figure 6.1, which shows a fan-shaped development since 1974. This development can be regarded as a mirror image of the development in foreign exchange rates illustrated in Figure 4.4. The increasing dispersion between national discount rates during the 1970s can be exemplified by the distance between the extreme values for the major OECD countries. At the end of 1971 the distance was a mere 1.75 percentage point; by the end of 1979 it was 16 percentage points.

Figure 6.1 Official discount rate 1970-84
End of the quarter, percentage per year

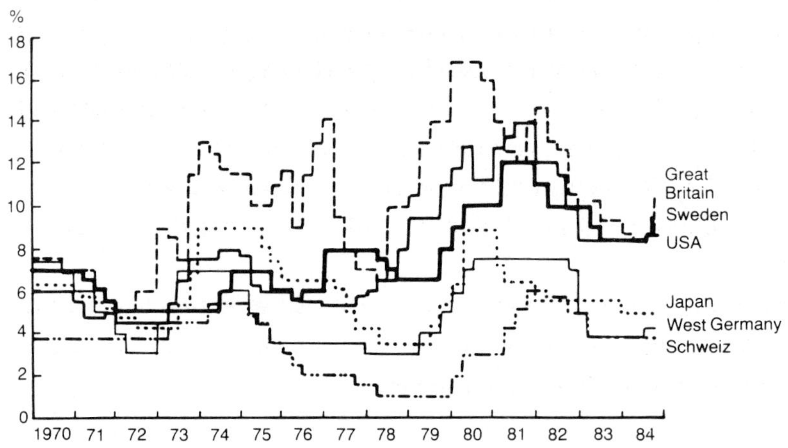

Note: For Great Britain the minimum lending rate is included for the period after 1979.

The discount rate is raised to prevent overheating at peaks in the business cycle

The cyclical fluctuations which may be traced in the discount rate development reveal the importance of this rate as an instrument of economic policy. But the way it is used varies from one country to another. In France and Spain, for example, no change was made in the discount rate between 1977 and 1984. In the countries represented in the figure, however, discount rate movements seem to belong to the economic policy toolbox. The picture shows that the rates converge after 1980, and that the increase which might have been expected from the cyclical pattern has been extremely modest during the latest periods of high business activity.

Swedish discount rate shows increasing pliancy in relation to the foreign development

Table 6.1 shows the major shifts in the discount rate development.[2] A major change in the development in the global interest level is generally followed within eight months by a corresponding change in the US rate. During the 1980s this time-lag appears to have dropped to about one month.

The responsiveness of the *Swedish* discount rate to major shifts in the global level has not been as good as this. During the 1970s shift in the Swedish development some times appeared more than a year later. Between 1966 and 1980 we can even see some shifts in the Swedish discount rate which had no equivalent in the global development.

A comparison of the Swedish and US discount rate developments shows that such "unmatched" development shifts became even more frequent. During 1980 there was also a downturn and then an upturn in the global trend and in the US trend, which had no equivalent in the Swedish discount rate. After that, however, Swedish responsiveness was high, except that the downturn in the global discount rate in July 1984 was not followed by any downturn in the Swedish discount rate until July 1985.

If we want to read a causal relationship into the adaptability between interest rates, we must be extremely cautious, particularly in any interpretation of the discount rate developments. It is very likely that any unilateral or mutual influence which we find may be spurious, and that possible parallels in discount rate developments are a function of the fluctuations in the global business cycle, as manifest in the economic developments in the respective countries. It so happens that the global level exhibits a procyclical trend. The lag which appears in Table 6.1 between the shift in the US rate, and the subsequent major shift in the Swedish discount rate, is also much the same as the time that passes before fluctuations in the business cycle generally culminates in Sweden compared with the United States.

Table 6.1 **Major shifts in the discount rate development 1966–84**
Months when bottom or top quotations are registered

	US interest rate		Global rate [a]		Interest rate in Sweden
Downturn	1967:3	(-2)	1966:12	(1)	1967:1
Upturn	1967:10	(1)	1967:9	(2)	1967:11
Downturn	–	–	–	–	1968:1
Upturn	–	–	–	–	1969:1
Downturn	1970:10	(4)	1970:6	(8)	1971:2
Upturn	1972:12	(15)	1972:5	(22)	1974:3
Downturn	1974:10	(9)	1974:8	(11)	1975:7
Upturn	–		1976:2	(3)	1976:5
Downturn	–		1976:10	(15)	1978:1
Upturn	1977:7	(23)	1977:10	(20)	1979:6
Downturn	1980:4		1980:4		–
Upturn	1980:8		1980:11		–
Downturn	1981:10	(-1)	1981:10	(-1)	1981:9
Upturn	1984:3	(2)	1984:3	(2)	1984:5
Downturn	1984:10	(9)	1984:7	(12)	1985:7

[a] The global interest rate here is a trade-weighted average of the discount rates in the 15 major OECD countries. Since it is calculated with trade weights, this interest rate is slightly less shaped by the US interest rate development than if the calculation had been based on capital market weights.

Note: The numbers in brackets show how many months passed before the shift in the development in the particular interest rate had an "equivalent" in the Swedish interest rate.

It took time for the relative strength of the currencies to be revealed in the interest rate pattern

A comparison of the exchange rate trend in Figure 4.4 and the discount rate trend in Figure 6.1 shows how much time passed before the sharply diverging exchange rates affected expectations in such a way that the relative strength of the currencies revealed itself in interest rates. This applies to the discount rate and to the other interest rates studied here. As we shall see later, the lag gave rise to large temporary deviations from the International Fisher Effect – at least as regards Swedish rates in relation to the West German and Swiss. We can find similar deviations in the relationship with the US rate after American monetary policy was tightened up in October 1979.

The role of the discount rate in Swedish economic policy has varied

Until the middle of the 1970s the Swedish discount rate was a political tool for regulating domestic construction activity (housing policy), rather than a means for regulating capital flows over the national borders. A change in policy could be discerned during the spring of 1974, when the discount rate was changed on the formal grounds that the measure was part of a package to encourage corporate borrowing on the international money and bond markets. In the later part of the studied period, however, the penalty rate began to supplement and even replace the discount rate as a tool of economic policy.

The substantial increase in the Swedish discount rate in the middle of 1979 started almost two years after the corresponding average upturn in the OECD countries and the United States. See Figures 6.2 and 6.3. The large number of increases between 1979 and 1981 were caused by a growing foreign exchange flow. In Figure 6.2 we can see that at the end of the period the Swedish discount rate was around two percentage points above the international discount rate.[3] We shall be analysing the content of this gap in greater detail in Chapter 8.

6.2.2 The rate on treasury bills/treasury discount notes

The rate on treasury bills is the most common rate of interest in international integration studies. Figures 6.4 and 6.5 show how the rate on Swedish treasury bills has adjusted to the weighted global interest level and the rate on US treasury discount notes.

Weak upwards trend in the Swedish interest rate on treasury bills

There is no marked trend in the global interest level over our period as a whole. On the other hand we can discern a weak upwards trend in the Swedish interest rate, and thus a weak trend in the interest gap.

Greater responsiveness to major shifts in the foreign development

The response of the Swedish interest rate to major shifts in the global interest development can be seen in Table 6.2. It is more difficult to get a comparative view over time here, because in July 1982 treasury discount notes were introduced in Sweden and a secondhand market appeared. Previously treasury bills were mainly acquired by banks

Figure 6.2 Sweden's official discount rate vis-à-vis the weighted average of the OECD countries' discount rates 1974-84
Percentage per year, observations at the end of each month

---- Sweden

—— an average[a] based on trade weights (in accordance with the Swedish currency basket) for the 15 largest OECD countries

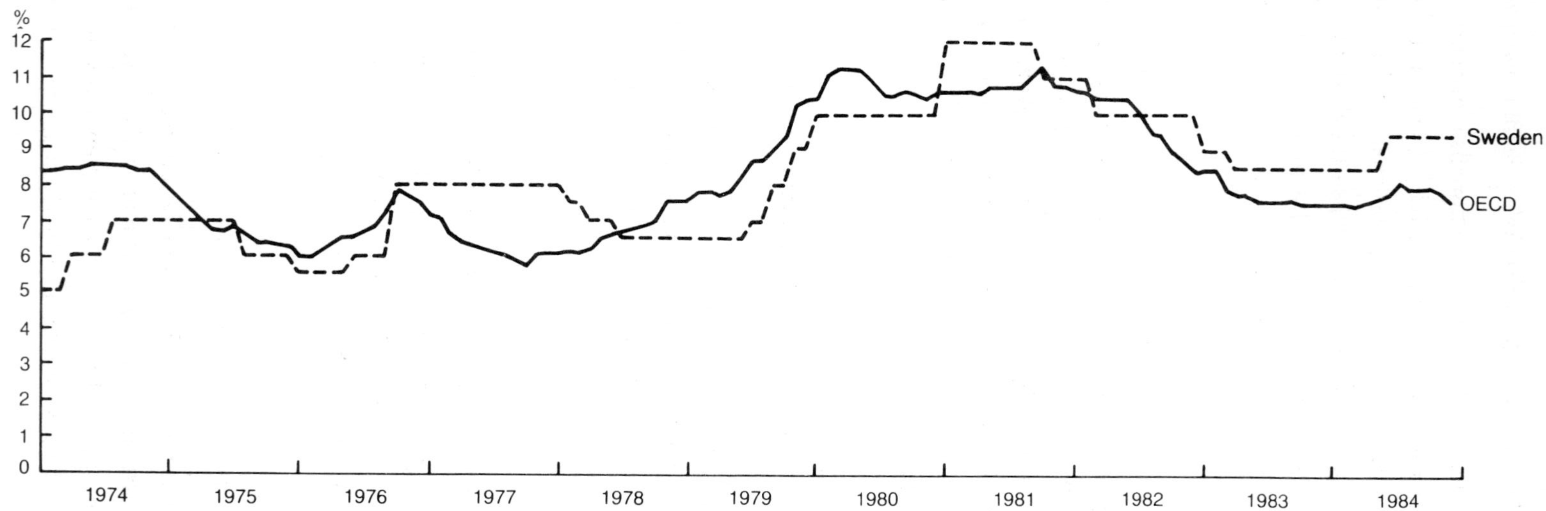

a If we weight with OECD's capital market weights instead of trade weights, the weighted average for the 1980s falls by about half a percentage point.

Figure 6.3 Sweden's official discount rate vis-à-vis the US discount rate 1974-84

Percentage per year, observations at the end of each month

Figure 6.4 Interest rate on Swedish three-month treasury bills/treasury discount notes vis-à-vis the weighted average for corresponding interest rates in some of the larger OECD countries 1974-84

Percentage per year, observations at the end of each month

- - - - Sweden[a]

—— Weighted[b] average for USA, Japan, Great Britain, West Germany[c], The Netherlands and Belgium

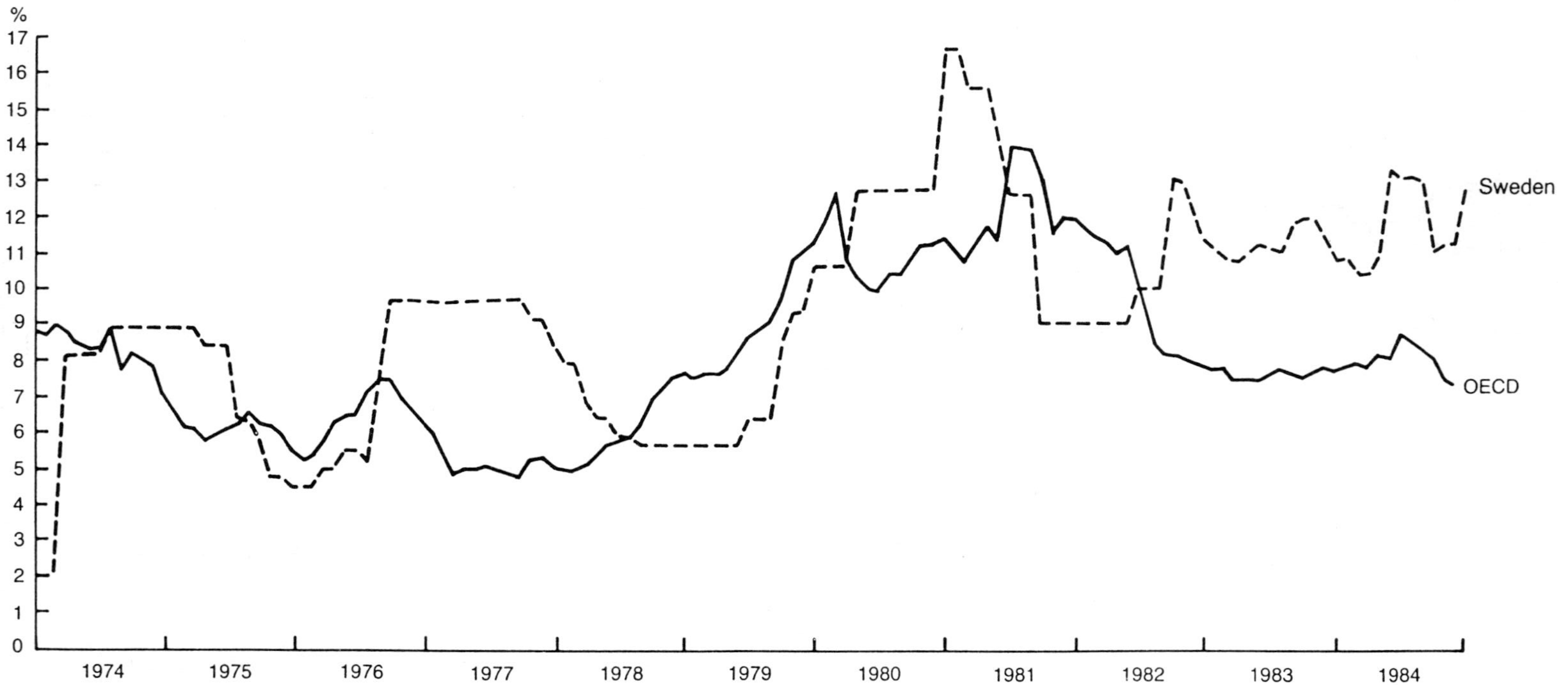

[a] From October 1982 the interest rate for treasury discount notes with 90 days outstanding maturity.
[b] Weighted with trade weights (in accordance with the Swedish currency basket). Using capital flow weights according to OECD we obtain a similar trend.
[c] From 1982 onwards the Frankfurt rate is used

Figure 6.5 Interest rate on Swedish three-month treasury bills/treasury discount notes vis-à-vis corresponding rate in the USA 1974-84
Percentage per year, observations at the end of each month

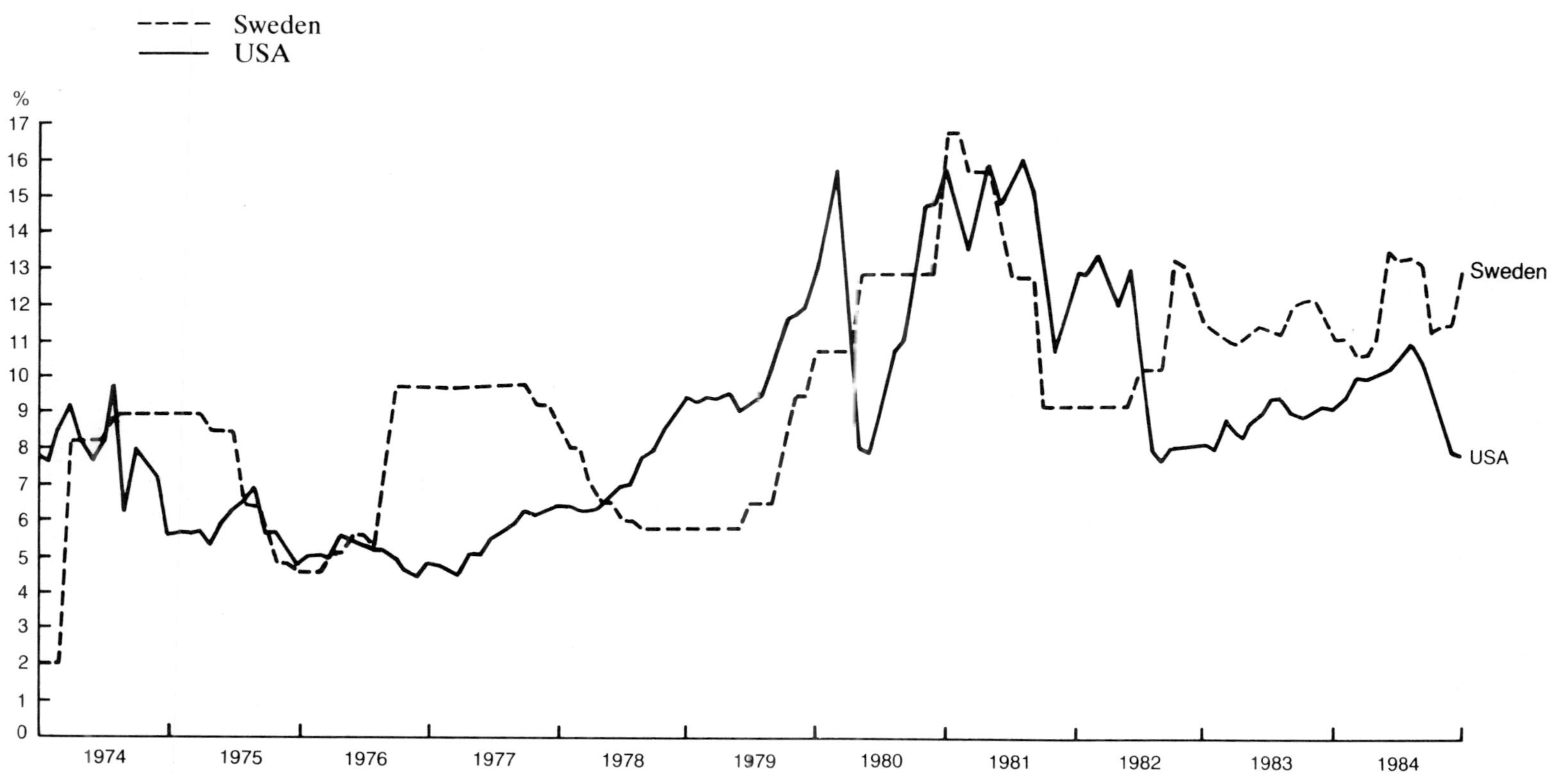

Table 6.2 Major shifts in the interest rate development for treasury bills/treasury discount notes 1974–84
Month when bottom and top quotations were registered

	US interest rate		Global interest rate[a]		Interest rate in Sweden
Downturn	1974:8	(8)	1974:3	(13)	1975:4
Upturn	–	–	1976:2	(1)	1976:3
Downturn	–	–	1976:10	(12)	1977:10
Upturn	1977:4	(26)	1977:10	(20)	1979:6
Downturn	1980:3	(15)	1980:3	(15)	1981:5
Upturn	1980:6	(24)	1980:7	(23)	1982:6
Downturn	1981:8	(14)	1981:7	(15)	1982:10
Upturn	1982:9	(7)	1983:6	(-2)	1983:4
Downturn	1984:8	(0)	1984:7	(1)	1984:8

[a]The global interest here is a weighted average, using trade weights, of the interest rate on treasury bills/treasury discount notes in the USA, Japan, England, West Germany, The Netherlands and Belgium. As a result of the use of trade weights, this interest rate is slightly less shaped by the development in the US interest rate than if the estimate had been made on a basis of capital market weights.

Note: The figures in brackets show how many months passed before the shift in the particular interest rate had its "equivalent" in the Swedish interest rate.

as a result of the central bank's investment requirements, but companies also sometimes bought these securities. Interest on 90-day (remaining) treasury discount notes was first quoted in October 1982[4]. It has been included in the figures from that date.

The pattern is not clear, and this makes it difficult to decide whether it is the US interest rate or the weighted global rate that initiated the reversals in the interest development. It used to be generally accepted that the US interest rates led the development, but Table 6.2 does not fully support this view. Rather, we seem to get confirmation of a kind of mutual "influence" between the US rate and the global rate.[5] Regardless of which of these two rates initiated a shift in the development, the Swedish shift appears only after some delay. Since the introduction of treasury discount notes, a foreign development shift affects the Swedish interest rate much sooner.

6.2.3 Prime rate development

The gap between the Swedish and foreign prime rates is sometimes very big

In Figures 6.6 and 6.7 the development in the Swedish interest rate on loans to first-class borrowers i.e. the prime rate, is compared with the global prime rate and the prime rate in the United States.[6] It appears from these figures that the gap between

Table 6.3 **Major shifts in the prime interest rate development 1974–84**
Month when bottom and top quotations were registered

	US interest rate		Global interest rate[a]		Interest rate in Sweden
Downturn	1974:9	(10)	1974:8	(11)	1975:7
Upturn	–	–	–	–	1976:9
Downturn	–	–	–	–	1978:1
Upturn	1976:12	(31)	1978:2	(17)	1979:7
Downturn	1980:3	(-2)	1980:3	(-2)	1980:1
Upturn	1980:7	(5)	1980:7	(5)	1980:12
Downturn	1981:8	(1)	1981:8	(1)	1981:9
Upturn	1984:2	(2)	1983:7	(9)	1984:4
Downturn	1984:8	(10)	1984:7	(11)	1985:6

[a] The global interest level here is a weighted average of the prime rate in the 11 largest OECD countries. As a result of the use of trade weights, this interest rate is slightly less shaped by the development in the US interest rate than if the estimate had been made on a basis of capital market weights.

Note: The figures in brackets show how many months passed before the shift in the particular interest rate had its "equivalent" in the Swedish interest rate.

the Swedish interest rate and the US rate in particular has sometimes been very big, occasionally as large as 10 percentage points.

Responsiveness to foreign development shifts has increased

Roughly speaking shifts in the development of the US rate and the global rate coincide, as can be seen from Table 6.3. Since the beginning of the 1980s the Swedish interest rate has responded to movements in this development fairly closely. The tendency is that a major shift abroad is reflected in an equivalent shift in the Swedish interest trend a month or so later.

6.2.4 Interest rate on government bonds/government notes

Swedish and foreign rates exhibit a parallel trend

Figures 6.8 and 6.9 show that since 1968 there has been an upward trend in the interest rate on Swedish government bonds/government notes. We can see a similar trend in the USA, albeit almost always on a slightly higher level. The weighted trend for the

Figure 6.6 Lending rate to first-class borrowers (prime rate) in Sweden vis-à-vis the weighted trend of the corresponding rates in the 11 largest OECD countries 1974-84
Percentage per year, observations at the end of each month

- - - - Sweden
——— weighted[a] trend in the 11 largest OECD countries

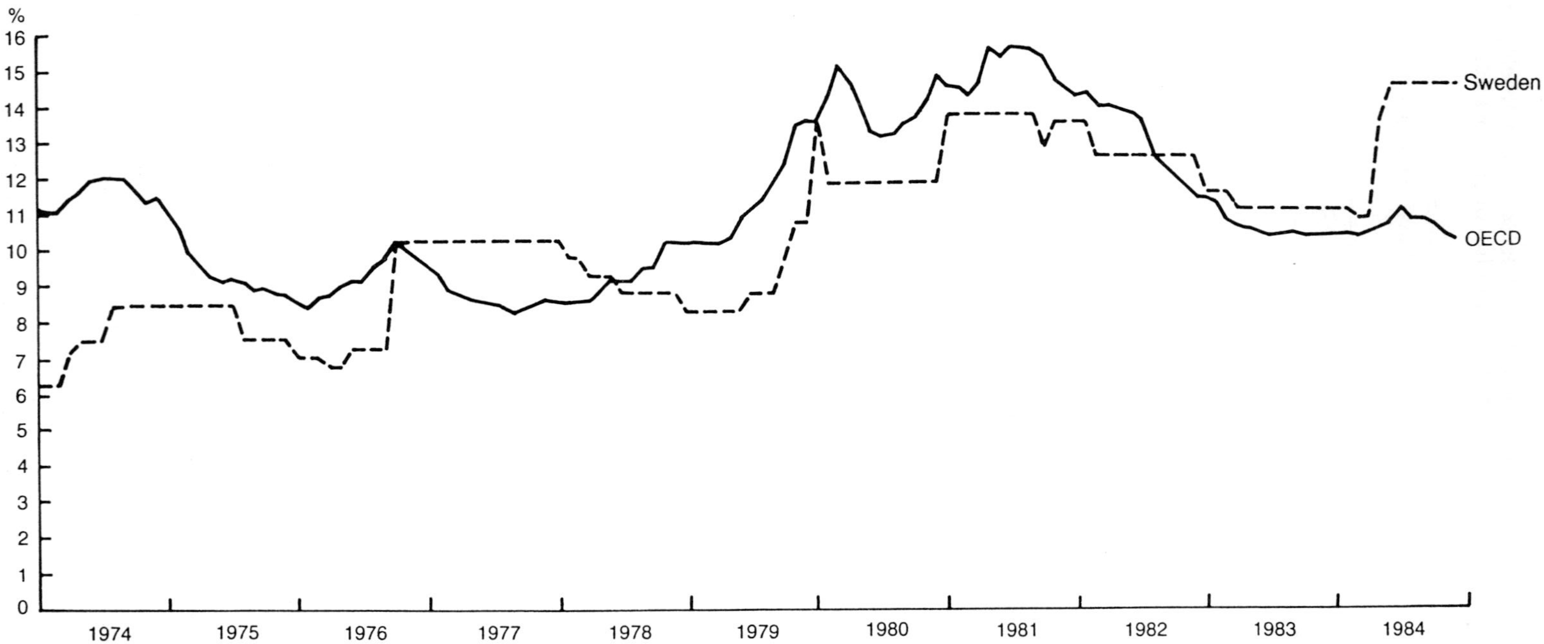

[a] Weighted with trade weights (in accordance with the Swedish currency basket). These weights give a weighted trend which in 1980-81 fell short of the trend given by capital flow weights by 0.5 percentage points, and in 1982-83 exceeds this trend by 0.5 percentage points.

Figure 6.7 Lending rate to first-class borrowers (prime rate) in Sweden vis-à-vis the corresponding rates in the USA 1974-84
Percentage per year, observations at the end of each month

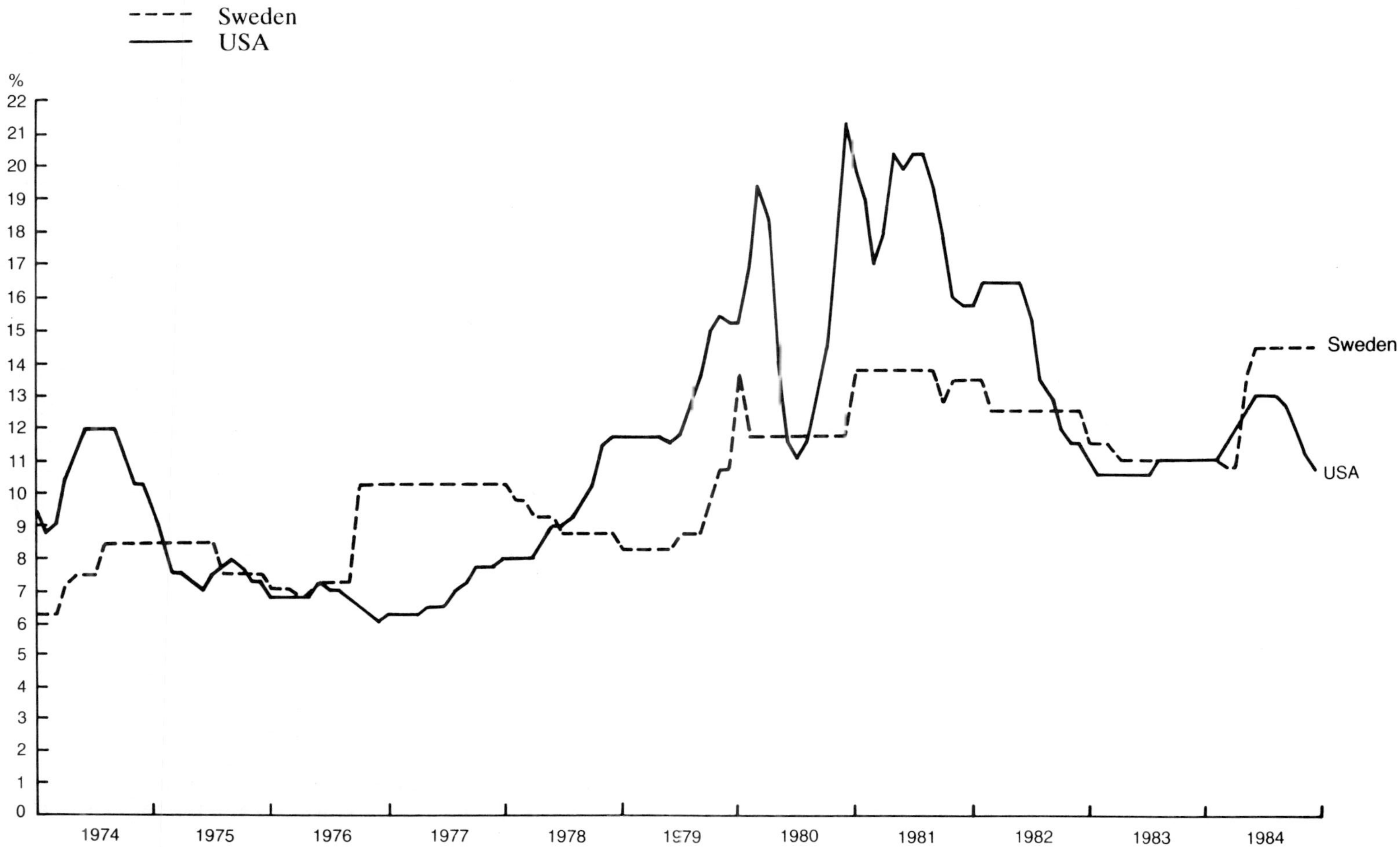

Figure 6.8 Interest rate on Swedish government bonds/government notes vis-à-vis the weighted rate for government bonds in the 11 largest OECD countries 1974-84

Percentage per year, observations at the end of each month

- - - - Sweden

——— Weighted[a] average for the 11 largest OECD countries

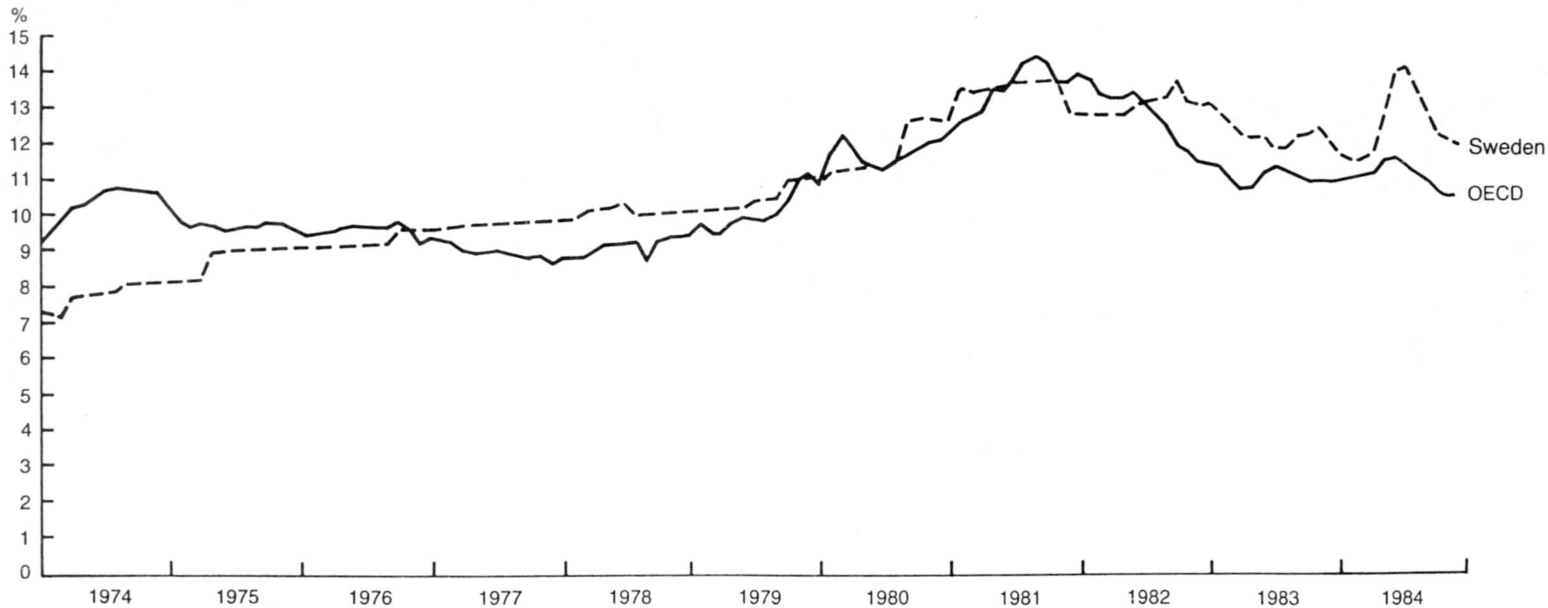

a Weighted with bilateral trade weights (in accordance with the Swedish currency basket). If OECD's capital market weights had been used, the curve of the weighted trend would have moved down one percentage point.

Figure 6.9 Interest rate on Swedish government bonds/government notes vis-à-vis the corresponding rate for the US government bonds 1974-84
Percentage per year, observations at the end of each month

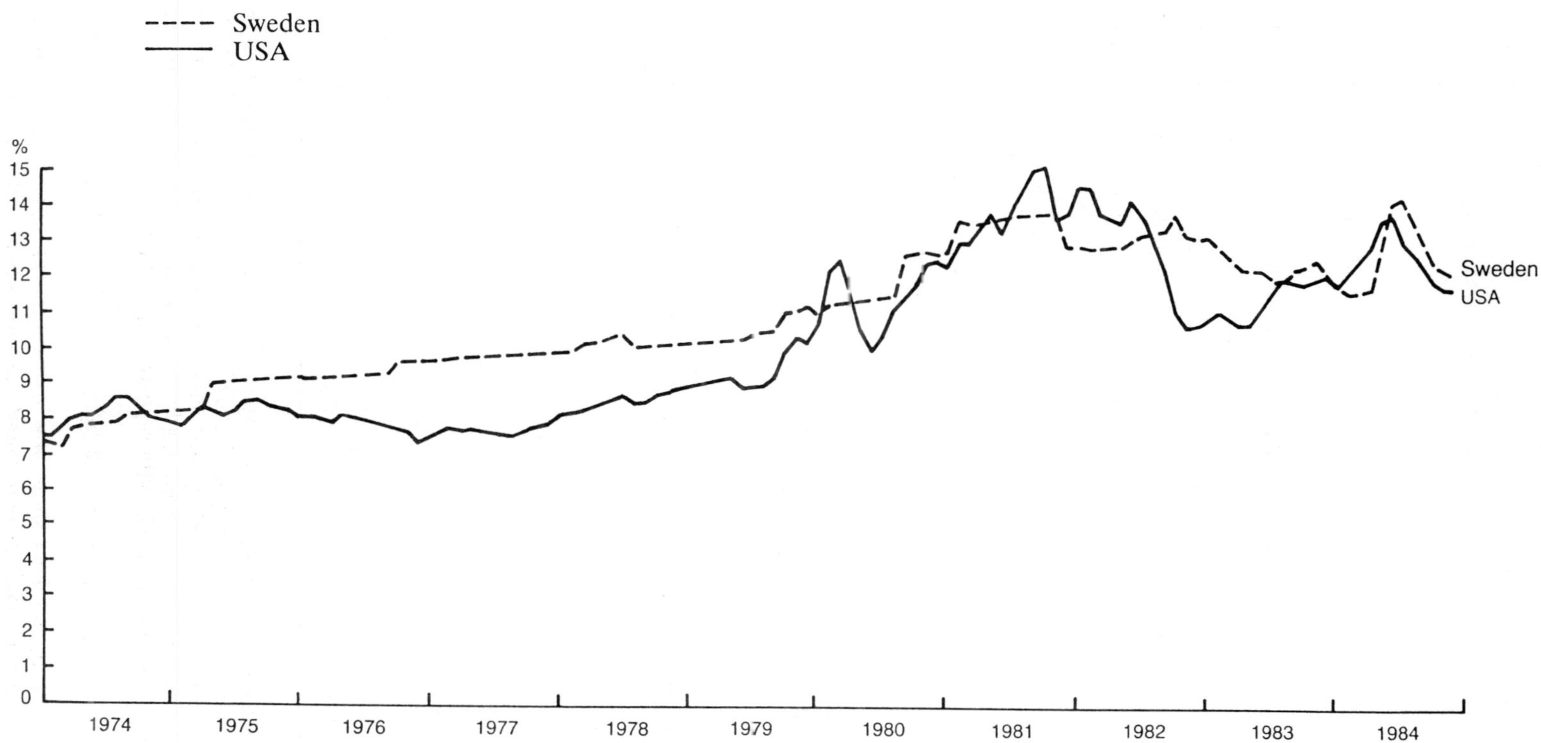

OECD countries is more cyclical in character, and there have sometimes been large gaps between this aggregate interest rate and the Swedish rate.

Only in recent years have major shifts in the foreign development been reflected in the Swedish interest rate

Table 6.4 shows major shifts in the interest development for government bonds in the period 1961–84. The major shifts in the US rate and the global rate match one another pretty well in timing, except in the middle of the 1970s when the lag between them amounted to 12 months. But the shifts in the US and global rates during 1968–81 are not reflected in the Swedish interest rate for government bonds. Since that time period, however, shifts in the global level appear to have made an impact in Sweden. This suggests that the integration of the government bond market has increased. Since the government bond rate is often used in corporate yield estimates as a measure for a risk-free rate, we can take this to mean that corporate requirements on rates of return on investments are being increasingly determined on the international financial markets.

Table 6.4 **Major shifts in the interest rate development for government bonds 1961–84**
Month when bottom and top quotations were registered

	US interest rate		Global interest rate[a]		Interest rate in Sweden
Upturn	1961:5	(21)	–	–	1963:2
Downturn	1970:6	–	1970:6	–	–
Upturn	1972:11	–	1972:2	–	–
Downturn	1975:9	–	1974:9	–	–
Upturn	1976:12	–	1977:10	–	–
Downturn	1980:3	–	1980:3	–	–
Upturn	1980:6	–	1980:7	–	–
Downturn	1982:1	(-2)	1981:9	(2)	1981:11
Upturn	1983:4	(10)	1983:4	(10)	1984:2
Downturn	1984:6	(1)	1984:6	(1)	1984:7

[a] The global rate is here a weighted average, using trade weights, of the interest rate on government bonds in the 11 largest OECD countries. As a result of the use of trade weights, this interest rate is slightly less shaped by the development in the US interest rate than if the estimate had been made on a basis of capital market weights. For technical reason the global rate is only reported since 1968.

[b] The Swedish rate since October 1983 refers to the interest rate on government notes.

Note: The figures in brackets show how many months passed before the shift in the particular interest rate had its "equivalent" in the Swedish interest rate.

6.2.5 *Interest rate on industrial bonds*

Since 1975 the Swedish interest rate has been systematically higher than the global interest level

Figure 6.10 shows that the nominal interest rate for Swedish industrial bonds used to deviate considerably from the weighted interest development in the major OECD countries. Since 1975 the Swedish interest rate has been almost consistently higher than the weighted OECD level, something which can hardly be regarded as the intended result of economic policy measures. Rather, it was a result of the market's expectations and its demands for premiums for various types of risk. The interest differential on industrial bonds in Sweden and the USA is illustrated in Figure 6.11. We can see that the interest gap has been very much smaller than the corresponding gap between the interest rates in Sweden and the OECD aggregate. A further difference is that the interest rate in the USA has sometimes been considerably higher than the rate on Swedish industrial bonds.

Table 6.5 Major shifts in the interest rate development for industrial bonds 1974–84
Month when bottom and top quotations were registered

	US interest rate		Global interest rate[a]		Interest rate in Sweden
Upturn	–		–		before 1974
Downturn	1974:9	–	1974:10	–	–
Upturn	1976:10	–	1978:1	–	–
Downturn	1980:3	–	1980:3	–	–
Upturn	1980:6	–	1980:6	–	–
Downturn	1981:9	(0)	1981:10	(-1)	1981:9
Upturn	1983:4	(11)	1983:4	(11)	1984:3
Downturn	1984:6	(5)	1984:6	(5)	1984:11

[a] The global rate is here a weighted average, using trade weights, of the interest rate in the USA, West Germany, the Netherlands, England, Switzerland and Japan. As a result of the use of trade weights, this interest rate is slightly less shaped by the development in the US interest rate than if the estimate had been made on a basis of capital market weights. Since the global rate is only estimated here for five countries apart from the USA, we can – other things being equal – expect greater similarity between the US rate and the global rate than in the case of the other types of interest rate I have discussed.

Note: The figures in brackets show how many months passed before the trend shift in the particular interest rate had its "equivalent" in the Swedish interest rate.

Figure 6.10 Interest rate on Swedish industrial bonds vis-à-vis the weighted average of the corresponding interest rate in the six largest OECD countries 1974-84

Percentage per year, observations at the end of each month

---- Sweden
—— Weighted average[a] of the interest rate for industrial bonds in the USA, West Germany, the Netherlands, Great Britain, Switzerland and Japan.

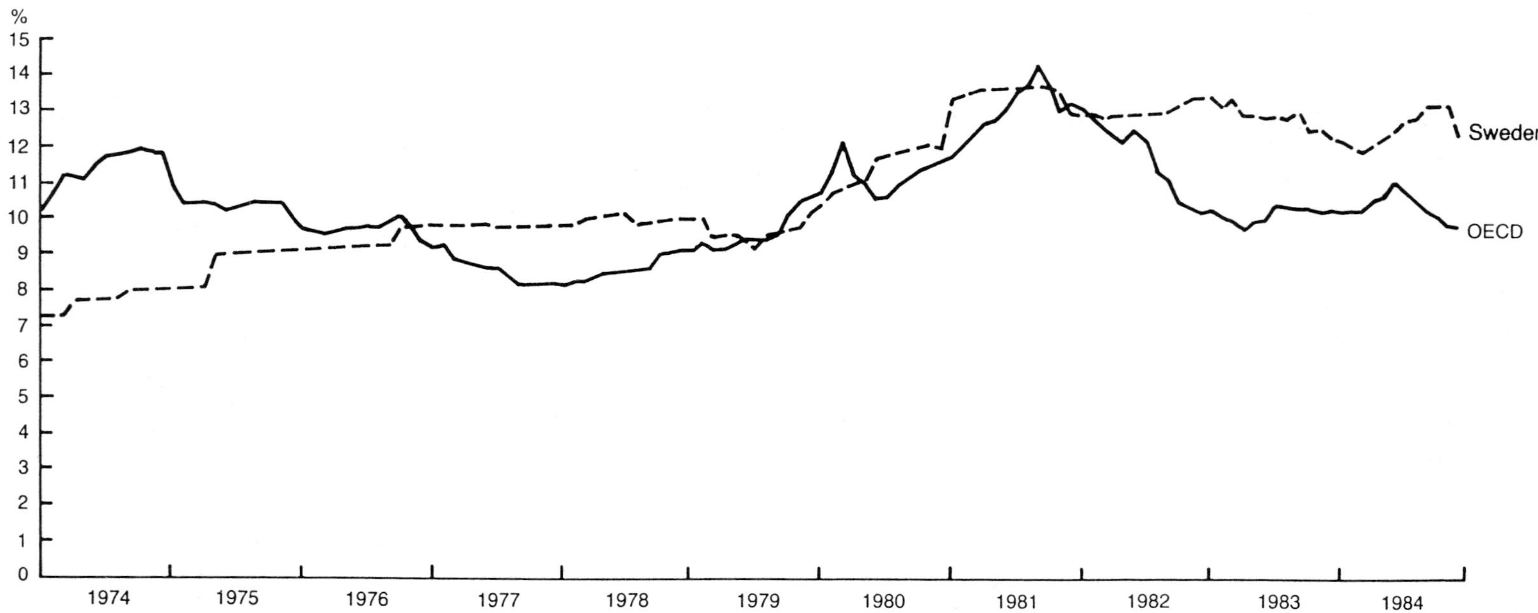

[a] Weighted with bilateral trade weights, in accordance with the Swedish currency basket.

Figure 6.11 Interest rate on Swedish industrial bonds vis-à-vis a corresponding rate for industrial bonds in the USA 1974-84
Percentage per year, observations at the end of each month

More immediate impact from major shifts in the foreign development during the 1980s

Table 6.5 shows the coincidence between major shifts in the US interest development and the global level. Up to September 1981 the major discernible shifts in these rates do not appear to have been reflected in the nominal Swedish interest rate for industrial bonds. Since then, however, they have made an impact on the Swedish interest level. This may be regarded as an indication of increasing integration in the Swedish market for industrial bonds.

The tendency towards a decreasing interest rate in the USA since 1984 can be explained to some extent by the abolition of the withholding tax on the lending interest rate. In 1984 this tax was also abolished in West Germany and France, which helped to reinforce the downward trend in the OECD aggregate.

6.2.6 Nominal interest rate fluctuations on the world market have increased in strength and frequency

Supplement 1 at the end of the book shows how the variability of the five interest rates studied here has changed over time. It appears that short-term interest rates are generally more variable than long-term rates, and that both kinds of interest have become more variable over time in most combinations of interest rate/country. In some cases, such as the prime rate in Denmark and the USA, the standard deviation has doubled or almost doubled between 1974–77 and 1978–84.

The variability of different interest rates has been extremely "contagious". And Mascaro and Meltzner (1983), describing the situation in the USA, have confirmed that the interventions of economic policy have not led to any reduction in risk in recent years. Further confirmation of this comes from the fact that since 1979 not only interest rates but also the growth in the money supply has become more variable.

We can also see from Supplement 1 that when it comes to the type of interest rate which reveals the greatest variability (treasury discount notes or prime rate), the picture is not the same in the different countries. In the largest OECD countries the prime rate exhibits the greatest variability, while in smaller countries such as Sweden and Belgium the most variable interest is the rate on treasury bills.[7]

As can be seen in Supplement 1, long-term interest rates – which are an important factor in the expectations on which most investments are based – fluctuate less than short-term rates. However, the variation in the interest rate on government bonds, for example, has been increasing worldwide since the end of 1960, as can be seen in Table 6.6.[8] In the last year of our period, however, there seems to have been a reversal in this trend, which contradicts Mascaro and Meltzer's (1983) results for the period immediately following 1979.

Table 6.6 **Standard deviations in interest rates on government bonds 1968–85**
Percentage per year, observations at the end of each month

	1968–70	1971–73	1974–76	1977–79	1980–82	1983–85
USA	0.6	0.5	0.3	0.8	1.5	0.9
Canada	0.6	0.4	0.5	0.7	1.7	0.9
Great Britain	0.8	1.1	1.0	1.0	1.3	0.2
Germany	0.9	0.8	1.2	0.9	1.0	0.4
Japan	0.1	0.5	0.3	1.0	0.6	0.3
France	1.0	0.5	0.8	0.8	1.5	1.0
Italy	1.1	0.5	1.7	0.5	2.5	3.5
Sweden	0.5	0.1	0.7	0.4	0.9	0.5

6.3 Deviations of Swedish real interest rates from foreign real interest rates

In perfectly totally integrated markets, in which international purchasing power parity and the International Fisher Effect obtain, expected real interest rates would be the same. However, in a foreign exchange system such as the Swedish, quite large temporary deviations from purchasing power parity can arise, and these are probably taken into account when the market forms its expectations. If these imbalances are not corrected during the period which the interest rate reflects, there will naturally be movements over time in the actual real interest rate.

Substantial differences between real interest rates in different currencies

An analysis of both short-term and long-term rates also reveals big differences in the real interest rates on securities in different currencies. In the case of short-term interest rates, for example the three-month interest rate, there have been substantial differences between the real interest rates for DEM and USD since the collapse of the Bretton Woods agreement. This applies to both actual and expected real interest rates. During the later 1970s the real interest rate in the USA was as much as 5 per cent lower than the corresponding German real interest rate. During the early 1980s, the reverse applied. Many researchers[9] have used these differentials in an attempt to explain exchange rate movements over the last decade. For quite long periods there is also a convincing connection between observed exchange movements and expected changes in the real interest rate differential.

Table 6.7 shows the real yield on industrial bonds, divided into different periods. We can see, for instance, that German industrial bonds generated the highest real yield[10] throughout the 1970s. The biggest country differentials appear in the years immediately after the collapse of the Bretton Woods system and the first oil crisis. During that period investors may have been affected by some confusion in assessing the choice of policy in different countries. Great Britain was conducting an expansive monetary policy, while West Germany and Switzerland, for example, preferred a more contractive approach. In such a situation the market was probably unable to form sufficiently realistic expectations about the subsequent inflation explosion. Big differences in real interest rates also appeared in the period immediately following the reorganization of economic policy in the United States in October 1979.

The gap between Swedish and foreign real interest rates has increased during the period of the analysis

The average gap between Swedish and foreign real interest rates has increased during the period of the analysis. During the period 1978–84 the actual Swedish real interest rate has been lower on an average than the real interest rate in the USA. Depending on the type of interest, this gap varies between 2 and 5 percentage points. The equivalent gap between the Swedish rate and the global rate is somewhat less, roughly between 1 and 3 percentage points. Figure 6.12 illustrates, as an example, the real yield on

Table 6.7 Real yield on industrial bonds 1965–84
Percentage per year, average for the period

	USA	Canada	Japan	Great Britain	West Ger–many	France	Italy	Bel-gium	Switz-erland	Sweden	Range
1965–69	1.8	2.6	2.1	3.1	4.7	3.2	4.3	3.2	1.0	2.4	3.7
1970–74	0.7	1.8	–3.4	1.0	3.2	1.3	–0.7	1.0	–1.3	0.2	6.6
1975–79	0.3	0.4	0.5	–2.2	3.0	0.5	–3.2	1.3	1.6	–0.1	6.2
1980–84	4.9	4.6	4.1	2.9	4.2	3.6	1.1	5.2	0.3	2.8	4.9
1983	8.1	5.9	5.6	6.2	4.6	4.9	2.9	4.1	1.2	3.5	6.9
1984	8.2	8.4	4.5	5.8	5.4	5.7	4.2	5.6	1.6	5.6	6.6

Note: The estimates are based on the yield on (long-term) industrial bonds at the close of every month, subtracted by the percentage change in the respective consumer price index during the immediately preceding twelve-month period. The column furthest to the right shows the range, i.e. the difference between the highest and lowest real interest rate for each period.

Figure 6.12 Real yield on industrial bonds 1960-84
Percentage per year, observations at the end of each quarter

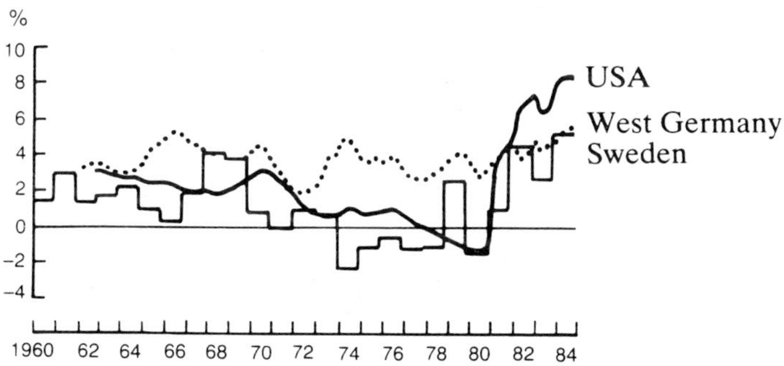

Note: The effective long-term interest rate on industrial bonds is given for West Germany and the USA. It is deflated by the annual average on the consumer price index. For Sweden the lowest issuing rate is given, and that too is deflated by the consumer price index.

Source: OECD, IUI.

industrial bonds in the USA and West Germany, compared with the situation in Sweden.

The standard deviation for actual and expected real interest rates in Sweden during the period 1978–84, was roughly the same as for the world rate, while for the real interest rate in the USA the standard deviation was generally twice as big.

6.4 What does this initial comparison suggest about financial integration?

Large and growing differentials between real interest rates indicate that *total* financial integration has diminished. This may be because monetary integration and/or the integration between goods markets has declined. Thus direct financial integration may not necessarily have been reduced.

Does this historical outline give us any indication that *direct* integration between the Swedish and foreign financial markets has increased? Indeed it does but in a weak form: the greater frequency with which major shifts in the US and global rates seem to lead to major shifts in Swedish interest rates, is such an indication. The figures have also revealed some responsiveness among nominal interest rates, albeit combined with big gaps. An interpretation of this data in terms of responsiveness to international interest rate movements leads to the initial impression that the direct financial integration of the Swedish financial market has increased. The substantial gaps between Swedish and foreign interest rates, however, give no grounds for any further inferences without the information that a detailed analysis could supply. Chapter 8 is intended to meet this need. But before embarking on such an analysis I shall first quantify the correlation between domestic and foreign interest rate movements in the next chapter.

Notes

1 Henceforth I shall refer to the weighted average of the OECD countries' interest rates as the "global interest level". The weights in the Swedish currency basket have been used.

2 I date major shifts in the development to the point at which there is a reversal of signs in the change, and when the discount rate development has changed direction in a "convincing" manner, i.e. there was no change back the next month.

3 Figures 6.2–6.11 showing the gaps between Swedish interest rates and the equivalent international rates all have the *same* scale, to make it easier to compare the different types of interest rates.

4 The substantial interest differentials that arise between the administratively determined interest rates on treasury bills and the market-determined treasury discount notes, gives an indication of financial protection, when rationing effects and the interest of the Dept Office in this instrument are taken into account. At the end of April 1985 the interest level on treasury bills was 7 per cent, which can be compared with a return of around 13.5 per cent on treasury discount notes.

5 Although the global rate is a constructed interest rate, I think we can still refer to possible influence on other interest rates as "caused" influence. Once more it should be pointed out that it is possible that the influence may be illusory, and that the changes in the two interest rates are symptoms of movements in a common exogenous factor.

6 The series of commercial bank lending rates to prime borrowers are used as standardized and published in World Financial Markets by Morgan Guaranty Trust Company.

7 In Sweden this can be explained in part by the introduction of the treasury discount notes as a modified form of treasury bill.

8 The trend-adjusted development shows an even more marked increase for each one of the eight countries. In 1980–82 the standard deviation in six of the countries is about three times greater than during 1968–70.

9 See, for example, Oxelheim (1982) for a description of the link between the SEK exchange rate and the deviations of the Swedish real interest rate from the foreign rates.

10 The calculation of the real interest rate is based on a simple approximation of the market's inflation expectations. Alternative measures such as official inflation forecasts, data from studies of the market's inflation expectations, time series analysis etc, all have their drawbacks and only seem to confirm the impression which the simple approximation gives us here.

CHAPTER 7

Swedish Interest Rate Dependence: A Correlation Analysis

7.1 Introduction

In Chapter 6 we obtained a visual impression of the responsiveness of Swedish interest rates to the development in international interest rates. In this chapter I shall measure in quantitative terms the relationship between foreign interest movements and changes in Swedish interest rates, and the time it takes for foreign movements to affect the Swedish rates. The importance of the lagged effect of foreign interest rate movements will thus become manifest. In the absence of a theory explaining this influence, our scrutiny of the data will determine our modelling of lagged influence in Chapter 8.

The analysis below will concern the Swedish interest rate and its relationship with the "global interest level" and the US rate. The analysis covers the period 1974–84, and is divided into subperiods. The analysis of the discount rate starts from 1964 and of the interest rate on government bonds from 1968. Trade weights in accordance with the weights in the Swedish currency basket and capital market weights are used to obtain a global interest rate level.

Section 7.2 discusses the covariation between real interest rates as a basis for an evaluation of the level of total financial integration.

Section 7.3 presents an analysis of the covariation between nominal Swedish interest rates and the corresponding rates abroad, with a lag of up to 36 months. Our earlier discussion has made it fairly clear that the way in which exchange rates develop must somehow be taken into account in a study of the international dependence of the Swedish interest rate. One way of keeping the problem of the exchange rate under control, is to study the relationship between the Swedish interest rate and the corresponding foreign rate covered on the forward market for foreign exchange. An analysis of this relationship is introduced in Section 7.4.

Section 7.5 consists of a summary of the results of the analysis, and an interpretation of these results in terms of total and direct financial integration.

7.2 Covariation between Swedish and foreign real interest rates

Equal expectations as regard real interest rates is our indication of *total* financial integration. We have already observed that Swedish expected real interest rates have varied over time. The question now is the extent to which they have covaried with expected real interest rates abroad.

Covariation between the Swedish and the global real interest level has been declining

Table 7.1 shows the correlation between the Swedish real interest *level* and the foreign real interest *level*. In the table I have divided the correlation into three periods, so that I can compare developments over time. As a general pattern throughout we find that correlation is strongest between the Swedish real interest rate and the global rate. We can also see that the correlation between actual real interest rates is higher than that for expected real interest rates. Moreover, the link between the Swedish real interest rate level and the level in the rest of the world has become weaker during the period of the analysis. For the 1981–84 period we find no significant correlation at all.

Covariation between Swedish and foreign real interest rate movements has also declined

In Table 7.2 we can see the correlation between *changes* in Swedish and foreign real interest rates. The pattern recalls the correlation between real interest rate levels. The covariation with the global interest level is still clearly the strongest. The difference as between actual and expected quantities, however, is not so marked as for real interest rate levels. For the period 1974–78 the highest correlation between changes appears for expected real long-term interest rates.[1] Here, a change in the expected global real interest rate for industrial bonds can explain over 50 per cent of the variation in the movements of the real interest rate for Swedish industrial bonds.[2]

The covariation between movements in Swedish real interest rates and foreign rates has declined substantially during the period of the analysis. This tendency holds globally, as the correlation between the global interest movements and changes in the US rate has also declined, albeit not so markedly.

The total integration of Sweden's financial markets has declined

My correlation studies of the real interest level and of changes in this level reveal that the covariation has declined, suggesting that the total integration of the Swedish financial market has also decreased. These observations accord well with my observations in Chapter 6 on the increasing gap between expected real interest rates in Sweden and abroad.

Table 7.1 Correlation between Swedish real interest level and corresponding real level for the global interest rate and the US interest rate, 1974–84

Correlation of Swedish real interest rate with:	1974–78 Actual real interest rate	1974–78 Expected real interest rate	1979–84 Actual real interest rate	1979–84 Expected real interest rate	1981–84 Actual real interest rate	1981–84 Expected real interest rate
Global discount rate	0.80*	0.44	0.63*	0.12	–0.50	–0.16
US discount rate	0.42	0.19	0.55*	0.23	–0.34	–0.33
Global interest rate for treasury bills	0.75*	–0.03	0.51*	–0.15	–0.18	–0.03
Interest rate for treasury bills in the USA	0.40	0.09	0.47*	–0.35	0.19	–0.16
Global prime rate	0.80*	0.41	0.66*	0.34	–0.47	–0.28
US prime rate	0.43	0.15	0.55*	0.29	–0.40	–0.14
Global interest rate for government bonds	0.75*	0.75*	0.59*	0.46*	–0.42	–0.15
Interest rate for US government bonds	0.38	0.39	0.57*	0.37	–0.46	–0.10
Global interest rate for industrial bonds	0.72*	0.84*	0.60*	0.57*	–0.48	0.11
US interest rate for industrial bonds	0.43	0.47*	0.59*	0.42	–0.56	–0.14

Note:* marks the significance in two-tailed tests at the 5 % level. The actual real interest rate is estimated as the rate at the beginning of the quarter minus actual inflation during the quarter. Expected real interest rate is estimated as the rate at the beginning of the quarter minus expected inflation in the shape of the inflation during the immediately preceding quarter. Weighting has been based on trade weights.

Table 7.2 **Correlation between Swedish real interest movements and corresponding movements in the global interest rate and the US interest rate, 1974–84**
Quarterly data

	1974–78		1979–84		1981–84	
Correlation between the Swedish real interest rate and:	Actual real interest rate	Expected real interest rate	Actual real interest rate	Expected real interest rate	Actual real interest rate	Expected real interest rate
Global discount rate	0.70*	0.51*	0.49*	0.50*	0.27	0.50
US discount rate	0.50*	0.42*	0.21*	0.11	0.24	0.28
Global interest rate for treasury bills	0.65*	0.44	0.43	0.07	0.36	0.19
Interest rate for treasury bills in the USA	0.34	0.38	0.19	–0.19	0.44	–0.16
Global prime rate	0.71*	0.49*	0.50*	0.34	0.41	0.50
US prime rate	0.53*	0.39	0.15	–0.04	0.36	0.29
Global interest rate for government bonds	0.70*	0.70*	0.40	0.43*	0.35	0.57
Interest rate for US government bonds	0.49*	0.52*	0.17	0.09	0.23	0.29
Global interest rate for industrial bonds	0.67*	0.72*	0.40	0.42	0.35	0.55
US interest rate for industrial bonds	0.50*	0.50*	0.15	0.01	0.21	0.15

Note: See note to Table 7.1.

7.3 Covariation between the Swedish nominal interest rate and the foreign rate

7.3.1 Correlation between interest levels

To what extent does the Swedish nominal interest rate covariate with the foreign rate? Table 7.3 shows the level of covariation between the global interest level and the interest level in the USA on the one hand and the Swedish rate on the other. The table exhibits the cross-correlation measured for terms of interest *levels.* I have calculated two averages for the global level here, one based on trade weights in accordance with the weights in the Swedish currency basket, and the other on OECD's capital market weights.

Three patterns are discernible

A general feature of all these types of interest rates is that the lagging by a significant number of months has declined. However, a closer analysis reveals that the correlation pattern is very heterogeneous. Three patterns can be discerned. They are illustrated in Figure 7.1.

Pattern *a* applies mainly to long-term interest rates for the various subperiods and to treasury bills for the period as a whole. According to this pattern significant coefficients are obtained for the correlation between the Swedish interest rate for the period and the foreign rate in the immediately preceding period. If the lag is increased, the coefficients become insignificant, and after a sufficiently long time they become significantly negative. Pattern *b* applies to long-term interest rates for the whole period of the study. Here the coefficients are significantly positive for all the early periods. Pattern *c* applies to the short-term interest rates, and here the coefficients are significantly positive for the most immediate period but are otherwise insignificant. The relationship between patterns *b* and *c* seems intuitively correct, in that successive quotations of the long-term rate should have a large common component which remains as a significant element very much longer than in the case of short-term interest rates. Pattern *a* could perhaps be explained by lags in the phases of the business cycle in Sweden in relation to the US and the global cycle respectively.

The lag which we see here is a dimension of my measure of direct financial integration. In order to be able to interpret it in terms of integration, further information is required about the size and degree of significance in the coefficients of correlation.

Table 7.3 **Cross-correlation pattern for Swedish interest rate/foreign rate with significant[a] lag in number of months (level), 1974–84**
Monthly observations

Interest rate	Period	Significant lag in number of months					
		"Global rate"				US rate	
		Trade-weighted		Capital market-weighted			
Treasury bills/ treasury discount notes[b]	Jan 1974–Dec 1984	0–22	(0–31)	0–27	(0–35)	0–34	(0–36)
	Jan 1978–Dec 1984	0–14	(0–16)	0–10	(0–15)	0–6	(0–8)
	Jan 1981–Dec 1984	–	(5–11)	–	(6–12)	–	(0.8–13)
Loan to first-class borrowers	Jan 1974–Dec 1984	0–26	(0–31)	0–22	(0–36)	0–36	(0–36)
	Jan 1978–Dec 1984	0–14	(0–16)	0–14	(0–16)	0–13	(0–15)
	Jan 1981–Dec 1984	17–24	(0–3, 14–27)	0–1 17–24	(0–4, 14–27)	0–3 18–24	(0–6, 15–28)
Government bonds/ government notes[c]	Jan 1968–Dec 1984	0–36	(0–36)	0–36	(0–36)	0–36	(0–36)
	Jan 1978–Dec 1984	0–16	(0–18)	0–16	(0–18.36)	0–15	(0–17, 32–36)
	Jan 1981–Dec 1984	0–3	(0–6, 20–27)	0–3	(0–9, 20–23, 26–28)	0–3	(0–11, 19–22)
Industrial bonds	Jan 1974–Dec 1984	0–21	(0–26)	0–25	(0–29)	0–30	(0–34)
	Jan 1978–Dec 1984	0–20	(0–22)	0–19	(0–21)	0–18	(0–20, 34–36)
	Jan 1981–Dec 1984	0–2 29–30	(0–14, 24–34)	0–1, 29–30	(0–14, 23–33)	–	(1–15, 22–32)
Official discount rate	Jan 1964–Dec 1984	0–36	(0–36)	0–36	(0–36)	0–36	(0–36)
	Jan 1978–Dec 1984	0–16, 33–36	(0–18, 29–36)	0–16, 32–36	(0–17, 27–36)	0–16 36	(0–18, 31–36)
	Jan 1981–Dec 1984	0–6	(0–9, 20–31)	0–6	(0–8, 20–32)	0–7	(0–9, 21–33)

[a] By a significant coefficient of cross-correlation is meant a coefficient which in absolute terms exceeds 3 standard deviations (the lag for coefficients which exceed 2 standard deviations is given in brackets).
[b] From October 1982 the Swedish interest rate is the rate on 90-day treasury discount notes.
[c] From November 1983 the Swedish interest rate is the rate for government bonds.

Figure 7.1 Empirical pattern of correlation

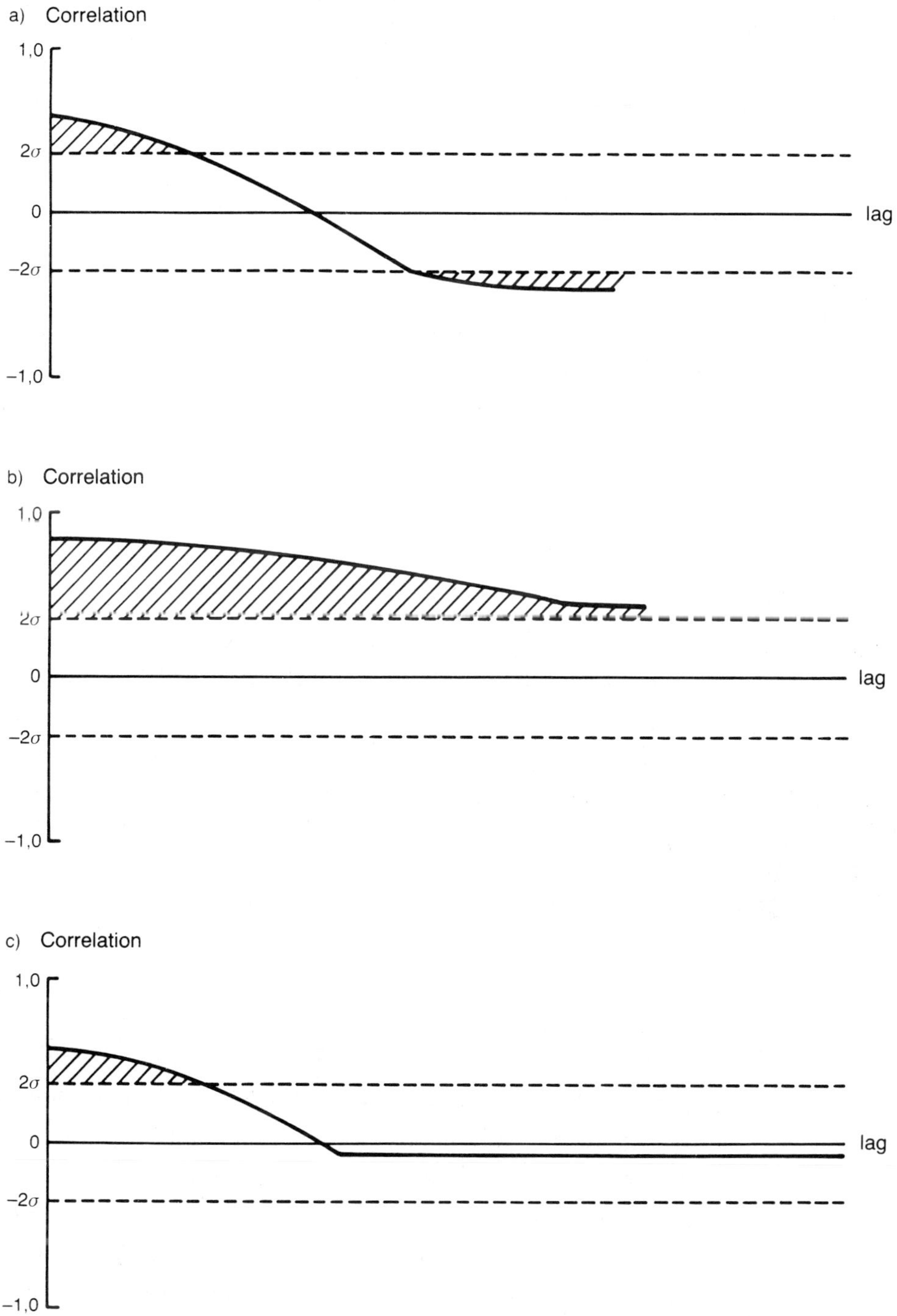

Correlation with the US rate differs from correlation with the global rate

The pattern for the correlation between the US interest rate and the Swedish rate differs somewhat from the pattern of the correlation between the global rate and the Swedish rate.[3] The pattern of correlation with the US rate seems to be less stable than the correlation pattern with the global rate, which may have a technical explanation in that, as an aggregate, the global rate has less variance.

7.3.2 Correlation between interest rate movements

Studies based on nominal interest levels rather than on interest movements can tempt us to infer an excessively high covariation. By studying the covariation between *changes* in the interest levels, we obtain a more realistic measure of the influence of foreign interest rates. Table 7.4 shows the lag expressed as the number of months that pass before the Swedish interest rate exhibits any significant responsiveness.

Changes in the US rate have become less influential in recent years

In the case of all five types of interest the degree of significant influence from the US rate has declined. This becomes clear from a comparison of the period 1981–84 with the period of the study as a whole. In earlier periods when there was a significant relationship, interest movements on the US market were reflected in Swedish interest rates after a delay of six to nine months. Changes in the interest rate on treasury bills were an exception to this; during the period 1978–84 there could be up to 18 months delay. Changes in the US prime rate showed no significant influence in any period. We find no indication of a significant relationship between US and Swedish interest movements in the most recent period, 1981–84 for any kind of interest rate. This may be due, for instance, to the widespread use of technicals in dollar trading.

Together the size and pattern of the lag provide an ambivalent sign of greater covariation

Table 7.5 shows that the linear relationship between Swedish and foreign interest movements has increased in recent years for most types of interest. Because of the presence of negative coefficients of correlation it is rather difficult to interpret the meaning of this increase. I regard a *positive* correlation as an indication of financial integration. Another problem is that the standard deviation in the coefficients of correlation has increased, which means that the degree of significance has declined in recent

in number of months (first differential), 1974–84
Monthly observations

Interest rate	Period	Significant lag in number of months					
		"Global rate"				US rate	
		Trade-weighted		Capital market-weighted			
Treasury bills/ treasury discount notes[b]	Jan 1974–Dec 1984	–	(9, 14, 15, 18, 20, 26, 35)	–	(9, 14, 15, 18, 19)	9	(0, 4, 9, 18)
	Jan 1978–Dec 1984	–	(9, 15, 18, 23)	9, 18	(9, 18)	9, 18	(8, 9, 18)
	Jan 1981–Dec 1984	3	(3, 36)	3	(3, 36)	–	(2, 4)
Loan to first-class borrowers	Jan 1974–Dec 1984	2	(1, 2, 4, 14, 20, 21, 36)	–	(1, 2, 4, 14, 20, 21)	–	(2, 3, 14)
	Jan 1978–Dec 1984	–	(1, 2, 14)	–	(1, 2, 14)	–	(2)
	Jan 1981–Dec 1984	–	(20, 21, 36)	–	(20, 21, 36)	–	(21, 31, 36)
Government bonds/ government notes[c]	Jan 1968–Dec 1984	1, 12	(0, 1, 11, 12, 17)	1	(0, 1, 2, 11, 12, 17, 27, 34)	1	(0, 1, 2, 5, 12, 22, 27, 34, 35)
	Jan 1978–Dec 1984	1, 12	(0, 1, 11, 12, 34)	1	(0, 1, 11, 12)	1	(0, 1, 5, 12)
	Jan 1981–Dec 1984	–	(1, 12)	–	(1, 19)	–	(1, 19)
Industrial bonds	Jan 1974–Dec 1984	–	(9, 11, 14, 15, 18, 30)	–	(9, 14, 15, 30)	9	(5, 9, 15, 22, 24, 28, 30)
	Jan 1978–Dec 1984	–	(4, 9, 15, 30)	–	(4, 9, 15, 30)	9	(9, 15, 22, 30)
	Jan 1981–Dec 1984	–	(30)	–	(30)	–	
Official discount rate	Jan 1964–Dec 1984	0	(0, 1, 2, 4, 11, 14, 25, 28)	4	(0, 1, 2, 4, 11, 14, 15, 25, 28)	4	(1, 2, 4, 14, 15)
	Jan 1978–Dec 1984	14	(2, 4, 11, 14, 28)	4, 14	(1, 2, 4, 11, 14)	4	(1, 2, 4, 14, 15)
	Jan 1981–Dec 1984	–	(15)	–	(4, 20)	–	(4, 14, 20, 23, 31)

[a] By a significant coefficient of cross-correlation is meant a coefficient which in absolute terms exceeds 3 standard deviations (the lag for coefficients which exceed 2 standard deviations is given in brackets).
[b] From October 1982 the Swedish interest rate is the rate on 90-day treasury discount notes.
[c] From November 1983 the Swedish interest rate is the rate for government bonds.

Table 7.5 **Maximal correlation between lagged interest movements, 1974–84**
Monthly observations; lag given in number of months

Interest rate	Period	Significant lag in number of months					
		"Global rate"				US rate	
		Trade-weighted		Capital market-weighted			
Treasury bills/ treasury discount notes[a]	Jan 1974–Dec 1984	0.17	(18)	0.21	(18)	0.25*	(9)
	Jan 1978–Dec 1984	0.27	(18)	–0.33*	(9)	–0.38*	(9)
	Jan 1981–Dec 1984	–0.51*	(3)	–0.44*	(3)	0.31	(4)
Loan to first-class borrowers	Jan 1974–Dec 1984	0.25*	(2)	0.22	(2)	0.16	(2)
	Jan 1978–Dec 1984	0.24	(2)	0.23	(2)	0.19	(2)
	Jan 1981–Dec 1984	–0.44	(21)	–0.43	(21)	–0.40	(21)
Government bonds/ government notes[b]	Jan 1968–Dec 1984	0.29*	(1)	0.34*	(1)	0.35*	(1)
	Jan 1978–Dec 1984	0.33*	(1)	0.36*	(1)	0.36*	(1)
	Jan 1981–Dec 1984	0.34	(1)	0.41	(1)	0.42	(1)
Industrial bonds	Jan 1974–Dec 1984	0.21	(15)	–0.23	(9)	–0.25*	(9)
	Jan 1978–Dec 1984	–0.24	(9)	–0.25	(9)	–0.28*	(9)
	Jan 1981–Dec 1984	–0.29	(30)	–0.30	(30)	–0.26	(30)
Official discount rate	Jan 1964–Dec 1984	0.24*	(0)	0.24*	(4)	0.24*	(4)
	Jan 1978–Dec 1984	0.38*	(14)	0.34*	(4)	0.37*	(4)
	Jan 1981–Dec 1984	–0.30	(15)	–0.33	(20)	0.35	(4)

a From October 1982 the Swedish interest rate is the rate on 90-day treasury discount notes.
b From November 1983 the Swedish interest rate is the rate for government bonds.

* Absolute deviations from zero greater than three standard deviations.

Note: The lag in number of months on which the reported coefficient of correlation is calculated is given in brackets. By (9), for example, is meant the correlation between the change in foreign interest level and the change in the corresponding rate in Sweden 9 months later.

years for most types of interest. This circumstance is particularly marked in the covariation between the Swedish interest rates and the corresponding US rates.

Changes have also occurred in the length of time before the strongest relationship becomes evident. A shorter time-lag can be taken as an indicator of greater integration. However, changes in the time-lag in the correlation analysis coincide either with the relationship becoming insignificant and/or with it becoming negative. Thus the signals are not unequivocal as regards a possible increase in the influence of foreign interest movements.

This ambivalence reflects changes in foreign exchange policy during the period of the analysis. When formally fixed or semi-fixed exchange rates obtain, or when there is little variation in the rates, it may be sufficient to examine the covariation between nominal uncovered interest rates. But when floating exchange rates obtain and there is great currency turbulence, as in 1981–84, such an approach can be expected to be inadequate. We now have confirmation that in any study of the international integration of Swedish financial markets, the fluctuations in foreign exchange must be taken into account.

An analysis that ignores foreign exchange effects provides no lead

Many researchers have used the size of the cross-correlation between domestic and foreign nominal interest rates as an expression of the level of direct financial integration. In our case, however, it seems obvious that the neglect of foreign exchange rate effects gives rise to difficulties in interpreting results. When I perform a simple regression analysis with changes in the Swedish interest rate as a function of earlier changes in foreign rates, I also find indications of misspecifications. Everything suggests that it is the exchange rate effects that are missing.[4] In the next section we will therefore allow for these effects by a simple device, in the form of the forward premium. It is also important, to allow for the premium for political risk, and in the multiple regression analysis in Chapter 8 this premium will be included, together with a term for the market's exchange rate expectations and its demands for a premium for exchange risk.

7.4 Covariation between the Swedish interest rate and the forward-covered foreign interest rate

One way of considering the impact of the exchange rate on the covariation between interest rates, is to study the correlation between the Swedish interest rate and the corresponding foreign rate which has been covered on the forward market for foreign exchange. By adopting this procedure we eliminate the problem of exchange rate expectations and exchange rate risk. The problem of political risk remains, since the comparison must be made between national interest rates, in the absence of a Euro-krona rate for the whole period of the study.

The great majority of the transactions on the Swedish forward market refer to three-month or shorter contracts, while the market is "thin" as regards longer contracts. I shall therefore limit myself to three-month forward transactions, and cross-correlation for short-term rates only, i.e. the interest rate on treasury discount notes and the prime rate.

7.4.1 Correlation between interest levels

In calculating a cross-correlation with the global interest level, the forward cover transaction refers to weighted forward premiums, i.e. I calculate the cross-correlation between the Swedish interest rate and a weighted forward-covered foreign interest rate.

More immediate impact from foreign interest movements in recent years

Table 7.6 shows this cross-correlation in the case of interest *levels*. The pattern that emerges is essentially different from the one we saw in Table 7.3. Thus the inclusion of exchange rate effects does alter our conclusions.

The pattern is fairly clear as regards the duration of the lag, during which there is significant cross-correlation. Compared with the period of the study as a whole, the period 1981–84 seems to represent a dramatic reduction in this respect. The speed with which foreign interest rates make an impact has increased considerably.

7.4.2 Correlation between interest rate movements

Table 7.7 shows the pattern of cross-correlation between *changes* in Swedish interest rates and earlier changes in foreign rates.

Table 7.6 **Cross-correlation pattern for Swedish interest rate/covered foreign rate with significant[a] lag in number of months (levels), 1974–84**
Monthly observations

Interest rate	Period	Significant lag in number of months					
		"Global rate"				US rate	
		Trade-weighted		Capital market-weighted			
Treasury bills/ treasury discount notes[b]	Jan 1974–Dec 1984	0–8	(0–9)	0–7	(0–9)	0–7	(0–8)
	Jan 1978–Dec 1984	0–9	(0–11)	0–8	(0–9)	0–8	(0–9)
	Jan 1981–Dec 1984	0–1	(0–4)	0–1	(0–4)	0–3	(0–4)
Loan to first-class borrowers	Jan 1974–Dec 1984	0–11	(0–13)	0–11	(0–14)	0–12	(0–14)
	Jan 1978–Dec 1984	0–12	(0–16)	0–13	(0–16)	0–13	(0–16)
	Jan 1981–Dec 1984	0–1	(0–7)	0–4	(0–8)	0–4	(0–8)

[a] By a significant coefficient of cross-correlation is meant a coefficient which in absolute terms exceeds 3 standard deviations (the lag for coefficients which exceed 2 standard deviations is given in brackets).
[b] Since October 1982, the interest on 90-day treasury discount notes.

Table 7.7 **Cross-correlation pattern for Swedish interest movements/covered foreign interest movements with significant[a] lag in number of months (first differential), 1974–84**
Monthly observations

Interest rate	Period	Significant lag in number of months					
		"Global rate"				US rate	
		Trade-weighted		Capital market-weighted			
Treasury bills/ treasury discount notes[b]	Jan 1974–Dec 1984	–	(0, 1)	–	(0, 1)	–	(0)
	Jan 1978–Dec 1984	–	(0, 4, 8, 9, 20, 21)	–	(0, 4, 8, 9, 20, 21)	0	(0, 8, 9, 17)
	Jan 1981–Dec 1984	8	(1, 4, 8, 20)	4	(1, 4, 8, 20)	–	(0, 1, 4, 8, 20)
Loan to first-class borrowers	Jan 1974–Dec 1984	30	(29, 30)	30	(29, 30)	30	(29, 30)
	Jan 1978–Dec 1984	–	(13)	–	(13)	–	(0, 8)
	Jan 1981–Dec 1984	8	(8, 13, 23)	–	(8, 13, 23)	–	(8, 13 23)

[a] By a significant coefficient of cross-correlation is meant a coefficient which in absolute terms exceeds 3 standard deviations (the lag for coefficients which exceed 2 standard deviations is given in brackets).
[b] Since October 1982, the interest on 90-day treasury discount notes.

The timing of the impact of foreign interest rate movements is unclear

The pattern has become a little more difficult to interpret than when we were looking at the correlation between changes in forward-covered interest levels. When we estimate the relationship for the period 1981–84, it turns out that changes in the global rates for treasury bills/treasury discount notes make a significant impact on the Swedish rate after 4–8 months. The delay varies according to the weights I use in the weighted global rate: trade weights in accordance with the weights in the Swedish currency basket give an 8-month lag and capital market weights a 4-month lag. For the period 1974–84 as a whole, there is no equivalent significant impact.

In the case of the prime rate we find a significant impact on the Swedish interest rate during the period 1981–84, occurring 8 months after a change in the global prime rate. This lag can be compared with a 30-month lag for the period as a whole.

US rate now has less impact on Swedish interest rates

Not only the speed of impact but also the size of the correlation is of interest to any study of the changing level of direct financial integration. Table 7.8 shows the highest correlation between changes in the Swedish interest rate and the lagged covered foreign rate. Here, unlike Table 7.5, there are no negative coefficients.[5]

The correlation pattern for changes in the interest rates on treasury bills is convincing. During the period 1981–84 the correlation increased dramatically, compared with the correlation for the period as a whole. The correlation of the Swedish interest rate against the global rate is significant for this period, but not for the period as a whole. As regards the cross-correlation between changes in the Swedish interest rate and in the US rate, the opposite development obtains. For the period 1978–84 we find a significant correlation with immediate impact. In the period 1981–84 the significance disappears and the impact is felt after a delay of 8 months.

The prime rates show a strong correlation for the period as a whole and for the subperiod 1981–84. If we compare these two periods, we find that the correlation has declined somewhat during the latter period, but on the other hand the delay before the most significant impact on Swedish interest rates appears has fallen from 30 months to 8. As in the case of the interest rate on treasury discount notes, the correlation between changes in the Swedish prime rate and in the corresponding rate in the US loses in significance, but this time the impact occurs sooner.

Table 7.8 Maximal correlation between lagged changes in Swedish interest rate and in covered foreign rate, 1974–84
Monthly observations; lag given in number of months

Interest rate	Period	Significant lag in number of months					
		"Global rate"				US rate	
		Trade-weighted		Capital market-weighted			
Treasury bills/ treasury discount notes[a]	Jan 1974–Dec 1984	0.21	(0)	0.22	(0)	0.26	(0)
	Jan 1978–Dec 1984	0.35	(0)	0.36	(0)	0.51*	(0)
	Jan 1981–Dec 1984	0.46*	(8)	0.48*	(4)	0.43	(8)
Loan to first-class borrowers	Jan 1974–Dec 1984	0.46*	(30)	0.46*	(30)	0.47*	(30)
	Jan 1978–Dec 1984	0.23	(13)	0.23	(13)	0.23	(0)
	Jan 1981–Dec 1984	0.43*	(8)	0.42	(13)	0.33	(13)

a Since October 1982, the interest on 90-day treasury discount notes.

* Absolute deviations from zero greater than three standard deviations.

Note: The lag in No. month on which the reported coefficient of correlation is calculated is given in brackets. By (9), for example, is meant the correlation between the change in foreign interest level and the change in the corresponding rate in Sweden 9 month later.

The size and timing of the covariation between the Swedish interest rate and the covered foreign rate indicates a stronger link

In view of the size of the covariation and the pattern of the lagged impact of covered foreign rates, I conclude that Swedish interest rates are being increasingly determined by the global interest level. It also turns out that the global rate has taken over the role of the US rate as the global interest leader.

7.5 The correlation analysis and direct financial integration

Declining total integration does not exclude an increase in direct financial integration

The analysis of the link between the Swedish and the global real interest rates shows that the *total* integration of the Swedish financial market has declined. We have observed this in the shape of a bigger gap between Swedish real interest rates and foreign rates. We have also seen it in the form of a lower correlation between these two rates. In Chapter 4 we found that the deviations from purchasing power parity had been roughly as frequent and as large in the later part of our period as they were in the period as a whole.[6] Thus, growing deviations from international purchasing power parity and disintegrated goods markets may not explain the decline in total financial integration. The variability in the nominal krona rates increased during the period, while the variability in the real effective exchange rate by and large remained the same. Thus we do not obtain any clear indication of whether monetary disintegration increased to such an extent as to explain the decline in total financial integration. On the other hand it seems to me that the political risks in the shape of the likelihood of Swedish government intervention did increase. If this increase and the accompanying risk premiums can explain the decline in total financial integration, then it is still possible that direct financial integration increased.

Ambivalent indications of direct financial integration from the correlation analysis of nominal uncovered interest rates

Before making any more definite inferences about direct financial integration I would have liked the analysis of the cross-correlation between the Swedish interest rate and earlier changes in foreign rates to have given us a clear and unambiguous indication about the strength of the impact of the foreign interest fluctuations and the length of time before it took effect. The correlation analysis described above between nominal uncovered interest rates gives us no such clear-cut picture.

The exchange rate must be taken into account in studies of the interest gap

An important lesson learnt from the analysis of the correlation between nominal interest rates, however, is that unless the market's exchange rate expectations and risk premiums are taken into account *simultaneously*, we cannot identify any clear relationship between Swedish interest rates and earlier changes in foreign rates. When both these factors are taken into account in a comparison between Swedish nominal interest rates and the corresponding foreign rates covered on the forward market, it turns out that changes in the forward-covered global interest level for the period 1981–84 can explain 20–23 per cent of the variance in Swedish interest movements four months later.[7] When the effect of all lagged movements in forward-covered global interest levels is taken into account in a correlation analysis in which interest movements are the sole explanatory variable, a cautious interpretation could be that the lagged movements as a whole can explain 35–40 per cent of the variation in Swedish interest movements.

The correlation between covered interest rates provides weak indications of greater direct financial integration

Does the correlation analysis using covered interest rates show that changes in the level of direct financial integration may have occurred in recent years? To provide grounds for such a conclusion, the analysis of these interest rates should show an *increased* positive correlation and/or *shorter* lags. The cross-correlation has increased, and the impact of foreign interest movements on Swedish rates has appeared more quickly in recent years. The analysis thus suggests that the level of direct integration has increased. However, before we could make an unreserved statement about increased direct financial integration on a basis of the link between Swedish interest rates and the global interest level, the signals would have to be more definite.

It turns out that the link between the Swedish interest rate and the US rate has become weaker in recent years. These observations accord well with the results of other studies, in which the declining importance of the US rate as "price leader" has been verified.

The correlation analysis must be extended

My observations in this chapter provide a point of departure for further analysis. In order to make a more qualified assessment, the correlation analysis must be complemented with a number of explanatory variables to give us further insight into the following question: why is the Swedish interest rate not linked more closely to the international level than these results seem to indicate? Variables that capture differences in the information content of different interest rate quotations must be included. An example of such a variable is the premium for political risk.

Notes

1 We should be cautious about interpreting the statistical measure. Long-term rates are more affected by developments in the business cycle and changes in business condition than short-term rates. A relatively large part of the covariation between long-term rates may thus be illusory and may come from some common underlying factor.

2 Obtained by squaring 0.72 from Table 7.2.

3 The pattern in the lagged effects seems to depend to a certain extent on the system of weights used in calculating the global interest level. If the pattern for the global rate is compared with that for the US rate, the global interest level based on capital market weights exhibits the greatest similarity. In view of the facts that the US rate weight is greatest in the weight system of capital market weights, this is also the result we would expect.

4 For example, for a regression analysis with changes in the Swedish interest rate on treasury bills as a function of earlier changes in trade-weighted rate on international treasury bills, and as a function of lagged US rates, the Durbin-Watson values will be as low as 0.4–0.5. In a regression analysis in which changes in Swedish interest rates are the dependent variable and changes in covered foreign rates the independent variable, the Durbin-Watson value is close to the expected value 2.

5 But negative coefficients do occur. They are not among the absolute largest, however, and are not therefore expressed in the table. Moreover they are insignificant.

6 This can be inferred from the figures in Chapter 4. Average value and variance are reported in Chapter 8.

7 These values are obtained from Table 7.8 in terms of squared coefficients of correlation.

CHAPTER 8

A Model-Based Analysis of Direct Financial Integration

8.1 Introduction

In Chapter 2 above I defined direct financial integration and specified the sources of market disintegration. I also formulated a model for the analysis of direct financial integration, after establishing that real interest rates vary over time and from one country to another. We can now test the model and measure any changes in the level of direct integration and in Sweden's interest autonomy. The reader may recall that the model is based on an extension of the International Fisher Effect.

In Chapter 2 a way of identifying and measuring an increase in the level of direct integration was also indicated. Two factors were discussed, which can be said to express such an increase: 1) a *reduction* in the differential between domestic and foreign interest rates, after all the risks have been priced and exchange expectations have been taken into account, 2) a *shorter* time-lag before the foreign interest movements make an impact on the Swedish rate. The correlation analysis was included in Chapter 7, as part of our study of this time-lag. We found that the lag had been reduced. We were also able to see how much time passed before the main foreign interest rate influences came into effect.

Section 8.2 contains a brief analysis of deviations from the International Fisher Effect. Section 8.3 consists of a similar analysis of deviations from the interest rate parity theory. In both these sections I limit myself to analysing the character of the deviations, i.e. whether they are systematic or random. Section 8.4 provides a brief analysis of the forward rate as an unbiased estimate of the future spot exchange rate, with a view to illustrating the size of the exchange risk premium. In Section 8.5 my model is presented together with the arguments underlying the choice of approximations for the variable included.

Sections 8.6–8.10 are devoted to an analysis of the model. Each of these sections is devoted to one of the five types of interest rates which we have been studying so far. In each case I examine the links with the global interest level and with the US rate.

8.2 Analysis of deviations from the International Fisher Effect

When we analyse *direct* financial integration we adopt a rate of return perspective, and look at the law of one price for interest rates. The International Fisher Effect expresses this law in terms of market expectations regarding future exchange rate movements. The investor is regarded here as being risk-neutral, and it is therefore assumed that different probability distributions with respect to exchange movements do not generate any demand for risk premiums. The same applies to premiums for any increase in uncertainty associated with political changes such as adjustments in exchange controls. If the assumption of risk neutrality holds, and the assumption that the gap between two interest rates corresponds at every moment in time to the exchange expectations, then the direct financial integration of the market is perfect.

Thus, if an empirical test of this integration is to be satisfactorily underpinned, we must have information about the market's exchange expectations. If we have no such information, we will have to make do (as is usual) with the actual (ex post) exchange rate movements. If the analysis is to have any point, this means we have to make some further assumptions.

8.2.1 The ex post analysis tests two hypotheses

In our discussion of formula (3.2) we noted that an analysis of the deviation between observed exchange rate movements and the exchange rate movements which the interest differential predicts, actually contains an analysis of two hypotheses. With our ex post data, we can now see whether the use of the International Fisher Effect as a forecasting tool produces any systematic error. If we do find such an error, the difficulty will be to choose one among the many probable explanations, where some agree with the hypothesis of efficient markets and others do not.

In our interview study we found that about half the business leaders interviewed placed great confidence in the International Fisher Effect, while the other half were equally convinced that the theory does not hold. This could mean that half the market also acts in accordance with its belief, while the other half provides one reason for the ex post deviations. On top of which, possible market inefficiencies also affect the outcome.

Substantial differences between the interest differential and actual exchange rate movements

A more detailed analysis of the forecasting error in the International Fisher Effect is presented in Oxelheim (1985), on a basis of the Swedish case. In our present context when the purpose is different, we can nonetheless use the results from my earlier analysis as a point of departure. The difference between actual exchange rate movements and the expected change according to the International Fisher Effect, can be designated d_{IFE} and defined as follows:

$$d_{IFE} = \left[\frac{S_{t+3} - S_t}{S_t} - \frac{r_{swe} - r_{for}}{1 + r_{for}}\right] \cdot 100 \qquad (8.1)$$

Figures 8.1 and 8.2 show the development of d_{IFE} for three-month prime rates. The broken line in the figures shows the predicted exchange rate change during the period concerned, and the unbroken line shows the actual outcome. The interest rates have been converted into quarterly figures. Thus the difference between the lines indicates the "forecasting error" in the interest differential.[1] The deviations, i.e. d_{IFE}, are registered at time t and refer to the changes between time t and t+3 months. The average value ($\bar{d}_{IFE}$) and the standard deviation (σ_{IFE}) in the error are shown in Table 8.1 for the interest rates on treasury bills/treasury discount notes, and in Table 8.2 for prime rates.[2]

We can see from the figures that in absolute numbers the expected exchange rate change proved to be small in relation to the actual outcome. We can also see that, according to the International Fisher Effect, expected exchange rate movements had the wrong sign in relation to the outcome for long periods at a time. For example, this applies to the SEK/USD rates from the middle of 1980 to the end of 1983, and to the SEK/GBP rates for most of the period 1978–80.[3]

These systematic errors appear in our analysis as autocorrelated error terms, which can usually be interpreted as a sign of an inefficient market. As we have already noted, many researchers may wrongly come to this conclusion when they work with ex post data. I shall try to avoid the same mistake, and simply point out that the errors could depend on several factors: the actors have perhaps used adaptive expectations, or they are not risk-neutral as I have assumed but are averse to risk,[4] or the so-called Peso problem which we discussed in Chapter 2, has come into the picture.

Few interest rate combinations with systematic deviations appear in the period of the study

In Table 8.1 we can see four significant deviations in the case of the *treasury bills rate*, which two refer to GBP. One of these is for the period 1974–76. But for the period as a whole only USD shows a systematic deviation. A further breakdown into subperiods

Figure 8.1 Deviations from the International Fisher Effect in an analysis of ex post data SEK/USD, 1974-84
Monthly observations, quarterly percentage

—— actual exchange rate change
– – – expected exchange rate change according to the difference between prime rates (3-month)

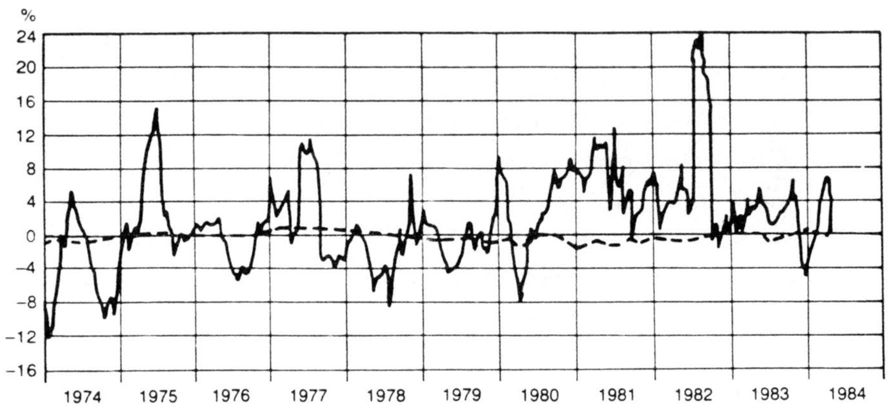

Figure 8.2 Deviations from the International Fisher Effect in an analysis of ex post data SEK/GBP, 1974-84
Monthly observations, quarterly percentage

—— actual exchange rate change
– – – expected exchange rate change according to the difference between prime rates (3-month)

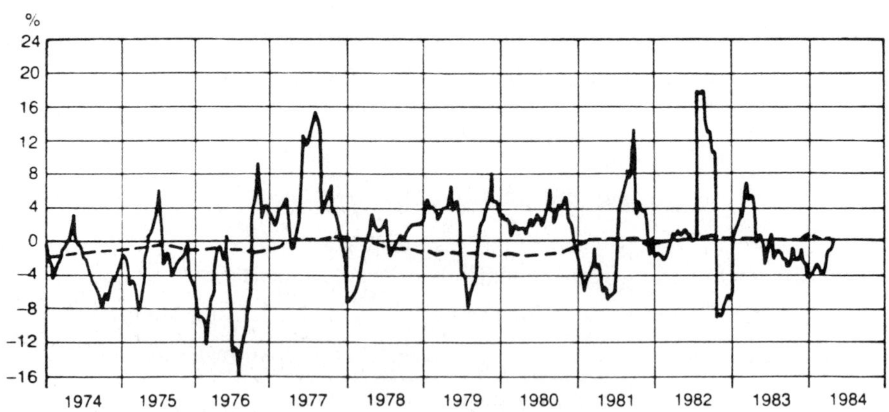

Source: Oxelheim (1985).

would show that over a longer period the USD deviation was not significant until after 1980. In the case of GBP, the interest differential certainly indicated the direction in which exchange rate movements occurred in 1974–76, but it greatly underestimated them. To balance the errors that thus arose with a negative sign, the interest differential after 1977 produced big forecasting errors with a positive sign. Thus what we can infer from Figures 8.1 and 8.2 and Table 8.1 is that substantial temporary deviations do occur, but that it is difficult to demonstrate systematic errors, i.e. average errors which significantly deviate from zero, in a longer perspective.

The comparisons of *prime rates* in Table 8.2 reveal the same pattern as we can see in Table 8.1. A few more currencies are significant for the whole period in an analysis at the 5 % level. But an analysis at the 0.1 % level gives us the same results as for treasury bills.

Table 8.1 **Mean ($\bar{d}_{IFE}$) and standard deviation (σ_{IFE}) in the deviation from the International Fisher Effect based on three-month treasury bill rates**
Monthly data, per cent/quarter, ex post analysis

	1974–84		1974–76		1978–84	
Currency	$\bar{d}_{IFE}$	σ_{IFE}	$\bar{d}_{IFE}$	σ_{IFE}	$\bar{d}_{IFE}$	σ_{IFE}
GBP	0.79	5.26	–2.03*	4.78	1.51*	4.81
USD	1.63*	5.43	–0.82	5.07	2.85*	5.19
DEM	0.62	4.72	–0.49	1.61	0.50	5.53
CHF	–	–	–	–	–	–
JPY	1.24	6.60	–0.77	4.75	1.44	7.13
Number of observations	123		36		75	

* Significant deviation from zero when analysed at 5 per cent level.
H_0: $\mu_{d_{IFE}} = 0$ is rejected.

Source: Oxelheim (1985).

The explanation of the significance which we find in an analysis of the prime rate in DEM, CHF and JPY for the 1974–84 period as a whole, lies in the events of 1977, in particular the Swedish devaluations. Not altogether surprisingly we find the largest positive and negative deviations in connection with adjustments to the parity of the

Swedish krona. The interest rates seem to reflect expected relative inflation, rather than the devaluation/revaluation potential in the form of cumulative inflation differentials (u). Here, as in other interest analyses based on monthly or quarterly observations, interpretations should be cautious in the absence of any knowledge of the market's timing.

Table 8.2 **Mean ($\bar{d}_{IFE}$) and standard deviation (σ_{IFE}) in the deviation from the International Fisher Effect based on three-month commercial bank prime lending rates**
Monthly data, per cent/quarter, ex post analysis

	1974–84		1974–76		1978–84	
Currency	$\bar{d}_{IFE}$	σ_{IFE}	$\bar{d}_{IFE}$	σ_{IFE}	$\bar{d}_{IFE}$	σ_{IFE}
GBP	0.82	5.26	–2.35*	4.81	1.49*	4.75
USD	1.78*	5.51	–0.89	5.09	2.94*	4.75
DEM	1.14*	4.59	0.07	1.39	0.83	5.39
CHF	1.58*	6.46	0.72	3.56	0.67	6.99
JPY	1.52*	6.75	–0.73	4.73	1.63	7.35
Number of observations	123		36		75	

* Significant deviation from zero when analysed at 5 per cent level.
H_0: $\mu_{d_{IFE}} = 0$ is rejected.

Source: Oxelheim (1985).

It is interesting to note that, unlike the other currencies in the study, USD and GBP exhibit systematic deviations for the period 1978–84. This observation could be worth following up as both USD and GBP are the currencies of countries where for most of the period concerned the policy was to control the development of the money supply, while the other three countries in the study adopted other monetary policy goals.

8.2.2 *Ex post analysis reveals substantial differences in actual loan costs, depending on the choice of currency*

Another way of illustrating the result of an ex post analysis of the International Fisher

Figure 8.3 Index of additional cost to a Swedish borrower of borrowing in USD or CHF as compared to SEK, 1974-84
Monthly observations, quarterly percentage

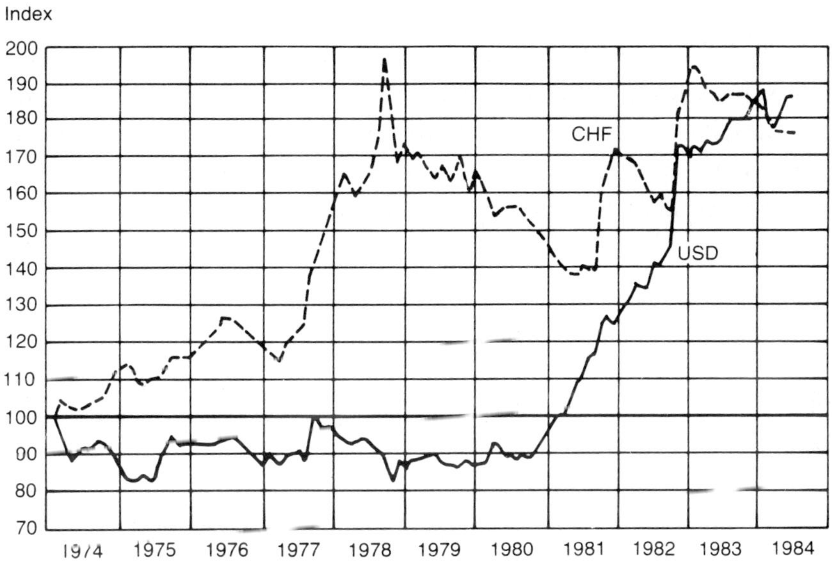

Source: Oxelheim (1985).

Effect with interest rates to first-class borrowers, is to estimate an additional cost index. Indexes of this kind are illustrated in Figure 8.3. They can be said to describe the *cumulative* validity (ex post) of the International Fisher Effect. From a base value of 100 a chain index is estimated for every month, which shows the extent to which the interest differentials have balanced actual exchange rate movements. It is a question here of (roll-over) loans which, it is assumed, are reborrowed every month at the prime rate. A value higher than 100 shows that loans denominated in some other currency after the "base time" has proved more expensive to a Swedish borrower than a loan in SEK. Parallel indexes over a given period show that the loans during the period have been equal in value from a cost point of view.

Figure 8.3 shows that a Swedish company which decided at the beginning of 1974 to borrow in CHF instead of SEK, would have had 85 per cent higher capital costs up to the end of 1983. We can also see that the additional cost of the loan would have been the same, if the company had decided instead to borrow in USD. However, this is just a crude description as we have not taken into account that the cost distribution over time in this second alternative is quite different from the case of CHF.

An analysis of the 1970s as a whole shows that throughout the period it was more expensive to borrow in a strong currency than in a weak one at a slightly higher interest rate. Several explanations suggest themselves; it is certainly probable that the actors' expectations were affected considering the long delay before the interest explosion followed the exchange rate explosion after the breakdown of the Bretton Woods agreement.

Table 8.3 **Additional cost of foreign loans for a Swedish borrower divided between an interest-rate component and a foreign exchange rate component**
Per cent per annum

	1969/70–1979/80		1973/74–1979/80		1977/78–1983/84	
Currency	Change in exchange rate	Interest rate differential	Change in exchange rate	Interest rate differential	Change in exchange rate	Interest rate differential
GBP	–3.0	1.6	–1.8	2.2	4.5	2.1
USD	–2.6	–0.8	–0.8	–1.3	9.5	2.0
DEM	5.4	–1.6	8.0	–2.9	4.7	–1.8
CHF	8.5	–3.2	12.9	–3.7	8.0	–5.6
JPY	2.1	–2.1	2.7	–3.1	9.9	–4.7

Table 8.3 shows the additional cost divided between exchange rate changes and interest differentials. We see here that both GBP and USD show the same sign for interest rate and exchange rate after 1977/78, instead of balancing opposite signs.

Many experts claim that shortage of capital rather than cost determines the investment level.[5] Nevertheless it seems likely that the ex post deviations from the International Fisher Effect, i.e. the cost spread which we can see here, is important to the "real" side in a society.

8.2.3 What does the International Fisher Effect tell us about the level of direct financial integration?

Large, temporary and (for some combinations of periods/currencies) systematic deviations can thus be seen, when the interest differential is compared with *actual* exchange rate movements. The analysis also shows that the forecasting errors are autocorrelated. However, these results can not be interpreted in terms of integration in any simple way. By using ex post data I have tested a composite hypothesis, and in order to be able to say anything about integration, I have to make assumptions about the actors. Thus I assume that the actors have rational expectations and are risk-neutral, i.e. all premiums for exchange risk and political risk are zero. Given these assumptions and on a basis of my observations, I can infer that there have been inefficiencies. I then take this as confirmation of imperfect direct financial integration, i.e. segmented credit markets.

This conclusion depends on the validity of my assumptions. I will have come to the wrong conclusion if, for example, the actors are adaptive in their expectations, or if they are averse to risk. How far my assumption are unreasonable – i.e. the deviations correspond to transactions cost[6], or risk premiums[7] or errors in the market's expectations, we shall see later in this chapter. In that part of my analysis I shall formalize the risks and examine the extent to which premiums for these risks can explain the interest differentials. I shall also model the investor's exchange expectations.

8.3 Analysis of deviations from interest rate parity

Deviations from interest rate parity indicate imperfect direct financial integration. If the absolute sum of a deviation also exceeds the transaction cost, we obtain an expression of general market inefficiency and/or politically induced inefficiency. We have seen that many researchers claim that deviations from interest rate parity with Eurorates are negligible, lying within the interval where arbitrage is not profitable in view of the transaction cost.[8] Regardless of how well these observations are supported, we would still need a Eurorate for the Swedish krona, if we were to be able to obtain comparable results. In the absence of any such rate, I use the interest rates for treasury bills/treasury discount notes and prime rates as in the previous section.

8.3.1 Diminishing deviations from interest rate parity with Swedish interest rates

Figures 8.4 and 8.5 give us some idea of the interest rate parity of USD and GBP

Figure 8.4 Deviations from interest rate parity, SEK/USD, 1974-84
Monthly data, per cent/quarter

—— Three-month forward premium
--- Differences in commercial bank prime lending rates (3-month)

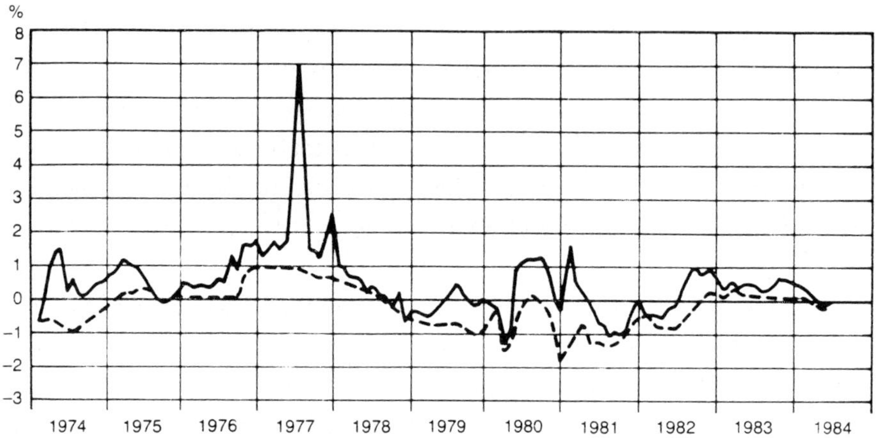

Figure 8.5 Deviations from interest rate parity, SEK/GBP, 1974-84
Monthly data, per cent/quarter

—— Three-month forward premium
--- Differences in commercial bank prime lending rates (3-month)

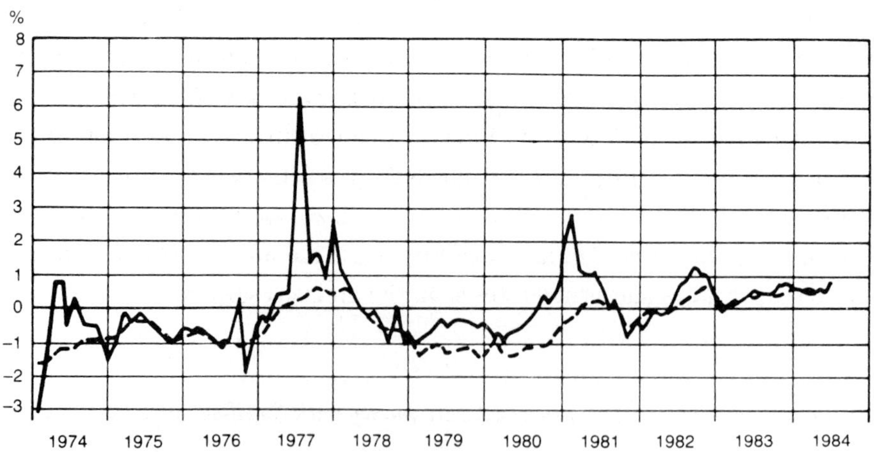

Source: Oxelheim (1985).

against SEK. The figures are based on prime rates. The difference between the forward premium (marked by an unbroken line) and the interest rate differential (indicated by broken lines) constitutes the deviation from interest rate parity. This deviation is defined according to formula (8.2) and is designated d_{CIP}. The deviation for period t to t+3 months is registered in the figure at time t. The interest rates are divided by 4 to give us the quarterly figures.

$$d_{CIP} = \left[\left(\frac{F_t(3)}{S_t} - 1\right) - \frac{r_{swe} - r_{for}}{1 + r_{for}}\right] \cdot 100 \tag{8.2}$$

where $F_t(3)$ is the three-month forward rate.

The figures strongly suggest that the deviation has been very slight during the later years of our period. We can take this as an indication of increasing direct financial integration.[9]

8.3.2 *Are there opportunities for risk-free profits as a result of covered interest arbitrage?*

Tables 8.4 and 8.5 show the average deviations ($\bar{d}_{CIP}$) and the standard deviations (σ_{CIP}) divided into subperiods. We can see that during the early years of the studied period at least, there were systematic deviations from interest rate parity. If for the sake of simplicity we assume that the transaction cost consists of the cost of currency transactions only, our yield will be reduced due to this cost by the factor $(1-T_S)\cdot(1-T_F)$.[10] The question is whether the deviations are still significant, when the transaction cost at 0.5 per cent is taken into account. The answer is yes! There have been a great many opportunities for risk-free profits as a result of covered interest arbitrage during the period 1974–84, for anyone who knew how to exploit the opportunities. The signals suggest an outflow of capital. There is a risk, however, that I overestimate the opportunities, partly because I use a conservative estimate of the transaction cost, which only takes into account the costs of the actual exchange operations, and partly because I ignore the possible premium for political risk.

However, as we can see in Figures 8.4 and 8.5, the number of significant economically exploitable opportunities for risk-free profits seems to have declined in recent years. Much of this decline in opportunities for safe arbitrage profit can probably be explained by computerization, which has made the market more efficient. One point that seems to confirm this, is that the diminishing gaps coincide in time with a period when money became dramatically more expensive. These trend shifts in both nominal and real interest rates have already been emphasized above.

Table 8.4 **Mean ($\bar{d}_{CIP}$) and standard deviation (σ_{CIP}) in the deviation from interest rate parity based on three-month treasury bill rates[a]**
Monthly data, per cent/quarter

	1974–84		1974–76		1978–84	
Currency	$\bar{d}_{CIP}$	σ_{CIP}	$\bar{d}_{CIP}$	σ_{CIP}	$\bar{d}_{CIP}$	σ_{CIP}
GBP	0.57*	0.74	0.22*	0.65	0.67*	0.40
USD	0.53*	0.72	0.48*	0.56	0.45*	0.42
DEM[a]	0.73*	0.82	0.54*	0.65	0.72*	0.59
JPY	0.46*	1.06	0.08	1.25	0.57*	0.65
Number of observations	126		36		78	

[a] For the most recent period Frankfurt rate has been used for Germany.

* Significant deviation from interest rate parity on a 5 per cent level.
H_0: $\mu_{d_{CIP}} = 0$ is rejected.

Source: Oxelheim (1985).

8.3.3 *What does the deviation from interest rate parity tell us about the level of direct financial integration?*

How far we can explain the deviation from interest rate parity in terms of inefficiency will thus depend on the size of the risk premium. By this is meant the premium for political risk, since the exchange risk is eliminated in cases of covered interest arbitrage. I find it difficult to determine the extent to which the observed deviation should be interpreted as an expression of inefficiencies in the market, as exchange controls, or as premiums for political risks. If we assume that the premium for political risk has not declined to any notable extent during the later part of the period studied, the smaller deviation could be interpreted as an expression of increased direct integration.

Thus the analysis of deviations from interest rate parity gives us only conditional indications of an increase in direct financial integration. These indications suggest that the Swedish money market really has assumed the form of a fairly free market, more firmly linked to interest rates in the rest of the world.

Table 8.5 Mean ($\bar{d}_{CIP}$) and standard deviation (σ_{CIP}) in the deviation from interest rate parity based on three-month commercial bank prime lending rates
Monthly data, per cent/quarter

	1974–84		1974–76		1978–84	
Currency	$\bar{d}_{CIP}$	σ_{CIP}	$\bar{d}_{CIP}$	σ_{CIP}	$\bar{d}_{CIP}$	σ_{CIP}
GBP	0.50*	0.89	–0.09	0.76	0.46*	0.64
USD	0.75*	0.77	0.41*	0.57	0.64*	0.55
DEM	1.19*	0.94	1.09*	0.81	0.96*	0.70
CHF	1.22*	1.08	1.10*	0.92	0.94*	0.87
JPY	0.63*	1.31	–0.04	1.49	0.61*	1.05
Number of observations	126		36		78	

* Significant deviation from interest rate parity when analysed at 5 per cent level. H_0: $\mu_{d_{CIP}} = 0$ is rejected.

Source: Oxelheim (1985).

8.4 The forward rate as an unbiased estimate of the future exchange rate

In the last two sections we have been discussing two of the five links which were numbered in Figure 1.1. A third relationship in the figure refers to the forward rate as an unbiased estimate of the future spot exchange rate. In this section, too, I shall use empirical results from Oxelheim (1985) as my point of departure in discussing direct financial integration.

In the previous section we found substantial deviations from interest rate parity for the period 1974–84 as a whole. We thus have reason to regard the International Fisher Effect and the theory of the forward rate as an unbiased estimate of the future exchange rate, as two different theories whose applicability should be evaluated empirically (see Figure 1.1).

When interest rate parity and the International Fisher Effect hold, the expected exchange rate is equal to the forward rate.[11] In Section 8.2 we were able to observe large temporary and in some cases systematic deviations from the International Fisher Effect in an ex post analysis. We interpreted these deviations as an expression of political and exchange risk premiums. In the analysis of interest rate parity, we found deviations which we also interpreted as an expression of a political risk premium. Thus in both cases we found deviations which can be explained by a political risk premium. Since this premium is a common factor, we can then estimate the exchange risk premium by assuming rational expectations and by running the following regression, on the same grounds as above:[12]

$$S_{t+3} = \alpha_1 + \beta_1 F_t(3) + \varepsilon_{t+3} \tag{8.3}$$

In order to avoid the problem that can result from non-stationarity, I suggest instead a test of relative changes with the help of the following equation:[13]

$$\hat{s}_{t,t+3} = \alpha_1 + \beta_1 \left[\frac{F_t(3)}{S_t} - 1\right] + \varepsilon_{t+3} \tag{8.4}$$

A test of non-overlapping three-month periods gives us the result presented in Table 8.6. It appears that we cannot reject the hypothesis ($\beta=1$) for any currency in the table. The coefficients of determination are low throughout, and only for GBP/SEK do we obtain significant regression. We find no clear evidence here indicating that the forward premium contains an exchange risk premium.

8.4.1 *What does the analysis of the exchange risk premium tell us about the level of direct financial integration?*

I have not found confirmation of the presence of an exchange risk premium. The existence of such a premium is important to the level of *total* financial integration, while it is of no importance to the level of *direct* financial integration. In this last case, however, its size is of interest when it actually comes to measuring the level of integration.

Hörngren and Vredin (1986) report tests very similar to those described above. They find evidence indicating the presence of a risk premium which they regard as a necessary albeit not a sufficient condition for a certain amount of Swedish monetary autonomy.[14] However, their tests are based on an index for the Swedish currency basket and refer to a different period, namely from November 1982 until December 1985 which might explain why their results differ from the results presented above. One more explanation which refers to differences in the test procedure is that Hörngren and Vredin use the forward premium in its absolute form ($F_t(3) - S_t$) like Fama (1984), while we are using the premium in its relative form in equation (8.4).

Table 8.6 **Relative three-month forward premium/discount as a forecast of relative changes in exchange rate, 1974–84**
Non-overlapping data

Currency	Equation of regression	R^2	F	D–W	Number of observa-tions
GBP	$\hat{s}_{t,t+3} = \underset{}{0.00} + \underset{(0.68)}{1.43} \left[\frac{F_t(3)}{S_t} - 1\right]$	0.10	4.46*	1.72	42
USD	$\hat{s}_{t,t+3} = 0.01 + \underset{(0.88)}{0.78} \left[\frac{F_t(3)}{S_t} - 1\right]$	0.03	0.77	1.61	42
DEM	$\hat{s}_{t,t+3} = 0.01 + \underset{(0.97)}{1.53} \left[\frac{F_t(3)}{S_t} - 1\right]$	0.07	2.50	1.91	42
CHF	$\hat{s}_{t,t+3} = 0.00 + \underset{(1.24)}{1.01} \left[\frac{F_t(3)}{S_t} - 1\right]$	0.02	0.66	1.95	42
JPY	$\hat{s}_{t,t+3} = 0{,}01 + \underset{(0.82)}{1.34} \left[\frac{F_t(3)}{S_t} - 1\right]$	0.06	2.67	1.94	42

* Significant regression at a 5 per cent level.

Standard deviations for different estimates are shown in parentheses.

Source: Oxelheim (1985).

8.5 Presentation of the model

We have now proceeded to a stage in our study of direct financial integration when we can no longer avoid the problem of explicitly determining the size of variable premiums for risk, in particular for political risk but even for exchange risk as well. Thus in the present section we will discuss the choice of approximations which satisfactorily reflect such things as variable risk premiums, market exchange expectations, etc. I shall also try to underpin a hypothesis about rational expectations. First, however, I must say a few words about my chosen method and its implications for my choice of proxy variables.

8.5.1 Choice of method

The point of departure for the empirical analysis is multiple linear regression. I have chosen to use stepwise regression with a backward elimination procedure. This means starting with a full set of variables and successively eliminating them one after the other, until the search targets are satisfied. This procedure is to be preferred to stepwise regression with forward selection.[15] One obvious reason for this is that the first mentioned method starts from a "complete" equation, which can be evaluated in terms of economic theory. Another reason is that it provides better opportunities for handling multicollinearity.

We seek a descriptive model

The search process and the extent to which the model-builder wants to reduce the equation, depends on the purpose of the model. If, as in our case, the idea is to *describe* a process with the help of a model, we try to select the smallest number of independent (explanatory) variables, which explain a satisfactorily large part of the variation in the dependent variable. In other situations the model-builder may be interested in forecasting or control. If the dominating interest is to *forecast*, variables will be chosen such that the mean squared error in the forecasts will be minimized. If the predominant interest is to *control* – perhaps the model-builder is thinking in terms of response functions and the necessary changes in the independent variable in order to generate a desired outcome in the dependent variable – then an equation will be chosen in which the coefficients for the independent variables are strictly accurate, i.e. where the standard error in the coefficients of regression is small.

The aim of the present investigation is descriptive. I thus choose the variables to be included in the model with a view to describing a sequence of events.

Multicollinearity must be kept under control

Even when the purpose is a descriptive one, we want as small a standard error in the regression coefficients as possible. One way of reducing the standard errors is to minimize the multicollinearity. This can be done with least effort by considering the covariation matrix for the explanatory variables. I also include here as an explicit part of the method, a high barrier to multicollinearity.[16] No other action is taken to deal explicitly with a possible covariation between independent variables. Even though we should not generally speaking use stepwise regression in cases of covariation between the explanatory variables, at least the procedure which starts backwards is the one which copes best with the covariation.[17]

Criteria for stepwise elimination

Cp is used for the choice of representative equation, and the significance level of 5 per cent is chosen throughout in eliminating variables from the base equation.[18] The elimination is made on a basis of the way in which Cp deviates from its expected value p (=number of parameters).

In choosing the "best" equation, the residuals are studied with reference to extreme values and autocorrelation. As a test of the first-order autocorrelation, the Durbin-Watson test will be used.

How often should observations be made?

We have already touched on the problem of the choice of interest rates for international comparisons, and the implications of the absence of a Eurorate for the krona. There are also two further problems connected with the collection of data. One of these concerns the *density of the observations.* Opportunities for arbitrage last for hours or minutes rather than weeks or months. In order to be able to capture this timing aspect, we thus require extremely frequent observations. The problem is that in economic contexts it is often a question of explanatory variables for which the data is only available from the national accounts, and observations cannot therefore be made more frequently than every quarter. This is also the case here, as I have to conduct my analysis of the structural models on a basis of quarterly data. In order to describe arbitrage realistically I use *market data,* where such is relevant, at a given point in time. Observations of price and balance-sheet data refer to the value of the variable at the end of the period.

What is a suitable length for the period of the analysis?

The second problem connected with data collection concerns the choice of *period for the analysis,* i.e. the choice of starting-point and suitable length. We can identify some points in time where institutional changes motivate an analysis of subperiods. Such dates are March 1973 with the collapse of the Bretton Woods agreement, August 1977 with a change in the Swedish foreign exchange arrangements, 8 October 1982, when the value of the Swedish krona was written down substantially with a devaluation which in some respects deviated from the pattern of previous devaluations during the 1970s and 1980s. October 1979, when the US economic policy was reorganized, is another important date. The difficulty in acquiring a sufficiently large number of observations prevents me from dividing the total period under investigation into several subperiods.[19] I shall thus take the period 1974–84 as the overall period to be studied. The period 1979–84 is the subperiod with which I make comparisons, to try to find out whether financial integration has increased. Other institutional or market changes in the model are captured with the help of dummy variables.

8.5.2 *Model for studying direct financial integration*

Multiple linear regression makes it possible for us to take into account *at the same time* the two previously mentioned indications of integration.

The analysis of five interest rates divided over subperiods provides many analytical combinations

Given the types of interest, the comparative rate and the period of the study, we obtain 20 different comparisons and analyses. The matrix in Table 8.7 indicates the sections in which I report the analyses of different combinations of these classification bases.

Basic form of the model

Thus I have chosen to use multiple *linear* regression. We could easily have envisaged another structural form. In the absence of hypotheses about any other form, and given the assumption that successive changes are small, it seems reasonable to use a linear approximation. This means among other things that different risk premiums will be additive in the model, it is also assumed that these premiums grow linearly.[20]

Table 8.7 Excerpt for presentation of analysis results

	Rate of interest				
Swedish market's links with	Official discount rate	Interest rate on treasury bills/treasury discount note	Prime rate	Interest rate on government bonds/government notes	Interest rate on industrial bonds
Global interest level	8.6.3	8.7.3	8.8.2	8.9.2	8.10.2
US interest level	8.6.4	8.7.4	8.8.3	8.9.3	8.10.3

Note: A complete list of the variables included in the analysis will be found in Supplement 2.

The model is based on the assumption of a market which is averse to risk. This aversion is represented for the market as a whole by an average aversion which is constant during the period.[21]

The basic equation in the form of a Fisher approach for markets with risk aversion, assumes the following general form, with some proxy variables inserted as examples:

$r_{swe,t} - r_{for,t} =$ (8.5)

$\beta_0 +$ (transactions cost, constant risk premium, inefficiency)

$+ \beta_1 u_t + \beta_2 RELINF^*_t +$ (exchange, rate effect)

$+ \beta_3 NFAGDP_t +$ (variable risk premium)

$+ \beta_4 CF_{t-1,t}/ER_t \ldots + \beta_{10} CF_{t-7,t-6}/ER_{t-6} +$

$+ \beta_{11} DVIC + \beta_{12} DV824 +$ (institutional changes)

$+ \beta_{13} \Delta r^{weighted}_{for,t-1} + \ldots + \beta_{18} \Delta r^{weighted}_{for,t-6} +$ (lagged interest effect)

$+ \varepsilon_t$ (error term)

where

$r_{swe,t}$	=	Swedish nominal interest rate at time t
$r_{for,t}$	=	Weighted nominal foreign interest rate at time t
u_t	=	Swedish krona's deviation from its weighted international purchasing power parity at time t
RELINF*	=	Forecast of the relative inflation for the maturity of the financial contract
$NFAGDP_t$	=	Sweden's net foreign assets as a percentage of Sweden's GDP at time
$CF_{t-1,t}/ER_t$	=	Capital flow during period t–1 to period t as a percentage of foreign exchange reserves at time t
DVIC	=	Dummy variable for the change in the Swedish exchange rate arrangements in August 1977
DV824	=	Dummy variable for quarter 4, 1982
$\Delta r^{weighted}_{for,t-1}$	=	Change in nominal foreign interest rate during period t–1 to t
ε_t	=	Random error with $E(\varepsilon_t) = 0$, $E(\varepsilon_{t-1}, \varepsilon_t) = 0$ and $Var(\varepsilon_t) = \sigma^2_\varepsilon$

Choice of dependent variable

The aim of the analysis is to identify the amount of influence from international financial markets. Since there appears to be a mutual influence between the US rate and other financial markets during the period of the investigation, we will study the direct financial integration between the Swedish market on the one hand and the world market and the US market respectively on the other. In the analysis the gap between the Swedish rate and the global rate, and the Swedish rate and the US rate, will be used as dependent variables. In all cases the US rate is included as one of the interest rates in the weighted global interest level. Weighting has been performed throughout with trade weights.

The intercept

In accordance with my definition, the constant risk-premium-adjusted intercept should be zero at every point in time, if we are to be able to confirm perfect direct financial integration.[22] If this is not the case, we will be able to measure changes in the adjusted intercept, in order to obtain confirmation of my hypothesis that the direct integration of the Swedish credit market has increased.

The intercept that remains after the adjustment contains transaction costs and inefficiencies. By comparing the intercept in this form for the total period of the study with the subperiod, we will get some idea of a possible increase or decrease in direct financial integration.[23] By also eliminating the transaction cost from the intercept, we can determine the general market efficiency and possible effects induced by Swedish interest rate policy.

8.5.3 Choice of approximations for the variables in the model

The basic model persists, but I am compelled to search for *proxy variables* as expressions of the risks, the expectations and the institutional changes included in it. Since it is a question of effects which are hard to model, I will give a brief exposition of my approach here.

Market exchange rate expectations

The market's expectations as regards exchange rate movements are included in the model, and it is important to find a good approximation for this quite sizable variable.

How this should be done has been hotly debated, and because of the difficulties several researchers have tried to avoid this component as soon as they find it possible to do so. I have chosen a market perspective, and must therefore somehow find an expression to use in the model. My interview study of the way in which exchange rate expectations are formed in Swedish multinationals has provided a basis for choosing a variable which expresses the deviation from purchasing power parity.

The use of a purchasing power parity model as a basis for expectations about exchange rate movements, seems intuitively consistent with the hypothesis of rational expectations, even though an evaluation would give us other signals in accordance with what we found in our discussion of the Peso problem. Thus my study provides confirmation of the suggestion that the actors sense the "right" model, and form their expectations accordingly. The investigation also shows we can assume the actors will avoid perception error due to misunderstanding the available information, since they match their own expectations, also in accordance with the rational expectation hypothesis, with the forecasts of the "expert" which are based on his estimation of the deviation from purchasing power parity.[24]

Given the character of the Swedish exchange rate arrangements, with the emphasis on stabilization under the currency snake and again under the basket, there is reason to assume in pursuing a PPP approach that these expectations are made up of two components. One of these consists of deviations already observed from purchasing power parity, u_t, in other words the depreciation or appreciation potential of the day,[25] and the other consists of an expressions of the estimated future inflation differential.

I use u_t in the model. Generally speaking there is uncertainty about the choice of index, starting-point and weighting system in specifying the size of this variable. However, the trend in the deviations from PPP has proved fairly robust to the choice of index in economies where the changes between internal relative prices are small. In the case of Sweden the choice of index does not appear to be a significant question. The next critical point concerns the identification of an equilibrium point or period. Here opinions can differ widely. Fortunately the way in which u_t is included in the model leaves the level without any impact. Weighting is the third critical factor. On this question both Swedish and international reports have shown that, despite all the extra work, highly developed multilateral weighting systems such as the MERM system following Artus and McGuire (1983), give results which accord well with simple weightings using bilateral trade weights. Thus, we will use these last weights in our present analysis. *The sign for the coefficient of regression for u_t can be expected to be negative*, which actually means that the more overvalued the Swedish krona, the more necessary is a high Swedish interest level to balance it.[26] However, the actors do not discount the PPP deviation altogether; they ascribe to it a probability. Thus my term in the model expresses the exchange rate expectation in the form of an expected adjustment to the PPP deviation.

It should be noted that u_t corresponds to the historical part only, in the shape of actual deviations from purchasing power parity. As has been mentioned, expectations of exchange rate movements have a second component. We must complement the u_t component with an estimate of the exchange rate movement which is motivated by changes in fundamental variables in the period covered by the interest comparison. One way of doing this is to persist in our purchasing power parity approach, by estimating the relative inflation change for the actual future period.

In the analysis I adopt two ways of complementing u_t. One is based on Frankel (1979a); expected inflation differentials are estimated on a basis of the difference between long-term bond interest rates. The advantage of the long-term interest differential is that it is capable of immediately reflecting the effect of new information, such as news about changes in the supply of money. However, this proxy cannot be used when our dependent variables are interest gaps which are more or less identical with the proxy variable. Frankel's approximation (RELBITW) – i.e. the differential in interests on government bonds – is consequently no good when we use the differential between government bond rates as our dependent variable in our model of the financial integration. The weighting is based here on trade weights, when the model refers to the Swedish rate's links with the global rate. *The sign for the coefficient of regression for the inflation differential can be expected to be positive.*

My alternative way of complementing u_t is to use the forward premium (or discount) (FP3TW). As we found in Chapter 4 this has proved to be the best forecast for changes in the krona rate, in the sense that it has been unbiased and has had a lower variance than other market-generated forecasts. *The sign for the coefficient of regression for the forward premium can be expected to be positive.*

It might be feared that the inclusion of the forward premium together with u_t could cause an increase in multicollinearity. However, we have already seen that the correlation between u_t and the three-month forward rate was very low during the period 1974–84.

As the forward rate is also a function of an interest rate differential i.e. between Eurorates, we have to consider – and avoid – the possibility that we have the same interest gap on both sides of our equation, thus producing some nonsensical correlations. In the current case, the forward premium is used when the correlation between the dependent variable, i.e. the interest gap and the forward premium is far from perfect.

Risk premiums

Another main group of variables in the equation consists of different expressions for risk premiums. These premiums can refer to compensation for the systematic component in the various risks such as inflation risk, exchange risk, default risk, political risk etc. In preparing my analysis I used matching to ensure that the compared interest rates are subject to the same basic conditions and risks associated with the underlying instrument. It then remains to model premiums for exchange risk including inflation risk and political risk.

The risk premium may have one fixed and one variable component

If we are to evaluate the level of direct financial integration correctly, we must allow for all types of risk premium. We have previously found reason to estimate these in the shape of one variable and one fixed or semi-fixed component.[27] It can be assumed that the fixed component is associated with fairly stable expressions of risk, such as the standard deviation in the deviation from purchasing power parity, etc. The variable component is associated with a source of risk that varies over time.

When it comes to the variable component, which must be expressed explicitly, the problem is to identify and formulate the risk variable.[28] The constant component, on the other hand, is expressed in the intercept. If we want to estimate the size of this component, we must be able to distinguish it from the transaction cost, from inefficiencies and from other disturbances.

Allowing for two important sources of risk

The model includes proxies for two variable risks. One of these, *the political risk*, is expressed in variable form in terms of *Swedish net foreign assets as a percentage of GDP*, (NFAGDP).[29] The standardization with GDP produces an expression that indicates the growth of the risk in "real" form. It is easy in a repayment perspective to understand intuitively the demand for a risk premium from someone making a loan to a country as debt-ridden as Sweden. But if it is only anxiety about repayment that is reflected in the premium, then this premium should be low, since Sweden gets top marks as a borrower on the global market. It is perhaps more difficult from this point of view to understand the demand for a risk premium from those who in some other way invest in Sweden. However, in both cases it is a question of a premium which is mainly intended to compensate for uncertainty about the rules of the market game in Sweden. The higher the value of the Swedish debt variable, the more imminent economic policy interventions and regulations can be expected. It may be made more difficult for investors to get their money out of the country (cash flow lag), or in extreme cases it may become impossible for them to get the whole of their investment out (the confiscation case). Here we can expect a *negative coefficient of regression*: the greater the Swedish debt (negative value for net assets), the higher the interest gap.

The other risk component of the variable kind is *exchange rate risk*. I have expressed this risk component as the *capital flow over national borders during a certain number of past periods, in relation to the size of the currency reserve at the end of the respective period, for instance* $CF_{t-1,t}/ER_t$. It actually signals the risk of two events, namely a change in the exchange rate and economic policy measures to support the exchange rate.[30] The risk includes the possibility of tighter exchange controls, an increase in interest rates etc, which can affect the size of the investor's yield as well as the repatriation situation. Part of the premium for this risk for the period under investigation is the market's demand for compensation for the authorities' willingness to use and possibly tighten up exchange controls.

The foreign exchange flow in this risk variable is related to the currency reserve, in order to create an impression of the "real" magnitude of the change. In the case of short-term interests it is reasonable to use speculative or interest-sensitive capital flows, rather than the flow that is linked to commercial transactions. In the case of long-term rates the total currency flow may be the flow that possesses the greatest value as a signal and which determines the market's risk premium. The market knows that the interest-sensitive capital flow reported by the central bank provides the basis for decisions of economic policy.[31] In view of the value of this flow as a *signal*, I have included it in my variable (CFISCER), which is used with up to six quarters' time-lag.[32] We can expect *positive coefficients of regression.*

The premium should reflect the relative risk

The risk premium in the model should express relative risks, something which is particularly important in bilateral studies. The political risk associated with the global interest rate can be assumed to be negligible. Thus, when I study the Swedish interest rate against the global rate, my variable for political risk expresses the Swedish risk only.[33] The same applies when I compare the Swedish rate with the US rate during the period 1974–84.[34]Since the risk to the USA measured in terms of NFAGDP is negligible in our period, all that remains is an expression of risks associated with Sweden.[35]

Institutional changes

Institutional changes represent yet another group of explanatory variables. One such is the change in the Swedish exchange rate arrangements in August 1977, for which I use a dummy variable (DVIC). This is underpinned by my interview study which showed that companies felt risk management had become easier to handle under the basket arrangement.[36] For example, this potential shift in the level of the risk premium can be expected to be captured by the dummy variable.

A dummy variable is also used for the fourth quarter of 1982 (DV824). The devaluation of the Swedish krona which was affected during this quarter, deviated from traditional patterns. For this reason a dummy variable is used to "lift" this observation out of the equation, in order to reduce the disturbance it causes.

Lagged influence from foreign interest movements

As a result of stickiness in the shape of adaptation costs, controls and so on, the realized change in the interest differential is perhaps only a fraction of the change that would have resulted from an immediate adjustment. I see this slowness to adapt as a measure of temporary segmentation, and would therefore like to find a way of measuring it.[37] By including lagged foreign interest rates in the model, I obtain an expression of the speed with which a foreign interest rate change makes an impact on the Swedish rate and the interest gap. The results of the correlation analysis of lagged foreign influence on Swedish interest rates (see Chapter 7), has given us a first indication of the pattern of this influence. Swedish interest rate movements at a particular moment in time showed traces of foreign interest movements that had mainly occurred during the immediately preceding 18 months.

In my model I include lagged foreign interest rate movements for the most recent six quarters as explanatory variables.[38] *The coefficient for lagged foreign interest rate changes is expected to be negative.*

The error term

There remains an error term ϵ_t in the model specification, which is analysed with the help of the Durbon-Watson test. Whenever we find signs of autocorrelation, the error term is analysed in order to reveal possible misspecifications of the model.[39]

Adjusted explanatory value

In using the equation I have chosen, which reflects changes over time, there is always a risk of obtaining a spuriously high explanatory value due to the existence of trends. However, if we look a little more closely at the individual variables, we find few such trends. The only variable with any secular development is the risk variable with Sweden's net foreign assets vis-à-vis the rest of the world (NFAGDP). But the importance of this variable in "forcing up" the explanatory value must be regarded as limited. Furthermore I shall also indicate the so-called "adjusted" explanatory value, i.e. a more cautious interpretation of the explanatory value.

The model can be extended to include a trend factor

A general problem in analysing structural models is that, at best, the data used can be broken down to the quarterly level. If we want to compare period averages as we do here, we also need fairly long periods to achieve reasonable certainty in the estimates. Thus, if we had a clear *a priori* idea about the way the interest gap would develop over time, we would be justified in including a trend factor in the model, thus simplifying the analysis. In order to do this we would only need to add a trend factor which could be expected to assume a negative value if integration increased over time.

Since it is only a hypothesis that the gap should have diminished, and since I have no clear *a priori* idea of the *sequence of events*, I have abstained from including a trend factor in my model. Moreover the model already contains a variable associated with a trend (NFAGDP). The insertion of a separate trend factor would complicate the interpretations of the results.

8.5.4 Guidelines for the analysis and the economic interpretation of the results

After this presentation of the model and the reasons for my choice of proxy variables, we can now summarize what the model can tell us about the level of direct financial integration. Using regression analysis, I will link the interest gap to the price of various risks and to exchange rate expectations. The interest gap can be subdivided as follows:

	↑ Exchange rate expectations				
	Exchange risk premium – variable component				
	Political risk premium – variable component				
	Temporary segmentation – lagged effects				
The interest rate gap	Risk premiums – constant component	1)			
	Transaction cost – inefficiency	Inter–			
	General market inefficiency	cept	2)	3)	
	↓ Permanent segmentation – inefficiency				4)

With a view to obtaining an expression for the average inefficiency and segmentation, I have to subtract constant risk premiums from the intercept (1).[39] There then remains that part of the average gap (2) which expresses all kinds of inefficiency – transaction cost, general market inefficiency, and the effect of politically determined segmentation.

The next stage is to eliminate the transaction cost from the intercept (2). There then remains general market inefficiency and politically determined segmentation (3). This can be seen as an upper limit to what in everyday usage we mean by market inefficiency. If the gap had been zero, we would have been dealing with an efficient market. The gap (3) gives us an upper limit for politically determined segmentation. If we assume not only rational expectations but also general market efficiency, the gap (4) is the same as the effect of all this segmentation. The size of the gap expresses one half of my measure of direct financial integration which has been mentioned previously. This permanent component in the gap represents genuine segmentation. How the central bank has succeeded in resisting the immediate impact of foreign interest rate movements represents the other half, and expresses temporary disintegration in the form of the number of months that we find with significant lag.

When I have to analyse the *change* in the interest gap over time, I run into problems because of the statistical constraint implied by my having only 18 observations in one subperiod, which means that I have to use a reduced equation for this period. I thus reduce the equation as regards the control variables in accordance with the model specification obtained from my stepwise regression for the whole of the period studied. However, in the initial position I chose six lagged interest rate changes, since I want to see whether there is any change in the structure of the lag when I compare subperiods with the total period. Thus, apart from this, the model specification has been retained. However, the new estimate generates new coefficients, which have to be analysed.

8.6 Analysis of the gap between Swedish and foreign discount rates

The first in the series of interest rates to be analysed will be the official discount rate. We have already noted that the role of the discount rate in the OECD countries has differed a great deal in the period as a whole. However, the development in the weighted average of the OECD countries' discount rates has often been used as an indicator of the trend in the global interest level. For the period 1964–84, the weighted OECD discount rate exhibits a weak upwards trend – a trend which can also be traced in both the Swedish and the US discount rates.

8.6.1 The penalty rate is excluded from the analysis

For a long time, as we have seen, there was a strong link in Sweden between the discount rate and various kinds of other domestic rates. For example, money market rates such as the interest on certificates of deposit and deposits on special conditions have been controlled by the discount rate/penalty rate in combination with liquidity requirements. When there have been changes in the discount rate, these have been intended to mark a major shift in the Swedish interest level. Up to June 1985 the banks' lending rates were linked to the discount rate by way of the central bank's interest recommendations, according to which a reasonable relationship should be maintained in the long run between the discount rate and the penalty rate. In my analysis in the present section I shall limit myself to studying the link between Swedish and foreign discount rates, disregarding the penalty rate. Although the role of the discount rate in Sweden has changed during the period of the analysis, I shall try to identify, even here, a model for the whole period in order to be consistent in my analysis of the five kinds of interest rates .

8.6.2 Nature of the basic model

The discount rate lacks a time dimension in the form of an agreed period of maturity, such as characterizes the other interest rates that we shall be analysing. This makes it difficult to decide which time horizon the exchange rate expectations should refer to. In the analysis I use the discount rate expressed in quarterly figures. Deviations from purchasing power parity (u) and the three-month forward premium (FP3TW) express the market's exchange rate expectations for this time horizon.[41]

Apart from the variables mentioned, my basic model also includes lagged interest-sensitive relative capital flows (CFISCER,CFISCER1,...,CFISCER6),[42] lagged changes in foreign interest rates (ΔDISCTW1–6 and ΔDISCUS1–6 respectively) and two dummy variables for institutional changes of the kind mentioned above (DVIC and DV824).

8.6.3 Deviations between Swedish and global discount rates[43]

The altered role of the discount rate in economic policy means that we can expect estimation problems. It is also difficult to find a satisfactory model for the discount gap, in an estimate covering the whole of the period. The problem appears in that the stepwise backward elimination of variables from the basic model produces a relatively low D-W value at an early stage.[44]

Table 8.8 Difference between the Swedish discount rate and the global discount rate, 1974–84
Dependent variable: DISCSWTW

Variance analysis

Source	Degrees of freedom	Sum of squares	Mean square	F–value	Probability
Model	4	1.89	0.47	13.65	0.0001
Error	34	1.17	0.03		
Total	38	3.06			

$R^2 = 0.62$ R^2 (adjusted) $= 0.57$
D–W = 1.22

Parameter estimates

Variable	Degrees of freedom	Parameter estimate	Standard error	t–value for H_0: parameter = 0	Probability $p > \|t\|$
Intercept	1	–0.22	0.05	–4.38	0.0001
FP3TW	1	0.24	0.04	5.23	0.0001
NFAGDP	1	–0.02	0.00	–5.01	0.0001
CFISCER	1	0.008	0.002	3.78	0.0006
ΔDISCTW5	1	–0.49	0.25	–1.99	0.0552

Best model of the gap between Swedish and global discount rates for the period gap 1974–84

The "best" model according to the criteria previously set, gives a significant regression between the discount gap and four variables. The Durbin-Watson value is at the limit of what we can accept. The explanatory variables can be seen in Table 8.8. All variables have the correct sign and are significant at the 5 per cent level in one-tailed tests.[45] We can see that Swedish indebtedness abroad means two points for each percentage that the net foreign debt increases as a percentage of GDP. The capital flow coefficient indicates an additional risk of 0.8 points for each percentage which the capital flow represented of the foreign exchange reserve during the latest quarter.[46] These are premiums that the investors require for the risk that the central bank might decide to balance an interest gap that is "too small" by altering the exchange rate. The third significant variable is the forward premium.

The three variables mentioned here are only control variables. Their actual incidence has no implications for our conclusions about the level of direct financial integration.[47] For such conclusions we are interested in the size of the intercept and the time that passes before foreign interest movements can be discerned in the gap between Swedish and foreign rates. The intercept is here significantly negative, and the same applies to the link with changes in the global discount rate five quarters back in time. I interpret the coefficient for the interest change as follows: of a change of one percentage point in the foreign discount rate, 0.49 percentage points still remain in the interest gap after five quarters. The economic interpretation of this is that when the world discount level is raised by one percentage point, the central bank succeeds in limiting the immediate impact of this increase to 0.51 percentage points, given that everything else in the model is constant.

The interpretation of the intercept – once all our "price" variables have been taken into consideration – is that on an average Sweden has had a discount rate 0.22 percentage points lower than the average in the 15 countries whose discount rates are included in our "global discount rate". I shall continue this argument in terms of direct financial integration later in the present section. First, however I would like to look at the model for the subperiod 1979–84, and at the gap between the Swedish and US discount rates.

Best model of the gap between Swedish and global discount rates for the period 1979–84

When stepwise elimination of variables is performed from a basic equation consisting of the three control variables included in the best model for the whole period and lagged interest changes for the six latest quarters, the model presented in Table 8.9 is obtained. We see that the only difference compared with the model for the whole period is that in the subperiod the variable ΔDISCTW5 is replaced by the variable ΔDISCTW4. The size of the remaining effect is much the same, except that the foreign interest rate change has an impact one quarter earlier. However, the coefficient does not significantly deviate from zero. The same applies to the intercept.

8.6.4 Deviations between Swedish and US discount rates

The only difference between this model and the model for the global discount rate, is that the forward premium FP3USA and lagged changes in the discount rate in the USA are now used.

Table 8.9 **Difference between the Swedish discount rate and the global discount rate, 1979–84**
Dependent variable: DISCSWTW

Variance analysis

Source	Degrees of freedom	Sum of squares	Mean square	F–value	Probability
Model	4	0.74	0.18	7.16	0.0020
Error	15	0.39	0.03		
Total	19	1.13			

$R^2 = 0.66$ R^2 (adjusted) $= 0.56$
D–W = 1.23

Parameter estimates

Variable	Degrees of freedom	Parameter estimate	Standard error	t–value for H_0: parameter = 0	Probability $p > \|t\|$
Intercept	1	–0.21	0.14	–1.45	0.1666
FP3TW	1	0.04	0.07	0.62	0.5472
NFAGDP	1	–0.02	0.01	–2.29	0.0365
CFISCER	1	0.004	0.002	1.81	0.0904
ΔDISCTW4	1	–0.48	0.37	–1.29	0.2172

Best model of the gap between Swedish and US discount rates for the period 1974–84

The best model here includes five control variables and the lagged effect of discount rate changes in the USA which occurred four or five quarters earlier, respectively. All the variables in Table 8.10 have the sign we would expect. Compared with the control variables in the model for the global discount rate, the interest-sensitive capital flow in the second last quarter also proves to be significant.[48]

The changes in the discount rate in the USA remain in the interest gap after six quarters, when 0.31 percentage points remain of a change in the discount rate in the USA of one percentage point. Unlike the coefficient for the discount rate change in the USA four quarters ago, however, this figure is not significant. With this lag, 0.43 percentage points remain of a change in the US discount rate of one percentage point.

The intercept is significantly negative and shows that on an average the Swedish discount rate was 0.38 percentage points below the discount rate in the USA, if we allow for the influence of the variables included in the equation.

Table 8.10 Difference between the Swedish discount rate and the US discount rate, 1974–84
Dependent variable: DISCSWUS

Variance analysis

Source	Degrees of freedom	Sum of squares	Mean square	F–valut	Probability
Model	7	5.95	0.85	18.42	0.0001
Error	30	1.39	0.05		
Total	37	7.34			

$R^2 = 0.81$ R^2 (adjusted) $= 0.77$
D–W = 1.64

Parameter estimates

Variable	Degrees of freedom	Parameter estimate	Standard error	t–value for H_0: para– meter = 0	Probability p > |t|
Intercept	1	–0.38	0.09	–4.30	0.0002
u	1	–0.01	0.01	–0.40	0.6960
FP3USA	1	0.31	0.04	7.62	0.0001
NFAGDP	1	–0.01	0.01	–1.76	0.0885
CFISCER	1	0.008	0.003	3.13	0.0039
CFISCER1	1	0.005	0.003	1.94	0.0623
ΔDISCUS4	1	–0.43	0.17	–2.45	0.0203
ΔDISCUS6	1	–0.31	0.19	–1.59	0.1223

Best model of the gap between Swedish and US discount rates for the period 1979–84

The best model possesses high explanatory value (see Table 8.11). The difference compared with the model for the period as a whole is that the lagged effect of discount changes in the USA has diminished in size, and is also somewhat more immediate. The coefficients are small and insignificant. The intercept, on the other hand, has increased in size from –0.38 to –0.91, and deviates significantly from 0. We did not find a corresponding increase in the average discount gap in our comparison with the global rate. Thus the reason for the bigger gap is probably not that the penalty rate – which was used in combination with the discount rate during the relevant subperiod – has been disregarded.

Table 8.11 **Difference between the Swedish discount rate and the US discount rate, 1979–84**
Dependent variable: DISCSWUS

Variance analysis

Source	Degrees of freedom	Sum of squares	Mean square	F–value	Probability
Model	7	1.66	0.24	22.54	0.0001
Error	11	0.12	0.01		
Total	18	1.78			

R^2 = 0.93 R^2 (adjusted) = 0.89
D–W = 2.34

Parameter estimates

Variable	Degrees of freedom	Parameter estimate	Standard error	t–value for H_0: parameter = 0	Probability $p > \|t\|$
Intercept	1	–0.91	0.14	–6.44	0.0001
u	1	–0.01	0.01	–1.28	0.2261
FP3USA	1	0.29	0.04	7.14	0.0001
NFAGDP	1	–0.04	0.01	–5.00	0.0004
CFISCER	1	0.004	0.002	2.12	0.0577
CFISCER1	1	0.008	0.002	3.86	0.0026
ΔDISCUS4	1	–0.06	0.11	–0.57	0.5822
ΔDISCUS5	1	–0.08	0.12	–0.61	0.5541

8.6.5 *What does the discount rate gap tell us about the level of direct financial integration?*

We have now acquired the quantitative basis for determining the level of direct financial integration in terms of the lagged effect of foreign interest movements and the size of the intercept in our model.

More immediate interest adjustments suggest an increased level of integration

Under perfect direct financial integration, a foreign interest movement would be followed immediately by a neutralizing domestic adjustment, maintaining a zero interest gap corrected for risk and exchange rate expectations. We have noted that this does not apply to the discount rate gap, which instead exhibits some dependence on lagged foreign discount rate changes. Our view here is that if there is a significant dependence lag, this delay will be shorter when integration is higher. In the case of the gap between the Swedish interest rate and the world discount rate for the period as a whole, there is a significant effect on the interest gap from the change in the global discount rate five quarters before. In the subperiod 1979–84 foreign interest movements make their impact more immediately. We can see a similar phenomenon in the link between the Swedish discount rate and the discount rate in the USA. Thus, what we have noted hitherto suggests that direct financial integration has increased.

In order to obtain a complete measure of direct financial integration, we will have to link our observations of the lag with observations of the intercept. Thus the intercept should give us the remaining component in our measure of the level of direct financial integration. However, we must first eliminate potential constant risk premiums from the intercept generated by the model.

The constant component in the exchange rate premium is negligible

The variable component in the premium for exchange risk is included in the model. When we want to analyse the intercept, a question arises as to whether the premium for exchange risk also has a constant component.[49] We have already noted that there is little help to be found in other studies of the presence or the character of this premium. If there is a constant component, however, there is reason to assume that it would be an expression of the relative variability in u, i.e. in the deviation from weighted purchasing power parity. We can see in Table 8.12 that this variability is largely unchanged for the Swedish krona as between 1974–84 and 1979–84. If we compared the variability of u for the Swedish krona with the weighted variability for the basket countries in order to obtain an expression of the relative risks, we would find that even the relative risks are largely unchanged. Given such an approach we would also find that the constant component in the risk premium is of negligible size.

If on the other hand we adopt a portfolio approach and consider the covariation between the weighted deviation from purchasing power parity in the different OECD countries, we may well find that the relative risk in our case is reduced to a risk consisting of the variability in the deviation of the Swedish krona from the weighted purchasing power parity. Thus, if there is a "constant" component in the premium for exchange risk, a more or less unchanged relative risk suggests that we can nevertheless compare the intercepts for the periods 1974–84 and 1979–84, to see whether integration has increased.

Table 8.12 Mean ($\bar{u}$) and standard deviation (σ_u) in the deviation from purchasing power parity (u) for the Swedish krona
Percentage

Period	$\bar{u}$	σ_u
1974–84	–2.6	5.2
1979–84	–0.2	4.9
1981–84	1.9	2.6

The intercept reveals imperfect direct financial integration

Given the assumption that the *constant* component in the exchange risk premium and the premium for political risk is negligible, the whole intercept remains as an expression of less than perfect direct integration.[50]

In the models of the gap between the Swedish discount rate and the global rate, a comparison between the total period and the subperiod 1979–84 reveals no change in the size of the intercept. However, during the subperiod it does not deviate significantly from zero,[51] which I regard as a weak sign of increasing direct integration.

The intercept in the gap between the Swedish discount rate and the discount rate in the United States appears to have developed quite differently. It is significant in both the periods, and is much greater for the subperiod, which suggests a decrease in direct integration.

Measures of direct financial integration

The results of the analysis of the gap between the Swedish discount rate and the global rate for the period as a whole yield the value (–0.22*, 5*) as a measure of direct financial integration, and for the subperiod 1979–84 the value (–0.21, 0).[52] I conclude from this that direct financial integration has increased. Both parts of the measure suggest that this is so, albeit weakly.

The study of the gap between the Swedish discount rate and the discount rate in the United States does not produce any similarly clear-cut results. The pattern in the lagged effect of foreign interest movements certainly suggests greater integration, but the intercept suggests the opposite. For the period 1974–84 we obtain the value (–0.38*, 4*) for direct financial integration. For the period 1979–84 the value is (–0.91*, 0).The zero reflects the fact that the lagged effect from discount changes in the United States is negligible. Furthermore the difference between the two intercepts is significant. Thus there is no question here of a random change between the periods.

In general I suggest that the intercept has greater weight in my measure. It expresses the permanent element in the disintegration of markets, while the pattern of lagged effects reflects a temporary phenomenon. Furthermore, we have found in this last case that the change in the pattern of lagged effects is not as certain, statistically speaking, as the change in the intercept. Thus I interpret my observations of the gap vis-à-vis the US discount rate as an expression of increased direct financial disintegration.

Does this tell us anything about the autonomy of Swedish interest rate policy?

The autonomy of monetary policy is often discussed in somewhat vague terms. So as to avoid any problems of interpretation, I shall limit myself here to statements regarding the autonomy of interest rate policy. The scope for an independent interest rate policy is determined by my measure of integration in a modified form.

In its unchanged version the pattern of lagged effects gives us some idea of the way in which foreign interest rate influence can be temporarily held off as part of an independent policy. But the intercept must be adjusted to allow for possible transaction costs in order to give us an opinion about the autonomy. "Unreasonably" large transaction costs in the shape of special costs for transactions in a particular country should be regarded as disintegrative, and must be allowed for. What remains after this adjustment are inefficiencies. These are of two kinds: general market inefficiencies, and inefficiency caused by economic policy controls. As we have already noted, these two types of inefficiency are difficult to separate. But without making any such distinction, we can regard the inefficiencies as a whole as an upper limit to what a government has succeeded in doing in the way of managing interest rates by its regulations etc. Assuming rational expectations and general market efficiency, we are even justified in regarding the remaining part of the intercept in this way.

In earlier chapters we noted that researchers disagree about the different components in the transaction cost. We found that in the simplest case the transaction cost could be equated with the cost of a buying spot transaction and a selling spot transaction on the foreign exchange market. According to my estimates for the period as a whole, these two costs together have averaged about 0.5 per cent for transaction in proportion to the weights in the Swedish currency basket as well as for the SEK/USD transactions. We have found reason in previous chapters to assume that transaction costs have been falling over the years. According to my estimates the average cost for the two foreign exchange transactions also fell to 0.4 per cent during the subperiod 1979–84.

As an upper limit to the transaction cost I take the gap between the Swedish rate and the forward covered foreign rate, after eliminating the variable premium for political risk. By adopting this estimate I also hope to cover the cost of information search and information management.

Since the discount rate in itself will not be the subject of direct arbitrage, this transaction-cost argument remains hypothetical. When I use the cost of the least complicated transaction – three-month interest rate speculation starting in cash – the analysis only generates one intercept, containing an expression of the inefficiency of the market. This intercept refers to the gap between the Swedish discount rate and the discount rate in the United States for the period 1979–84. When the transaction cost has been eliminated we get an average inefficiency of 0.51 per cent. In economic terms I regard this as an expression of increased autonomy in interest policy in this particular segment.

The Swedish central bank's success in keeping the discount rate at an average level about half a percentage point under the discount rate in the United States during the period 1979–84, after allowing for risk premiums and exchange rate expectations, might be due to the fact that the US discount rate had lost its role as the indicator of the global rate, and that the weighted OECD discount rate which we have used here constitutes a better description of this interest level.

One objection to my conclusion that disintegration vis-à-vis the US has increased, could be that I have disregarded the importance of the penalty rate as a complement to the discount rate during the subperiod 1979–84. However, the objection does not hold up since, if it were true, the phenomenon should also have been revealed in the analysis of the global interest level.

It seems to me that observations of the intercept in the model of the link with the US discount rate provide a strong indication of increasing interest rate autonomy in this particular segment. However, the temporary element in the interest rate autonomy declined, and disappeared altogether during the subperiod.

In the link with the global level, there was no permanent interest rate autonomy during the period as a whole or during the subperiod. On the other hand temporary scope for interest rate management by the Swedish central bank did occur, but this was somewhat less during the subperiod than during the period of the study as a whole.

8.7 Analysis of the gap between Swedish and foreign interest rates on treasury discount notes

In this section we will analyse the gap between interest rates of the kind which are most common in the general debate on financial integration.

8.7.1 The paucity of observations of the interest rate on the new treasury discount notes is a drawback

In order to obtain enough quarterly observations for an analysis of the period 1974–84, data series can be chosen in two ways. We could apply our analysis to a complete series of quotations on treasury bill rates. Or we could apply it to a series of quotations on treasury bill rates up to September 1982 and on treasury discount notes after that date. In my analysis I have used this second series. Both have their evident drawbacks. It is obvious that the rate on treasury discount notes drew the attention of the government and the market from October 1982 onwards. From that date the quotations on treasury bill rates appear to have been ill suited to attracting investors.

We have already noted that the Swedish rate on treasury bills/treasury discount notes has varied, revolving round the equivalent global level. In three periods in particular since 1974 (the last one from mid-1983 to the end of the period), the Swedish interest rate has been considerably higher than the global level. We will now eliminate the influence of the control variables and see whether the intercept indicates any systematic difference between the Swedish and foreign rates.

8.7.2 Nature of the basic model

The basic model looks exactly the same as the model for analysing the discount gap, except that the interest variables here refer to rates on treasury bills/treasury discount notes. To start with, I have 18 variables including all lagged quantities.

8.7.3 Deviations between the Swedish interest rate on treasury bills/treasury discount notes and the corresponding global interest rate [53]

Stepwise elimination of variables from the basic model will help us to choose the best model as a basis for our analysis of integration.

Best model of the gap between Swedish and global rates for the period 1974–84

The best model can be seen in Table 8.13.[54] We find significant regression with an explanatory value of over 70 percent, and a Durbin-Watson value which is perfect.

For the period as a whole we find that exchange expectations make a significant contribution to the interest gap. We can see that these expectations consist of two parts: the forward premium and a fraction of the deviation from purchasing power parity. We also find that the political risk premium increases the interest gap by 4 points for each percentage point by which the Swedish net assets are reduced in relation to GDP.

In the table we also find a significant coefficient for DVIC. This coefficient means that the gap between the Swedish and foreign rates after the third quarter of 1977 – the point at which Sweden introduced the currency basket – has changed by 0.58 percentage points. If we add this change to the intercept, we find that on an average, and after the elimination of all price elements, the Swedish interest level has fallen short of the foreign rates by about one percentage point between 1974 and 1977:3 and by about 0.4 percentage points after that.

Foreign interest movements appear to be significant in the interest gap after a lag of 4 or 5 quarters.

Best model of the gap between Swedish and foreign interest rates 1979–84

As we can see from Table 8.14, the best model for the period 1979–84 has a Durbin-Watson value which does not suggest any misspecification and which has a good explanatory value. But only few variables are significant. The explanation of this may be: few degrees of freedom, high multicollinearity, or the fact that this subperiod largely consists of a fifty-fifty distribution of observations between rates of treasury bills and treasury discount notes. If the explanation had been a high degree of multicollinearity, this would also have been revealed in our analysis. But this is not the case. The explanation is rather that the observations have been divided between an administratively determined rate (on treasury bills) and a market rate (on treasury discount notes).

Bearing this observation in mind, we can note that the intercept is still negative but that it no longer deviates significantly from zero. The lagged influence of earlier foreign interest movements exhibits the same pattern as in the period as a whole.

Table 8.13 **Difference between the Swedish interest rate on treasury bills/treasury discount notes and the corresponding global interest rate, 1974–84**
Dependent variable: TBRSWTW

Variance analysis

Source	Degrees of freedom	Sum of squares	Mean square	F–value	Probability
Model	9	13.51	1.50	11.56	0.0001
Error	29	3.77	0.13		
Total	38	17.28			

$R^2 = 0.78$ R^2 (adjusted) = 0.71
D–W = 2.02

Parameter estimates

Variable	Degrees of freedom	Parameter estimate	Standard error	t–value for H_0: parameter = 0	Probability $p > \|t\|$
Intercept	1	–1.02	0.33	–3.10	0.0043
u	1	–0.05	0.03	–2.05	0.0492
FP3TW	1	0.77	0.09	8.20	0.0001
NFAGDP	1	–0.04	0.01	–4.16	0.0003
CFISCER	1	0.013	0.005	2.85	0.0080
CFISCER1	1	0.006	0.005	1.30	0.2054
DVIC	1	0.58	0.28	2.10	0.0450
DV824	1	0.02	0.45	0.04	0.9651
ΔTBRTW4	1	–0.58	0.23	–2.54	0.0166
ΔTBRTW5	1	–0.95	0.27	–3.59	0.0012

8.7.4 Deviations between the Swedish interest rate on treasury bills/treasury discount notes and the corresponding rate in the USA

This basic model differs from the previous model in that the forward premium FP3USA is used instead of FP3TW. Further, lagged changes in the US rate rather than in the global rate are now included.

Best model of the gap between Swedish and US interest rates 1974–84

The result of the stepwise elimination is reported in Table 8.15. As the table shows, we obtain a model with a high explanatory value and no sign of misspecification. The

Table 8.14 **Difference between the Swedish interest rate on treasury bills/treasury discount notes and the corresponding global interest rate, 1979–84**
Dependent variable: TBRSWTW

Variance analysis

Source	Degrees of freedom	Sum of squares	Mean square	F–value	Probability
Model	8	5.93	0.74	5.02	0.0103
Error	10	1.48	0.15		
Total	18	7.41			

$R^2 = 0.80$ R^2 (adjusted) $= 0.65$
D–W = 1.95

Parameter estimates

Variable	Degrees of freedom	Parameter estimate	Standard error	t–value for H_0: parameter = 0	Probability $p > \|t\|$
Intercept	1	–0.20	0.56	–0.36	0.7295
u	1	–0.04	0.04	–0.90	0.3556
FP3TW	1	1.20	0.25	4.89	0.0006
NFAGDP	1	–0.02	0.03	–0.63	0.5416
CFISCER	1	0.01	0.007	1.39	0.1960
CFISCER1	1	0.015	0.008	2.00	0.0730
DV824	1	0.12	0.59	0.21	0.8413
ΔTBRTW4	1	–0.55	0.29	–1.93	0.0824
ΔTBRTW5	1	–1.11	0.34	–3.24	0.0089

model greatly resembles the one we obtained for the gap between the Swedish rate and the global rate.

The intercept in the model is significantly negative and shows that for the period as whole the Swedish interest level – after the elimination of risk premiums and exchange rate expectations – fell short of the US level on an average by about half a percentage point. This result accords well with our observations regarding the gap between the Swedish rate and the global rate after the third quarter of 1977.[55] As in the case of the global rate gap, foreign interest movements appear to be significant after a lag of 4 and 5 quarters respectively.

Table 8.15 **Difference between the Swedish interest rate on treasury bills/treasury discount notes and the corresponding US interest rate, 1974–84**
Dependent variable: TBRSWUS

Variance analysis

Source	Degrees of freedom	Sum of squares	Mean square	F–value	Probability
Model	9	17.71	1.97	13.58	0.0001
Error	28	4.06	0.14		
Total	37	21.77			

$R^2 = 0.81$ R^2 (adjusted) $= 0.75$
D–W = 1.84

Parameter estimates

Variable	Degrees of freedom	Parameter estimate	Standard error	t–value for H_0: parameter = 0	Probability $p > \|t\|$
Intercept	1	–0.56	0.15	–3.86	0.0006
u	1	–0.02	0.02	–1.31	0.2020
FP3USA	1	0.57	0.07	8.00	0.0001
NFAGDP	1	–0.04	0.01	–3.85	0.0006
CFISCER	1	0.009	0.006	1.52	0.1406
CFISCER6	1	0.007	0.004	1.73	0.0954
DV824	1	0.15	0.52	0.29	0.7741
ΔTBRUS4	1	–0.32	0.15	–2.14	0.0416
ΔTBRUS5	1	–0.29	0.16	–1.82	0.0789
ΔTBRUS6	1	–0.26	0.16	–1.61	0.1196

Best model of the gap between Swedish and US interest rates 1979–84

The model is presented in Table 8.16. As we can see, we no longer have a significant relationship between the interest gap and previous foreign interest movements. The intercept is unchanged in relation to the total period of the study, except that it no longer deviates significantly from zero.

8.7.5 *What does the gap between the interest rate on treasury bills/treasury discount notes tell us about the level of direct financial integration?*

Changes in the global rate make an impact after a certain time-lag

As regards the gap between the Swedish rate and the global rate, the pattern of lagged

Table 8.16 **Difference between the Swedish interest rate on treasury bills/treasury discount notes and the corresponding US interest rate, 1979–84**
Dependent variable: TBRSWUS

Variance analysis

Source	Degrees of freedom	Sum of squares	Mean square	F–value	Probability
Model	6	6.77	1.13	10.36	0.0006
Error	11	1.20	0.11		
Total	17	7.97			

$R^2 = 0.85$ R^2 (adjusted) = 0.77
D–W = 1.57

Parameter estimates

Variable	Degrees of freedom	Parameter estimate	Standard error	t–value for H_0: parameter = 0	Probability $p > \|t\|$
Intercept	1	–0.56	0.49	–1.12	0.2858
u	1	–0.01	0.03	–0.16	0.8751
FP3USA	1	0.89	0.15	6.00	0.0001
NFAGDP	1	–0.04	0.03	–1.29	0.2244
CFISCER	1	0.016	0.006	2.54	0.0274
CFISCER6	1	0.014	0.006	2.45	0.0325
DV824	1	–0.49	0.55	–0.89	0.3909

effects shows no sign of increasing integration. On the other hand we obtain such a sign from a study of the gap between the Swedish rate and the US rate. The lagged effect for the period as a whole disappears for this gap in the subperiod 1979–84, which suggests growing integration. Here the pattern accords well with our earlier observations regarding the gap between the Swedish discount rate and the US rate.

The size of the intercepts indicates growing integration

Given our assumption of negligible constant risk premiums, we can interpret the intercept in terms of disintegration. The intercept in the form derived from the model has decreased for both types of interest gap. In the case of the global level the average gap fell from one per cent in the period before the third quarter of 1977 to just under half a per cent in the subsequent period. According to my estimates this decline continued during 1979–84, reaching –0.21. Thus, after risk premium and exchange rate expectations have been taken into account, we find that on an average the Swedish level has remained below the foreign level, but the gap has been successively shrinking. Here we have an indication of increased direct financial integration. We can see similar developments in the gap between the Swedish and the US rates, albeit they are less clear-cut. Here the change consists of a move away from an intercept which deviates significantly from zero to an intercept of the same size but not deviating significantly from zero.

Measures of direct financial integration

The measure of the direct financial integration from an analysis of the gap between the Swedish and the global rate is (–1.02*, 5*) for the period up to the third quarter of 1977. If we take the DVIC variable into account, we find that the measure changes to (–0.44, 5*) for the period from the third quarter of 1977. For the period 1979–84 we obtain the value (–0.20, 5*). The corresponding measure for the gap between the Swedish and US rates is (–0.56*, 5*) for the period as a whole, and (–0.56, 0) for the subperiod.

Interest rate policy autonomy has disappeared

If we adjust the above integration measure by considering the transaction cost, we obtain an expression of average interest rate policy segmentation. Using our earlier estimate of the transaction cost of 0.5 per cent, we find that the signs of interest rate policy autonomy that were obtained up to and including the third quarter of 1977, have disappeared. What remains for the central bank is the possibility of varying the interest rate within an interval which, in view of the transaction cost, is not economically interesting to investors.

The intercept obtained from the analysis of the gap between the Swedish and US rates reveals small average scope for segmentation, but this is not significant. Here, as in the case of the link to the global rate, there is the possibility of temporary segmentation for the period as a whole. However, this time the possibility disappears in the subperiod.

The deviation from interest rate parity can help our interpretation

The analysis of the deviation from covered interest rate parity can serve two purposes here. First, we can get some idea of the validity of our estimate of political risk with the help of the variable NFAGDP, and secondly we acquire an alternative estimate of transaction costs in the form of the average deviation when the political risk is taken into account.

Tables 8.17–20 show the regression, with the gap between the Swedish and the covered foreign rates as the dependent variable and Sweden's net foreign indebtedness (NFAGDP) as the explanatory variable. If, as in these cases, we compare national interest rates, we could expect to find market demands for a compensatory premium for political risk. The empirical estimates of the variable premium for political risk accord well with the estimates from our earlier models.

The intercept provides a broader estimate of the transaction cost. I expect it to include information costs and so on. However, obviously the intercept can also include general market inefficiency. Thus, I assume here that when it exceeds 0.5 percentage points, it can be used as an upper limit for the transaction cost. As a result of this assumption I hope to obtain more reliable signals of possible interest rate autonomy.

On a basis of the transaction costs (the intercepts) reported in Tables 8.17–20, I conclude from the gap between the Swedish and global rates that there was scope for interest rate policy generated permanent segmentation in the period up to the third quarter of 1977. After this quarter the scope is no longer significant in the model for the total period of the study. Nor is there any such scope in the period 1979–84.

As regards the gap between the Swedish and US rates, there are no significant effects from the central bank's management of interest rates here in terms of permanent segmentation, either for the period as a whole or for the period 1979–84.

We should note that these conclusions are not affected by our choosing one or the other of our transaction costs in the analysis.

Table 8.17 **Difference between the Swedish interest rate on treasury bills/treasury discount notes and the corresponding covered global rate, 1974–84**
Dependent variable: TBRSWTWF

Variance analysis

Source	Degrees of freedom	Sum of squares	Mean square	F–value	Probability
Model	1	2.99	2.99	8.49	0.0057
Error	42	14.81	0.35		
Total	43	17.80			

$R^2 = 0.17$ R^2 (adjusted) = 0.15
D–W = 1.70

Parameter estimates

Variable	Degrees of freedom	Parameter estimate	Standard error	t–value for H_0: parameter = 0	Probability $p > \|t\|$
Intercept	1	–0.28	0.11	–2.57	0.0139
NFAGDP	1	–0.03	0.01	–2.91	0.0057

Table 8.18 **Difference between the Swedish interest rate on treasury bills/treasury discount notes and the corresponding covered global rate, 1979–84**
Dependent variable: TBRSWTWF

Variance analysis

Source	Degrees of freedom	Sum of squares	Mean square	F–value	Probability
Model	1	2.57	2.57	10.38	0.0039
Error	22	5.45	0.25		
Total	23	8.02			

$R^2 = 0.32$ R^2 (adjusted) = 0.29
D–W = 2.02

Parameter estimates

Variable	Degrees of freedom	Parameter estimate	Standard error	t–value for H_0: parameter = 0	Probability $p > \|t\|$
Intercept	1	–0.60	0.23	–2.63	0.0152
NFAGDP	1	–0.04	0.01	–3.22	0.0039

Table 8.19 **Difference between the Swedish interest rate on treasury bills/treasury discount notes and the corresponding covered US rate, 1974–84**
Dependent variable: TBRSWUSF

Variance analysis

Source	Degrees of freedom	Sum of squares	Mean square	F–value	Probability
Model	1	4.31	4.31	10.86	0.0020
Error	42	16.65	0.40		
Total	43	20.96			

$R^2 = 0.21$ R^2 (adjusted) = 0.19
D–W = 1.60

Parameter estimates

Variable	Degrees of freedom	Parameter estimate	Standard error	t–value for H_0: parameter = 0	Probability $p > \|t\|$
Intercept	1	–0.52	0.12	–4.49	0.0001
NFAGDP	1	–0.03	0.01	–3.30	0.0020

Table 8.20 **Difference between the Swedish interest rate on treasury bills/treasury discount notes and the corresponding covered US rate, 1979–84**
Dependent variable: TBRSWUSF

Variance analysis

Source	Degrees of freedom	Sum of squares	Mean square	F–value	Probability
Model	1	1.61	1.61	10.01	0.0045
Error	22	3.55	0.16		
Total	23	5.16			

$R^2 = 0.31$ R^2 (adjusted) = 0.28
D–W = 1.34

Parameter estimates

Variable	Degrees of freedom	Parameter estimate	Standard error	t–value for H_0: parameter = 0	Probability $p > \|t\|$
Intercept	1	–0.58	0.18	–3.14	0.0048
NFAGDP	1	–0.03	0.01	–3.16	0.0045

8.8 Analysis of the gap between Swedish and foreign prime rates

The next analysis to be undertaken also concerns a three-month interest gap. This time it is the gap between the banks' rates on lending to first-class borrowers.

8.8.1 Nature of the basic model

This basic model deviates from both the previous models in that I now use a complete purchasing power parity approach as a description of the market's exchange rate expectations.[56] As before I use the deviation from purchasing power parity at a certain point in time as an expression of cumulative imbalance, but I now combine this deviation with an expression for the change in relative inflation during the coming period rather than with the forward premium. This is still compatible with our experience among other things of the way in which multinationals form their expectations about future exchange rate movements.[57]

8.8.2 Deviations between the Swedish prime rate and the corresponding global prime rate [58]

By eliminating step-wise variables from the basic model, I seek the best description of the interest gap.

Best model of the gap between Swedish and global interest rates for the period 1974–84

It can be seen from Table 8.21 that the best model of the prime rate gap for the period as a whole contains almost all the control variables from the basic model. But of the lagged foreign interest movements there remains only the change during the very last period. Furthermore, this change is not significant.

The explanatory value of the model as a whole is high, and the large number of variables proves to be justified when we interpret the difference between total and adjusted explanatory value. Perhaps, however, some variable is missing, as the low D–W value rings a warning bell about a possible misspecification.

Table 8.21 Difference between the Swedish prime rate and the corresponding global interest rate, 1974–84
Dependent variable: CBLRSWTW

			Variance analysis		
Source	Degrees of freedom	Sum of squares	Mean square	F–value	Probability
Model	12	7.56	0.63	11.17	0.0001
Error	25	1.41	0.06		
Total	37	8.97			

$R^2 = 0.84$ R^2 (adjusted) $= 0.77$
D–W = 1.28

			Parameter estimates		
Variable	Degrees of freedom	Parameter estimate	Standard error	t–value for H_0: parameter = 0	Probability $p > \|t\|$
Intercept	1	–1.54	0.38	–4.08	0.0004
u	1	–0.07	0.02	–3.24	0.0034
RELBITW	1	2.07	0.26	8.00	0.0001
NFAGDP	1	–0.05	0.01	–4.49	0.0001
CFISCER	1	0.009	0.004	2.44	0.0221
CFISCER1	1	0.018	0.005	3.82	0.0008
CFISCER2	1	0.011	0.004	2.88	0.0081
CFISCER3	1	0.012	0.004	3.25	0.0033
CFISCER4	1	0.005	0.003	1.41	0.1717
CFISCER5	1	0.003	0.003	0.85	0.4014
CFISCER6	1	0.003	0.003	0.88	0.3867
DVIC	1	0.47	0.26	1.84	0.0776
ΔCBLRTW1	1	–0.40	0.24	–1.67	0.1075

Among the control variables we find that the complete purchasing power parity approach as an expression of the market's exchange rate expectations, is significant. Net indebtedness to the rest of the world also reveals itself in a significant way in the interest gap. For every percentage point by which the net indebtedness increases as a percentage of GDP, the interest rate rises by 5 points.

The interest-sensitive capital flow during the four immediately preceding quarters, is also reflected in a significant way in the interest gap.

The interest gap declined after the third quarter of 1977

Our intercept is significantly negative, and shows that on an average Sweden was able to maintain an interest rate which was about 1.5 percentage points lower than the weighted global rate, when the influence from the control variables is taken into account.[59] The dummy variable for change in the exchange rate arrangements in the third quarter of 1977 (DVIC) is significant, and shows that after that quarter the interest gap shrank by about one half of a percentage point.

Best model of the gap between Swedish and global interest rates for the period 1979–84

The idea behind my search for the best model for the subperiod, is that in the initial equation I included the control variables which are in the best model for the total period of the study. Thus, given these control variables, it is a question of finding the relevant pattern for the lagged effects of foreign interest movements. However, the large number of control variables in the model for the overall period of the study suggests that there may be estimation problems for the subperiod. The best model, which is reported in Table 8.22, shows by 4 significant variables that this concern is excessive. As we can see from the table, the explanatory value is high. However, the D–W value is over 3, and on the high side. If we change the control variables so as to eliminate the insignificant variables for interest-sensitive capital flows from the model for quarter numbers 2, 4, 5 and 6, we obtain a D-W value of about 2. We then no longer see any signs of misspecifications.

Otherwise both models produce much the same estimates. The complete purchasing power parity element is significant, as in the case of the total study period. The same is true of the coefficient for Swedish net indebtedness abroad.

Both models also show that there is no longer any influence on the size of the interest gap from lagged foreign interest movements.

The intercept is significantly negative and amounts to about two percentage points.[60] Thus we find that after taking the influence of the control variables into account the Swedish interest rate was lower than the global rate by an average of two percentage points.

8.8.3 Deviations between Swedish and US prime rates

This basic model is the same as the model for the total period of the study, except that I now use the forward premium (FP3USA) instead of relative inflation, as a complement to the historical deviation from purchasing power parity. Furthermore lagged changes in the US prime rate are now included instead of changes in the global rate.

Table 8.22 **Difference between the Swedish prime rate and the corresponding global interest rate, 1979–84**
Dependent variable: CBLRSWTW

Variance analysis

Source	Degrees of freedom	Sum of squares	Mean square	F–value	Probability
Model	10	4.26	0.43	10.24	0.0027
Error	7	0.29	0.04		
Total	17	4.55			

$R^2 = 0.94$ R^2 (adjusted) $= 0.84$
D–W = 3.08

Parameter estimates

Variable	Degrees of freedom	Parameter estimate	Standard error	t–value for H_0: parameter = 0	Probability $p > \|t\|$
Intercept	1	–2.02	0.32	–6.30	0.0004
u	1	–0.09	0.03	–2.93	0.0219
RELBITW	1	1.25	0.52	2.39	0.0485
NFAGDP	1	–0.11	0.02	–5.52	0.0009
CFISCER	1	0.007	0.006	1.17	0.2800
CFISCER1	1	0.016	0.008	1.86	0.1048
CFISCER2	1	0.003	0.009	0.36	0.7287
CFISCER3	1	0.008	0.010	0.81	0.4424
CFISCER4	1	0.001	0.008	0.13	0.8970
CFISCER5	1	–0.002	0.006	–0.39	0.7087
CFISCER6	1	0.003	0.006	0.48	0.6482

Best model of the gap between Swedish and US prime rates for the period 1974–84

The model is presented in Table 8.23. We find that the forward premium contributes significantly to an explanation of the size of the interest gap. The risk premium for net indebtedness abroad is lower than when we made an estimate of the gap between the Swedish and the global rates. Significantly lagged effects from an interest movement in the USA occur only in the very last quarter. The intercept is significantly negative and is roughly the same size as it was after the third quarter of 1977 in the model for the gap between the Swedish and the global rates. Thus, taking risk premium and exchange rate expectation into account, we find that on an average the Swedish prime rate has been lower than the US prime rate by one percentage point.

Table 8.23 **Difference between the Swedish prime rate and the corresponding US rate, 1974–84**
Dependent variable: CBLRSWUS

Variance analysis					
Source	Degrees of freedom	Sum of squares	Mean square	F–value	Probability
Model	8	19.64	2.45	12.05	0.0001
Error	29	5.91	0.20		
Total	37	25.55			

$R^2 = 0.77$ R^2 (adjusted) $= 0.70$
D–W = 1.60

Parameter estimates					
Variable	Degrees of freedom	Parameter estimate	Standard error	t–value for H_0: parameter = 0	Probability $p > \|t\|$
Intercept	1	–0.95	0.16	–5.94	0.0001
FP3USA	1	0.53	0.08	6.23	0.0001
NFAGDP	1	–0.03	0.01	–2.93	0.0066
CFISCER1	1	0.014	0.005	2.71	0.0111
CFISCER3	1	0.015	0.006	2.67	0.0123
CFISCER5	1	0.008	0.005	1.54	0.1355
CFISCER6	1	0.011	0.005	2.28	0.0301
DV824	1	–0.32	0.51	–0.63	0.5324
ΔCBLRUS1	1	–0.31	0.13	–2.35	0.0257

Best model of the gap between Swedish and US prime rates for the period 1979–84

The best model for the period 1979–84 is given in Table 8.24. We find here that the forward premium and net indebtedness to the rest of the world are still significant. For this second variable the coefficient has increased substantially – a pattern which we also observed in our estimates of the gap between the Swedish and the global rates. Movements in prime rates in the United States still have a significant effect on the interest gap one quarter later.

In absolute terms the intercept has risen substantially and amounts to –2.20. During the period 1979–84 the Swedish prime rate has thus on an average been lower than the US prime rate by two percentage points, without there having been any corresponding demand for compensation from the market.

Table 8.24 Difference between the Swedish prime rate and the corresponding US rate, 1979–84
Dependent variable: CBLRSWUS

Variance analysis

Source	Degrees of freedom	Sum of squares	Mean square	F–value	Probability
Model	8	11.27	1.41	14.32	0.0003
Error	9	0.89	0.10		
Total	17	12.16			

$R^2 = 0.93$ R^2 (adjusted) $= 0.86$
D–W = 1.61

Parameter estimates

Variable	Degrees of freedom	Parameter estimate	Standard error	t–value for H_0: parameter = 0	Probability $p > \|t\|$
Intercept	1	–2.20	0.30	–7.37	0.0001
FP3USA	1	0.62	0.15	4.13	0.0026
NFAGDP	1	–0.09	0.02	–5.84	0.0002
CFISCER1	1	0.004	0.007	0.65	0.5298
CFISCER3	1	–0.008	0.008	–0.91	0.3884
CFISCER5	1	–0.011	0.007	–1.55	0.1549
CFISCER6	1	0.002	0.006	0.43	0.6776
DV824	1	0.16	0.41	0.39	0.7064
ΔCBLRUS1	1	–0.24	0.13	–1.86	0.0964

8.8.4 What does the gap between the prime rates tell us about the level of direct financial integration?

Foreign prime rate movements make a quick impact

Changes in the global prime rate make a more or less immediate impact. In this case there is no significant lagged influence. However, this pattern does not apply to the link between the Swedish and US prime rates, where the impact takes longer. In the whole period as well as in the subperiod there is a significant effect for this gap from interest movements in the immediate preceding quarter. As regards temporary segmentation, we thus find indications that the link between the Swedish prime rate with the global rate and the corresponding link with the US rate, is unchanged.

The intercepts suggest decreasing direct financial integration

A comparison of the subperiod with the whole period shows that after the control variables have been taken into account, the average gap between the Swedish prime rate and the global prime rate has increased by half to one percentage point in quarterly terms. The change deviates significantly from zero, and shows that direct financial integration has declined. This conclusion applies equally to the link between the Swedish and the US prime rates.

Measures of direct financial integration

For the period up to 1977:3 we find a value of (–1.54*, 0) for the link between the Swedish and the global prime rates. The period following this quarter produces a value of (–1.07*, 0). The corresponding value for the subperiod 1979–84 is (–2.02*, 0). On the basis of these measures I would claim that direct financial integration in this interest segment has diminished significantly.[61]

The values for the link between the Swedish and the US prime rates are (–0.95*,1*) and (–2.20*,1*) for the whole period and the subperiod respectively. For this relationship, too, the measures show that direct financial integration has diminished significantly.

Interest rate policy autonomy persists

On the assumption that constant risk premiums are negligible, we can determine the average segmentation as before by correcting the intercept for the size of the transaction cost. If we use the estimate of 0.5 percentage points for the transaction cost, we find what we have previously defined as a significant indication of scope for interest rate policy autonomy. Given the lower transaction cost 0.4 for the subperiod, we can also conclude that the interest rate policy autonomy has increased, regardless of whether we take the global rate or the US rate as the global price setter or "interest rate leader".

The absence of any lagged influence from movements in the global rate on the Swedish prime rate suggests that the scope for autonomy is of a permanent kind only, and is not a question of temporary protection against foreign interest rate movements.

As in the case of the rate on treasury bills and treasury discount notes, we can also make an analysis of covered interest parity, in order to get some idea of the upper limit of the transaction cost plus a possible constant premium for political risk. Tables 8.25–28 show the models for regression, with the gap between the Swedish and the covered foreign prime rate as the dependent variable and the political risk variable NFAGDP as the explanatory variable. The regression give us intercepts which deviate significantly from zero. They also give us coefficients for the variable political risk, which accord well with our earlier estimates. However, if we compare the coefficient for the subperiod with the coefficient for the total period, we find that the increase is not as substantial as before.

If we use the intercept from the interest rate parity analysis as an upper limit for transaction costs with all the related costs, we find that our conclusion changes somewhat.[62] The effects of interest policy controls still prove significant in terms of permanent segmentation for the Swedish prime rate's link with the global rate both in the period as a whole and in the subperiod. But the result differs from the analysis with a lower transaction cost for the link with the US rate, in that the effects of central bank's management of interest rates are not demonstrable for the period of the study as a whole, but they are still demonstrable for the subperiod. Moreover, the discernible effects of interest rate management have increased significantly in the case of the link between the Swedish and the US prime rates, as well as the link with the global rate.

8.9 Analysis of the gap between the Swedish interest rate on government bonds/government notes and the corresponding foreign rate

We now come to the case of long-term interest rates, with the difference between annual rates as the dependent variable. As we have seen in Chapter 6, the Swedish interest rate on government bonds/governments notes has been higher than the corresponding foreign rate for almost the whole of the period. We shall now see whether this gap persists after we have taken our "price variables" into account.

8.9.1 Nature of the basic model

The basic model contains the same variables as the earlier models, but there are a few alterations.[63] One such adjustment is that the forward premium now refers to the 12-month term. Admittedly the Swedish forward market must be regarded as thin when it comes to such long contracts, but we will have to accept this uncertainty. The alternative would be to estimate exchange rate expectations on a basis of the differential between government bond rates, as Frankel (1979a) prescribes, which would not be suitable here.

Table 8.25 Difference between the Swedish prime rate and the correponding covered global rate, 1974–84
Dependent variable: CBLRSWTWF

Variance analysis

Source	Degrees of freedom	Sum of squares	Mean square	F–value	Probability
Model	1	3.92	3.92	11.91	0.0013
Error	42	13.81	0.33		
Total	43	17.73			

$R^2 = 0.22$ R^2 (adjusted) = 0.20
D–W = 1.56

Parameter estimates

Variable	Degrees of freedom	Parameter estimate	Standard error	t–value for H_0: parameter = 0	Probability p > |t|
Intercept	1	–0.78	0.11	–7.33	0.0001
NFAGDP	1	–0.03	0.01	–3.45	0.0013

Table 8.26 Difference between the Swedish prime rate and the corresponding covered global rate, 1979–84
Dependent variable: CBLRSWTWF

Variance analysis

Source	Degrees of freedom	Sum of squares	Mean square	F–value	Probability
Model	1	2.47	2.47	8.95	0.0067
Error	22	6.07	0.28		
Total	23	8.54			

$R^2 = 0.29$ R^2 (adjusted) = 0.26
D–W = 1.04

Parameter estimates

Variable	Degrees of freedom	Parameter estimate	Standard error	t–value for H_0: parameter = 0	Probability p > |t|
Intercept	1	–1.03	0.24	–4.27	0.0003
NFAGDP	1	–0.04	0.01	–2.99	0.0067

Table 8.27 **Difference between the Swedish prime rate and the corresponding covered US rate, 1974–84**
Dependent variable: CBLRSWUSF

Variance analysis

Source	Degrees of freedom	Sum of squares	Mean square	F–value	Probability
Model	1	2.35	2.35	6.50	0.0145
Error	42	15.18	0.36		
Total	43	17.53			

$R^2 = 0.13$ R^2 (adjusted) = 0.11
D–W = 1.32

Parameter estimates

Variable	Degrees of freedom	Parameter estimate	Standard error	t–value for H_0: parameter = 0	Probability $p > \|t\|$
Intercept	1	-0.86	0.11	–7.76	0.0001
NFAGDP	1	–0.02	0.01	–2.55	0.0145

Table 8.28 **Difference between the Swedish prime rate and the corresponding covered US rate, 1979–84**
Dependent variable: CBLRSWUSF

Variance analysis

Source	Degrees of freedom	Sum of squares	Mean square	F–value	Probability
Model	1	2.75	2.75	12.34	0.0020
Error	22	4.91	0.22		
Total	23	7.66			

$R^2 = 0.36$ R^2 (adjusted) = 0.33
D–W = 1.22

Parameter estimates

Variable	Degrees of freedom	Parameter estimate	Standard error	t–value for H_0: parameter = 0	Probability $p > \|t\|$
Intercept	1	–1.29	0.22	–5.94	0.0001
NFAGDP	1	–0.05	0.01	–3.51	0.0020

Another difference concerns the capital flows. Initial estimates using the same interest-sensitive capital flows that we used for the short-term rates gave signals of misspecifications. It appears plausible that in analysing government bonds, the market actors look rather at the total foreign exchange flow as this flow provides signals of the state of economy as a whole. In the present section I thus use as explanatory variables the lagged values of the total exchange flow in a particular period in relation to the foreign exchange reserves at the end of the same period.

8.9.2 *Deviations between the Swedish rate on government bonds and the corresponding global rate* [64]

The step-wise elimination of variables from the basic model helps us to find the best description of the interest gap.

Best model of the gap between Swedish and global rates for the period 1974–84

Table 8.29 shows the most important variables explaining the gap between the Swedish rate on government bonds and the corresponding global rate. We find that the lagged influence on the gap from earlier movements in the global rate are not significant in any of the cases.

The model gives us an intercept which is negative but not significant. From the coefficient for DVIC we obtain a significant indication that after the third quarter of 1977 the interest gap changed from an average of -0.5 percentage units to 0.8 percentage units.

The deviation from purchasing power parity proves not to have any explanatory value, when the total foreign exchange flow is included in the model. The deviations from purchasing power parity are also strongly correlated with the total foreign exchange flow, and are thus to a large extent expressed in the size of this flow.

Best model of the gap between Swedish and global rates 1979–84

Table 8.30 shows that the explanatory value is high, and there are no signs of misspecifications. The effects of earlier movements in the global rate are if possible weaker than for the period as a whole. The intercept is positive but not significant. After the control variables have been allowed for, we find that on an average the Swedish rate was 0.7 percentage points higher than the global level for the period 1979–84.

Table 8.29 **Difference between the Swedish interest rate on government bonds and the corresponding global rate, 1974–84**
Dependent variable: BONDSWTW

Variance analysis					
Source	Degrees of freedom	Sum of squares	Mean square	F–value	Probability
Model	9	20.57	2.29	11.16	0.0001
Error	28	5.74	0.20		
Total	37	26.31			

$R^2 = 0.78$ R^2 (adjusted) = 0.71
D–W = 1.91

Parameter estimates					
Variable	Degrees of freedom	Parameter estimate	Standard error	t–value for H_0: parameter = 0	Probability $p > \|t\|$
Intercept	1	–0.51	0.30	–1.70	0.1004
u	1	–0.00	0.03	–0.05	0.9590
FP12TW	1	0.14	0.03	4.68	0.0001
NFAGDP	1	–0.03	0.01	–2.00	0.0557
EFTER	1	0.024	0.006	3.92	0.0005
EFTER6	1	0.021	0.006	3.83	0.0007
DVIC	1	1.33	0.33	4.04	0.0004
ΔBONDTW1	1	–0.23	0.18	–1.27	0.2145
ΔBONDTW2	1	–0.21	0.18	–1.19	0.2454
ΔBONDTW6	1	–0.16	0.16	–0.95	0.3499

8.9.3 Deviations between the Swedish rate on government bonds and the corresponding rate in the USA

Here I replace the weighted 12-month forward premium FP12TW in the basic model by the bilateral forward premium FP12USA. However, u is still estimated multilaterally. Further, the lagged influence of movements in the US rate rather than the global rate is now included.

Table 8.30 **Difference between the Swedish interest rate on government bonds and the corresponding global rate, 1979–84**
Dependent variable: BONDSWTW

Variance analysis

Source	Degrees of freedom	Sum of squares	Mean square	F–value	Probability
Model	7	13.56	1.94	10.46	0.0007
Error	10	1.85	0.19		
Total	17	15.41			

$R^2 = 0.88$ R^2 (adjusted) = 0.80
D–W = 2.45

Parameter estimates

Variable	Degrees of freedom	Parameter estimate	Standard error	t–value for H_0: parameter = 0	Probability $p > \|t\|$
Intercept	1	0.68	0.72	0.94	0.3696
u	1	–0.01	0.05	–0.17	0.8670
FP12TW	1	0.20	0.08	2.47	0.0332
NFAGDP	1	–0.03	0.04	–0.84	0.4182
EFTER	1	0.011	0.01	1.07	0.3114
EFTER6	1	0.034	0.01	3.44	0.0064
ΔBONDTW4	1	–0.23	0.26	–0.91	0.3865
ΔBONDTW6	1	–0.18	0.21	–0.87	0.4031

Best model for analysing the gap between the Swedish rate on government bonds and the corresponding rate in the USA 1974–84

Table 8.31 shows that the lagged effect of interest movements in the USA is negligible. The intercept is significantly positive at 0.8 percentage points. The coefficient for DVIC shows that the average Swedish rate was roughly another half percentage point above the rate on government bonds in the USA after the third quarter of 1977.

Best model for analysing the gap between the Swedish rate on government bonds and the equivalent rate in the USA 1979–84

As we can see from Table 8.32, the model for 1979–84 shows no significant link between the interest gap and earlier changes in the US rate on government bonds.

Table 8.31 Difference between the Swedish interest rate for government bonds and the corresponding US rate, 1974–84
Dependent variable: BONDSWUS

Variance analysis

Source	Degrees of freedom	Sum of squares	Mean square	F–value	Probability
Model	7	28.72	4.10	10.23	0.0001
Error	30	12.03	0.40		
Total	37	40.75			

$R^2 = 0.70$ R^2 (adjusted) $= 0.64$
D–W = 1.59

Parameter estimates

Variable	Degrees of freedom	Parameter estimate	Standard error	t–value for H_0: parameter = 0	Probability $p > \|t\|$
Intercept	1	0.80	0.27	3.00	0.0054
FP12USA	1	0.13	0.03	4.25	0.0002
EFTER	1	0.017	0.008	2.31	0.0283
EFTER6	1	0.033	0.008	4.04	0.0003
DVIC	1	0.46	0.31	1.47	0.1515
DV824	1	0.41	0.73	0.56	0.5776
ΔBONDUS2	1	–0.06	0.14	–0.41	0.6868
ΔBONDUS3	1	–0.03	0.13	–0.24	0.8093

According to the model the average Swedish rate, after risk premiums and exchange rate expectations have been taken into account, was about 0.7 percentage units above the corresponding rate in the USA. The gap is about half a percentage point lower than the estimate for the period following the third quarter of 1977. Thus the average gap for the subperiod is the same size, regardless of whether we measure the Swedish rate against the global rate or the US rate.

8.9.4 What does the gap between the interest rates on government bonds tell us about the level of direct financial integration?

No lagged effect can be discerned

The gap between the interest rates on government bonds shows no significant link with

Table 8.32 **Difference between the Swedish interest rate on government bonds and the corresponding US rate, 1979–84**
Dependent variable: BONDSWUS

Variance analysis

Source	Degrees of freedom	Sum of squares	Mean square	F–value	Probability
Model	6	14.19	2.36	6.38	0.0042
Error	11	4.08	0.37		
Total	17	18.27			

$R^2 = 0.78$ R^2 (adjusted) = 0.66
D–W = 1.81

Parameter estimates

Variable	Degrees of freedom	Parameter estimate	Standard error	t–value for H_0: parameter = 0	Probability $p > \|t\|$
Intercept	1	0.69	0.35	1.95	0.0773
FP12USA	1	0.24	0.07	3.34	0.0066
EFTER	1	0.012	0.011	1.09	0.3004
EFTER6	1	0.021	0.016	1.28	0.2268
DV824	1	0.92	0.78	1.18	0.2630
ΔBONDUS2	1	–0.08	0.19	–0.42	0.6833
ΔBONDUS3	1	–0.14	0.15	–0.90	0.3879

previous changes in the corresponding foreign rates. The size of the lagged influence is negligible and there is no need to discuss the nature of the changes. I take this to mean that any foreign interest movements are quickly balanced by a Swedish movement of such a size as to leave the gap unchanged.

The intercept suggests increasing integration

After taking risk premiums and exchange rate expectations into account, we find that on an average Swedish rates have been above the global level. However, the difference is not significantly greater than zero in the subperiod. A comparison of the total period with the period 1979–84 shows that the intercept decreased – a sign, albeit a weak one, of increasing integration. The decrease is not significant.

As compared to the US rate we find, after having allowed for the control variables, that for the whole period of the study, the average Swedish rate has been significantly higher. It was also higher during the period 1979–84, albeit not significantly. We have here confirmation of disintegration. A comparison of the intercepts shows that disintegration has decreased, but not significantly.

Measures of direct financial integration

For the period after 1977:3 the link between the Swedish rate and the global rate can be expressed as (0.82*, 0), and before that date as (–0.51, 0). For the subperiod 1979–84 we obtain the value (0.68, 0). The corresponding values for the link between the Swedish rate and the US rate are (0.80*, 0), (1.26*, 0) and (0.69, 0) for 1974:1 to 1977:3, 1977:3 to 1984:4 and 1979:1 to 1984:4 respectively.

No evidence of interest rate autonomy after 1977

In order to determine the scope for an independent interest rate policy, we have to subtract the transaction cost from the intercept. I shall use the same estimates as before.[65] If we allow for a transaction cost, we find that the intercept for the gap between the Swedish and global rates is much the same size as the transaction cost for the period of the study as a whole. There is no significant evidence of interest rate autonomy here. The same applies to the period 1979–84. A comparison of the total period and the subperiod reveals effects which indicate a decrease in interest rate autonomy. But the decrease is not significant.

As regards the gap between the Swedish and US rates, the model for the total period provides no significant confirmation of interest rate autonomy up to the third quarter of 1977. Nor do we find any such confirmation for the subperiod 1979–84.

8.10 Analysis of the gap between Swedish and foreign interest rates on industrial bonds

In Chapter 6 we observed a growth trend in the nominal interest rate on Swedish industrial bonds in the period 1974–81 and a growth trend in the global level during 1978–81. Looking at the period 1974–84 as a whole, we find that the Swedish rate has for periods of three years at a time been higher and lower than the global level. The Swedish rate has also weakly reflected the downturn in the global rate which started in mid-1981. During the period 1982–84, however, the nominal gap between the Swedish and the global rates was considerable.

8.10.1 Nature of the basic model

In connection with the basic model we have already discussed the possibility of using alternative expressions for the market's exchange rate expectations.[66] It has mainly been a question of the choice of complementary expressions for u. Here, as in the case of the prime rate, I use an expression for future relative inflation, RELBITW. This variable as a way of creating a complete purchasing power parity approach must generally be used with caution, as misleading results could be generated. In this case, however, a check on the correlation matrix reveals that the variable can be used as a proxy.

In the basic model the interest-sensitive capital flows reported by the central bank for the last six quarters are included as the explanatory variable.[67]

8.10.2 Deviations between interest rate *on Swedish industrial bonds and the corresponding global rate* [68]

By eliminating step-wise variables from the basic model we obtain the best description of the interest gap.

Best model of the gap between Swedish and global interest rates for the period 1974/84

The best model, which is presented in Table 8.33, gives us a high explanatory value and no signals of misspecification. It contains many variables, all except one of which are significant in one-tail tests at the 5 per cent level.

We see here a significant impact on the interest gap from movements in the global rates during the last six quarters. The intercept is significantly negative up to the third quarter of 1977, showing that during the period the average Swedish rate after the control variables have been taken into account, was 1.75 percentage points under the global level. After the third quarter of 1977 we see a significant change of 1.84 percentage points, which leads us to conclude that during this period the average Swedish rate, after the control variables have been allowed for, was on a level with the global rate.

Best model of the gap between Swedish and global interest rates for the period 1979–84

As we can see from Table 8.34 the model for the subperiod shows statistical qualities largely as good as the model for the period as a whole, except that fewer coefficients prove to be significant. This last is not surprising, in view of the large number of estimates in relation to the number of observations.

The lagged effect of global interest movements is considerable. However, compared with the model for the period as a whole, the influence of changes six quarters ago is no longer significant.

Table 8.33 Difference between the Swedish interest rate on industrial bonds and the corresponding global rate, 1974–84
Dependent variable: DCBRSWTW

Variance analysis

Source	Degrees of freedom	Sum of squares	Mean square	F–value	Probability
Model	12	55.49	4.62	34.07	0.0001
Error	25	3.39	0.14		
Total	37	58.88			

$R^2 = 0.94$ R^2 (adjusted) $= 0.91$
D–W = 1.87

Parameter estimates

Variable	Degrees of freedom	Parameter estimate	Standard error	t–value for H_0: parameter = 0	Probability $p > \|t\|$
Intercept	1	–1.75	0.47	–3.76	0.0009
u	1	–0.12	0.04	–3.22	0.0035
RELBITW	1	0.73	0.10	7.39	0.0001
NFAGDP	1	–0.05	0.01	–4.64	0.0001
CFISCER1	1	0.01	0.005	1.90	0.0698
DVIC	1	1.84	0.42	4.41	0.0002
DV824	1	0.54	0.50	1.07	0.2953
ΔDCBRTW1	1	–0.67	0.11	–6.04	0.0001
ΔDCBRTW2	1	–0.36	0.12	–3.04	0.0055
ΔDCBRTW3	1	–0.40	0.12	–3.23	0.0034
ΔDCBRTW4	1	–0.53	0.12	–4.48	0.0001
ΔDCBRTW5	1	–0.47	0.12	–3.87	0.0007
ΔDCBRTW6	1	–0.39	0.13	–3.10	0.0048

The intercept is positive and shows that, allowing for all the market demands for compensation, the average Swedish rate was about one percentage point higher than the global level. However, the intercept does not deviate significantly from zero.

8.10.3 Deviations between the rate on Swedish industrial bonds and the corresponding rate in the USA

Relative inflation, RELBIUSA, is now calculated bilaterally between Sweden and the USA. I also change the model by replacing lagged effects from changes in the global rate by lagged effects from changes in the US rate. On the other hand I still calculate u multilaterally, since this quantity is supposed to express the devaluation/appreciation potential of the Swedish krona.

Best model of the gap between interest rates in Sweden and the USA for the period 1974–84

Stepwise elimination still leaves many variables in the model, as can be seen from Table 8.35. The explanatory value is very high and there are no signs of misspecifications.

The model shows a significant impact on the interest gap from earlier interest movements in the USA. However, the link is not as strong as the one we found for the global level in the shape of the trade-weighted interest rate.

The intercept shows that over the period as a whole, and after risk premiums and exchange rate expectations have been allowed for, the average Swedish rate was 1.2 percentage points lower than the US rate. For the period after 1977:3 the change in level was only nine points and was insignificant. Thus we find that the gap persists. There is a difference here compared with the gap between the Swedish and the global rates, which last was eliminated after 1977:3 in the model for the total period.

Best model of the gap between interest rates in Sweden and the USA for the period 1979–84

We now come up against the problem that the best model for the whole period contains many control variables. Since these variables must be included in the basic equation for the subperiod, together with all the lagged interest rate movements, the standard errors – given the small number of observations – will be great. Nonetheless many variables prove significant, as Table 8.36 shows.

Table 8.34 **Difference between the Swedish interest rate on industrial bonds and the corresponding global rate, 1979–84**
Dependent variable: DCBRSWTW

Variance analysis

Source	Degrees of freedom	Sum of squares	Mean square	F–value	Probability
Model	10	25.65	2.57	12.97	0.0007
Error	8	1.58	0.20		
Total	18	27.23			

$R^2 = 0.94$ R^2 (adjusted) $= 0.87$
D–W = 2.83

Parameter estimates

Variable	Degrees of freedom	Parameter estimate	Standard error	t–value for H_0: parame– ter = 0	Probability $p > \|t\|$
Intercept	1	0.95	0.69	1.37	0.2067
u	1	–0.03	0.06	–0.45	0.6640
RELBITW	1	0.65	0.15	4.30	0.0026
NFAGDP	1	–0.01	0.04	–0.18	0.8623
CFISCER1	1	0.009	0.008	1.12	0.2954
DV824	1	–0.43	0.65	–0.66	0.5277
ΔDCBRTW1	1	–0.55	0.16	–3.41	0.0092
ΔDCBRTW2	1	–0.31	0.16	–1.93	0.0897
ΔDCBRTW3	1	–0.35	0.16	–2.17	0.0618
ΔDCBRTW4	1	–0.61	0.16	–3.69	0.0061
ΔDCBRTW5	1	–0.45	0.17	–2.64	0.0299

The lagged impact of changes in the US rate are weaker than for the period as a whole. We can now only discern any significant influence from foreign interest rate movements from the last four quarters. The intercepts show that, after the control variables have been allowed for, the average gap between the rates in Sweden and the USA has increased. During the period 1979–84 the Swedish rate has been almost two percentage points below the US rate, which can be compared with our observations of the Swedish rate versus the global rate for that period, when it was almost one percentage point above. A comparison of the total period and the subperiod shows that, after allowing for the control variables, the average gap between the Swedish and the US rates has increased. But the increase is not significant.

Table 8.35 **Difference between the interest rate on Swedish industrial bonds and the corresponding US rate, 1974–84**
Dependent variable: DCBRSWUS

Variance analysis

Source	Degrees of freedom	Sum of squares	Mean square	F–value	Probability
Model	13	79.90	6.15	37.05	0.0001
Error	25	4.15	0.17		
Total	38	84.05			

$R^2 = 0.95$ R^2 (adjusted) $= 0.93$
D–W = 2.19

Parameter estimates

Variable	Degrees of freedom	Parameter estimate	Standard error	t–value for H_0: parame– ter = 0	Probability $p > \|t\|$
Intercept	1	–1.21	0.51	–2.39	0.0245
u	1	–0.01	0.03	–0.22	0.8271
RELBIUSA	1	1.17	0.10	11.64	0.0001
NFAGDP	1	–0.02	0.02	–1.12	0.2746
CFISCER	1	0.007	0.005	1.33	0.1954
CFISCER1	1	0.012	0.007	1.78	0.0868
CFISCER3	1	0.010	0.006	1.65	0.1113
CFISCER5	1	0.009	0.005	1.82	0.0802
DVIC	1	0.09	0.40	0.22	0.8288
DV824	1	–1.29	0.58	–2.23	0.0350
ΔDCBRUS1	1	–0.16	0.08	–2.11	0.0446
ΔDCBRUS3	1	–0.17	0.09	–1.94	0.0641
ΔDCBRUS4	1	–0.30	0.09	–3.19	0.0038
ΔDCBRUS5	1	–0.20	0.08	–2.41	0.0239

8.10.4 What does the gap between the interest rates on industrial bonds tell us about the level of direct financial integration?

In the case of the rates on industrial bonds we have found a large significant lagged influence from foreign interest movements. There are thus indications here of central bank generated effects in the shape of temporary segmentation. However, a comparison of the subperiod and the period as a whole shows that the time span for this form of segmentation became shorter.

Table 8.36 **Difference between the interest rate on Swedish industrial bonds and the corresponding US rate, 1979–84**
Dependent variable: DCBRSWUS

Variance analysis

Source	Degrees of freedom	Sum of squares	Mean square	F–value	Probability
Model	11	39.35	3.58	13.83	0.0010
Error	7	1.81	0.26		
Total	18	41.16			

$R^2 = 0.96$ R^2 (adjusted) $= 0.89$
D–W = 2.34

Parameter estimates

Variable	Degrees of freedom	Parameter estimate	Standard error	t–value for H_0: parameter = 0	Probability $p > \|t\|$
Intercept	1	–1.91	0.83	–2.30	0.0554
u	1	–0.12	0.08	–1.43	0.1962
RELBIUSA	1	1.49	0.20	7.58	0.0001
NFAGDP	1	–0.06	0.05	–1.35	0.2199
CFISCER	1	0.019	0.01	1.87	0.1044
CFISCER1	1	0.044	0.015	2.98	0.0206
CFISCER3	1	0.050	0.018	2.76	0.0283
CFISCER5	1	0.033	0.014	2.29	0.0556
DV824	1	–2.15	1.21	–1.78	0.1186
ΔDCBRUS3	1	–0.29	0.13	–2.27	0.0578
ΔDCBRUS4	1	–0.36	0.14	–2.53	0.0395
ΔDCBRUS5	1	–0.22	0.12	–1.83	0.1096

The intercept suggests a stronger link with the global level

Up to the third quarter of 1977 the average Swedish rate, after control variables have been allowed for, was 1.75 percentage points below the global level, which I see as a strong indication of direct financial disintegration. After 1977:3 this average rate was the same as the global rate. For the period 1979–84 our model shows that the average Swedish rate, after risk premiums and exchange rate expectations have been taken into account, was one percentage point higher than the global rate. However, the interest gap for the subperiod is not significant. I conclude that direct financial integration has increased, and that there is no demonstrable effect in the shape of permanent segmentation after the third quarter of 1977. The increased integration is not significant.

The interest gap between the Swedish rate and the US rate developed quite differently. Here we find a significant gap which increased during the subperiod 1979–81. Thus in this interest segment direct financial integration between Sweden and the United States has declined. However, the decline is not significant.

Measures of direct financial integration

The link between the Swedish and the global rates seems to have been weak up to the third quarter of 1977; it can be expressed as (–1.75*, 6*). After the third quarter of 1977 it can be expressed as (0.09, 6*), which indicates that effects of permanent segmentation are negligible, but that temporary segmentation does occur. The measure for 1979–84 is (0.95, 5*). Compared with the period up to the third quarter of 1977, permanent segmentation as well as temporary segmentation have thus declined.

The link with the US rate is weaker than the link with the global rate. Average inefficiencies are also over one per cent here. The measure is (–1.21*, 5*) for the period up to the third quarter of 1977, and (–1.12*, 5*) afterwards. For the period 1979–84 we get (–1.91*, 4*). Permanent segmentation has increased, while temporary segmentation has diminished.

The scope for interest rate policy autonomy has increased

In the case of industrial bonds we have found that the link between the Swedish rate and the global rate has become stronger. The question is whether any scope remains for an independent interest rate policy. The answer is that opportunities do exist for temporarily withstanding foreign interest movements, although this possibility has become weaker over time. There was also significant scope for permanent segmentation up to and including the third quarter of 1977. But in the model for the whole period of the study and after the control variables have been allowed for, we cannot see any significant signs that the average Swedish interest rate deviated from the foreign rate after that date. The estimate for the subperiod 1979–84 yields the same indications. I take this to mean that there is no longer any scope for permanent segmentation. The reduction in this scope is significant.

The link between the Swedish and the US interest rates shows signs of becoming weaker. However, when we take the transaction costs into account there is no indication of permanent segmentation, either in the period as a whole or in the subperiod 1979–84.

Notes

[1] i.e. the deviation between the forecast of exchange rate movements as expressed in the interest differential, and the actual outcome.

[2] In statistical contexts the Greek letters are often reserved for the designation of parameters. I break with this tradition here and use σ to designate standard deviations in the random sample, since the traditional designation s has been used here for the relative exchange rate change, and the designation for estimate "ˆ" has been used for change.

[3] The international currency designations are listed in Supplement 2.

[4] The presence of a variable risk premium.

[5] See, for example, Greenwald, Stiglitz and Weiss (1984).

[6] In so far as possible transaction costs contribute to the non-occurrence of those transactions, which would mean that the exchange rate change becomes equal to the interest differential.

[7] Since I have found empirically that long periods of overestimation are followed by long periods of underestimation, this can be taken to mean, assuming rational expectations, that the risk premium are variable over time.

[8] See, for example, Branson (1969), Levich (1979), McCormick (1979), Frenkel and Levich (1981) and others. Bahmani-Oskooe and Das (1985), on the other hand, claim that the transaction cost plays a diminishing role as an explanation of deviations from interest rate parity. In their view the explanation has to be sought in other factors.

[9] Assuming among others things a non negative political risk premium. In bilateral studies a negative premium cannot be disregarded. See, for example, Kouri (1983).

[10] T_S refers to the transaction cost for the spot transaction, and T_F for the transaction on the forward exchange market.

[11] This result is obtained by combining the formulae (A2.6) and (A2.19) from the Appendix to Chapter 2.

[12] Like Frenkel (1979) for example, who accepted the hypothesis (a=0, β=1).

[13] Cumby and Obstfeldt (1984), Fama (1984) and others have used various methods to test variants of this equation. With the US dollar as the base currency they reject the forward rate (premium) as an unbiased estimate of the exchange rate (the change); others accept it.

[14] Like Fama (1984) they obtain significant negative β-values. Such values arise according to Fama when the variance in the risk premium exceed the variance in the expected change in the exchange rate.

[15] See, for example, Chatterjee and Price (1977).

[16] An alternative which is included in most standard programs.

[17] See, for example, Mantel (1970).

[18] Cp for an equation with p explanatory variables measures the way in which these variables work in terms of standardized mean square error in the fitting procedure. It takes account of the systematic error (bias) as well as the variance. The extent to which Cp deviates from its expected value p, can be regarded as a measure of the systematic error. For a more detailed explanation, see Daniel and Wood (1971).

[19] Previously in this book we have used two subperiods, which was possible since we had monthly observations and thus a larger number of observations as a basis for the estimates.

[20] This approach is also motivated by the results of my study of the decision process in

Swedish multinational companies, where I found no confirmation of the application of an explicit portfolio approach.

21 For a discussion of the problems connected with aggregating market actors to be represented by an average, see Rubinstein (1974).

22 The intercept in the form in which it occurs in the presentations of the model, reflects the average interest gap when all the explanatory variables assume a value of zero. The intercept in this form is often only of technical interest, but since it is not a question here of an extrapolation – in that the zero value of our explanatory variables is within the interval in which we have made observations – the economic interpretation of the intercept is in fact relevant. During the subperiod 1979–84 there is no value as low as zero for the variable NFAGDP, but there are values that come very close to zero.

23 If we cannot assume unchanged "constant" risk premiums, these will have to be estimated if we are to be able to say anything about the direction of the integration/disintegration.

24 I also assume no constant term in the stochastic process generating the expected exchange rate.

25 When it is a case of the study of the weighted global rate, a parity change is required if the imbalance in the Swedish exchange rate is to be adjusted within the shorter periods, and we can then speak of devaluation or revaluation potentials instead.

26 The overvaluation is measured as a negative deviation from purchasing power parity.

27 The evidence for a constant premium varies from country to country. Domowitz and Hakkio (1985), e.g., demonstrate a constant risk premium for England and Japan for the period 1973–82, while finding no confirmation of such a premium for Germany, France or Switzerland.

28 The identification should be compatible with the hypothesis of rational expectations.

29 Which can also be interpreted in terms of underlying budget deficit.

30 This premium contains compensation for a currency risk that borders on a political risk.

31 In recent years the central bank has influenced the flow situation by transactions on the forward market, which the market actors came to recognize after about a year's delay. This circumstance does not thus reduce the value of the variable as a signal in the period of the investigation.

32 The principle underlying the variable designations introduced in this chapter, is that they should show how the variable has been created. CFISCER thus stands for *c*apital *f*low-*i*nterest-*s*ensitive and *c*entral-bank-reported in relation to the foreign *e*xchange *r*eserve.

33 This could have been created more exactly by using Eurorates for all the foreign rates involved, but due to the lack of some of these rates this approach was not adopted.

34 My expression is an approximation, since the USA's large foreign stock of assets gives the market forces greater scope than if NFAGDP was zero, and means less risk of intervention.

35 During the last few years the USA's increasing foreign debt has changed this situation.

36 Even if the currency snake gave the companies opportunities for almost risk-free profits in an intervention situation.

37 The average value of lagged foreign interest movements is very close to zero throughout, which means that we do not have to make any extra adjustment in order to give the intercept the form we want.

[38] The variables are designated Δ + interest designation + quarter when the change occurred. Δ DISCTW1 thus stands for the change in the *disc*ount rate (*t*rade-*w*eighted) that occurred in the most recent quarter.

[39] Cumby and Obstfelt (1984) warn us of problems in analysing financial markets with a variance σ_{ε}^2 which varies with the size of the explanatory variables (heteroscedasticity). The diagnostic analysis which I have conducted reveals no equivalent problems in the present study. However, such an analysis is uncertain when both autocorrelation and heteroscedasticity obtain.

[40] The average value of lagged foreign interest rate changes is here zero. If this were not the case, we would make the necessary adjustment with the help of a simple calculation.

[41] A summary of the variable designations is given in Supplement 2.

[42] The capital flow in the most recent quarter is designated CFISCER, in the next most recent CFISCER 1, etc.

[43] An average based on trade weights for the 15 major OECD countries. For a further description see Table S1.A in Supplement 1.

[44] If instead of the *change* in the foreign rate the *level* is used as an explanatory variable, a good econometric description is obtained. However, the economic interpretation would not be as clear-cut.

[45] The probability value in the table refers to two-tailed tests and should be halved for one-tailed tests and compared with 5 per cent.

[46] I have previously explained why I regard the interest-sensitive capital flow as reported by the central bank as most appropriate in analysing the gap between short-term rates. This choice is important, since the test with different types of exchange flows/capital flows – total, interest-sensitive flows reported by the central bank, and interest-sensitive flows reported by SCB – show different links. Thus the models reveal no significant relationship with the total currency flow, no significance for the most recent or next most recent exchange flow according to the central bank's reports, and no significance for the next most recent quotation of the exchange flow according to SCB's reports.

[47] In an argument regarding the *total* financial integration, however, they are important. Under perfect total integration the coefficients for all quantities apart from exchange rate expectations would be zero. The coefficient for exchange expectation would be such that it always gave us an exchange change rate corresponding to purchasing power parity.

[48] One-tailed test at the 5 per cent level.

[49] The intercept may also contain a constant component in a political risk premium. Moreover, this premium is difficult to distinguish from the constant component in the premium for exchange risk, since in their constant forms both these premiums reflect more or less the same phenomena.

[50] The assumption that the constant component is negligible means that in cases when the constant component is not negligible for Sweden or the Swedish krona, we will overestimate the level of disintegration. In the special case of Sweden being regarded as a "safe haven", we would expect a reverse sign for the premium compared with the previous case; thus, given a constant risk premium, we would underestimate the level of disintegration.

[51] This could be explained by the small number of degrees of freedom in the subperiod. This may have meant that the standard error in the estimate for the subperiod was three time higher than for the period as a whole, and that the estimate was thus no longer significant.

[52] * marks the significance at the 5 per cent level from a two-tailed test of the intercept

and a one-tailed test of the lagged effect of foreign interest rate changes.

53 The global interest level is estimated as a trade-weighted average of the rates in the USA, Japan, Great Britain, West Germany (the Frankfurt rate), the Netherlands and Belgium. For a further description see Table S1:B in Supplement 1.

54 The interest rates in the model are expressed in quarterly terms, so that the gap should indicate the size of the inefficiency over the relevant period of maturity.

55 This can of course be largely explained by the fact that the weighted rate consists of only six rates here, making the US rate very important to the aggregate.

56 The interest rates in the model are expressed in quarterly terms.

57 In test runs of a basic model with the forward premium as the explanatory value I obtain a D-W value of less than 1, which is a clear sign that the model is misspecified.

58 With trade-weighted interest based on the prime rates in the 11 largest OECD countries. For a further description see Table S1:C in Supplement 1.

59 In quarterly terms.

60 In the alternative model for the period 1979–84, the intercept is significantly negative at –1.58.

61 Significantly, because the difference in the intercept deviates significantly from zero.

62 We take it as the upper limit, because, as was stressed before, we know that the average can also include inefficiencies. The Durbin-Watson values in some of the analyses are low, but I nonetheless feel justified in using the estimated intercept here as a rough indication of the transaction cost.

63 Interest rates in the model are expressed in annual terms.

64 A trade-weighted average of the interest rate on government bonds in the 11 largest OECD countries. From November 1983 onwards the Swedish quotations refer to the interest on government notes. For a further description see Table S1:D in Supplement 1.

65 These estimates are probably somewhat excessive, since the exchange cost can be assumed to be amortized over the maturity of the investment, i.e. over several years. On the other hand we have not included any cost of information here.

66 The interest rates in the model are expressed in annual terms.

67 When RELBITW is included in the model, it turns out that the total foreign exchange flow is unsuitable as an explanatory variable. This is because of the correlation between this flow and the gap between government bond interest rates which we have previously observed.

68 The global level is estimated here as the weighted average of the interest rate on industrial bonds in the USA, West Germany, the Netherlands, England, Switzerland and Japan. As before, trade weights (TW) are used. For a further description, see Table S1:E in Supplement 1.

CHAPTER 9

Interest Rate Autonomy and the Foreign Dependence of the Swedish Financial Market – A Summary

With increasing international trade, deregulation, improvements in communications and other structural changes in society, it has become generally accepted today that integration between countries is growing. The meaning attached to the concept of integration in such claims is very broad, and the increase is never verified. For this reason I asked in the introduction to the present book whether it is in fact possible to measure the level of integration in general and of financial integration in particular, and thus to confirm the increase which – according to my hypothesis – has been taking place over the last few decades.

We must define what we include in "integration"

To succeed in measuring the level of integration, we must obviously specify what we include in the concept. We can speak of "total financial integration", and then subdivide this into "direct" and "indirect" financial integration. Given these classifications, it is also possible under imperfect direct financial integration, i.e. with segmented capital markets, to determine under certain assumptions the amount of government-induced segmentation. We can thus obtain an expression for the autonomy of monetary policy or, in a narrower sense, of interest rate policy. We have found that this expression consists of two parts: one, which we call *permanent*, is a measure of a country's ability to maintain an interest rate which, after all the demands of the market have been allowed for, deviates on an average from the global rate; the other, which we call *temporary*, is a measure of the length of time during which a country can temporarily protect its interest rate from the influence of foreign interest movements.

It is also important to reflect correctly the way the market forms its expectations

In order to make successful measurements we have also found it necessary to adopt an expectations perspective, rather than using ex post data. Given this perspective, we are compelled to determine the size of the exchange rate change expected by the market, and of the premiums for various risks. An interview study was conducted to discover more about the way the market behaves and to provide a basis for modeling the formation of market expectations. Among other things this study provided some support for an assumption regarding rational expectations.

Earlier Swedish studies have measured the interest elasticity of the capital flow

The measurement process has been illustrated by an example based on data concerning the international integration of the Swedish financial market. A review of the literature shows that in most earlier studies of the foreign dependence of Swedish markets, attempts have been made to determine the level of financial integration on a basis of the interest-sensitivity of the capital flow. The studies have produced a variety of conclusions. The lack of agreement can often be explained by differences in model specifications and in the choice of period, but the most important explanation is the uncertainty embedded in the actual determination of the size of the capital flow. And this is an uncertainty which can be expected to increase with the introduction of new financial instruments. This problem makes it impossible to use the capital flow as the dependent variable in a modelling context. We have therefore studied financial integration here on a basis of the difference between Swedish and foreign interest rates, and the study has been restricted to modelling and analysing the integration of the credit market.

We must study many interest segments before making inferences about the Swedish credit market as a whole

Some Swedish interest rates are administratively determined, or have been so at some time during the period studied. Other rates are determined by the market. Our analysis of the relationship between the different Swedish rates shows that this relationship is not sufficiently strong for us to be able to make any inferences that are valid for the market or the country as a whole, on a basis of studying a *single* interest rate, i.e. one segment of the Swedish credit market. This is a problem common to all methods for analysing financial integration. To provide grounds for conclusions about the level of international integration on the Swedish credit market as a whole, we have analysed five different interest rates representing five interest rate segments. In so far as we see unequivocal signals from all five segments, we are justified in speaking of a change in the level of integration and in the scope for interest rate policy autonomy.

It is assumed that Swedish interest rates are influenced by a "global rate"

For a long time the US interest rate was regarded as the exclusive "leader" which dictated the interest level in the rest of the world. Interest rates in small open economies were adjusted to movements in this US rate. However, according to several studies in recent years, the leading role of the US rate has been undermined; its role has been taken over by something that is described as an average of the interest rates of the major OECD countries. Both these rates have their advocates today, each group claiming that "their" rate is the price leader, i.e. that it determines the global level. To avoid the risk of drawing the wrong conclusions from our study of the links between Swedish and foreign interest rates, we have analysed the links between the Swedish rate and both the US rate *and* the weighted average of the OECD rates.

The link is weak between nominal interest rates and expected inflation

Our empirical analysis has shown that changes in inflation expectations in Sweden are not fully reflected, as classical theory claims, in higher or lower nominal rates. Rather it is the real rate and expected inflation that covariate. Thus the real rate varies, in contrast to the prescriptions of classical theory, between countries and over time. This seems to suggest that the market's real rate requirements in a small open economy such as the Swedish, are to a large extent determined by the expected real rate which the international markets can offer.

Foreign exchange regulations should be evident in the market's demand for a political risk premium

Have the Swedish foreign exchange controls succeeded in inserting a wedge between Swedish and foreign interest rates, by restricting the actors' scope for action? One way of finding an answer to this question is to study the extent to which the main actors – the large multinational companies – have perceived the foreign exchange controls as restrictive.

Our interview study of the largest Swedish multinational companies shows that during the period of our study these companies felt restricted on three counts as a result of the controls: 1) they were compelled to finance direct investments abroad by five-year borrowing abroad, 2) they were unable to amortize a loan prematurely without raising a new loan abroad to an equivalent amount, and 3) they were only able to cover on the forward market the last six months of their financial loans.[1] Other regulations were seen as administrative inconveniences which were not insuperable but which simply generated extra costs. From this we can perhaps conclude that Swedish companies may have demanded compensation for repatriating foreign capital to invest in Sweden.[2] And this conclusion is explicitly supported by the interview respondents. The compensation for the restriction involved in repatriating capital and being unable to employ it with optimal efficiency, revealed itself in the size of the gap between Swedish and foreign rates in the shape of a political risk premium.

It may seen paradoxical that foreign exchange controls give rise to demands for higher risk premiums. But we can perhaps expect that part of the greater political risk which in our view is created by the foreign exchange controls, would be compensated by a reduction in exchange risk. However, there are no research results suggesting that the systematic exchange risk is less when foreign exchange controls are being imposed than it is in periods of non-regulation.

Total financial integration is decreasing globally

Under global *total* financial integration, the size of the "expected real interest rate" is the same all over the world. Moreover, interest rate theory speaks of "constant real rates". The empirical evidence is that the level of the OECD countries' real rates, as well as the gap between them, has varied to an increasing extent during the 1980s. We have noted that these rates fluctuate very much. The question then is whether there is any relationship between real interest rate movements in different countries. The answer is in the affirmative. The 1970s exhibit significant correlations between real interest rate levels as well as between real interest rate movements. As a global tendency towards decreasing total financial integration, however, the correlation decreased during the period of our investigation.

Whatever perspective we adopt in relation to real interest rate developments, the conclusion is that during the first half of the 1980s total financial integration decreased compared with the immediately preceding decade. Total financial integration consists of three forms of integration, so that it is not possible from this single observation to exclude the possibility that global capital market integration has increased.

Perfect total financial integration requires that goods markets, foreign exchange markets and credit markets are all perfectly integrated. Thus the explanation of the decline in total financial integration may lie in the fact that deviations from PPP (in the case of the US dollar, for example) have been considerable during the first half of the 1980s. We have seen the real effective value of the dollar increase by about 40 per cent between 1979 and the end of our period.[3] Apart from increasing disintegration between goods markets, a greater disintegration on the foreign exchange market with adjacent increasing foreign exchange risk premiums and an incidence of political risk premiums, may all help to explain the decrease in total financial integration.

The total integration of the Swedish financial market is also declining

During the 1980s there have been big gaps between the Swedish real rate on the one hand and the weighted average of the real rates of the OECD countries and the US real rate on the other. Thus the total integration of the Swedish financial market has declined.

The correlation between Swedish real rates on the one hand and the real global rate and the real US rate on the other was also smaller in 1981–84 than it had been during the 1970s. Thus the correlation analysis confirms our conclusion that the *total* integration of the Swedish financial market has declined.

Major shifts in foreign interest rates are reflected more quickly in the Swedish rates

An analysis of major foreign and Swedish shifts in interest rate developments since 1974, shows that a foreign shift is reflected in a Swedish shift after even shorter intervals. This tendency can be seen in all the five types of interest rate that we have studied. This can be taken as an indication that the temporary segmentation of the Swedish credit market has declined.

The correlation between Swedish interest rates and forward covered foreign rates indicates an increase in credit market integration

The analysis of the correlation between nominal interest levels and interest movements respectively, shows that we cannot make any inferences about the level of integration unless we *simultaneously* consider exchange rate movements and risk premiums. One way of allowing for exchange rate expectations and eliminating the exchange risk, is to study the correlation between Swedish rates and forward covered foreign rates. We have made such an analysis, and have also allowed for lagged foreign forward-covered interest movements. Our conclusion, based on the size of the covariation and the pattern of lagged effects from covered foreign interest, is that Swedish rates are increasingly determined by the global level in the shape of the weighted average of the OECD rates.

Model-based analysis indicates a weak increase in direct financial integration

In order to make a simultaneous study of the effects of all the market demands which must be covered by the interest gap, we have formulated a model as an extension of the

International Fisher Effect. The model is based on observations of the formation of expectations on the market, and it divides the interest gap into its constituent parts.

The estimates in the model show that the market demands a premium for political risk amounting on an average to three points for every percentage point by which Sweden's net foreign debt is increased in relation to GDP. Swedish foreign indebtedness is used in the model as a source of political risk. Our interview study indicated this result and the logic is that a bigger debt implies less domestic scope for action, and heralds political intervention. Furthermore, the presence of functioning foreign exchange controls signals a willingness to intervene. As we have noted, the premium is to be regarded as the market actor's way of compensating for the perceived risk of being unable to manage his capital in an economically optimal way.

With its intercept adjusted for constant risk premiums, the model provides a measure of permanent disintegration. An intercept that deviates significantly from zero provides a strong indication of segmented capital markets. The model also provides a measure for the lagged effect of foreign interest movements, or temporary disintegration. Observed values of both components can be seen in Table 9.1 for the different interest segments. By comparing the measures for the period 1974–84 with those for 1979–84, we can judge how the level of direct financial integration has changed. Table 9.2 summarizes the changes.

Taking the Swedish credit market as a whole, and after allowing for risk premium and exchange rate expectations, we find that the tables provide significant evidence of deviations from the *global interest level.* Swedish quotations for government bonds and to some extent for industrial bonds have been higher than the corresponding global quotations. In other cases the Swedish rates have been below the global level. The deviations were less during the period 1979–84 compared with the period as a whole, but not significantly so. The pattern varies somewhat for the different interest segments. Direct integration in the shape of the link between the Swedish rate and the global interest level, can be said to have increased for the Swedish credit market as a whole, but only slightly.

After allowing for risk premium and exchange rate expectation, we find that the interest rate level on the Swedish credit market as a whole has differed significantly from the *interest rate level in the USA*. Moreover, the gaps have increased during the subperiod compared with the period as a whole. However, the development differs in the different interest rate segments. Direct integration in the shape of the link between the Swedish rate and the US rate can be said to have declined on the Swedish credit market as a whole.

Table 9.1 **Measure of direct financial integration based on models for the periods 1974–84 and 1979–84**

Interest gap	1974:1–1984:4		1979:1–1984:4
	1974:1–1977:3	1977:4–1984:4	
Swedish discount rate - corresponding global rate	–0.22*,5*		–0.21,0
Swedish discount rate – US discount rate	–0.38*,4*		–0.91*,0
Swedish interest rate on treasury bills/treasury discount notes - corresponding global rate	–1.02*,5*	–0.44,5*	–0.20,5*
Swedish interest rate on treasury bills/treasury discount notes - corresponding US rate	–0.56*,5*		–0.56,0
Swedish prime rate - corresponding global rate	–1.54*,0	–1.07*,0	–2.02*,0
Swedish prime rate - corresponding US rate	–0.95*,1*		–2.20*,1*
Swedish interest rate on government bonds/government notes – corresponding global rate	–0.51,0	0.82*,0	0.68,0
Swedish interest rate on government bonds - corresponding US rate	0.80*,0	1.26*,0	0.69,0
Swedish interest rate on industrial bonds - corresponding global rate	–1.75*,6*	0.09,6*	0.95,5*
Swedish interest rate on industrial bonds - corresponding US rate	–1.21*,5	–1.12*,5*	–1.91*,4*

* = significant at the 5 per cent level.
Note: Under perfect direct financial integration we can expect the value pair (0, 0). The first figure in the pair represents the average difference between interest rates after elimination of the average effect of exchange rate expectations and premiums for risk. This figure indicates the size of the inefficiency. In the case of short interest rates the gap between interest rates expressed in a quarterly rate applies. For long interest rates the gap is expressed in annual terms. The second figure represents the highest significant number of quarters during which foreign interest rate changes affect the interest gap.

Table 9.2 **Degree of direct financial integration during the whole of the studied period 1974–84 and changes in relation to the period 1979–84**

	Global interest level		US interest rate	
Segment of the credit market	Permanent disinte-gration	Temporary disinte-gration	Permanent disinte-gration	Temporary disinte-gration
Discount rate	Significant gap which diminishes weakly	Long lag which dis-appears	Significant gap which increases strongly	Medium long lag which disappears
Treasury bills/ treasury discount notes	Significant gap that diminishes strongly	Long lag which re–mains intact	Significant gap that diminishes weakly	Long lag which dis–appears
Lending to first class borrowers	Significant gap that increases strongly	Non existent lag which remains non existent	Significant gap that increases strongly	Short term lag which remains intact
Government bonds/ government notes	Significant gap that diminishes weakly	Non existent which re–mains non existent	Significant gap that diminishes weakly	Non existent lag which remains non existent
Industrial bonds	Non existent gap which increases weakly	Long lag which is getting shorter	Significant gap that increases weakly	Long lag which is getting shorter
Trend for Sweden's total credit market	Significant gap that remains un-changed or diminishes weakly	Lagged in-fluence from foreign interest rate changes is diminish-ing and dis-appearing in some cases	Significant gap that increases	Lagged in–fluence from foreign interest rate changes is diminishing and disappear-ing in some cases

Note: For each combinations of rows and columns there is an inference about the direct financial integration in the studied period as a whole, and about the way this has changed between this period and the subperiod 1979–84. As regards permanent disintegration, it is shown how the average interest gap less the market's demands has changed between the periods. Strong changes are significant, unlike weak changes.

In the case of temporary disintegration the number of quarters is indicated for which lag there is a significant correlation between foreign interest changes and the interest gap. A short lag implies about one quarter, while a long one implies 5–6 quarters.

Few indications of Swedish interest rate policy autonomy

Before we can determine the scope for an autonomous interest rate policy, we have to eliminate the transaction cost from the measure of permanent segmentation presented in Table 9.1. Our lower limit for calculating the average transaction cost during the period as a whole, is 0.5 per cent. This cost refers to the cost of foreign exchange transactions in interest rate speculation starting from cash. In the subperiod 1979–84 this transaction cost fell to 0.4 per cent.

We have also calculated as upper limit for the transaction cost in terms of the cost of covered arbitrage at short term interest rates. This transaction cost is calculated as the intercept in a regression with the gap between the Swedish rate and the covered foreign rate as the dependent variable and a political risk variable as the explanatory variable. We expect this intercept, which can be seen in Table 9.3, to provide us with a rough estimate of a transaction cost including the information cost. However, it may also contain inefficiencies in the shape of deviations from covered interest parity which are not to be regarded as part of the transaction cost. For this reason we regard the estimate of the transaction cost as an upper limit.

What remains of our expression of disintegration after eliminating the transaction cost, gives us a measure of the effect of interest rate policy autonomy and of general market inefficiency. If we assume that this last type of inefficiency is non-existent, we can see the whole expression as a sign of autonomous action. In order to evaluate more accurately how far the government has succeeded in its policy, we need to know what goals were set up.

Table 9.3 Deviations from covered interest rate parity as an estimate of the arbitrage cost
Percentage points

	1974–84	1979–84
Arbitrage costs under covered interest arbitrage with the global treasury bill rate	0.28*	0.60*
Arbitrage costs under covered interest arbitrage with the US treasury bill rate	0.52*	0.58*
Arbitrage costs under covered interest arbitrage with the global prime rate	0.78*	1.03*
Arbitrage costs under covered interest arbitrage with the US prime rate	0.86*	1.29*

* = significantly deviating from zero in an analysis at a 5 per cent level.

Assuming that general market inefficiency is non-existent, we evaluate Swedish interest rate autonomy in accordance with the description in Table 9.4. The conclusions in the table prove robust for deviations from this assumption. The conclusions regarding the short-term interest rates are based on the upper transaction-cost limit; where the use of the lower limit alters the result, this is noted in the table.

Table 9.4 shows that in few cases only does the deviation of the Swedish rate from the *global rate* contain any inefficiency apart from the transaction cost. However, in the case of the interest rate on industrial bonds we found a significant inefficiency of this kind for the period 1974:1–1977:3, but it subsequently disappeared. The only rate which exhibits significant inefficiency for the whole of the period as well as during the subperiod 1979:1–1984:4, is the prime rate. For this type of interest rate we see significant and persistent evidence of interest rate autonomy.

Taking the Swedish credit market as a whole and the total period of the study, we thus find *one* significant indication of interest rate autonomy vis-à-vis the global rate only. The indication persists in an analysis of the subperiod 1979–84.

In the case of the Swedish rate vis-à-vis the *US rate*, our conclusions are mostly the opposite. Taking the period of the study as a whole we find no indication of interest rate autonomy. However, during the period 1979–84 we find a significant increase, in the case of the discount rate and the prime rate, in the Sweden - US gap due to inefficiencies. While we see even fewer signs that the government has succeeded in steering Swedish rates away from the level dictated by the global rate, we see more signs of the Swedish rate deviating from the corresponding rate in the USA. This agrees with the general pattern noted in international studies, where it has been found that the global rate has taken over as "interest leader" for interest rates in small open economies.

No difference between long-term and short-term interest rates as regards interest rate autonomy

Because of the way in which foreign exchange controls function and in view of the results of the interview study, we might have expected greater segmentation and interest policy autonomy in the case of the long-term rates. After allowing for risk premium and exchange rate expectation, we expected to see the average long-term interest rates, which are such an important incentive to investment, lying below the level in the rest of the world. However, the results of the study show no difference between long-term and short-term rates in the context of successful central-bank management of interest rates.

Table 9.4 **Indications of Swedish interest policy autonomy for the whole studied period 1974–84 and changes in this compared with the subperiod 1979–84**

	Vis-à-vis the global rate		**Vis-à-vis the US rate**	
Segment of the financal market	Permanent segmentation	Temporary segmentation	Permanent segmentation	Temporary segmentation
Discount rate	No indication and no change	See Table 9.1	No indication which significantly becomes an indication	See Table 9.1
Treasury bills/ treasury discount notes [a]	No indication and no change	See Table 9.1	No indication and no change	See Table 9.1
Lending to first class borrowers	Indication that remains [b]	See Table 9.1	No indication that significantly becomes an indication [c]	See Table 9.1
Government bonds/government notes	No indication and no change	See Table 9.1	No indication and no change [d]	See Table 9.1
Industrial bonds	Indication that significantly diminishes and disappears after 1977:3	See Table 9.1	No indication and no change	See Table 9.1
Trend for all segments	One indication for the whole of the studied period, which also persists in 1979–84	See Table 9.1	No indication for the studied period as a whole but two indications for 1979–84	See Table 9.1

[a] The conclusions are the same regardless of whether we choose the upper or the lower limit for the estimate of transaction cost.

[b] The conclusions are the same regardless of whether we choose the upper or the lower limit for the estimate of transaction cost. The change refers to 1979:1–1984:4 compared with 1974:1–1977:3.

[c] The conclusions refer to the case of the higher transaction cost. Given the lower estimate we would get an indication which becomes significantly stronger for the studied period as a whole.

[d] The conclusions refer to 1974:1–1977:3 compared with 1979:1–1984:4, and the change from the first to the second of these periods.

Note: By "indication" is meant here that the total inefficiency less the transaction cost significantly deviates from zero at the 5 per cent level. The actual change itself is also analysed to see whether it significantly deviates from zero at the 5 per cent level.

As applied during the period 1979–84 the value of the foreign exchange controls as a way of creating interest rate policy autonomy can be questioned. Looking at the links with the global rate, and after allowing for compensation for risk and exchange expectation, we find that in only one of the five interest segments – and then only for a short-term rate – is there any strong economic indication that Sweden has succeeded in maintaining lower average rates than the rest of the world.

Thus, paradoxically, our empirical results show quite clearly that foreign exchange controls do not give the central bank the intended interest rate policy independence as regards long-term interest rates, while they generate a relatively higher interest rate level by evoking demands for premiums for political risk.[4]

An increase in the links between interest rates contributes indirectly to connecting national stock markets with one another

In the empirical analysis we have not discussed the stock market as a segment of the financial market. However, the growing links on the credit market have the indirect effect – other things being equal – that developments on national stock markets will be more closely connected. Thus, after allowing for differences in industrial structure, we claim that the returns on the Swedish stock market are probably determined largely on the global market. The same applies to return requirements in Swedish companies. As to the links between the Swedish and foreign stock markets, we find inefficiency in the shape of "unreasonably" high special costs in Sweden, which means that the Swedish stock market still cannot be regarded as fully integrated with the "global stock market".

What has happen since 1984?

An important change occurred in 1986 when the central bank abolished the requirement regarding the foreign financing of direct corporate investment abroad. The abolition of this requirement, which the large multinationals regarded as the most serious restriction associated with the foreign exchange controls, now gives companies a better chance of using their capital in an economically optimal way.

The intention to abolish all the regulations before the end of 1989 was expressed in the annual plan issued by the Ministry of Finance and published in early January 1989. To show that the intention was serious, certain parts of the foreign exchange control regulations were abolished a week later. The rate at which abolition could be affected depended on finding acceptable ways of registering capital flows for tax control purposes. In May these problems were settled and a more or less complete abolition of exchange controls was announced for 1 July 1989. The Swedish market rates fell on publication of the plan for the almost complete abolition of all exchange controls. The interest gap decreased by around 1.5 per cent – ceteris paribus. This drop can be interpreted in the terminology of the present book as a reduction in the market's demand for a political risk premium, since the signals suggested that intervention had become less likely.

Immediately before the drop in interest rates took place, our model estimated the political risk premium as approximately 2 percentage points. A Eurokrona loan (a World Bank loan) placed on the market shortly after the drop, showed a rate about 0.5 percentage points lower than a corresponding domestic Swedish rate. Thus if we combine these results we get an impression of fairly realistic out-of-the-sample estimates from the model – at least as regards the political risk premium. The Swedish exchange controls were finally abolished on July 1989. However, transaction procedures are still regulated. New estimates of the degree of financial integration along the lines suggested in the present book would call for another dummy variable, to try to capture the implications of the abolition.

Suggestions for further research

Many interesting research problems remain in the field which this book has tried to chart. One general issue for further research concerns the extent to which there is a connection between the level of integration and the size of the average global real rate. If there is such a relationship, what shape does it assume? More specifically, there is a need for further research into issues in the three following subject areas.

A *first* set of issues revolves round the approach suggested in the present book. Because of the paucity of observations, we have been compelled to disregard many interesting questions. One such question concerns the importance of the business cycle. It would be interesting to continue the analysis of financial integration, and to introduce economic booms and recessions. It would also be interesting to subdivide the studied period according to whether fiscal policy or monetary policy has been the dominating instrument of control. Moreover, it would be interesting to study the possible existence of asymmetrical[5] intervention, which has been a subject of debate during the 1980s. Given a larger number of observations these questions could be studied with the help of dummy variables within the framework of the model presented here.

A *second* group of research problems concerns the importance of what is happening on the global financial markets today. The tremendous flow of innovations and the evolution of many new financial instruments, are together opening up interesting perspectives.

For example, do these innovations lead to higher levels of integration? Theoretically the answer should be in the affirmative, since every instrument effects an increase in efficiency in its own little segment. However, in practice integration probably decreases as a result of difficulty in pricing risks correctly. In Chapter 2 we saw that the job still remains of clarifying the character and size of the risk premiums both theoretically and empirically. Just as the problem of pricing the political risk resulted in the present debt crisis, many researchers believe that the pricing of the new instruments may lead to a crisis in the shape of a breakdown in the international banking system. Thus the connection between financial integration and the spread of crisis in the banking system represents another urgent subject for research.

The new instruments also complicate the study of the links between the level of financial integration and the autonomy of monetary policy. The new set of tools for managing risk results in a supereffective financial market in which adjustments are immediate, but which in the long run can give rise to an ineffective total economy. These instruments make it more difficult for those who have to make the economic decisions to achieve a broad overview, as they add to the uncertainty of registered flows of various kind etc as "signals" for economic policy control. There is therefore every reason to investigate what can be achieved by conducting a stabilization policy under these conditions.

A *third* group of research problems concerns the development of alternative ways of studying and measuring financial integration. One alternative to the use (as here) of statistical methods for studying and comparing developments over *long* periods, for example, would be to study what happens in a small open economy just before and after a shock or disturbance on the global market.

Notes

1 These restrictions have now all ceased to apply.

2 The foreign exchange controls establish formal requirements regarding the extent to which companies must repatriate further capital according to the so-called Höganäs condition. In practice, however, the companies have considerable scope for action.

3 The real exchange rate change was closer to 50 percent, before it once more turned downwards in 1985. This turnaround can to same extent explain why real interest rates converged so powerfully in 1986.

4 Some people claim that a higher political risk premium indicates an independent monetary policy. However, it is difficult to see the purpose of managing the markets by way of increased risk premiums.

5 When the global rate is high domestic politicians want to lower the national rate. But when the global rate is low, they do not necessarily want to lower the national rate further. Cf. Table 2.1.

SUPPLEMENT 1

Mean and standard deviation in international interest rates 1974–84

Table S1:A Official discount rate (DISC) 1974–84

	1974–78					1979–84					1981–84				
	N	Mean	Standard deviation	Minimum value	Maximum value	N	Mean	Standard deviation	Minimum value	Maximum value	N	Mean	Standard deviation	Minimum value	Maximum value
USA	20	6.53	1.21	5.25	9.50	24	10.58	1.98	8.00	14.00	16	10.25	2.18	8.00	14.00
Japan	20	6.33	2.08	3.50	9.00	24	5.85	1.34	3.50	9.00	16	5.48	0.44	5.00	6.25
Great Britain[a]	20	10.34	2.20	6.00	14.00	24	12.34	2.75	8.50	17.00	16	10.88	1.87	8.50	14.50
Belgium	20	7.20	1.35	5.50	9.00	24	11.52	2.24	6.00	16.00	16	11.94	1.99	9.00	16.00
Denmark	20	8.88	0.83	7.50	10.00	24	9.73	2.03	7.00	13.00	16	9.09	1.89	7.00	11.00
France	20	10.08	1.58	8.00	13.00	24	9.50	0.00	9.50	9.50	16	9.50	0.00	9.50	9.50
West Germany	20	4.15	1.43	3.00	7.00	24	5.79	1.59	4.00	7.50	16	5.66	1.64	4.00	7.50
Italy	20	10.40	2.61	6.00	15.00	24	16.37	2.64	10.50	19.00	16	17.72	1.22	15.50	19.00
The Netherlands	20	5.55	1.49	3.50	8.00	24	7.02	1.95	3.50	9.50	16	6.38	1.97	3.50	9.00
Norway	20	5.88	0.67	5.00	7.00	24	8.46	0.72	7.00	9.00	16	8.56	0.51	8.00	9.00
Sweden	20	6.80	0.92	5.00	8.00	24	9.52	1.44	6.50	12.00	16	9.91	1.25	8.50	12.00
Switzerland	20	2.88	1.73	1.00	5.50	24	3.77	1.45	1.00	6.00	16	4.59	0.78	4.00	6.00
Austria	20	5.30	0.92	4.00	6.50	24	5.26	1.39	3.75	6.75	16	5.27	1.33	3.75	6.75

[a] Minimum lending rate 1981–84.

Table S1:B Interest rate on three month treasury bills/treasury discount notes (TBR) 1974–84

	1974–78					1979–84					1981–84				
	N	Mean	Standard deviation	Minimum value	Maximum value	N	Mean	Standard deviation	Minimum value	Maximum value	N	Mean	Standard deviation	Minimum value	Maximum value
USA	20	6.28	1.29	4.41	9.08	24	10.99	2.57	7.64	15.85	16	10.83	2.52	7.64	15.32
Japan	20	5.34	1.28	3.39	6.83	24	5.36	0.69	3.39	6.82	16	5.34	0.33	4.91	5.93
Great Britain	20	9.98	2.33	5.37	13.98	24	12.16	2.67	8.59	16.95	16	11.05	2.31	8.59	16.26
Belgium	20	8.35	2.16	5.75	13.00	24	12.70	2.44	7.90	17.50	16	12.77	2.27	9.25	16.00
West Germany[a]	20	3.61	1.25	2.67	7.12	24	6.85	2.08	3.68	12.50	16	7.40	2.14	5.45	12.50
The Netherlands	20	6.21	2.70	2.50	13.50	24	7.93	2.54	4.50	13.80	16	7.18	2.39	4.50	12.00
Sweden[b]	20	7.43	2.16	2.01	9.77	24	11.03	2.54	5.75	15.73	16	9.07	2.79	7.00	15.73

[a] Frankfurt rate from 1981.

[b] Up to October 1982 the series refers to the interest rate on three month treasury bills. After that date it refers to the interest rate on the secondhand market for three month treasury discount notes.

Table S1:C Prime rate (three month commercial bank lending rates to prime borrowers) (CBLR) 1974–84

	1974–78					1979–84					1981–84				
	N	Mean	Standard deviation	Minimum value	Maximum value	N	Mean	Standard deviation	Minimum value	Maximum value	N	Mean	Standard deviation	Minimum value	Maximum value
USA	20	8.30	1.92	6.00	12.00	24	14.09	3.40	10.50	21.50	16	13.80	3.26	10.50	20.00
Japan	20	7.80	1.52	4.50	9.56	24	6.56	1.16	4.44	9.27	16	6.37	0.59	5.71	7.74
Great Britain	20	11.48	1.92	8.00	15.00	24	12.80	3.19	8.50	19.00	16	11.02	1.97	8.50	14.50
Belgium	20	10.26	1.97	8.00	14.00	24	15.17	2.33	9.00	18.75	16	15.51	1.76	12.50	18.00
Denmark	20	11.63	1.11	9.00	14.00	24	12.81	2.22	9.50	15.75	16	12.52	2.24	10.00	15.50
France	20	11.95	1.26	10.80	14.45	24	13.12	1.29	10.95	15.90	16	13.16	1.35	11.50	15.90
West Germany	20	7.59	2.38	5.50	12.50	24	9.85	2.46	6.00	14.25	16	10.00	2.68	7.75	14.25
Italy	20	16.84	2.89	11.00	21.00	24	19.34	2.30	15.00	22.50	16	20.50	1.93	17.00	22.50
The Netherlands	20	8.85	2.60	6.00	14.00	24	9.53	2.83	5.00	15.00	16	8.53	2.73	5.00	13.75
Norway	20	8.67	1.11	7.50	11.00	24	12.90	1.26	11.00	14.50	16	13.66	0.60	12.50	14.50
Sweden	20	8.60	1.27	6.25	10.25	24	11.93	1.82	8.25	14.50	16	12.72	1.36	10.75	14.50
Switzerland	20	7.35	0.99	5.00	8.50	24	6.09	0.87	5.00	8.00	16	6.47	0.81	5.50	8.00

Table S1:D Interest rate on government bonds (BOND) 1974–84

	1974–78					1979–84					1981–84				
	N	Mean	Standard deviation	Minimum value	Maximum value	N	Mean	Standard deviation	Minimum value	Maximum value	N	Mean	Standard deviation	Minimum value	Maximum value
USA	20	8.06	0.40	7.30	8.90	24	11.88	1.66	8.91	15.07	16	12.60	1.28	10.62	15.07
Japan	20	8.12	1.35	6.03	9.60	24	7.95	0.96	6.30	10.00	16	7.70	0.74	6.36	9.02
Great Britain	20	13.74	1.39	11.16	17.18	24	12.60	1.77	10.23	15.65	16	12.07	2.03	9.89	15.65
Belgium	20	8.75	0.38	8.09	9.35	24	12.15	1.41	8.83	14.06	16	12.74	0.95	11.46	14.06
Denmark	20	13.38	1.58	9.65	15.91	24	16.88	2.70	12.00	21.65	16	17.10	3.00	12.43	21.65
France	20	9.53	0.82	8.33	11.74	24	13.50	2.24	8.34	17.41	16	14.61	1.35	12.70	16.84
West Germany	20	7.67	1.76	5.20	10.70	24	8.52	1.14	6.90	11.10	16	8.78	1.20	7.17	11.10
Italy	20	12.67	1.76	7.80	14.81	24	17.42	2.87	13.74	22.37	16	18.75	2.49	15.23	22.37
The Netherlands	20	8.65	0.84	7.35	10.43	24	9.63	1.30	7.72	12.30	16	9.59	1.45	7.72	12.30
Norway	20	7.51	0.58	6.22	8.54	24	11.58	1.66	8.25	13.27	16	12.58	0.50	11.57	13.27
Sweden[a]	20	9.17	0.87	7.15	10.33	24	12.23	1.02	10.15	13.73	16	12.82	0.70	11.50	14.01
Switzerland	20	5.16	1.51	3.03	7.41	24	4.68	0.68	3.22	6.13	16	4.69	0.53	4.22	6.13

[a] Interest on government notes from November 1983.

Table S1:E Interest rate on national industrial bonds (DCBR) 1974–84

	1974–78					1979–84					1981–84				
	N	Mean	Standard deviation	Minimum value	Maximum value	N	Mean	Standard deviation	Minimum value	Maximum value	N	Mean	Standard deviation	Minimum value	Maximum value
USA	20	8.62	0.57	7.35	9.60	24	12.79	2.02	9.15	16.63	16	13.60	1.61	11.63	16.63
Japan	20	8.65	2.08	5.59	12.28	24	7.71	0.62	6.21	8.75	16	7.46	0.55	6.21	8.22
Great Britain	20	14.70	1.95	11.88	19.50	24	13.46	1.63	11.29	17.23	16	13.29	1.89	11.29	17.23
West Germany	20	7.99	1.87	5.68	11.73	24	8.84	1.34	7.10	11.90	16	9.04	1.51	7.20	11.90
The Netherlands	20	8.63	1.07	7.15	10.78	24	9.63	1.44	7.51	12.48	16	9.47	1.57	7.51	12.48
Sweden	20	9.18	0.88	7.25	10.16	24	12.17	1.33	9.47	13.74	16	12.93	0.54	11.84	13.74
Switzerland	20	6.23	1.26	4.76	8.59	24	5.66	0.60	4.85	7.12	16	5.71	0.70	4.85	7.12

Sources: IMF, *International Financial Statistics*; OECD, *Main Economic Indicators*, Morgan Guaranty Trust, *World Financial Markets*, National central bank reports.

SUPPLEMENT 2

List of variables and abbreviations

1 *General designations*

r_i	=	nominal intrest rate
r_F	=	risk-free interest rate
r_M	=	return on market portfolio
r^R	=	real rate of interest
d_i	=	maturity in number of days for period i
$\wedge$	=	change
$*$	=	market expectation
$\cdot$	=	after tax
c	=	tax rate
σ^2	=	variance
E ( ) =		expectation operator
ρ	=	coefficient of correlation
cov	=	covariance
z	=	risk
U	=	utility function
π	=	Arrow—Pratt's risk premium
X_i	=	share of portfolio
x	=	initial wealth
$\hat{P}$	=	inflation
PPP	=	purchasing power parity
u	=	deviation from purchasing power parity
S	=	nominal spot exchange rate
S^{sell}	=	exchange rate – spot selling quotation
$\hat{s}$	=	relative change in exchange rate
f	=	relative forward exchange premium/discount
F_t	=	forward exchange rate
T	=	transaction cost – borrowing
T_S	=	transaction cost – buying/selling on the spot exchange market
T_F	=	transaction cost – buying/selling on the forward exchange market
T_L	=	transaction cost – lending

2 International currency codes

SEK	=	Swedish krona
GBP	=	Pound sterling
USD	=	US dollar
DEM	=	Deutsche mark
FRF	=	French franc
BEC	=	Belgium franc (commercial)
CHF	=	Swiss franc
NLG	=	Dutch florin
DKK	=	Danish krona
NOK	=	Norwegian krona
FIM	=	Finnish mark
ITL	=	Italian lira
ATS	=	Austrian schilling
CAD	=	Canadian dollar
ESP	=	Spanish peseta
JPY	=	Japanese yen
SDR	=	special drawing rights
ECU	=	European currency unit

Other abbreviations

EMS	=	European Monetary System
IMF	=	International Monetary Fund

3 List of variables in the analysis in Chapter 8

General designations

TW	= trade weight
u_t	= deviation from purchasing power parity
NFAGDP	= net foreign assets in relation to gross domestic product
$CF_{t-1,t}$	= capital flow for period t–1 to t
ER_t	= foreign exchange reserv at time t
$EFTER_{t-1,t}$	= total foreign exchange flow for period t–1 to t

CFISCER	=	non-government capital flow as reported by the central bank for a period in relation to the exchange reserve at the end of that period
DVIC	=	dummy variable for change in the Swedish exchange rate arrangement in August 1977
DV824	=	dummy variable for the devaluation of the Swedish krona in October 1982
RELINF	=	relative inflation
RELBITW	=	relative inflation estimated as the difference between Swedish and trade weighted foreign interest rates on government bonds
RELBIUSA	=	relative inflation estimated as the difference between the interest rate on Swedish and US government bonds
FP3TW	=	three-month forward premium, SEK/trade weighted currency basket
FP12TW	=	twelve-month forward premium, SEK/trade-weighted currency basket
FP3USA	=	three-month forward premium, SEK/USD
FP12USA	=	twelve-month forward premium, SEK/USD

Interest rate connotations

DISCSW	=	official discount rate, Sweden, per cent
DISCTW	=	official discount rate, foreign, trade-weighted
DISCUS	=	official discount rate, USA
DISCSWTW	=	difference between Swedish and trade-weighted foreign discount rate
DISCSWUS	=	difference between Swedish and US discount rate
ΔDISCTW1–6	=	change in trade weighted foreign discount rate, quarter t-6 to t-1
ΔDISKUS1–6	=	change in US discount rate, quarter t-6 to t-1
TBRSW	=	interest rate on treasury bills, Sweden, from October 1982 interest rate on 90-days treasury notes
TBRTW	=	interest rate on treasury bills, foreign, trade-weighted
TBRUS	=	interest rate on treasury bills, USA
TBRSWTW	=	difference between Swedish rate on treasury bills/notes and corresponding foreign trade weighted rate
TBRSWUS	=	difference between Swedish rate on treasury bills/notes and corresponding US rate
ΔTBRTW1–6	=	change in trade-weighted foreign rate on treasury bills, quarter t-6 to t-1
ΔTBRUS1–6	=	change in interest rate on US treasury bills, quarter t-6 to t-1

TBRSWTWF	=	difference between Swedish interest rate and covered trade-weighted foreign rate on treasury bills/notes
TBRSWUSF	=	difference between Swedish and covered US rate on treasury bills/notes
CBLRSW	=	prime rate – commercial bank lending rate to first-class borrowers, Sweden, per cent
CBLRTW	=	prime rate, foreign, trade-weighted
CBLRUS	=	prime rate, USA
CBLRSWTW	=	difference between Swedish prime rate and corresponding trade-weighted foreign rate
CBLRSWUS	=	difference between Swedish and US prime rates
ΔCBLRTW1–6	=	change in trade-weighted foreign prime rate, quarter t-6 to t-1
ΔCBLRUS1–6	=	change in US prime rate, quarter t-6 to t-1
CBLRSWTWF	=	difference between Swedish and covered trade-weighted foreign prime rate
CBLRSWUSF	=	difference between Swedish and covered US prime rate
BONDSW	=	interest rate on government bonds, Sweden, from November 1983 interest rate on government notes, per cent
BONDTW	=	interest rate on trade-weighted foreign government bonds
BONDUS	=	interest rate on US government bonds
BONDSWTW	=	difference between interest rate on Swedish government bonds and corresponding trade-weighted foreign rate
BONDSWUS	=	difference between interest rate on Swedish government bonds and corresponding interest rate on US bonds
ΔBONDTW1–6	=	change in trade-weighted foreign interest rate on government bonds, quarter t-6 to t-1
ΔBONDUS1–6	=	change in interest rate on US government bonds, quarter t-6 to t-1
DCBRSW	=	interest rate on industrial bonds, Sweden, per cent
DCBRTW	=	interest rate on trade-weighted foreign industrial bonds
DCBRUS	=	interest rate on US industrial bonds
DCBRSWTW	=	difference between interest rate on Swedish industrial bonds and corresponding trade-weighted foreign rate
DCBRSWUS	=	difference between Swedish rate on industrial bonds and corresponding US rate
ΔDCBRTW1–6	=	change in trade-weighted foreign interest rate on industrial bonds, quartert t-6 to t-1
ΔDCBRUS1–6	=	change in interest rate on US industrial bonds, quarter t-6 to t-1.

INDEX

BIBLIOGRAPHY

Adler, M. and Dumas, B., 1975, Optimal International Acquisitions, *Journal of Finance*, Vol. 30, March, pp. 1–20.

Adler, M. and Dumas, B., 1983, International Portfolio Choice and Corporation Finance: A Synthesis, *Journal of Finance*, Vol. 38, No. 3, pp. 925–984.

Agmon, T., 1972, The Relations among Equity Markets. A Study of Share Price Co-movements in the United States, United Kingdom, Germany, and Japan, *Journal of Finance*, Vol. 27, September, pp. 839–855.

Aharoni, Y., 1966, *The Foreign Investment Decision Process*, Harvard University.

Aliber, R., 1973, The Interest Rate Parity Theorem: A Reinterpretation, *Journal of Political Economy*, Vol. 31, No. 6, pp. 1451–1459.

Aliber, R., 1974, Attributes of National Monies and the Interdependence of National Monetary Policies; in Aliber, R. (ed.), *National Monetary Policies and the International Financial System*, University of Chicago, Studies in Business and Society, Series 3, Chicago, London, pp. 111–126.

Aliber, R., 1975, Exchange Risk, Political Risk, and Investor Demand for External Currency Deposits, *Journal of Money, Credit and Banking*, May.

Aliber, R., 1978a, *Exchange Risk and Corporate International Finance*, Macmillan, London.

Aliber, R., 1978b, The Integration of National Financial Markets: A Review of Theory and Findings, *Weltwirtschaftliches Archiv*, Band 114, Heft 3, pp. 448–480.

Allen, P.R. and Kenen, P.B., 1976, Portfolio Adjustment in Open Economies: A Comparison of Alternative Specifications, *Weltwirtschaftliches Archiv*, Band 112, pp. 33–72.

Allen, P.R. and Kenen, P.B., 1980, *Asset Markets, Exchange Rates and Economic Integration*, Cambridge University Press.

Amano, A., 1982, A Structural Approach to Capital Flows and Exchange Rates, *Discussion Paper* No. 179, Kyoto Institute of Economic Research, August.

Andersson, O.D., 1976, *Time Series Analysis and Forecasting*, Butterworth, London.

Argy, V. and Hodjera, Z., 1973, Financial Integration and Interest Rate Linkages in Industrial Countries, 1958–71, *IMF Staff Papers*, Vol. 20, Washington D.C., pp. 1–77.

Arrow, K., 1965, *Aspects of the Theory of Risk Bearing*, The Yrjö Jahnsson Foundation, Helsinki.

Artus, J.R., 1978, Methods of Assessing the Long-Run Equilibrium Value of an Exchange Rate, *Journal of International Economics*, Vol. 8, pp. 277–299.

Artus, J.R. and McGuire, A., 1982, A Revised Version of the Multilateral Exchange Rate Model, *IMF Staff Papers*.

Askari, H. and Modigliani, F., 1977, A Note on Capital Movements on the Relation of Spread in Spot and Forward Rates to Variations in the Short-Term Interest Differential, *Kyklos*, Vol. 30.

Auerbach, A.J. and King, M.A., 1983, Taxation, Portfolio Choice, and Debt-Equity Ratios: A General Equilibrium Model, *Quarterly Journal of Economics*, Vol. XCVIII, No. 4.

Bachelier, L., 1900, *Théorie de la Spéculation*. Also published in Cootner, P. (ed.) (1964).

Bahmani-Oshooe, M. and Das, P., 1985, Transactions Costs and the Interest Parity Theorem, *Journal of Political Economy*, August, pp. 793–799.

Balassa, B., 1964, The Purchasing Power Parity Doctrine: A Reappraisal, *Journal of Political Economy*, No. 6, pp. 584–596.

Bank for International Settlements 1977–87, *Forty-Seventh Annual Report – Fifty-Seventh Annual Report*, Basel.

Barro, R.J., 1976, Rational Expectations and the Role of Monetary Policy, *Journal of Monetary Economics*, Vol. 2, April, pp. 1–32.
Barro, R.J., 1980, A Capital Market in an Equilibrium Business Cycle Model, *Econometrica*, Vol. 48, pp. 1373–1417.
Barsky, R.B., 1987, The Fisher Hypothesis and the Forecastability and Persistence of Inflation, *Journal of Monetary Economics*, Vol. 19, pp. 3–24.
Barthold, T.A. and Dougan, W.R., 1985, The Fisher Hypothesis under Different Monetary Regimes, *Review of Economics and Statistics*, Vol. LXVIII, No. 4.
Basi, I., 1963, *Determinants of United States Private Direct Investment in Foreign Countries*, Kent State University.
Baxter, M., 1985, The Role of Expectations in Stabilization Policy, *Journal of Monetary Economics*, Vol.15, No. 3.
Begg, D., 1982, *The Rational Expectation Revolution in Macroeconomics: Theory and Evidence*, Philip Allan, Oxford.
Bergstrand, J., 1984, Short-Run Domestic Monetary Control in an International Money Market, *New England Economic Review*, July/August, pp. 29–38.
Bhagwati, I., 1969, *Trade, Tariffs and Growth*, Werdenfeld and Nicholson.
Bhandari, J.S., Driskill, R. and Frenkel, J.A., 1984, Capital Mobility and Exchange Rate Overshooting, *European Economic Review*, Vol. 24, pp. 309–320.
Bhandari, J.S. and Genberg, H., 1989, Exchange Rate Movements and the International Interdependence of Stock-Markets, *IMF Working Papers* 89/44.
Bilson, J., 1978, The Monetary Approach to the Exchange Rate – Some Empirical Evidence, *IMF Staff Papers*, Vol. 25, March, pp. 48–75.
Black, S., 1973, *International Money Market and Flexible Exchange Rates*, Princeton Studies in International Finance, No. 32, Princeton University.
Black, S., 1974, International Capital Market Equilibrium with Investment Barriers, *Journal of Financial Economics*, Vol. 1, December, pp. 337–352.
Black, S., 1980, *Central Bank Interventions and the Stability of Exchange Rates*, Institute for International Economic Studies, Stockholm.
Blanchard, O.J. and Summers, L.H., 1984, Perspectives on High World Real Interest Rates, *Brookings Papers on Economic Activity*, No. 2, pp. 273–324, The Brookings Institution, Washington D.C.
Bloch, E. and Schwartz, R., 1979, *Impending Changes for Securities Markets*, New York.
Bohi, D.R., 1972, The International Interdependence of Interest Rates, *Kyklos*, Vol. 25, No. 3, pp. 597–600.
Boonekamp, C., 1978, Inflation, Hedging and the Demand for Money, *American Economic Review*, Vol. 68, No. 5, December.
Boothe, P., 1983, Speculative Profit Opportunities in the Canadian Foreign Exchange Market, 1974–78, *Canadian Journal of Economics*, Vol. XVI, No. 4.
Boothe, P. and Glassman, D., 1987, The Statistical Distribution of Exchange Rates, *Journal of International Economics*, Vol. 22, pp. 297–319.
Borenstein, E.R., 1959, Alternative Hypotheses about the Excess Return of Dollar Assets, *IMF Staff Papers*, Vol. 34, No. 1.
Boughton, J.M., 1984, Exchange Rate Movements and Adjustment in Financial Markets: Quarterly Estimates for Major Currencies, *IMF Staff Papers*, Vol. 31, No. 3.
Box, G. and Jenkins, G., 1978, *Model Building Using GJP's Univariate Stochastic Programs*, London.
Bradley, M., Jarrell, G.A. and Kim, E.H., 1984, On the Existence of an Optimal Capital Structure: Theory and Evidence, *Journal of Finance*, Vol. 39, No. 3.
Branson, W., 1968, *Financial Capital Flows in the U.S. Balance of Payments*, North-Holland, Amsterdam.
Branson, W., 1969, The Minimum Covered Interest Differential Needed for International Arbitrage Activity, *Journal of Political Economy*, Vol. 77, No. 6.
Branson, W., 1972, *Macroeconomic Theory and Policy*, Harper and Row, New York.
Branson, W., 1979, *Exchange Rate Dynamics and Monetary Policy*; in Lindbeck, A. (ed.) (1979).
Branson, W., Halttunen, H. and Masson, P., 1977, Exchange Rate in the Short Run,

The Dollar-Deutschmark Rate, *European Economic Review*, Vol. 10, December, pp. 303–324.
Branson, W., and Hill Jr., R.D., 1971, *Capital Movements in the OECD Area, An Econometric Analysis*, OECD Economic Outlook. Occasional Studies, OECD Publications, Paris.
Brealey, R. and Myers, S., 1984, *Principles of Corporate Finance*, McGraw Hill.
Brealey, R. and Schaefer, S., 1977, Term Structure and Uncertain Inflation, *Journal of Finance*, Vol. 32, May, pp. 277–290.
Breeden, D.T., 1979, An Intertemporal Asset Pricing Model with Stochastic Consumption and Investment Opportunities, *Journal of Financial Economics*, Vol. 7, September, pp. 265–296.
Brewer, T., 1983, Political Sources of Risk in the International Money Market, *Journal of International Business Studies*, Vol. 14, spring/summer, pp. 161–164.
Brick, J.R. and Thompson, H.E., 1978, Time Series Analysis of Interest Rates: Some Additional Evidence, *Journal of Finance*, Vol. 33, No. 1, pp. 93–103.
Brock, W.A., 1982, Asset Prices in a Production Economy; in McCall, J.T. (ed.), *The Economics of Information and Uncertainty*, University of Chicago Press, pp. 1–43.
Bromwich, M., 1976, *The Economics of Capital Budgeting*, Harmondsworth, Middlesex.
Browne, F., 1983, Departures from Interest Rate Parity, *Journal of Banking and Finance*, Vol. 7, pp. 253–272.
Browne, F., 1984, The International Transmission of Inflation to a Small Open Economy under Fixed Exchange Rates and Highly Interest-Sensitive Capital Flows, *European Economic Review*, Vol. 25, No. 2, pp. 187–212.
Buiter, W., 1983, *Implications for the Adjustment Process of International Assets Risks*; in Hawkins, R., Levich, R. and Wihlborg, C. (eds.) (1983).
Buiter W., 1987, Borrowing to Defend the Exchange Rate and the Timing and Magnitude of Speculative Attacks, *Journal of International Economics*, Vol. 23, No. 3/4.
Bulkley, G., 1984, Does Inflation Uncertainty Increase with the Level of Inflation? *European Economic Review*, Vol. 25, No. 2, pp. 213–221.
Cagan, P., 1956, *The Monetary Dynamics of Hyperinflation*; in Friedman, M. (ed.) (1956).
Campbell, J.Y. and Shiller, R.J., 1984, The Determinants of Interest Rates: Old Controversies Reopened. A Simple Account of the Behavior of Long-Term Interest Rates, *American Economic Review*, Vol. 74, No. 2.
Canterbery, E.R., 1965, Foreign Exchange Capital Flows and Monetary Policy. *Princeton Studies in International Finance*, Department of Economics, Princeton University.
Carlson, J.A., 1977, Short-Term Interest Rates as Predictors of Inflation: Comment, *American Economic Review*, pp. 469–475.
Carmichael, J. and Stebbing, P.W., 1983, Fisher's Paradox and the Theory of Interest, *American Economic Review*, September.
Cassel, G., 1916, The Present Situation of the Foreign Exchanges, *Economic Journal*, March.
Cassel, G., 1922, *Money and Foreign Exchanges after 1914*, Constable & Co., London.
Caves, R.E. and Feige, E., 1980, Efficient Foreign Exchange Markets and the Monetary Approach to the Exchange Rate Determination, *American Economic Review*, Vol. 70, March, pp. 120–134.
Chacholiades, M., 1978, *International Monetary Theory and Policy*, New York.
Chatterjee, S. and Price, B., 1977, *Regression Analysis by Example*, John Wiley & Sons, New York.
Chen, N.-F, Roll, R. and Ross, S.A., 1986, Economic Forces and the Stock Market, *Journal of Business*, Vol. 59, No. 3, pp. 383–403.
Cho, C., Eun, C. and Senbet, L., 1984, International Arbitrage Pricing Theory: An Empirical Investigation, *Working Paper*, Graduate School of Business, University of Wisconsin – Madison, October.
Chown, J., 1982, The Tax Treatment of Foreign Exchange Fluctuations in the United States and the United Kingdom, *George Washington Journal of International Law and Economics*, Vol. 16, No. 2, pp. 201–237.

Coe, D.T. and Golub, S.S., 1986, Exchange Rates and Real Long-Term Interest-Rate Differentials: Evidence for Eighteen OECD Countries, *OECD Department of Economics and Statistics, Working Paper No. 28*, February.
Conybeare, J., 1984, International Bank Lending: Political Risk and Portfolio Diversification, *Journal of Business Research*, Vol. 12, No. 3, pp. 363–375.
Cooper, R.N., 1968, *The Economics of Interdependence: Economic Policy in the Atlantic Community*, McGraw Hill.
Cooper, R.N., 1971, *Towards an International Capital Market in North American and Western European Economic Policies*; in Kindleberger, C.P. and Shonfield, A. (eds.) (1971).
Cootner, P. (ed.), 1964, *The Random Character of Stock Market Prices*, the MIT Press.
Corden, W.M., 1977, *Inflation, Exchange Rates and the World Economy*, Clarendon Press, Oxford.
Cornell, W.B., 1977, Spot Rates, Forward Rates and Exchange Market Efficiency, *Journal of Financial Economics*, Vol. 5, pp. 55–65.
Cornell, W.B., 1979a, Relative Price Changes and Deviations from Purchasing Power Parity, *Journal of Banking and Finance*, Vol. 3, September, pp. 263–279.
Cornell, W.B., 1979b, Determinants of the Bid–Ask Spread on Forward Foreign Exchange Contracts under Floating Exchange Rates, *Journal of International Business Studies*, autumn, pp. 33–41.
Cosset, J.C., 1984, On the Presence of Risk Premiums in Foreign Exchange Markets, *Journal of International Economics*, Vol. 16, pp. 139–154.
Culbertson, J.M., 1957, The Term Structure of Interest Rates, *Quarterly Journal of Economics*, Vol. 71, November.
Cumby, R.E. and Mishkin, F., 1984, The International Linkages of Real Interest Rates: the European–US Connection, *NBER Working Paper No. 1423*, New York.
Cumby, R.E. and Mishkin, F., 1986, The Internationational Linkage of Real Interest Rates: The European–U.S. Connection, *Journal of International Money and Finance* 5, pp. 5–29.
Cumby, R.E. and Obstfeld, M., 1981, A Note of Exchange Rate Expectations and Nominal Interest Differentials: A Test of the Fisher Hypothesis, *Journal of Finance*, Vol. 36, June, pp. 697–704.
Cumby, R.E. and Obstfeld, M., 1984, International Interest Rate and Price Level Linkages under Flexible Exchange Rates: A Review of Recent Evidence; in Bilson, J.F.O. and Marston, R.C. (eds.), 1984, *Exchange Rate Theory and Practice*, University of Chicago Press, NBER, Chicago, pp. 121–152.
Daniel, C. and Wood, F., 1971, *Fitting Equations to Data*, John Wiley & Sons, New York.
Darby, M., 1975, The Financial and Tax Effects of Monetary Policy on Interest Rates, *Economic Inquiry*, Vol. 13, June, pp. 266–276.
Demery, D., 1984, Exchange Rate Dynamics, *European Economic Review*, Vol. 24, pp. 1–159.
Dhrymes, P.J., Friend, I. and Gultekin, N.B., 1984, A Critical Reexamination of the Empirical Evidence on the Arbitrage Pricing Theory, *Journal of Finance*, Vol. 39, No. 2.
Domowitz, I. and Hakkio, C.S., 1985, Conditional Variance and the Risk Premium in the Foreign Exchange Market, *Journal of International Economics*, Vol. 19, pp. 47–66.
Dooley, M.P., 1983, A Portfolio-Balance Rational-Expectations Model of the Dollar-Mark Exchange Rate, *Journal of International Economics*, Vol. 12, May, pp. 257–276.
Dooley, M.P., Frankel, J. and Mathieson, D.J., 1987, International Capital Mobility: What Do Saving-Investment Correlations Tell Us? *IMF Staff Papers*, Vol. 34, No. 3, pp. 503–530.
Dooley, M.P. and Isard, P., 1980, Capital Controls, Political Risk, and Deviations from Interest-Rate Parity, *Journal of Political Economy*, Vol. 88. No. 21, pp. 370–384.
Dooley, M.P. and Isard, P., 1982, The Role of the Current Account in Exchange Rate

Determination: A Comment on Rodriguez. *Journal of Political Economy*, Vol. 90, No. 6.

Dooley, M.P. and Isard, P., 1983, The Portfolio-Balance Model of Exchange Rates and Some Structural Estimates of the Risk Premium, *IMF Staff Paper*, Vol. 30, pp. 683–702.

Dooley, M.P. and Isard, P., 1986, *Country Preferences and Exchange Rate Determination*, IMF, Washington.

Dornbusch, R., 1976a, Expectations and Exchange Rate Dynamics, *Journal of Political Economy*, Vol. 84, No. 12, pp. 1161–1176.

Dornbusch, R., 1976b, Exchange Rate Expectations and Monetary Policy, *Journal of International Economics*, August, pp. 231–244.

Dornbusch, R., 1980, *Open Economy Macroeconomics*, Basic Book Publisher Inc., New York.

Dornbusch, R., 1982, Exchange Risk and the Macroeconomics of Exchange Rate Determination; in Hawkins, R. et al. (eds.), *The Internationalization of Financial Markets and National Economic Policy*, JAI Press, Greenwich, CT.

Dornbusch, R., 1983, Real Interest Rates, Home Goods, and Optimal External Borrowing, *Journal of Political Economy*, Vol. 91, No. 1, pp. 141–153, The University of Chicago.

Dornbusch, R. and Fischer, S., 1978, *Macroeconomics*, McGraw-Hill, New York.

Dornbusch, R. and Fischer, S., 1980, Exchange Rates and the Current Account, *American Economic Review*, Vol. 70, No. 5, pp. 960–971.

Dornbusch, R., and Krugman, P., 1976, Flexible Exchange Rates in the Short Run, *Brookings Papers on Economic Activity*, Vol. 3.

Dotan, A. and Ravid, S.A., 1985, On the Interaction of Real and Financial Decisions of the Firm under Uncertainty, *Journal of Finance*, Vol. XI, No. 2, June, pp. 501–517.

Driskill, R. and Shefferin, S., 1981, On the Mark: Comment, *American Economic Review*, Vol. 11, No. 5, pp. 1068–1074.

Driskill, R. and McCafferty, S., 1987, Exchange-Rate Determination: An Equilibrium Approach with Imperfect Capital Substitutability, *Journal of International Economics*, Vol. 23, pp. 241–261.

Dufey, G. and Giddy, I., 1978, *The International Money Market*, Prentice Hall Foundations of Finance Series, Englewood Cliffs, New Jersey.

Dufey, G. and Giddy, I., 1984, Eurocurrency Deposit Risk, *Journal of Banking and Finance*, Vol. 8, December, pp. 567–589.

Dumas, B., 1977, Discussion, *Journal of Finance*, Vol. 32, No. 2, pp. 512–515.

Easley, D. and Jarrow, R., 1983, Consensus Beliefs Equilibrium and Market Efficiency, *Journal of Finance*, Vol. 38, No. 3, pp. 903–911.

Eaton, J. and Turnovsky, S.J., 1983a, Exchange Risk, Political Risk and Macroeconomic Equilibrium, *American Economic Review*, Vol. 73, No. 1, pp. 183–189.

Eaton, J. and Turnovsky, S.J., 1983b, Covered Interest Parity, Uncovered Interest Parity and Exchange Rate Dynamics, *The Economic Journal*, Vol. 93, No. 371, September, pp. 555–575.

Eaton, J. and Turnovsky, S.J., 1984, The Forward Exchange Market, Speculation, and Exchange Market Intervention, *Journal of Economics*, Vol. XCIX, No. 1.

Eaton, J., Gersovitz, M. and Stiglitz, J., 1986, The Pure Theory of Country Risk, *European Economic Review*, Vol. 30, pp. 481–513.

Edwards, S., 1984, LDC Foreign Borrowing and Default Risk: An Empirical Investigation 1976–80, *American Economic Review*, Vol. 74, pp. 726–734.

Einzig, P., 1961, *A Dynamic Theory of Forward Exchange*, Macmillan, London.

Einzig, P., 1962, *The History of Foreign Exchange*, Macmillan, London.

Eken, S., 1984, Integration of Domestic and International Financial Markets: The Japanese Experience, *IMF Staff Papers*, Vol. 31, No. 3.

Eliasson, G. et al., 1985, *De svenska storföretagen – en studie av internationaliseringens konsekvenser för den svenska ekonomin,* IUI, Stockholm.

Enders, W. and Lapan, H.E., 1983, On the Relationship between the Exchange Regime and the Portfolio Rules of Optimizing Agents, *Journal of International Economics*, Vol. 15, No. 3/4.

Engel, C. and Frankel, J., 1984, Why Interest Rates React to Money Announcements. An Explanation from the Foreign Exchange Market, *Journal of Monetary Economics*, Vol. 13, pp. 31–39.

Englund, P., McPhee, S. and Viotti, S., 1985, Ränteparitet och ränteberoende, *Ekonomisk Debatt*, No. 4. pp. 275–288.

Englund, P. and Wallander, J., 1983, Repliker och kommentarer: Svar till Lars Wohlin, *Ekonomisk Debatt*, No. 2, pp. 123–130.

Englund, P. et al., 1987, Penningmarknad, räntebildning och valutaflöden, *Långtidsutredningen*, App. 14, Stockholm.

Errunza, V. and Losq, E., 1985, International Asset Pricing under Mild Segmentation: Theory and Test, *Journal of Finance*, Vol. 40, March, pp. 105–124.

Ettlin, F., et al., 1979, *The STEP 1 Quarterly Econometric Model of Sweden*, EFI, Stockholm.

Eun, C. and Resnick, B., 1987, *International Diversification under Estimation Risk: Actual versus Potential Gains*; in Khoury, S. and Gosh, A. (eds.), (1987).

Evans, P., 1985, Do Large Deficits Produce High Interest Rates? *The American Economic Review*, Vol. 75, No. 1, pp. 68–87.

Everett, R.M., Georges, A.M. and Blumberg, A., 1980, Appraising Currency Strengths and Weaknesses: An Operational Framework for Calculating Parity Exchange Rates, *Journal of International Business Studies*, Autumn, pp. 80–91.

Fama, E.F., 1970, Efficient Capital Markets, *Journal of Finance*, Vol. 25. No. 2.

Fama, E.F., 1975, Short-Term Interest Rates as Predictors of Inflation, *American Economic Review*, Vol. 65, June.

Fama, E.F., 1979, Efficient Capital Markets: A Review of Theory and Empirical Work, *Journal of Finance*, Vol. 34, No. 2, pp. 1129–1139.

Fama, E.F., 1984, Forward Spot Exchange Rates, *Journal of Monetary Economics*, Vol. 14. pp. 319–338.

Fama, E.F. and Farber, A., 1979, Money, Bonds and Foreign Exchange, *American Economic Review*, September, pp. 639–649.

Fama, E.F. and Gibbons, M.R., 1984, A Comparison of Inflation Forecasts, *Journal of Monetary Economics*, Vol. 13, No. 3, pp. 327–348.

de Faro, C. and Jucker, J., 1973, The Impact of Inflation and Devaluation on the Selection of an International Borrowing Source, *Journal of International Business Studies*, Vol. IV, No. 2.

Fase, M.M.G., 1973, A Principal Components Analysis of Market Interest Rates in the Netherlands, 1962–1970, *European Economic Review*, Vol. 4, pp. 107–134.

Fase, M.M.G., 1976, The Interdependence of Short-Term Interest Rates in the Major Financial Centres of the World: Some Evidence for 1961–1972, *Kyklos*, Vol. 29, pp. 63–96.

Feder, G. and Just, R.E., 1977, A Study of Debt Servicing Capacity Applying Logit Analysis, *Journal of Development Economics*, Vol. 4, pp. 23–58.

Feder, G. and Ross, S., 1981, Project Debt Servicing Capacity of Developing Countries, *Journal of Financial and Quantitative Analysis*, December, pp. 651–669.

Feige, E. and Pearce, D., 1979, The Causal Relationship between Money and Income: Some Caveats for Time Series Analysis. *Review of Economics and Statistics*, Vol. 61, November, pp. 521–533.

Feiger, G. and Jacquillat, B., 1979, Currency Option Bonds, Puts and Calls on Spot Exchange and the Hedging of Contingent Foreign Earnings, *Journal of Finance*, December, pp. 1129–1139.

Feldstein, M., 1976, Inflation, Income Taxes and the Rate of Interest, *American Economic Review*, Vol. 66, December.

Fieleke, N., 1975, Exchange Rate Flexibility and the Efficiency of the Foreign Exchange Markets, *Journal of Financial and Quantitative Analysis*, Vol. 10, No. 3–5, pp. 409–426.

Fisher, I., 1896, Appreciation and Interest, *Publications of the American Economic Association*, Vol. 9, No. 4, pp. 331–442.

Fisher, I., 1930, *The Theory of Interest*, Macmillan, New York.

Flavin, M., 1983, Excess Volatility in the Financial Markets: A Reassessment of Empirical Evidence, *Journal of Political Economy*, Vol. 91, No. 6, pp. 929–956.

Fleming, I., 1962, Domestic Financial Policy under Fixed and Floating Exchange Rate, *IMF Staff Papers*, Vol. 9, November, pp. 369–379.
Flood, R.P. and Hodrick, R.J., 1986, Asset Price Volatility, Bubbles, and Process Switching, 1986, *Journal of Finance*, Vol. XLI, No. 4, pp. 831–842.
Fortune, J.N., 1985, Expected Purchasing Power Parity, *Weltwirtschaftliches Archiv*, Band 121, Heft 1.
Frank, C. and Cline, W., 1971, Measurement of Debt Servicing Capacity: An Application to Discriminant Analysis, *Journal of International Economics*, March.
Frankel, J.A., 1979a, On the Mark: A Theory of Floating Exchange Rates Based on Real Interest Differentials, *American Economic Review*, September, pp. 610–622.
Frankel, J.A., 1979b, The Diversifiability of Exchange Risk, *Journal of International Economics*, September.
Frankel, J.A., 1982, In Search of the Exchange Risk Premium. A Six-Currency Test Assuming Mean-Variance Optimization, *Journal of International Money and Finance*, Vol. 14, pp. 319–338.
Frankel, J.A. (ed.), 1983, *Exchange Rates and International Macroeconomics*, University of Chicago Press, pp. 113–142.
Frankel, J.A., 1985a, The Implications of Mean-Variance Optimization for Four Questions in International Macroeconomics, *NBER Working Paper No. 1617*, May, New York.
Frankel, J.A., 1985b, International Capital Mobility and Crowding Out in the US Economy. Imperfect Integration of Financial Markets or of Goods Markets? *NBER Working Paper No. 1773*, December, New York.
Frankel, J.A. and Froot, K., 1986, Understanding the Dollar in the Eighties, Rates of Return, Risk Premium, Speculative Bubbles and Chartists and Fundamentalists, *Discussion Paper* No. 155, Centre for Economic Policy Research, Australian National University, Canberra.
Frankel, J.A. and MacArthur, A., 1988, Political vs Currency Premia in International Real Interest Differentials, *European Economic Review*, Vol. 32, pp. 1083–1121.
Franzén, T., 1987, *The Forward Exchange Market*, Sveriges Riksbank, Stockholm
Franzén, T. and Markowski, A., 1983, Valutaflöde och kreditpolitiken, *Seminar Paper*, May, Bäckaskog.
Franzén, T. and Markowski, A., 1985, Valutaflöden och kreditpolitik, en ekonometrisk studie, app. 2 in *Översyn av valutaregleringen*, SOU 1985:52, Stockholm.
Franzén, T. and Rosenberg, I., 1983, Valutakursstyrning i Sverige, *Kredit- och valutaöversikt* 1983:1, pp. 28–44.
Franzén, T. and Uggla, M., 1978, Valutaoron sommaren 1977 – en analys av de förväntningsstyrda valutarörelserna, *Ekonomisk Debatt*, No. 2.
Frenkel, J.A., 1973, Elasticities and the Interest Parity Theory, *Journal of Political Economy*, Vol. 81, May/June, pp. 741–747.
Frenkel, J.A., 1977, The Forward Exchange Rate, Expectations, and the Demand for Money. The German Hyperinflation, *American Economic Review*, September.
Frenkel, J.A., 1978, *A Monetary Approach to the Exchange Rate: Doctrinal Aspects and Empirical Evidence*; in Frenkel, J.A. and Johnson, H.G. (eds.), (1978).
Frenkel, J.A., 1979, *A Test of the Existence of the Risk Premium in the Foreign Exchange Market vs the Hypothesis of Perfect Substitutability*, Boards of Governors of the Federal Reserve System.
Frenkel, J.A., 1981, The Collapse of Purchasing Power Parities during the 1970s, *European Economic Review*, Vol. 16, May, pp. 145–165.
Frenkel, J.A., 1982, *Interest Rates, Exchange Rates and the Emerging Strength of the US Dollar*, University of Chicago Press.
Frenkel, J.A. (ed.), 1983, *Exchange Rates and International Macroeconomics*, University of Chicago Press, pp. 113–142.
Frenkel, J.A. and Aizenman, J., 1982, Aspects of the Optimal Management of Exchange Rates, *Journal of International Economics*, Vol. 13, pp. 231–256.
Frenkel, J.A. and Johnson, H.G. (eds.), 1978, *The Economics of Exchange Rates: Selected Studies*, Addison Wesley.
Frenkel, J.A. and Levich, R., 1975, Covered Interest Arbitrage: Unexploited Profits? *Journal of Political Economy*, April, pp. 325–338.

Frenkel, J.A. and Levich, R., 1977, Transaction Costs and Interest Arbitrage: Tranquil versus Turbulent Periods, *Journal of Political Economy*, Vol. 85, No. 6, pp. 1209–1226.
Frenkel, J.A. and Levich, R., 1981, Covered Interest Arbitrage in the 1970s, *Economic Letters*, Vol. 8, pp. 267–274.
Frenkel, J.A. and Razin, A., 1985, Government Spending, Debt and International Economic Interdependence, *Economic Journal*, Vol. 95, September, pp. 619–636.
Frenkel, J.A. and Rodriguez, C., 1982, Exchange Rate Dynamics and the Overshooting Hypothesis, *IMF Staff Papers*, Vol. 29, No. 1, pp. 1–30.
Friedman, M., 1956, *Studies in the Quantity Theory of Money*, Chicago University Press.
Friedman, M., 1962, *Capitalism and Freedom*, Chicago University Press.
Fukao, M. and Okubo, T., 1983, International Linkage of Interest Rates: The Case of Japan and the United States, *Discussion Paper* No. 13, Bank of Japan, Tokyo.
von Furstenberg, G.M., 1983, Changes in U.S. Interest Rates and Their Effects on European Interest and Exchange Rates; in Bigman, D. and Taya, T. (eds.), 1983, *Exchange Rate and Trade Instability: Causes, Consequences, and Remedies*, Ballinger, Cambridge, Mass., pp. 257–282.
Gaab, W., Granziol, M.J. and Horner, M., 1986, On Some International Parity Conditions: An Empirical Investigation, *European Economic Review*, No. 30. pp. 683–713.
Genberg, H., 1976, *Aspects of the Monetary Approach to the Balance of Payments Theory. An Empirical Study of Sweden*; in Frenkel, J.A. and Johnson, H.G. (eds.), 1976, The Monetary Approach to the Balance of Payment, University of Toronto Press, pp. 298–325.
Genberg, H., Salemi, M.K. and Swoboda, A., 1987, The Relative Importance of Foreign and Domestic Disturbances for Aggregate Fluctuations in the Open Economy, *Journal of Monetary Economics*, Vol. 19, pp. 45–67.
Geweke, J. and Feige, E., 1978, Some Joint Tests of the Efficiency of Markets for Forward Foreign Exchange, *Review of Economics and Statistics*, March.
Giddy, I.H., 1976, An Integrated Theory of Exchange Rate Equilibrium, *Journal of Financial and Quantitative Analysis*, Vol. 9, December, pp. 883–892.
Giddy, I.H., Dufey, G. and Min, S., 1979, Interest Rates in the U.S. and Eurodollar Markets, *Weltwirtschaftliches Archiv*, Band 115, pp. 51–67.
Glosten, L.R., 1987, Components of the Bid-Ask Spread and the Statistical Properties of Transaction Prices, *Journal of Finance*, Vol. XLII, No. 5, pp. 1293–1307.
Goldstein, M. and Young, J., 1979, Exchange Rate Policy, Some Current Issues, *Finance and Development*, March, pp. 7–10.
Goodwin, T., Farsio, F. and Willett, T, 1989, The Dollar and the DOW, *Working Paper*, Claremont Graduate School.
Gordon, R.H., 1984, Inflation, Taxation, and Corporate Behavior, *Quarterly Journal of Economics*, Vol. XCIX, No. 2.
Granger, C.W.J., 1968, Investigating Causal Relations by Econometric Models and Cross-Spectral Methods, *Econometrica*, Vol. 27, July, pp. 424–438.
Granger, C.W.J., 1983, Co-integrated Variables and Error-correcting Models, Unpublished *Discussion paper*, No. 83–139, University of California, San Diego.
Grauer, F.L.A., Litzenberger, R.H. and Stehle, R.E., 1976, Sharing Rules and Equilibrium in an International Capital Market under Uncertainty, *Journal of Financial Economics*, Vol. 3, pp. 233–256.
Greenberg, E., Marshall, W.J. and Yawitz, J.B., 1983, Firm Behavior Under Conditions of Uncertainty and the Theory of Finance, *Quarterly Review of Economics and Business*, Vol. 23, No. 2, pp. 6–21.
Greenwald, B., Stiglitz, J.E. and Weiss, A., 1984, Informational Imperfections in the Capital Market and Macroeconomic Fluctuations, *American Economic Review*, Vol. 74, No. 2.
Greenwood, J. and Kimbrough, K.P., 1987, An Investigation in the Theory of Foreign Exchange Controls, *Canadian Journal of Economics*, Vol. 20, No. 2, pp. 271–288.
Grossman, S.J., Kratchman, S.H. and Welker, R.B., 1983, Translate-Restate vs Restate-Translate: Pragmatism Overrides Theory, *Ohio CPA Journal*, Vol. 42, No.

3, pp. 131–137.
Grossman, S.J. and Stiglitz, J.E., 1976, Information and Competitive Price Systems, *American Economic Review*, Vol. 66, pp. 246–253.
Grossman, S.J. and Stiglitz, J.E., 1980, On the Impossibility of Informationally Efficient Markets, *American Economic Review*, Vol. 70, pp. 393–407.
Grubel, H.G., 1966, *Forward Exchange, Speculation and the International Flow of Capital*, Stanford University Press, Stanford.
Grubel, H.G., 1968, International Diversified Portfolios: Welfare Gains and Capital Flows, *American Economic Review*, December.
Grubel, H.G. and Fadner, K., 1971, The Interdependence of International Equity Markets, *Journal of Finance*, March.
Gylfason, T., and Schmid, M., 1983, Does Devaluation Cause Stagflation?, *Canadian Journal of Economics*, Vol. XVI, No. 4.
Hansen, L. and Hodrick, R., 1980, Forward Exchange Rates as Optimal Predictors of Future Spot Rates: An Econometric Analysis, *Journal of Political Economy*, Vol. 88, pp. 829–853.
Hansen, L. and Hodrick, R., 1983, *Risk Averse Speculation in the Forward Foreign Exchange Market: An Econometric Analysis of Linear Models*; in Frenkel, J. (ed.) (1983).
Hansson, I., and Stuart, C., 1986, The Fisher Hypothesis and International Capital Markets, *Journal of Political Economy*, Vol. 94, No. 6, pp. 1330–1337.
Hardouvelis, G.A., 1987, Reserves Announcements and Interest Rates: Does Monetary Policy Matter?, *Journal of Finance*, Vol. XLII, No. 2, pp. 407–422.
Hartman, D., 1984, The International Financial Market and US Interest Rates, *Journal of International Money and Finance*, Vol. 3, pp. 91–103.
Hawkins, R., 1972, *Intra-EEC Capital Movements and Domestic Financial Markets*; in Machlup, F., Salant, W. and Tarshis, L. (eds.) (1972).
Hawkins, R., Levich, R. and Wihlborg, C. (eds.), 1983, *Research in International Business and Finance*, JAI Press.
Haynes, S. and Stone, J., 1981, On the Mark: Comment, *American Economic Review*, Vol. 11, No. 5, pp. 1060–1067.
Heikensten, L. and Viotti, S., 1985, Statsskuldspolitiken – utveckling och problem, *Skandinaviska Enskilda Bankens kvartalsskrift*, No. 1, pp. 19–24.
Heitger, B., 1987, Purchasing Power Parity under Flexible Exchange Rates – The Impact of Structural Change, *Wertwirtschaftliches Archiv*, Band 123, Heft 1, pp. 149–156.
Hendershott, P., 1967, The Structure of International Interest Rates: The US Treasury Bill Rate and the Eurodollar Deposit Rate, *Journal of Finance*, Vol. 39, No. 3, pp. 685–696.
Hendershott, P., 1984, Expectations, Surprises and Treasury Bill Rates 1960–82, *Journal of Finance*, Vol. 39, No. 3, pp. 685–696.
Henderson, D.W. and Rogoff, K., 1982, Negative Net Foreign Asset Positions and Stability in a World Portfolio Balance Model, *Journal of International Economics*, Vol. 13, pp. 85–104.
Henning, C.N., Pigott, W. and Scott, R.H., 1978, *International Financing Management*, New York.
Henrekson, M., 1987, Valutaregleringen och den liberaliserade terminshandeln, *Skandinaviska Enskilda Bankens kvartalsskrift*, No. 4, pp. 100–105.
Herin, J., Lindbeck, A. and Myhrman, J., 1977, *Flexible Exchange Rates and Stabilization Policy*, Macmillan.
Herring, R.J. and Marston, R.C., 1977, National Monetary Policies and International Financial Markets, *Contributions to Economic Analysis* No. 104, North-Holland, Amsterdam.
Hesheth, B., 1979, To What Extent Can Forecasters "Outpredict" the Forward Markets? The Track Record of Forex Research, *Managerial Finance*, Vol. 4, No. 2.
Hicks, J.R., 1939, *Value and Capital, An Inquiry into Some Fundamental Principles of Economic Theory*, Clarendon Press, Oxford.
Hillard, I., 1979, The Relationship between Equity Indices on World Exchanges, *Journal of Finance*, March, pp. 103–113.

Himarios, D., 1987, Devaluation, Devaluation Expectations and Price Dynamics, *Economica*, Vol. 54, No. 215, pp. 299–313.
Hodjera, Z., 1973, International Short-Term Capital Movements, A Survey of Theory and Empirical Analysis, *IMF Staff Papers*, Vol. 20, pp. 683–740, Washington D.C.
Hodjera, Z., 1976, Alternative Approaches in the Analysis of International Capital Movements, A Case Study of Austria and France, *IMF Staff Papers*, Vol. 23, pp. 598–623.
Hodrick, R., 1987, *The Evidence on the Efficiency of Forward and Futures Foreign Exchange Markets*, Harwood Press, New York.
Hodrick, R. and Srivastava, S., 1984, An Investigation of Risk and Return in Forward Foreign Exchange, *Journal of International Money and Finance*, Vol. 3, pp. 5–29.
Hoelscher, G.P., 1983, Federal Borrowing and Short Term Interest Rates, *Southern Economic Journal*, Vol. 50, No. 2.
Honohan, P., 1984, Monetary Restraint and the Exchange Rate, *Economica*, Vol. 51, May, pp. 163–176.
Hooper, P., 1984, International Repercussions of the US Budget Deficit, *Federal Reserve Board International Finance Discussion Paper*, No. 246, September.
Hooper, P. and Kohlhagen, S., 1978, The Effect of Exchange Rate Uncertainty on the Prices and Volume of International Trade, *Journal of International Economics*, Vol. 8.
Hooper, P. and Morton, J.E., 1982, Fluctuations in the Dollar: A Model of Nominal and Real Exchange Rate Determination, *Journal of International Money and Finance*, No. 1, pp. 39–56.
Huang, R., 1984, Exchange Rate and Relative Monetary Expansions: The Case of Simultaneous Hyperinflation and Rational Expectations, *European Economic Review*, Vol. 24, No. 2, pp. 189–195.
Huizinga, J. and Mishkin, F.S., 1984, Inflation and Real Rates on Assets with Different Risk Characteristics, *Journal of Finance*, Vol. 39, No. 3, pp. 699–711.
Huizinga, J. and Mishkin, F.S., 1986, Monetary Policy Regime Shifts and the Unusual Behavior of Real Interest Rates, *Carnegie-Rochester Conference Series on Public Policy*, Vol. 24, pp. 231–274, North-Holland, Amsterdam.
Hutchison, M.M., 1984, Official Japanese Intervention in Foreign Exchange Markets. Leaning Against the Wind? *Economic Letters*, Vol. 15, pp. 115–120, North-Holland, Amsterdam.
Hörngren, L. and Vredin, A., 1986, The Foreign Exchange Risk Premium: A Review and Some Evidence from a Currency Basket System, *Working Paper* No. 14, May, FIEF, Stockholm.
Ibrahimi, F., Oxelheim, L. and Wihlborg, C., 1989, International Stock Markets and Fluctuations in Exchange Rates and Other Macroeconomic Variables, *IUI Working Paper* No. 244, Stockholm.
International Monetary Fund, 1977, *Annual Report.*
International Monetary Fund, 1981, *Annual Report.*
International Monetary Fund, 1987, *International Financial Statistics*, July.
Isard, P., 1977, How Far Can We Push the Law of One Price? *American Economic Review*, Vol. 67, December, pp. 942–948.
Isard, P., 1978, Exchange-Rate Determination: A Survey of Popular Views and Recent Models, *Princeton Studies in International Finance*, No. 42, Princeton University.
Isard, P., 1987, Lessons from Empirical Models of Exchange Rates, *IMF Staff Papers*, Vol. 34, No. 1, pp. 1–28.
Ito, T., 1983, Capital Controls and Covered Interest Parity, *NBER Working Paper* No. 1187, August, Cambridge Mass.
Jacobs, R.L., Leamer, E.E. and Ward, M.P., 1979, Difficulties with Testing for Causation, *Economic Inquiry*, Vol. 17, July, pp. 401–413.
Jaffe, D.M. and Modigliani, F., 1969, A Theory and Test of Credit Rationing, *American Economic Review*, December.
Jenkins, G., 1979, *Practical Experience with Modelling and Forecasting Time Series*, London.
Jenkins, P. and Walsh, C.E., 1987, Real Interest Rates, Credit Markets and Economic

Stabilization, *Journal of Macroeconomics*, Vol. 9, No. 1, pp. 95–108.
Jilling, M., 1978, *Foreign Exchange Risk Management in US Multinational Corporations*, UMI Research Press, Stanford.
Johnson, R.B., 1979, Some Aspects of the Determination of Eurocurrency Interest Rates, *Bank of England, Quarterly Bulletin*, March.
Johnston, J., 1972, *Econometric Methods*, 2nd edition, McGraw-Hill.
Jonung, L., 1981, Perceived and Expected Rates of Inflation in Sweden, *American Economic Review*, Vol. 71, December.
Jordan, J.S., 1983, On the Efficient Markets Hypothesis, *Econometrica*, Vol. 51, No. 5.
Kaen, F. and Hachey, G., 1983, Eurocurrency and National Money Market Interest Rates, *Journal of Money, Credit and Banking*, Vol. 15, No. 3, pp. 327–338.
Kane, A., Rosenthal, L. and Ljung, G., 1983, Tests of the Fisher Hypothesis with International Data: Theory and Evidence, *Journal of Finance*, Vol. 38, No. 2.
Kaserman, D., 1973, The Forward Rate, Its Determination and Behavior as a Predictor of the Future Spot Rate, *Proceedings of the American Statistical Association*.
Kaufman, G.G., Mote, L.R. and Rosenblum, H., 1984, Consequences of Deregulation for Commercial Banking, *Journal of Finance*, Vol. 39, No. 3.
Kenen, P.B., 1965, Trade, Speculation and the Forward Exchange Rates; in Baldwin, R.E. et al. (eds.), *Trade, Growth and the Balance of Payments*, Rand MacNally, Chicago.
Kenen, P.B., 1976, Capital Mobility and Financial Integration: A Survey, *Princeton Studies of International Finance*, No. 39, Princeton University.
Kenen, P.B., 1978, *A Model of the US Balance of Payments*, Lexington Books, Lexington.
Kesselman, J., 1971, The Role of Speculation in Forward-Rate Determination, *Canadian Journal of Economics*, August, pp. 279–298.
Kettel, B., 1979, The Forward Rate as an Accurate Predictor of Future Spot Rates, *Managerial Finance*, Vol. 4, No. 2.
Keynes, J.M., 1923, *A Tract of Monetary Reform*, Macmillan, London.
Keynes, J.M., 1936, *The General Theory of Employment, Interest and Money*, Macmillan, London.
Kim, B.J.C., 1987, Do the Foreign Exchange Rates Really Follow a Random Walk?: An Empirical Question Revisited, *Economics Letters*, Vol. 23, pp. 289–293, North-Holland.
Kimbrough, K.P., 1982, Real Disturbances, the Current Account, and the Exchange Rate, *Journal of International Economics*, Vol. 13, pp. 291–300.
Kindleberger, C.P. and Shonfield, A., 1971, *North American and Western Economic Policies*, Macmillan, St. Martin's Press.
Kobrin, S., 1979, Political Risk: A Review and Reconsideration, *Journal of International Business Studies*, Vol. 10, spring/summer, pp. 67–80.
Kobrin, S. et al., 1980, The Assessment and Evaluation of Noneconomic Environments by American Firms: A Preliminary Report, *Journal of International Business Studies*, Vol. 11, spring/summer, pp. 32–47.
Koh, A.–T., 1984, Money Shocks and Deviations from Purchasing Power Parity, *Journal of Monetary Economics*, Vol. 14, No. 1.
Kohlhagen, S.W., 1975, Evidence on the Cost of Forward Cover in a Floating System, *Euromoney*, September.
Kohlhagen, S.W., 1976, *The Forward Rate as an Unbiased Predictor of the Future Spot Rate*, University of California, Berkeley.
Kohlhagen, S.W., 1978, The Behavior of Foreign Exchange Markets: A Critical Survey of the Empirical Literature, *Monograph 1978–3*, Salomon Brothers Center for the Study of Financial Institutions, New York University.
Kohlhagen, S.W., 1983, *Overlapping National Investment Portfolios. Evidence and Implications of International Integration of Secondary Markets for Financial Assets*; in Hawkins, R., Levich, R. and Wihlborg, C. (eds.) (1983).
Khoury, S., Dodin, B. and Takada, H., 1986, *Multiple Time Series of National Stock Markets and Their Structure: Some Implications*; in Khoury, S. and Gosh, A. (eds.)

(1987).
Khoury, S. and Gosh, A. (eds.), 1987, *Recent Development in International Banking and Finance*, Vol. 1, Lexington Books.
Korajczyk, R.A., 1985, The Pricing of Forward Contracts for Foreign Exchange, *Journal of Political Economy*, Vol. 93, No. 2, pp. 347–366.
Kouri, P.J.K., 1976a, *The Determinants of the Forward Premium*, Institute for International Economic Studies, Stockholm.
Kouri, P.J.K., 1976b, *International Investment and Interest Rate Linkages under Flexible Exchange Rates*, Institute for International Economic Studies, Stockholm.
Kouri, P.J.K., 1976c, The Exchange Rate and the Balance of Payments in the Short Run and in the Long Run, *Scandinavian Journal of Economics*, Vol. 78, No. 2, pp. 280–304.
Kouri, P.J.K., 1977, International Investment and Interest Linkages under Flexible Exchange Rates: in Aliber, R.Z. (ed.), *The Political Economy of Monetary Reform*, Allenheld, N.J., pp. 74–96.
Kouri, P.J.K., 1983, *The Effect of Risk on Interest Rates. A Synthesis of the Macroeconomic and Financial Views*; in Hawkins, R., Levich, R. and Wihlborg, C. (1983).
Kouri, P.J.K. and Porter, M.G., 1974, International Capital Flows and Portfolio Equilibrium, *Journal of Political Economy*, Vol. 82, Chicago, Ill., pp. 443–467.
Kravis, I.B. and Lipsey, R.E., 1978, Price Behavior in the Light of Balance of Payments Theories, *Journal of International Economics*, Vol. 8, pp. 193–246.
Kumcu, M.E., 1983, Are Exchange Rate Movements a Random Walk?, *Economics Letters*, Vol. 13, North-Holland, Amsterdam.
Kwack, S., 1971, The Structure of International Interest Rates: An Extension of Hendershott's Tests, *Journal of Finance*, Vol. XXVI, pp. 897–900.
Kwack, S. and Schink, G.R., 1975, A Disaggregated Quarterly Model of the United State Trade and Capital Flows, Simulations and Test of Policy Effectiveness; in Fromm, G. and Klein, L. (eds.), *The Brookings Model, Perspective and Recent Developments*, North-Holland, Amsterdam.
Kvist, A., Nyberg, L. and Wissén, P., 1985, *Penningmarknaden*, SNS, Stockholm.
Lawrence, C., 1987, The Impact of Supply Shocks on Exchange Rates and Interest Rates: Does the Marshall – Lerner Condition Matter?, *Journal of International Economics*, Vol. 22, pp. 321–337.
Leamer, E. and Stern, R., 1972, *Problems in the Theory and Empirical Estimation of International Capital Movements*, National Bureau of Economic Research, New York.
Leavy, B., 1984, Assessing Country Risks for Foreign Investment Decisions, *Long-Range Planning*, Vol. 17, No. 3, pp. 141–150.
Lessard, D.R., 1976, World, Country, and Industry Relationships in Equity Returns, *Financial Analysts Journal*, Vol. 32, pp. 32–38.
Lessard, D.R., 1983, *Comments on Buiter*; in Hawkins, R., Levich, R. and Wihlborg, C. (1983).
Leventakis, J.A., 1987, Exchange Rate Models: Do They Work?, *Weltwirtschaftliches Archiv*, Band 123, Heft 2, pp. 363–376.
Levi, M.D., 1977, Taxation and 'Abnormal' International Capital Flows, *Journal of Political Economy*, Vol. 85, No. 3, pp. 635–646.
Levi, M.D. and Makin, J.H., 1979, Fisher, Phillips, Friedman and the Measured Impact of Inflation on Interest, *Journal of Finance*, Vol. 34, March.
Levich, R.M., 1978, Test of Forecasting Models and Market Efficiency in the International Money Market; in Frenkel, J and Johnson, H.G. (1978).
Levich, R.M., 1979, *The International Money Market*, JAI Press Inc., New York.
Levin, J.H., 1974, The Eurodollar Market and the International Transmission of Interest Rates, *Canadian Journal of Economics*, pp. 205–224.
Levy, H. and Sarnat, M., 1970, International Diversification of Investment Portfolios, *American Economic Review*, Vol. 60, September, pp. 668–675.
Lewellen, W.G. and Ang, J.S., 1984, Inflation, Currency Exchange Rates, and the International Securities Markets, *Journal of Business Research*, Vol. 12, No. 1.
Lindbeck, A., 1976, Approaches to Exchange Rate Analysis, *Scandinavian Journal of*

Economics, Vol. 78, No. 2, pp. 133–145.
Lindbeck, A. (ed.), 1979, *Inflation and Employment in Open Economies*, North-Holland, Amsterdam.
Lintner, J., 1965, The Valuation of Risk Assets and the Selection of Risky Investments in Stock Portfolios and Capital Budgets, *Review of Economics and Statistics*, Vol. 47, February, pp. 12–37.
LLewellyn, D., 1980, *International Financial Integration*, John Wiley & Sons, New York.
Logue, D.E., Salant, M.A. and Sweeney, R.J., 1976, International Integration of Financial Markets: Survey, Synthesis, and Results; in Stern, C.C., Makin, J.H. and Logue, D.E. (eds.), *Eurocurrencies and the International Monetary System*, American Enterprise Institute, Washington, D.C.
Lucas, R.E., 1976, Econometric Policy Evaluation. A Critique; in Brunner, K. and Meltzer, A. (eds.), *Carnegie-Mellon Conference Series on Public Policy*, 1, pp. 19–46, North-Holland, Amsterdam.
Lucas, R.E., 1978, Asset Prices in an Exchange Economy, *Econometrica*, Vol. 46, pp. 1429–1445.
Lucas, R.E., 1982, Interest Rates and Currency Prices in a Two Country World, *Journal of Monetary Economics*, Vol. 10, November, pp. 335–359.
Lutz, F.A. and Lutz, V.C., 1951, *The Theory of Investment in the Firm*, Princeton University Press, Princeton.
Lybeck, J., 1975, *A Disequilibrium Model of the Swedish Financial Sector*, EFI, Stockholm.
Lybeck, J., 1987, *Finansstrategi*, Rabén & Sjögren, Stockholm.
Lybeck, J. et al., 1984, A Comparison of the Dynamic Properties of Five Nordic Macroeconometric Models. *Scandinavian Journal of Economics*, Vol 86, No. 1, pp. 35–51.
Machlup, F., Salant, W. and Tarshis, L. (eds.), 1972, *International Mobility and Movement of Capital*, Universities – National Bureau Conference Series 24, New York and London.
Maenning, W.G.Ch. and Tease, W.J., 1987, Covered Interest Parity in Non-Dollar Euromarkets, *Weltwirtschaftliches Archiv*, Band 123, Heft 4, pp. 606–617.
Makin, J.H., 1977, Flexible Exchange Rates, Multinational Corporations and Accounting Standards, *Federal Reserve Bank of San Francisco Economic Review*, autumn, pp. 44–45.
Makin, J.H., 1978, Portfolio Theory and the Problem of Foreign Exchange Risk, *Journal of Finance*, May.
Makin, J.H., 1983, Real Interest, Money Surprises, Anticipated Inflation and Fiscal Deficits, *Journal of Money, Credit and Banking*, Vol. 10, August.
Makin, J.H. and Tanzi, V., 1983, The Levels and Volatility of Interest Rates in the United States: The Role of Expected Inflation, Real Rates, and Taxes. *NBER Working Paper No. 167*, Cambridge, Mass.
Makin, J.H. and Tanzi, V., 1984, *Level and Volatility of Interest Rates in the United States: Roles of Expected Inflation, Real Rates, and Taxes*; in Tanzi, V. (ed.) (1984), pp. 110–142.
Mankiw, N.G., 1986, The Term Structure of Interest Rates Revisited, *Brookings Papers on Economic Activity*, No. 1, pp. 61–96.
Mandelbrot, B., 1966, Forecasts of Future Prices, Unbiased Markets and Martingale Models, *Journal of Business*, Vol. 39, pp. 242–255.
Mantel, N., 1970, Why Stepdown Procedures in Variable Selection?, *Technometrics*, Vol. 12, pp. 591–612.
Mark, N.C., 1985a, On Time Varying Risk Premia in the Foreign Exchange Market: An Econometric Analysis, *Journal of Monetary Economics*, Vol. 16, No. 3–18, North-Holland.
Mark, N.C., 1985b, Some Evidence on the International Inequality of Real Interest Rates, *Journal of International Money and Finance* 4, pp. 189–208.
Markowitz, H., 1952, Portfolio Selection, *Journal of Finance*, Vol. 7, March.
Markowitz, H., 1959, *Portfolio Selection. Efficient Diversification of Investments*, John Wiley & Sons, New York.

Marston, R.C., 1983, *Comments on Kohlhagen* (1983); in Hawkins, R., Levich, R. and Wihlborg, C. (1983).

Mascaro, A. and Meltzer, A., 1983, Long- and Short-Term Interest Rates in a Risky World, *Journal of Monetary Economics*, Vol. 12. No. 4, pp. 485–518.

Masson, P., 1981, Dynamic Stability of Portfolio Balance Models of the Exchange Rate, *Journal of International Economics*, November.

McCallum, B.T., 1977, The Role of Speculation in the Canadian Forward Exchange Market: Some Estimates Assuming Rational Expectations, *Review of Economics and Statistics*, May, pp. 145–151.

McCormick, F., 1975, *Transaction Costs in the Foreign Exchange Market under Fixed and Floating Exchange Rates*, University of California, Berkeley.

McCormick, F., 1979, Covered Interest Arbitrage: Unexploited Profits?, Comment, *Journal of Political Economy*, Vol. 87, April, pp. 411–417.

McCullogh, I.H., 1975, Operational Aspects of the Siegel Paradox, *Quarterly Journal of Economics*, Vol. 86, pp. 303–309.

McCullogh, R., 1983, Unexpected Real Consequences of Floating Exchange Rates, *Essays in International Finance*, Princeton University, Princeton.

McFarland, J.W., Pettit, R.R. and Sung, S.K., 1982, The Distribution of Foreign Exchange Price Changes: Trading Day Effects and Risk Measurement, *Journal of Finance*, Vol. 37, June, pp. 693–716.

McKinnon, R., 1979, *Money in International Exchange*, Oxford University Press, Oxford.

Meese, R.A. and Rogoff, K., 1983, Empirical Exchange Rate Models of the Seventies – Do They Fit Out of Sample?, *Journal of International Economics*, Vol. 14, pp 3–24.

Meese, R.A. and Rogoff, K., 1986, Was It Real? The Exchange Rate-Interest Differential Relation 1973–84, *Journal of Economic Dynamics and Control* 10, pp. 297–298.

Meese, R.A. and Singleton, K.J., 1983, Rational Expectations and the Volatility of Floating Exchange Rates, *International Economic Review*, Vol. 24, No. 3.

Meiselman, D., 1962, *The Term Structure of Interest Rates*, Prentice-Hall.

Melard, G. and Rouland, O., 1979, *Une méthode de sélection d'un algorithme* à *court terme*, Université Libre de Bruxelles.

Merrick, J.J., Jr. and Saunders, A., 1986, International Expected Real Interest Rates: New Tests of the Parity Hypothesis and US Fiscal Policy Effects, *Journal of Monetary Economics*, No. 3–86, pp. 313–322.

Merton, R., 1974, On the Pricing of Corporate Debt: The Risk Structure of Interest Rates, *Journal of Finance*, Vol. 29, May, pp. 449–470.

Miles, J.A., 1983, Taxes and the Fisher Effect: A Clarifying Analysis, *Journal of Finance*, Vol. 38, No. 1.

Mills, R.H., 1973, Structural Changes in the Eurodollar Market: Evidence from a Two-Equation Model, *Discussion Paper* No. 33, Board of Governors of the Federal Reserve System.

Min, S., 1976, *Determinants of Interest Differential between the U.S. and Eurodollar Credit Markets – An Empirical Investigation* (PhD dissertation), University of Michigan.

Mishkin, F.S., 1981, Monetary Policy and Long-Term Interest Rates: An Efficient Markets Approach, *Journal of Monetary Economics*, Vol. 7, January, pp. 29–55.

Mishkin, F.S., 1984a, The Real Interest Rate: A Multicountry Empirical Study, *Canadian Journal of Economics* 17, No. 2, pp. 283–311.

Mishkin, F.S., 1984b, Are Real Interest Rates Equal across Countries? An empirical investigation of international parity conditions, *Journal of Finance* 39, pp. 1345–1358.

Modigliani, F. and Grunberg, E., 1954, The Predictability of Social Events, *Journal of Political Economy*, Vol. 62, pp. 465–478.

Modigliani, F. and Sutch, R., 1966, Innovations in Interest Rate Policy, *American Economic Review, Papers and Proceedings*, Vol. 56, pp. 178–197.

Modigliani, F. and Sutch, R., 1967, Debt Management and the Term Structure of Interest Rates, *Journal of Political Economy*, Vol. 75, pp. 569–589.

Modjtahedi, B., 1987, An Empirical Investigation into the International Real Interest Rate Linkages, *Canadian Journal of Economics*, Vol. XX, No. 4, pp. 833–854.
Mossin, J., 1966, Equilibrium in a Capital Asset Market, *Econometrica*, Vol. 34, October, pp. 768–783.
Mundell, R.A., 1963a, Capital Mobility and Stabilization Policy Under Fixed and Flexible Exchange Rates, *Canadian Journal of Economics and Political Science*, Vol. 29, pp. 475–485.
Mundell, R.A., 1963b, Inflation and Real Rates, *Journal of Political Economy*, Vol. 71, No. 3, pp. 280–283.
Mundell, R.A., 1968, *International Economics*, Macmillan, New York.
Mussa, M., 1976, The Exchange Rate, the Balance of Payments and Monetary and Fiscal Policy under a Regime of Controlled Financing, *Scandinavian Journal of Economics*, May.
Mussa, M., 1979, Empirical Regularities in the Behavior of Exchange Rates and Theories of the Foreign Exchange Market, *Carnegie-Rochester Conference Series on Public Policy*, Vol. 11.
Mussa, M., 1982, A Model of Exchange Rate Dynamics, *Journal of Political Economy*, Vol. 90, February, pp. 74–104.
Muth, J.F., 1961, Rational Expectations and the Theory of Price Movements, *Econometrica*, Vol. 29, pp. 315–335.
Nelson, C., 1972, The Prediction Performance of the FRB–MIT–PENN Model of the US Economy, *American Economic Review*, Vol. 62, No. 5.
Nelson, C., 1973, *Applied Time Series Analysis*, Holden-Day, San Francisco.
Niehans, J., 1983, Financial Innovation, Multinational Banking, and Monetary Policy, *Journal of Banking and Finance*, Vol. 7, pp. 537–551.
Nordiska Ekonomiska Forskningsrådet, 1987, *Penningpolitiken i Norden*, pp. 9–16.
Obstfeld, M., 1986, Capital Controls, the Dual Exchange Rate, and Devaluation, *Journal of International Economics*, Vol. 90, No. 1/2, pp. 1–20.
Obstfeld, M. and Rogoff, K., 1984, Exchange Rate Dynamics with Sluggish Prices under Alternative Price-Adjustment Rules, *International Economic Review*, Vol. 25, No. 1.
OECD, 1977, *Towards Full Employment and Price Stability*, The McCracken Report, June.
OECD, 1979, *Regulations Affecting International Banking Operations*, Paris.
OECD, 1984, *Multinational Modelling of Financial Linkages and Exchange Rates*, No. 2.
Officer, L., 1976, The Purchasing-Power-Parity Theory of Exchange Rates: A Review Article, *IMF Staff Papers*, March, pp. 1–60.
Officer, L., 1982, *Purchasing Power Parity and Exchange Rates: Theory, Evidence and Relevance*, JAI Press Inc.
OPTICA Report 2, 1977, Inflation and Exchange Rates, *Evidence Guidelines for the European Community*, Brussels.
Oxelheim, L., 1980, *Box-Jenkins modeller för beskrivning och prognosticering av valutakurser*, Lunds universitet, Lund.
Oxelheim, L., 1981, *Företagens utlandslån – Valuta- och redovisningsaspekter*, Liber, Malmö.
Oxelheim, L., 1982, *Företagets valutaplanering*, Liber, Malmö.
Oxelheim, L., 1983a, *Jämviktsvalutakurs och extern balans*, (mimeo), March, IUI, Stockholm.
Oxelheim, L., 1983b, *Valutastyrning*, Børsens forlag og Foreningen av Danske Civiløkonomers forlag, Kopenhagen.
Oxelheim, L., 1983c, *Frågor kring företagets beslut under valutaosäkerhet*, Scandinavian Institute for Foreign Exchange Research, Stockholm.
Oxelheim, L., 1984a, *Företaget och valutaregleringen*, Scandinavian Institute for Foreign Exchange Research, February.
Oxelheim, L., 1984b, *Exchange Risk Management in the Modern Company – A Total Approach*, Scandinavian Institute for Foreign Exchange Research, Stockholm.
Oxelheim, L., 1984c, Country Risks and Industrial Structure in a Nordic Perspective, *Unitas*, Helsinki.

Oxelheim, L., 1984c, Country Risks and Industrial Structure in a Nordic Perspective, *Unitas*, Helsinki.
Oxelheim, L., 1985, *International Financial Market Fluctuations*, John Wiley & Sons, Chichester.
Oxelheim, L., and Wihlborg, C., 1987, *Macroeconomic Uncertainty – International Risks and Opportunities for the Corporations*, John Wiley & Sons, Chichester.
Panton, D.B., Lessig, V.P. and Maurice, J.O., 1976, Comovements of International Equity Markets: A Taxonomic Approach, *Journal of Financial and Quantitative Analysis*, Vol. II, pp. 415–431, Seattle, Washington.
Papadia, F., 1981, Forward Exchange Rates as Predictors of the Future Spot Rates and the Efficiency of the Foreign Exchange Market, *Journal of Banking and Finance*, Vol. 5, June, pp. 217–240.
Papadia, F., 1984, Estimates of ex ante Real Rate of Interest in the EEC Countries and in the United States 1973–82, *Journal of Money Credit and Banking*, Vol. 16, August.
Pesando, J.E., 1979, On the Random Walk Characteristics of Short- and Long-Term Interest Rates in an Efficient Market, *Journal of Money, Credit and Banking*, Vol. 11, November, pp. 455–466.
Phaup, D., 1981, A Reinterpretation of the Modern Theory of Forward Exchange Rates, *Journal of Money, Credit and Banking*, June, pp. 477–484.
Phylaktis, K. and Wood, G.E., 1984, *An Analytical and Taxonomic Framework for the Studies of Exchange Controls*; in Black, J. and Durance, G.S. (eds.), Problems in International Finance, Macmillan.
Pippenger, J., 1972, Spot Rates, Forward Rates, and Interest-Rate Differentials, *Journal of Money, Credit and Banking.*, Vol. IV, pp. 375–383.
Pippenger, J., 1978, Interest Arbitrage between Canada and the United States: A New Perspective, *Canadian Journal of Economics*, May, pp. 183–193.
Pope, R.D., 1984, A Comment on Two Concepts of Risk Premia and Certainty Equivalents, *Economic Letters*, No. 3–4.
Porter, M.G., 1971, A Theoretical and Empirical Framework for Analyzing the Term Structure of Exchange Rate Expectations, *IMF Staff Papers*, Vol. 18, pp. 613–645, Washington, D.C.
Prachowny, M.F., 1970, A Note on Interest Parity and the Supply of Arbitrage Funds, *Journal of Political Economy*, Vol. 78, May/June, pp. 540–545.
Pratt, J., 1964, Risk Aversion in the Small and in the Large, *Econometrica*, Vol. 32, pp. 122–136.
Predex Corporation, 1975, *Predex Forecast*, New York.
Protopapadakis, A. and Stoll, H., 1983, Spot and Future Prices and the Law of One Price, *Journal of Finance*, Vol. 38, No. 5, pp. 1431–1455.
Putnam, B.H., 1983, *Comments on Kohlhagen (1983)*; in Hawkins, Levich and Wihlborg (1983).
Roberts, H.V., 1967, Statistical versus Clinical Prediction of the Stock Market, *Seminar Paper*, University of Chicago, May.
Robock, S., 1971, Political Risk: Identification and Assessment, *Columbia Journal of World Business*, July/August, pp. 6–20.
Rodriguez, C., 1982, The Role of Trade Flows in Exchange Rate Determination: A Rational Expectations Approach, *Journal of Political Economy*, Vol. 88, No. 6, pp. 1148–1158.
Roley, V.V. and Walsh, C.E., 1984, Unanticipated Money and Interest Rates, *American Economic Review*, Vol. 74, No. 2, May.
Roll, R., 1970, *The Behavior of Interest Rates: An Application of the Efficient Market Model to U.S. Treasury Bills*, Basic Books Inc.
Roll, R., 1977, Critique of the Asset Pricing Theory's Tests, *Journal of Financial Economics*, Vol. 4, No. 2, pp. 1–48.
Roll, R. and Ross, S., 1980, An Empirical Investigation of the Arbitrage Pricing Theory, *Journal of Finance*, Vol. 35, December, pp. 1073–1103.
Roll, R. and Solnik, B., 1977, A Pure Foreign Exchange Asset Pricing Model, *Journal of International Economics*, Vol. 7, pp. 161–179.
Roper, D.E., 1975, The Role of Expected Value Analysis for Speculative Decisions in

the Forward Currency Market, *Quarterly Journal of Economics*, No. 1.
Ross, S., 1976, The Arbitrage Theory of Capital Asset Pricing, *Journal of Economic Theory*, Vol. 13, December, pp. 341–360.
Rubinstein, M., 1974, An Aggregation Theorem for Securities Markets, *Journal of Financial Economics*, Vol. 1.
Rugman, A.M., 1976, Risk Reduction by International Diversification, *Journal of International Business Studies*, Vol. 7, pp.75–80, Newark, N.J.
Sachs, J.D., 1985, The Dollar and the Policy Mix: 1985, *Brookings Papers on Economic Activity*, No. 1.
Samuelson, P.A., 1965, Proof that Properly Anticipated Prices Fluctuate Randomly, *Industrial Management Review*, Vol. 6, pp. 41–49.
Saracoglu, R., 1984, Expectations of Inflation and Interest Rate Determination, *IMF Staff Papers*, Vol. 31, No. 1, pp. 141–178.
Sargent, T., 1978, Estimation of Dynamic Labor Demand Schedules under Rational Expectations, *Journal of Political Economy*, December, pp. 1009–1044.
SCB, 1987, *Beräkningar av bytesbalansen – en skenbar exakthet*, Stockholm.
Shaefer, J.R. and Loopesko, B.E., 1983, Floating Exchange Rates after Ten Years, *Brookings Papers on Economic Activity* 1, pp. 1–87.
Shanken, J., 1982, The Arbitrage Price Theory: Is It Testable, *Journal of Finance*, Vol. 37, December, pp. 1129–1140.
Sharpe, W.F., 1964, Capital Asset Prices: A Theory of Market Equilibrium under Conditions of Risk, *Journal of Finance*, Vol. 19, September, pp. 425–442.
Sharpe, W.F., 1978, Comment, *Journal of Finance*, June.
Siegel, J., 1972, Risk, Interest Rates, and the Forward Exchange, *Quarterly Journal of Economics*, Vol. 86, pp. 303–309.
Sjöö, .B, 1990, *Monetary Policy in a Continuous Time Dynamic Model for Sweden*, mimeo, Department of Economics, University of Gothenburg, Sweden.
Sohmen, E., 1969, *Flexible Exchange Rates*, University of Chicago (revised edition).
Solnik, B., 1973, *European Capital Markets, Towards a General Theory of International Investment*, Lexington Books.
Solnik, B., 1974a, An International Market Model of Security Price Behavior, *Journal of Financial and Quantitative Analysis*, Vol. 9, pp. 537–554, Seattle, Washington.
Solnik, B., 1974b, The International Pricing of Risk: An Empirical Investigation of the World Capital Market Structure, *Journal of Finance*, May.
Solnik, B., 1974c, Equilibrium in an International Capital Market, *Journal of Economic Theory*, August.
Solnik, B, 1977, Testing International Asset Pricing: Some Pessimistic Views., *Journal of Finance*, Vol. 32, May, pp. 503–511.
Solnik, B., 1983, International Arbitrage Pricing Theory, *Journal of Finance*, Vol. 38, No. 2.
Solnik, B., 1987, Using Financial Prices to Test Exchange Rate Models: A Note, *Journal of Finance*, Vol. XLII, No. 1, pp. 141–149.
SOU 1978:11, *Kapitalmarknadsutredningen.*
SOU 1980:51, *Valutaregleringen och ekonomisk politik.* Expertrapporter från valutakommittén.
SOU 1982:53, *Kreditpolitiken. Fakta, teorier och erfarenheter.*
SOU 1984:4, *Långtidsutredningen LU 84.*
SOU 1984:89, *Statsskuldspolitiken – samordningsfrågor.* Delbetänkande från statsskuldspolitiska kommittén.
SOU 1985:52, *Översyn av valutaregleringen.* Slutbetänkande av valutakommittén.
SOU 1987:3, *Långtidsutredningen LU 87.*
Stehle, R., 1977, An Empirical Test of the Alternate Hypotheses of National and International Pricing and Risky Assets. *Journal of Finance*, Vol. 32, May, pp. 493–502.
Stern, R.M., 1973, *The Balance of Payments, Theory and Economic Policy*, MacMillan, Chicago.
Stern, R.M. et al., 1977, *The Presentation of the US Balance fo Payments: A Symposium*, Essays in International Finance, No. 123, Princeton.
Stockman, A.C., 1978, *Risk, Information and Forward Exchange Rates*; in Frenkel

and Johnson (1978), pp. 159–178.
Stockman, A.C., 1980, A Theory of Exchange Rate Determination, *Journal of Political Economy*, Vol. 88, pp. 673–698.
Stockman, A.C. and Dellas, H., 1986, *Journal of International Economics*, Vol. 21, pp. 199–213.
Stoll, H.P., 1968, An Empirical Study of the Forward Exchange Market under Fixed and Flexible Exchange Rate System, *Canadian Journal of Economics*, February, pp. 55–78.
Stoll, H.P., 1972, Causes of Deviations from Interest Rate Parity, *Journal of Money Credit and Banking*, Vol. 4, February, pp. 113–117.
Stulz, R.M., 1981, On the Effects of Barriers to International Investment, *Journal of Finance*, Vol. 36, September, pp. 923–934.
Stulz, R.M., 1984, Currency Preferences, Purchasing Power Risks, and the Determination of Exchange Rates in an Optimizing Model, *Journal of Money, Credit and Banking*, Vol. 16, No. 3.
Ståhl, I., 1980, *Realräntans utveckling i Sverige 1900–1978*; in Dahmén, E. and Eliasson, G. (eds.), 1980, Industriell utveckling i Sverige, IUI, Stockholm.
Summers, L., 1983, The Non-Adjustment of Nominal Interest Rates: A Study of the Fisher Effect, *NBER Working Paper* No. 836, New York.
Svensson, L., 1983, Money and Asset Prices in a Cash-in-advance Economy, *IIES Seminar Paper* No. 267.
Svensson, L., 1985, Currency Prices, Terms of Trade and Interest Rates. A General Equilibrium Asset Pricing, Cash in Advance Approach, *Journal of International Economics*, Vol. 18, pp. 17–41.
Sveriges Riksbank, *Kredit- och valutaöversikt* 1984:2, 1984:3, 1984:4, 1986:1, 1986:2, 1986:4, 1987:1, *Årskrönika* 1987.
Södersten, J., 1987, Lönsamhet i svensk industri, *SE–bankens kvartalsskrift*, No. 2, Stockholm.
Söderström, H., 1980, *Valutaregleringen och reala kapitalrörelser*, SOU 1980:51, pp. 216.
Tanzi, V., 1984, *Taxation, Inflation and Interest Rates*, IMF, Washington.
Taylor, M.P., 1987, Risk Premia and Foreign Exchange: A Multiple Time Series Approach to Testing Uncovered Interest-Rate Parity, *Weltwirtschaftliches Archiv*, Band 123, Heft 4, pp. 579–591.
Teräsvirta, T., 1987, Usefulness of Proxy Variables in Linear Models with Stochastic Regressors, *Journal of Econometrics*, Vol. 36, pp. 377–382.
Thygesen, N., 1977, Inflation and Exchange Rates, *Journal of International Economics*, Vol. 8, pp. 301–317.
Tinic, S.M. and West, R., 1986, Risk, Return, and Equilibrium: A Revisit?, *Journal of Political Economy*, Vol. 94, No. 1, pp. 127–147.
Tobin, J., 1958, Liquidity Preferences as Behavior Towards Risk, *Review of Economic Studies*, Vol. 25, February.
Tobin, J., 1965, Money and Economic Growth, *Econometrica*, Vol. 33, No. 4, pp. 671–684.
Tobin, J., 1969, A General Equilibrium Approach to Monetary Theory, *Journal of Money, Credit and Banking*, February, pp. 15–29.
Tobin, J., 1980, Stabilization Policy Ten Years After, *Brookings Paper on Economic Activity*, No. 1, pp. 19–78.
Treynor, J., 1965, *Towards a Theory of the Market Value of Risky Assets* (mimeo).
Tsiang, S.C., 1959, The Theory of Forward Exchange and the Effects of Government Intervention on the Forward Market, *IMF Staff Papers*, Vol. 7, No. 1.
Turnovsky, S.J., 1983, Wage Indexation and Exchange Market Intervention in a Small Open Economy, *The Canadian Journal of Economics*, Vol. XVI, No. 4.
Turnovsky, S.J. and Ball, K.M., 1983, Covered Interest Parity and Speculative Efficiency: Some Empirical Evidence for Australia, *Economic Record*, No. 166, Melbourne.
Turnovsky, S.J. and Bhandari, J.S., 1982, The Degree of Capital Mobility and the Stability of an Open Economy under Rational Expectations, *Journal of Money, Credit and Banking*, Vol. 14, No. 3, pp. 303–326.

Wallander, J., 1982, En effektivare kreditpolitik, *Ekonomisk Debatt*, Vol. 10, No. 8.
Vinso, J.D. and Rogalski, R.J., 1978, Empirical Properties of Foreign Exchange Rates, *Journal of International Business Studies*, Autumn, pp. 69–80.
Virén, M., 1987, Inflation, Hedging and the Fisher Hypothesis, *Journal of Macroeconomics*, Vol. 9, No. 1, pp. 45–57.
Volker, P.A., 1980, Interest Rate Harmonisation among Selected Industrial Countries 1961(1)–1970(12), *European Economic Review*, pp. 361–376.
Vredin, A., 1988, *Macroeconomic Policies and the Balance of Payments*, EFI, Stockholm.
Wasserfallen, W. and Zimmermann, H., 1985, The Behavior of Intra-Daily Exchange Rates, *Journal of Banking and Finance*, Vol. 9, No. 1, pp. 55–72.
Wihlborg, C., 1978, Currency Risks in International Financial Markets, *Princeton Studies in International Finance*, No. 44, Princeton.
Wihlborg, C., 1979, *Flexible Exchange Rates, Currency Risks and the Integration of Capital Markets*; in Lindbeck, A. (ed.) (1979).
Wihlborg, C., 1982, Interest Rates, Exchange Rate Adjustments and Currency Risks, *Journal of Money, Credit and Banking*, Vol. 14, No. 1, February.
Wilcox, J.A., 1983, Why Real Interest Rates Were So Low in the 1970's, *American Economic Review*, Vol. 73, March, pp. 44–53.
Winkler, R. and Makridakis, S., 1983, The Combination of Forecasts, *Journal of the Royal Statistical Society*, Vol. 146, part 2, pp. 150–157.
Wohlin, L., 1983, Kreditpolitik i omvandling, *Ekonomisk Debatt*, Vol. 11, No. 1.
Wolff, Ch.C.P., 1987, Forward Foreign Exchange Rates, Expected Spot Rates, and Premia: A Signal-Extraction Approach, *Journal of Finance*, Vol. XLII, No. 2 pp. 395–406.
Wood, G.E., 1985, Valutaregleringar i Storbritannien, *SE-bankens kvartalstidskrift*, No. 3, pp. 64–69.
Wyplosz, Ch.A., 1983, The Exchange and Interest Rate Term Structure under Risk Aversion and Rational Expectations, *Journal of International Economics*, Vol. 14, pp. 123–139.
Zellner, A., 1979, *Causality and Econometrics*; in Brunner, K., and Meltzer, A.H. (eds.),Three Aspects of Policy and Policymaking: Knowledge, Data and Institutions, Carnegie-Rochester Conference Series, 10, pp. 9–54, North-Holland, Amsterdam.
Zellner, A. and Palm, F., 1975, Time Series Analysis and Simultaneous Equation Econometric Models, *Journal of Econometrics*, Vol. 3.
Zetterberg, J., 1980, *Kapitalrörelsernas bestämningsfaktorer och partiella kapitalkontrollsystem*, SOU 1980:51.
Åkerholm, J. and Tarkka, J., 1987, Kan de nordiska länderna föra en självständig penningpolitik?;in *Nordiska Ekonomiska Forskningsrådets Årsbok 1986*, pp. 79–115.